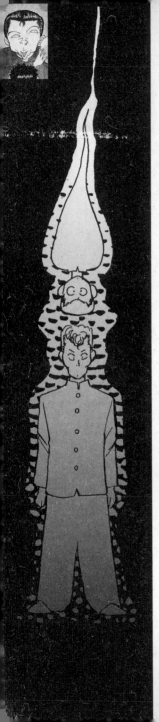

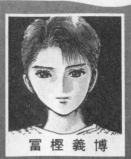

冨樫義博

"IF I COULD BE REINCARNATED AS ANYONE, WHO WOULD I BE" PART 1: A REALLY GOOD-LOOKING MAN. INNUMERABLE WOMEN HAVE PROFESSED THEIR LOVE TO ME, MY FIRST VICTIM BEING MY BABYSITTER FROM WHEN I WAS 4 YEARS OLD. AT AGE 13, I AM DISCOVERED BY A SCOUT FOR THE ENTERTAINMENT INDUSTRY, AND END UP BECOMING A MAJOR SINGER AND ACTOR. MY NAME IS REGULARLY PLASTERED ON SCANDAL SHEETS DUE TO RUMORS OF MY INVOLVEMENT WITH ACTRESSES AND IDOL SINGERS. AT AGE 22, I MARRY A BEAUTIFUL FEMINIST WRITER WHO IS SEVEN YEARS OLDER THAN ME, IN A VEGAS-STYLE HIGH-SPEED WEDDING. WE ARE DIVORCED TWO MONTHS LATER. AFTER THAT, I HAVE THREE MORE MARRIAGES, BUT THEY ALL RESULT IN DIVORCE WITHIN HALF A YEAR. AT AGE 36, I DIE IN AN ACCIDENT. THE PHOTO ABOVE IS A PICTURE OF ME WHEN I AM 20 YEARS OLD.
—YOSHIHIRO TOGASHI, 1991

Yoshihiro Togashi's manga career began in 1986 when, at the age of 20, he won the coveted Tezuka Award for new manga artists. He debuted in the Japanese Weekly Shonen Jump magazine in 1989 with the romantic comedy Tende Shôwaru Cupid. From 1990 to 1994 he wrote and drew the smash hit manga YuYu Hakusho, which was followed by the darkly humorous science-fiction series Level E and the adventure story Hunter x Hunter. In 1999 he married the manga artist Naoko Takeuchi.

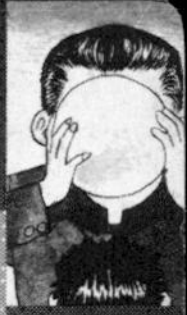

YUYU HAKUSHO VOL. 1
The SHONEN JUMP Graphic Novel Edition

This graphic novel contains material that was originally published in English in SHONEN JUMP #1-4.

STORY AND ART BY
YOSHIHIRO TOGASHI

ENGLISH ADAPTATION BY
GARY LEACH

Translation/Lillian Olsen
Touch-Up Art & Lettering/Cynthia Dobson
Initial Cover Design/Izumi Evers
Final Cover & Graphic Design/Sean Lee
Senior Editor/Jason Thompson

Managing Editor/Elizabeth Kawasaki
Director of Production/Noboru Watanabe
Vice President of Publishing/Alvin Lu
Vice President & Editor in Chief/Yumi Hoashi
Sr. Director of Acquisitions/Rika Inouye
Vice President of Sales & Marketing/Liza Coppola
Publisher/Hyoe Narita

Printed in the U.S.A.

Published by VIZ Media, LLC

P.O. Box 77010 • San Francisco, CA 94107

The SHONEN JUMP Graphic Novel Edition
10 9 8 7 6 5
First printing, May 2003
Fifth printing, January 2006

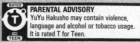

www.viz.com

PARENTAL ADVISORY
YuYu Hakusho may contain violence, language and alcohol or tobacco usage. It is rated T for Teen. RATED T TEEN

THE WORLD'S MOST POPULAR MANGA

www.shonenjump.com

SHONEN JUMP GRAPHIC NOVEL

YuYu HAKUSHO™

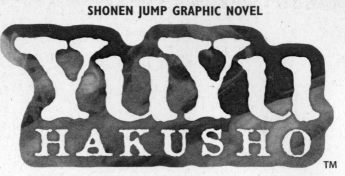

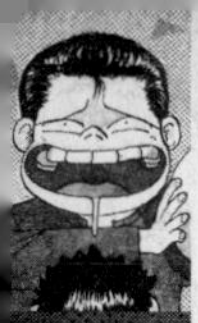

Vol. 1

GOODBYE, MATERIAL WORLD!

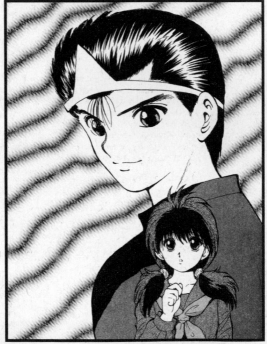

STORY AND ART BY

YOSHIHIRO TOGASHI

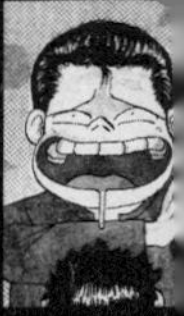

CONTENTS

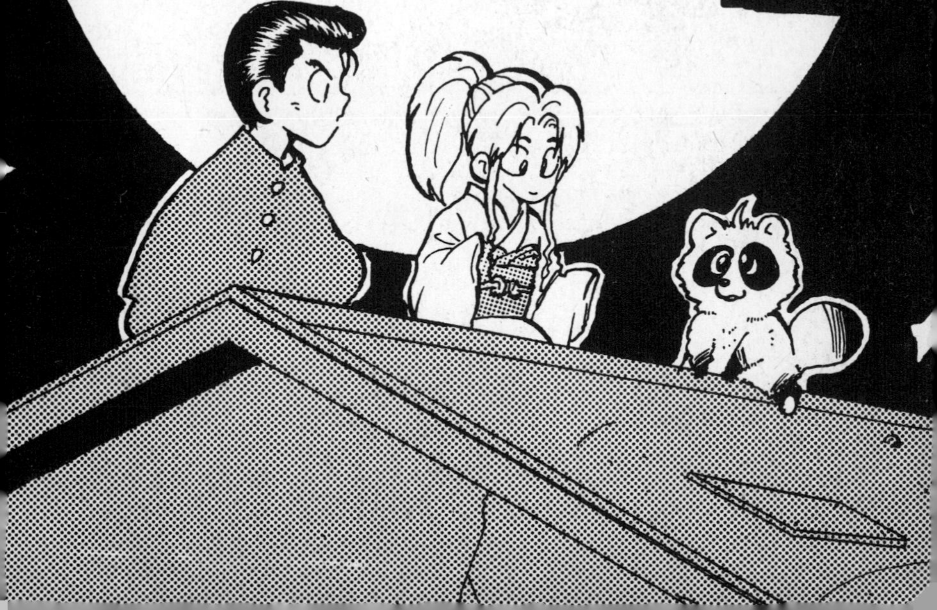

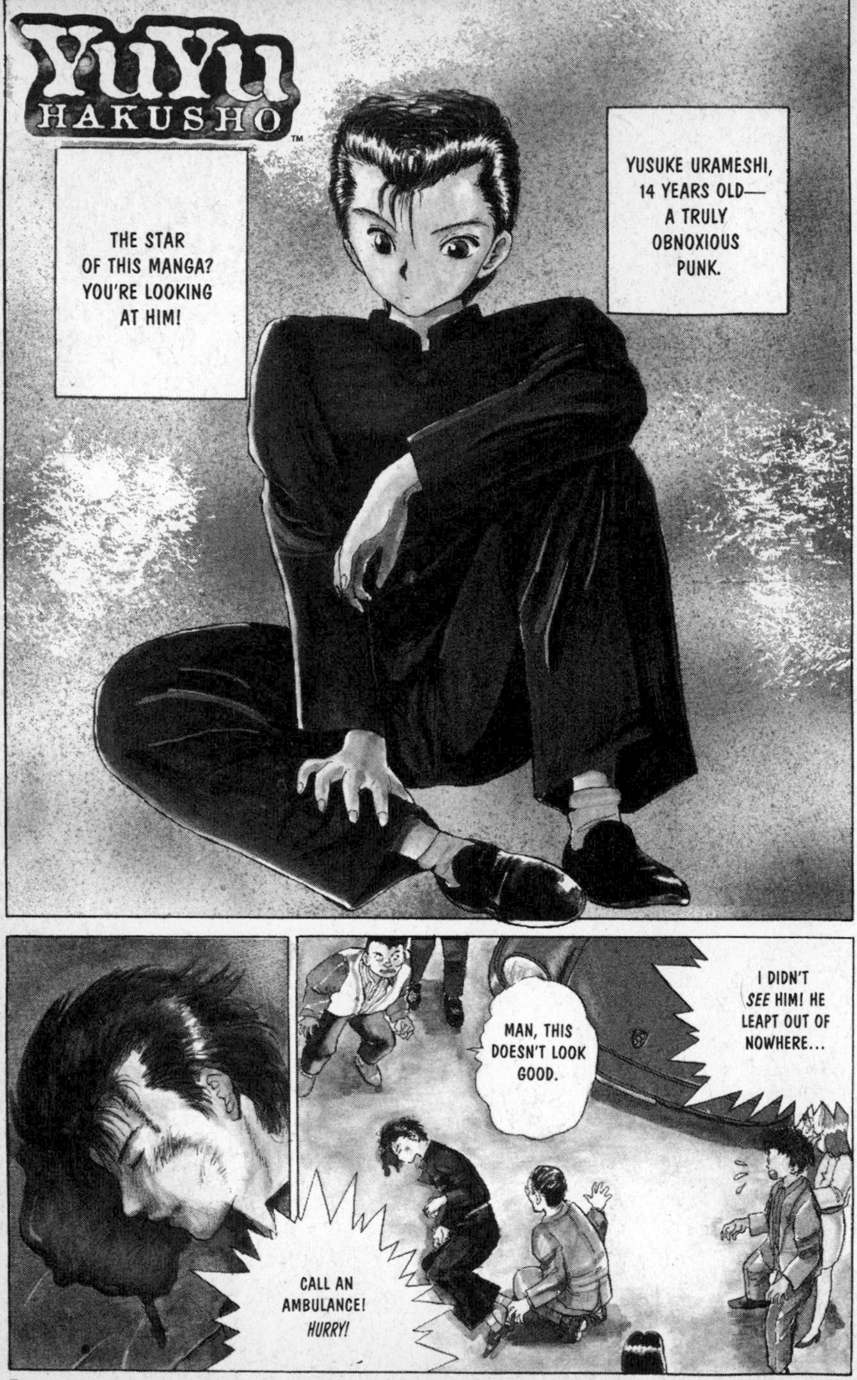
YUYU HAKUSHO™
YUSUKE URAMESHI, 14 YEARS OLD— A TRULY OBNOXIOUS PUNK.
THE STAR OF THIS MANGA? YOU'RE LOOKING AT HIM!
I DIDN'T *SEE* HIM! HE LEAPT OUT OF NOWHERE...
MAN, THIS DOESN'T LOOK GOOD.
CALL AN AMBULANCE! *HURRY!*

*YUYU HAKUSHO MEANS "GHOST FILES" OR "POLTERGEIST REPORT."

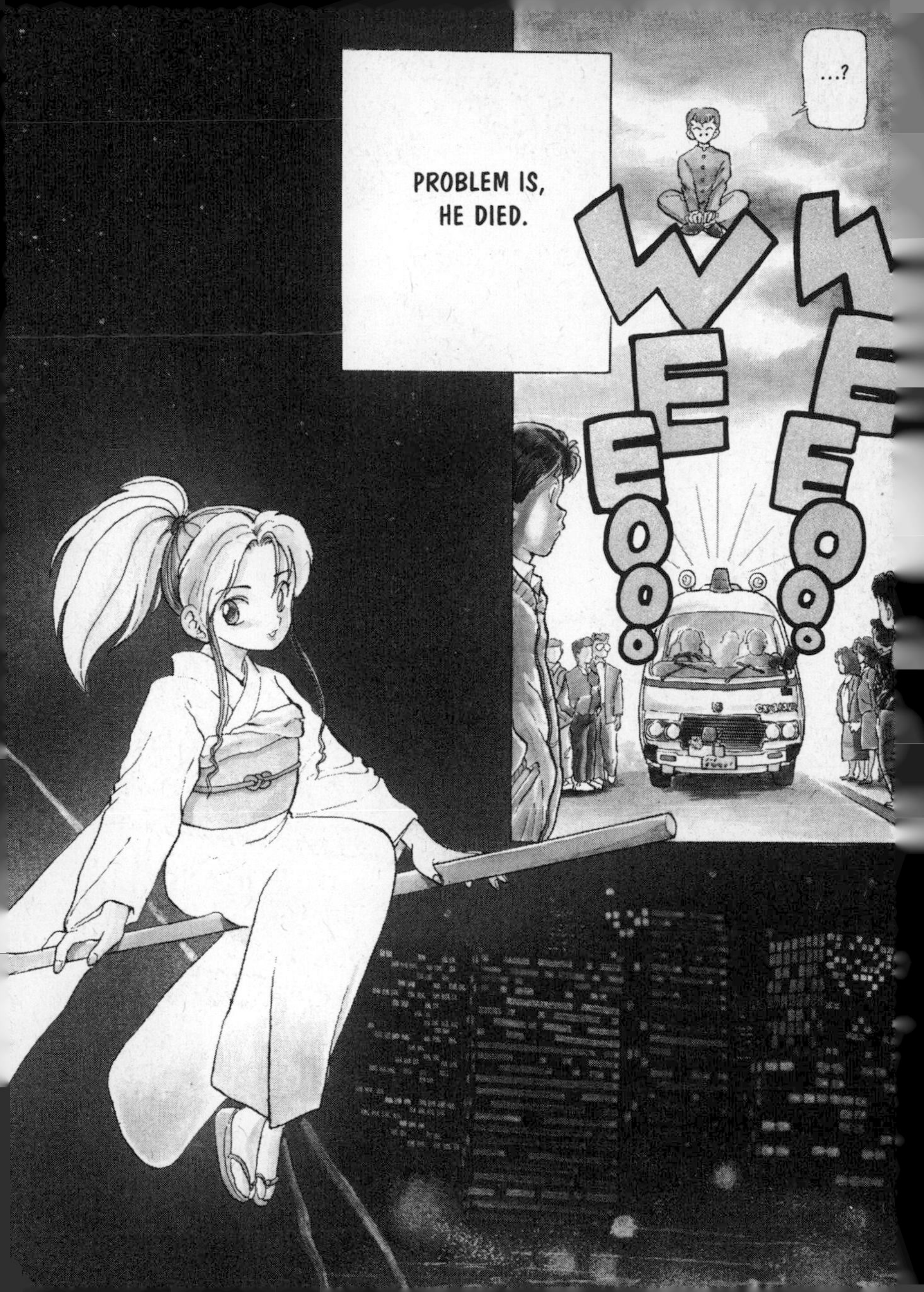

...?
WEEOOO
WEEOOO
PROBLEM IS, HE DIED.

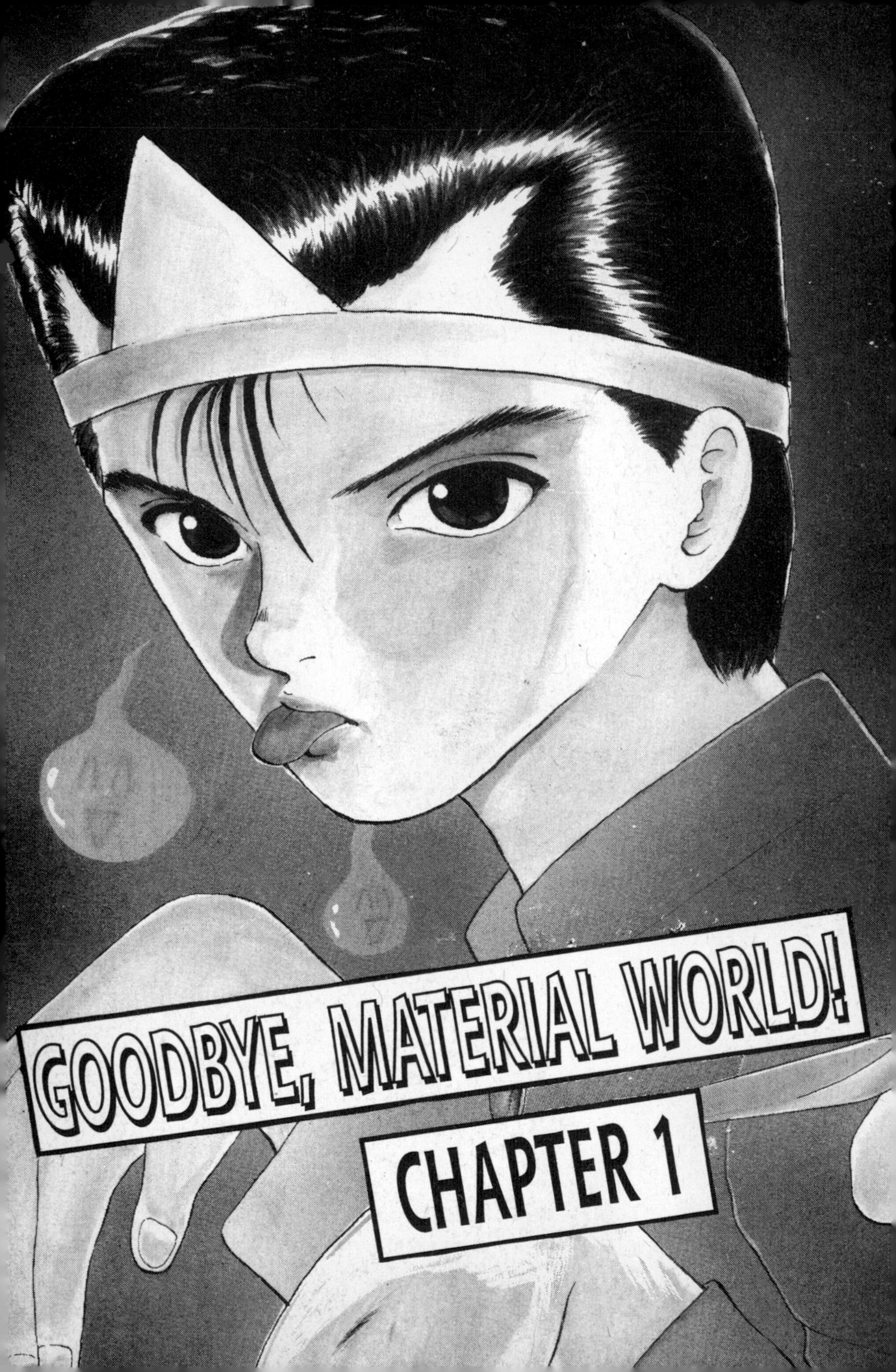
GOODBYE, MATERIAL WORLD!
CHAPTER 1

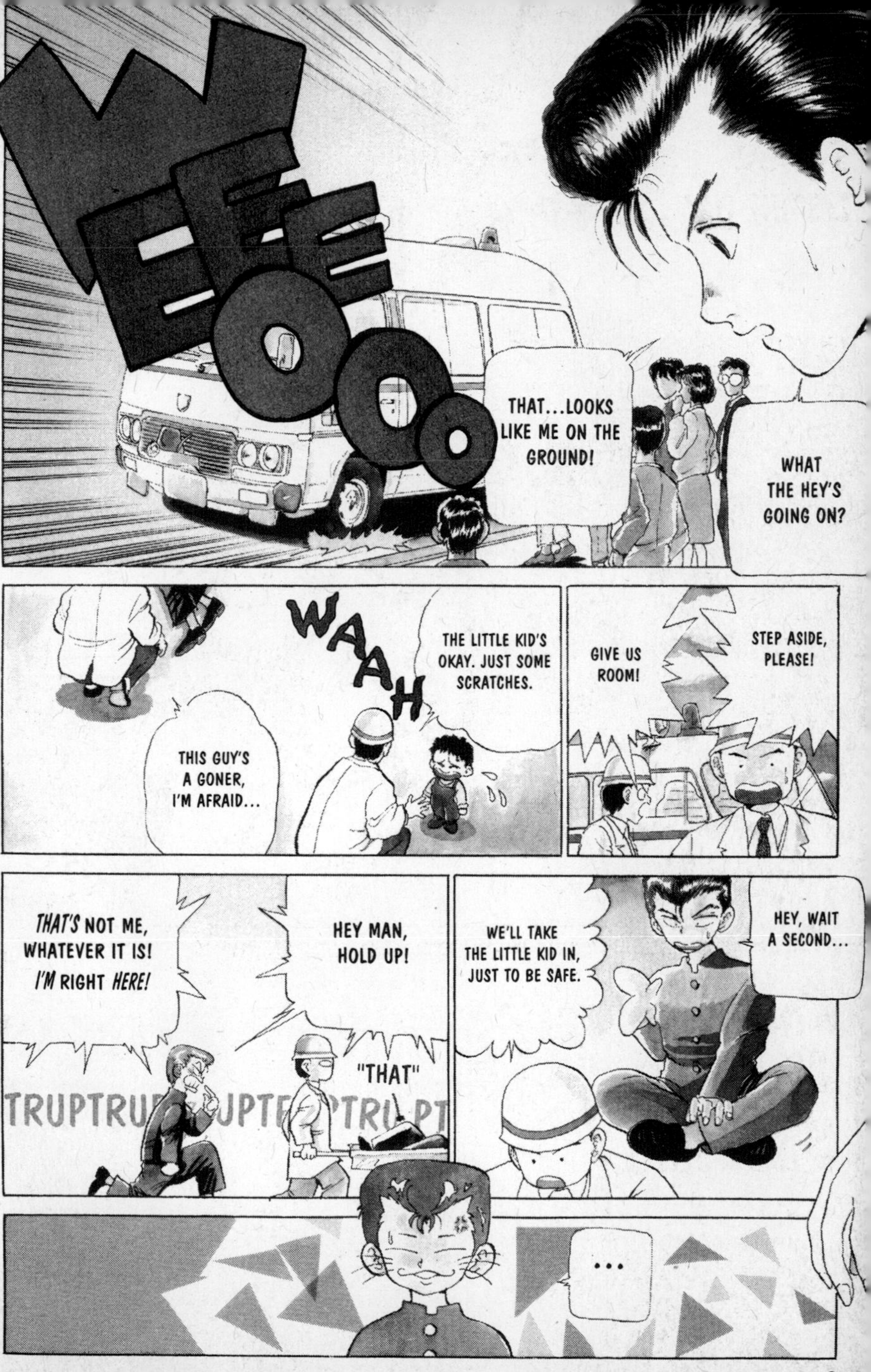

WHAT THE HEY'S GOING ON?
THAT...LOOKS LIKE ME ON THE GROUND!
WEEEOOO
STEP ASIDE, PLEASE!
GIVE US ROOM!
THE LITTLE KID'S OKAY. JUST SOME SCRATCHES.
WAAH
THIS GUY'S A GONER, I'M AFRAID...
HEY, WAIT A SECOND...
WE'LL TAKE THE LITTLE KID IN, JUST TO BE SAFE.
HEY MAN, HOLD UP!
THAT'S NOT ME, WHATEVER IT IS! *I'M* RIGHT *HERE!*
"THAT"
TRUPTRU
UPTR
PTRU PT
...

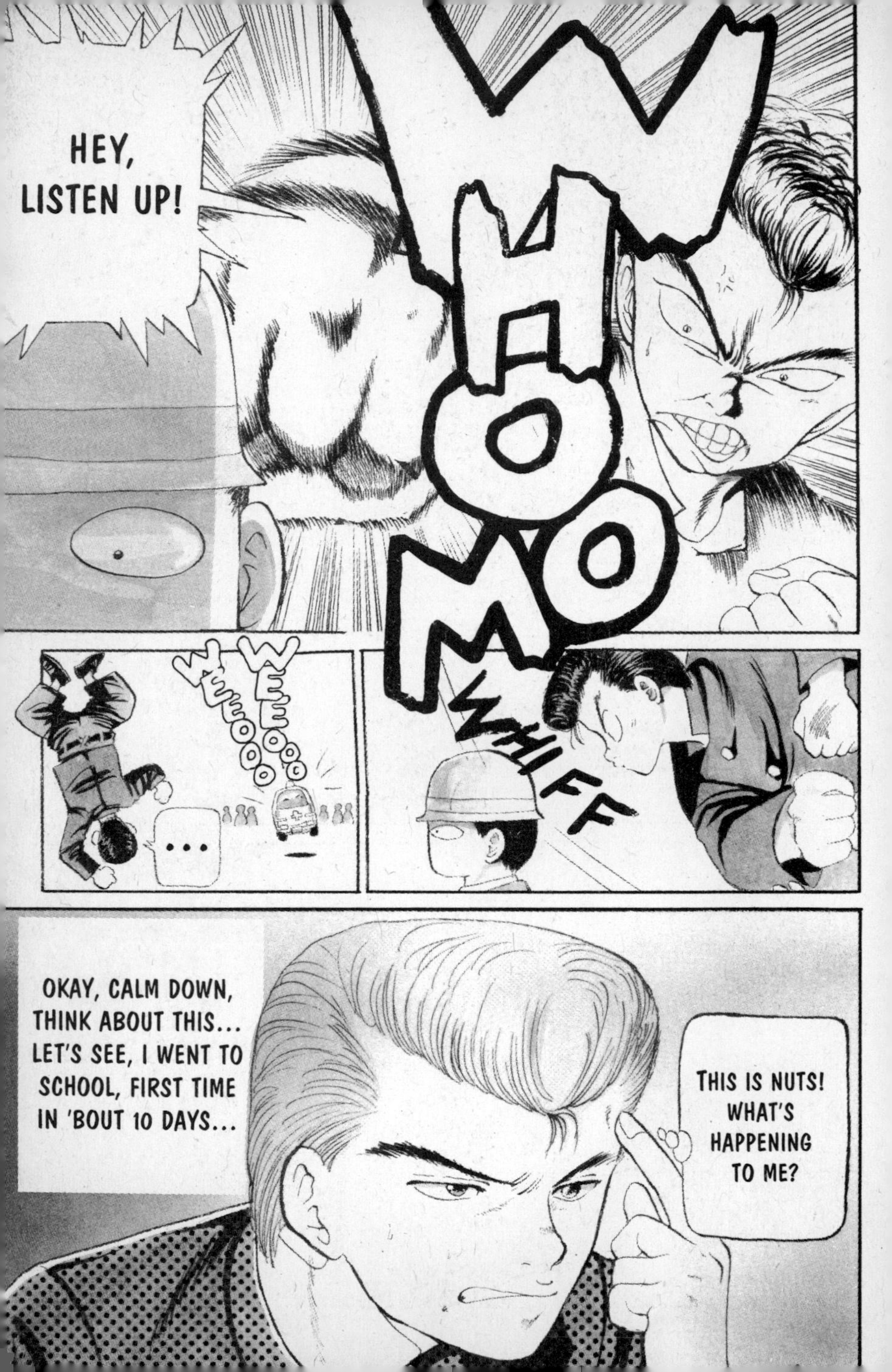

HEY, LISTEN UP!
WHOOMM
WHIFF
WEEOOO
WEEOOO
...
THIS IS NUTS! WHAT'S HAPPENING TO ME?
OKAY, CALM DOWN, THINK ABOUT THIS... LET'S SEE, I WENT TO SCHOOL, FIRST TIME IN 'BOUT 10 DAYS...

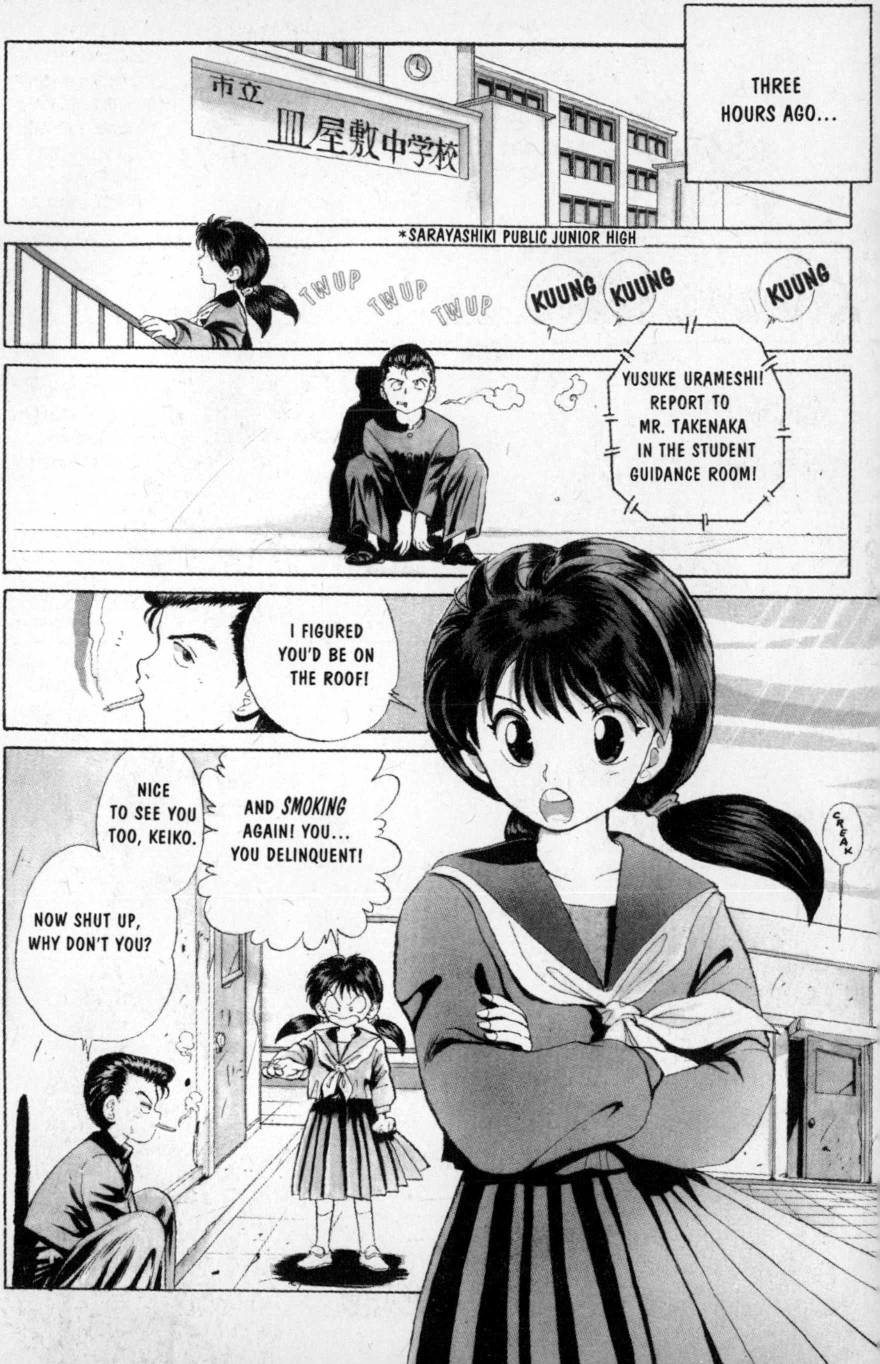
THREE HOURS AGO...
市立
皿屋敷中学校
*SARAYASHIKI PUBLIC JUNIOR HIGH
KUUNG
KUUNG
KUUNG
TWUP
TWUP
TWUP
YUSUKE URAMESHI! REPORT TO MR. TAKENAKA IN THE STUDENT GUIDANCE ROOM!
I FIGURED YOU'D BE ON THE ROOF!
CREAK
AND *SMOKING* AGAIN! YOU... YOU DELINQUENT!
NICE TO SEE YOU TOO, KEIKO.
NOW SHUT UP, WHY DON'T YOU?

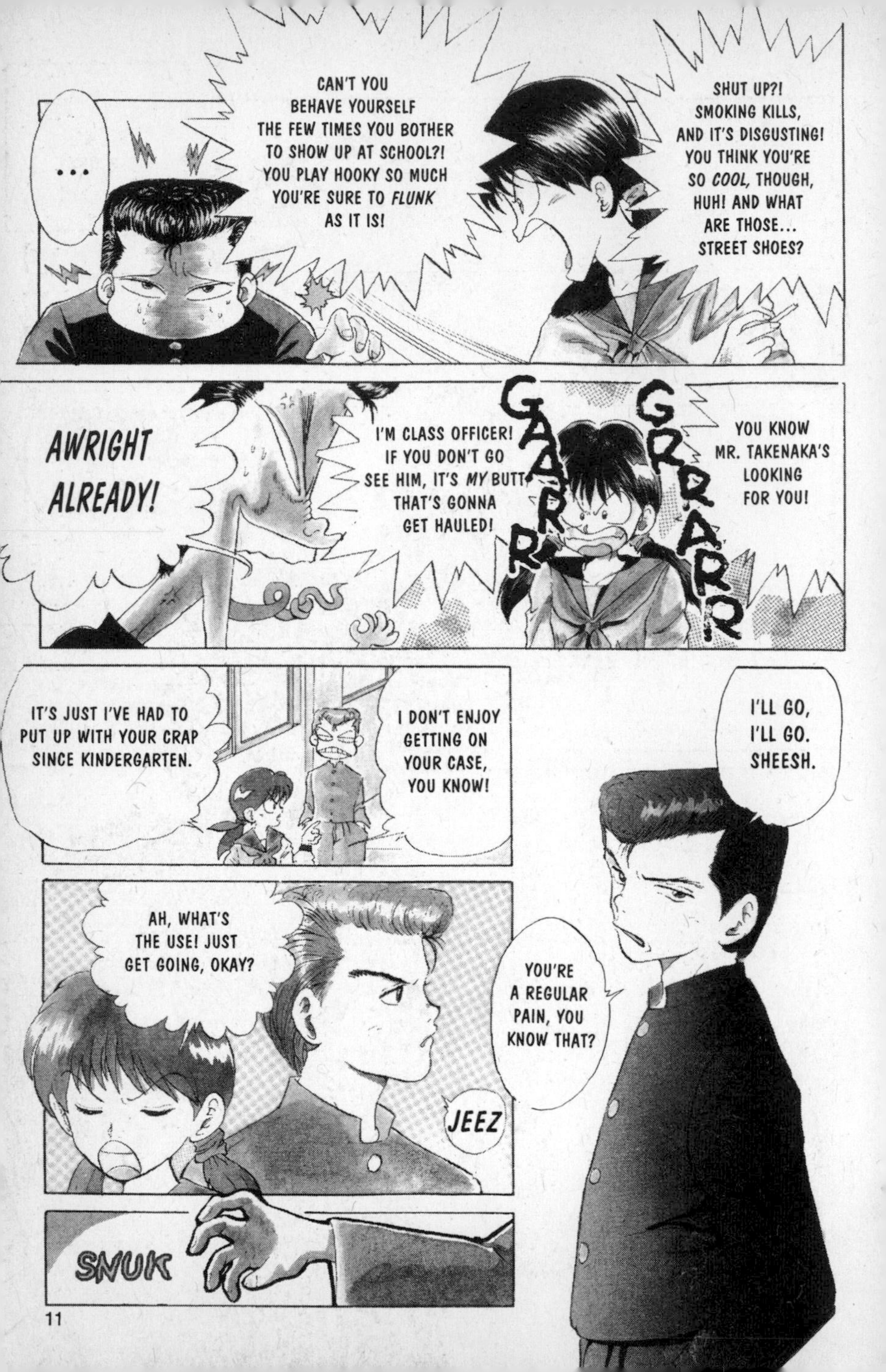
SHUT UP?! SMOKING KILLS, AND IT'S DISGUSTING! YOU THINK YOU'RE SO *COOL,* THOUGH, HUH! AND WHAT ARE THOSE... STREET SHOES?
CAN'T YOU BEHAVE YOURSELF THE FEW TIMES YOU BOTHER TO SHOW UP AT SCHOOL?! YOU PLAY HOOKY SO MUCH YOU'RE SURE TO *FLUNK* AS IT IS!
...
YOU KNOW MR. TAKENAKA'S LOOKING FOR YOU!
GRRARR
GAARR
I'M CLASS OFFICER! IF YOU DON'T GO SEE HIM, IT'S *MY* BUTT THAT'S GONNA GET HAULED!
AWRIGHT ALREADY!
I'LL GO, I'LL GO. SHEESH.
YOU'RE A REGULAR PAIN, YOU KNOW THAT?
I DON'T ENJOY GETTING ON YOUR CASE, YOU KNOW!
IT'S JUST I'VE HAD TO PUT UP WITH YOUR CRAP SINCE KINDERGARTEN.
JEEZ
AH, WHAT'S THE USE! JUST GET GOING, OKAY?
SNUK

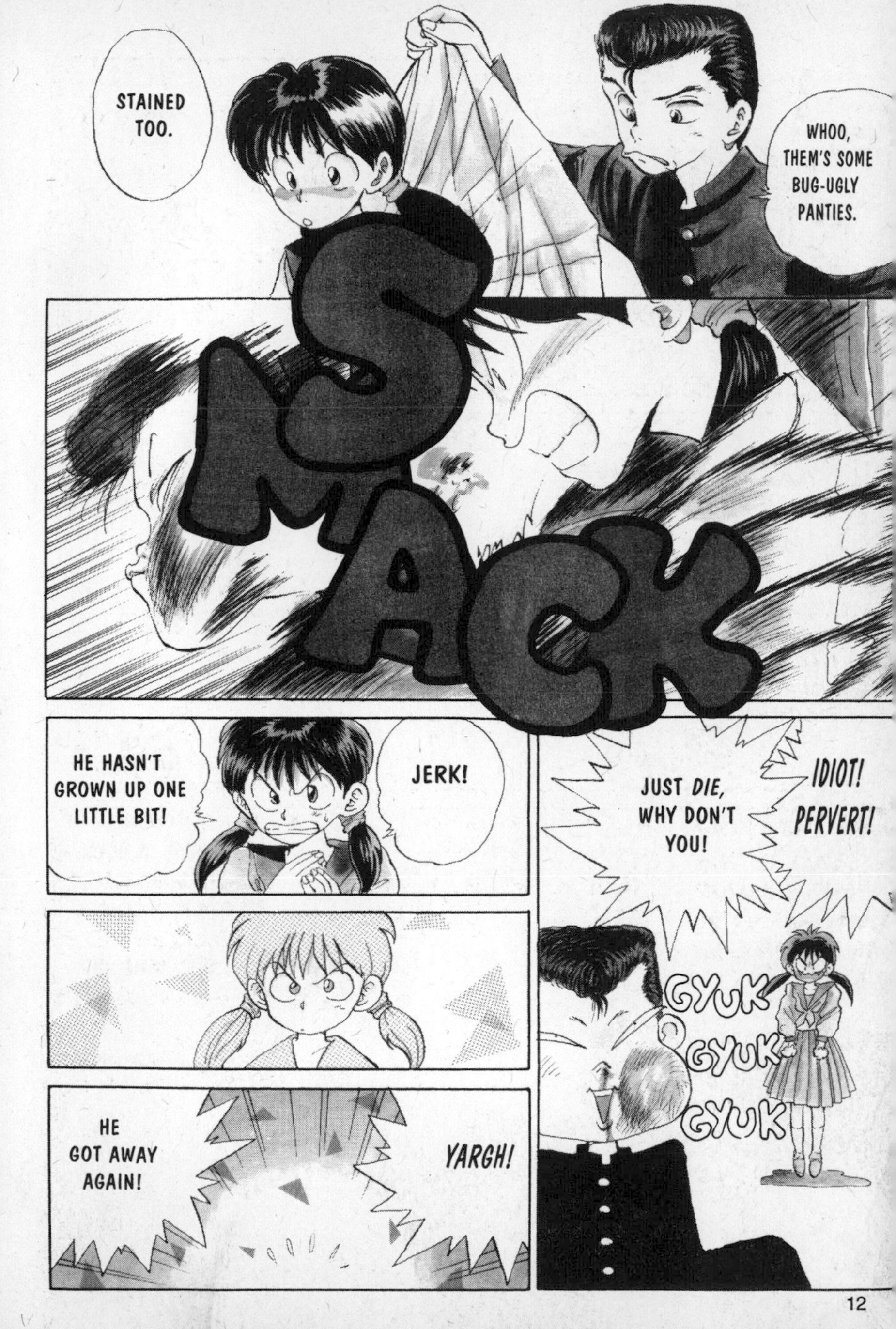
WHOO, THEM'S SOME BUG-UGLY PANTIES.
STAINED TOO.
SMACK
IDIOT! PERVERT!
JUST *DIE*, WHY DON'T YOU!
GYUK
GYUK
GYUK
JERK!
HE HASN'T GROWN UP ONE LITTLE BIT!
YARGH!
HE GOT AWAY AGAIN!

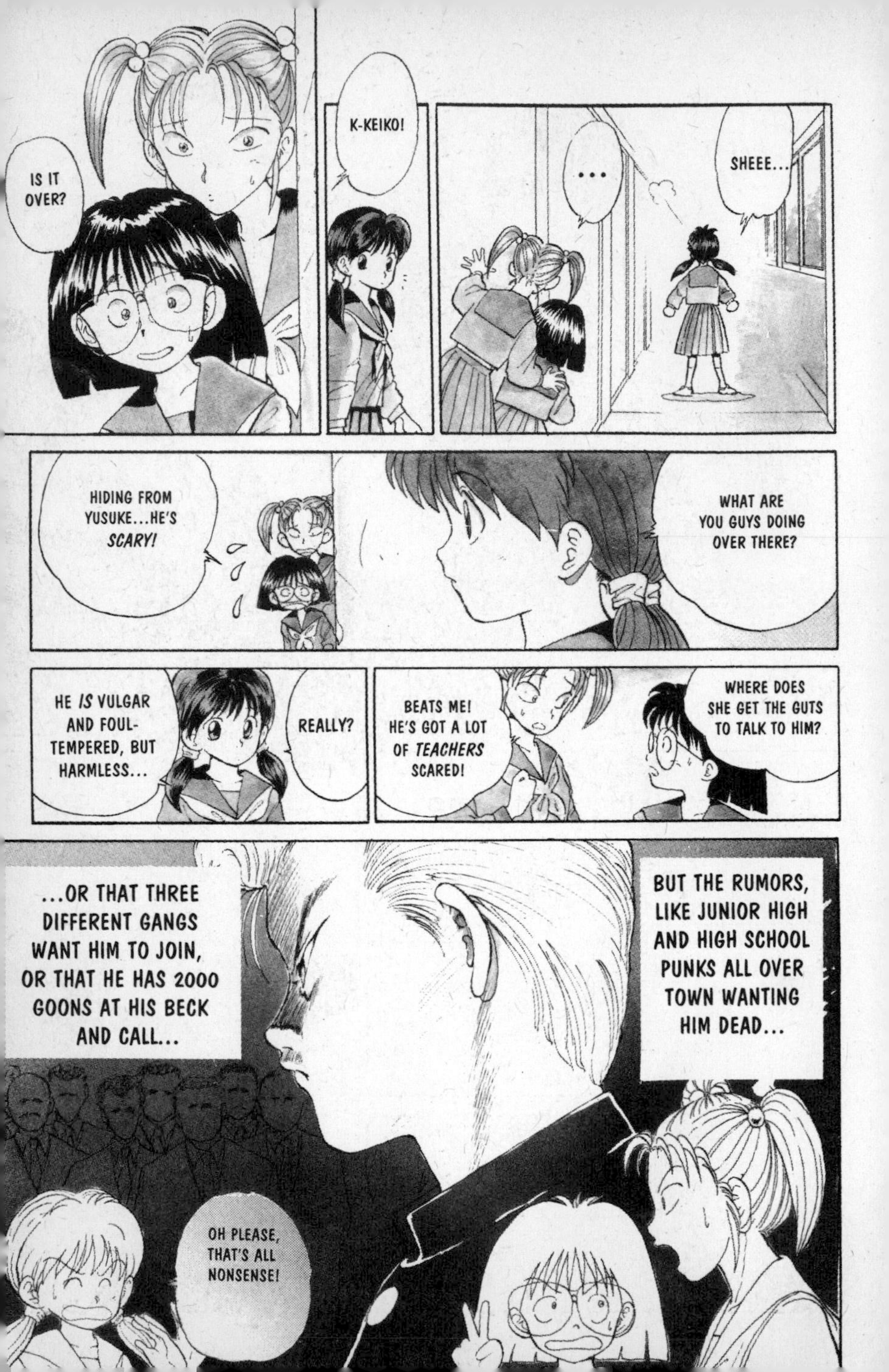
SHEEE...
...
K-KEIKO!
IS IT OVER?
WHAT ARE YOU GUYS DOING OVER THERE?
HIDING FROM YUSUKE...HE'S *SCARY!*
WHERE DOES SHE GET THE GUTS TO TALK TO HIM?
BEATS ME! HE'S GOT A LOT OF *TEACHERS* SCARED!
REALLY?
HE *IS* VULGAR AND FOUL-TEMPERED, BUT HARMLESS...
BUT THE RUMORS, LIKE JUNIOR HIGH AND HIGH SCHOOL PUNKS ALL OVER TOWN WANTING HIM DEAD...
...OR THAT THREE DIFFERENT GANGS WANT HIM TO JOIN, OR THAT HE HAS 2000 GOONS AT HIS BECK AND CALL...
OH PLEASE, THAT'S ALL NONSENSE!

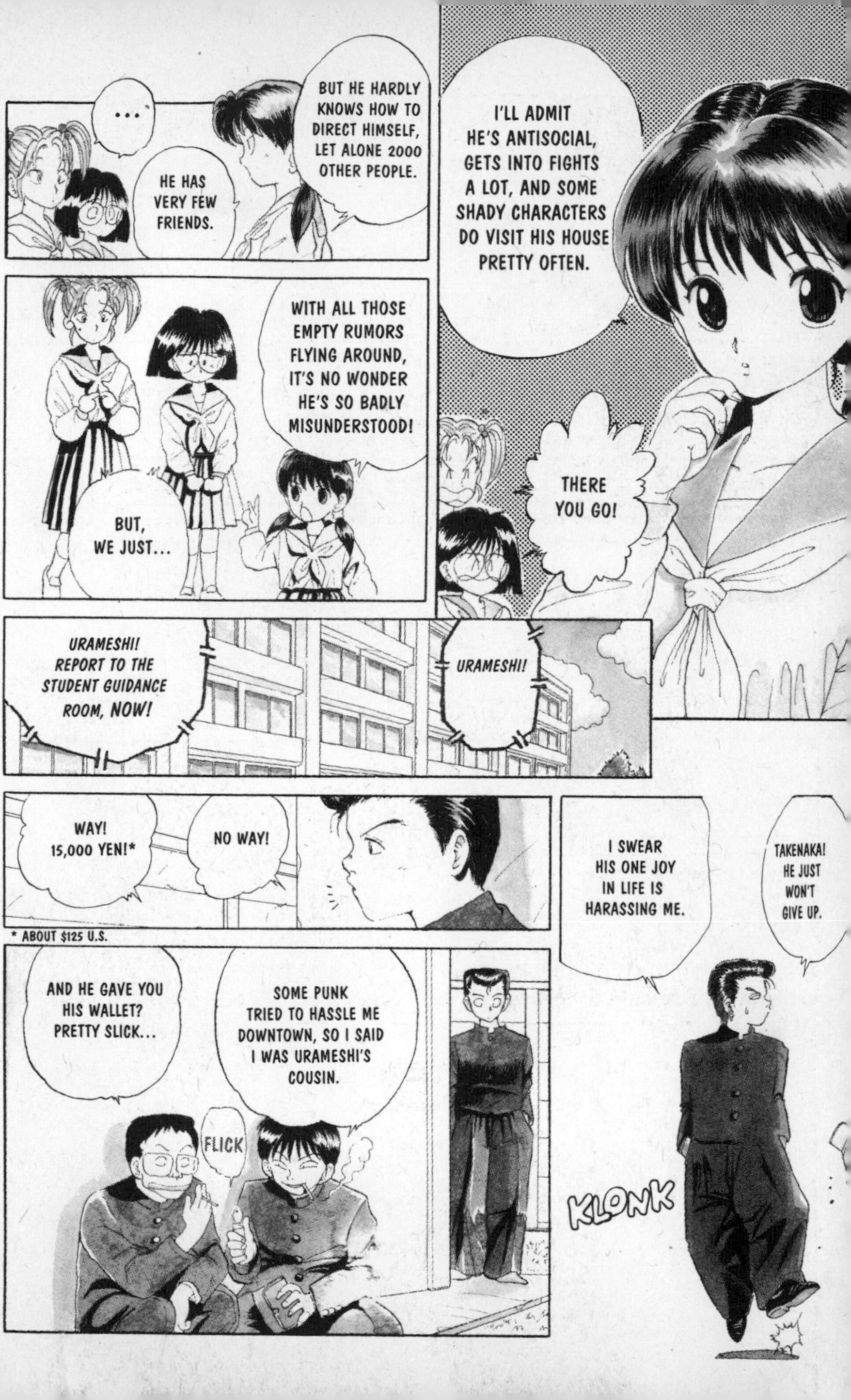
I'LL ADMIT HE'S ANTISOCIAL, GETS INTO FIGHTS A LOT, AND SOME SHADY CHARACTERS DO VISIT HIS HOUSE PRETTY OFTEN.
THERE YOU GO!
BUT HE HARDLY KNOWS HOW TO DIRECT HIMSELF, LET ALONE 2000 OTHER PEOPLE.
...
HE HAS VERY FEW FRIENDS.
WITH ALL THOSE EMPTY RUMORS FLYING AROUND, IT'S NO WONDER HE'S SO BADLY MISUNDERSTOOD!
BUT, WE JUST...
URAMESHI!
URAMESHI! REPORT TO THE STUDENT GUIDANCE ROOM, NOW!
TAKENAKA! HE JUST WON'T GIVE UP.
I SWEAR HIS ONE JOY IN LIFE IS HARASSING ME.
KLONK
NO WAY!
WAY! 15,000 YEN!*
* ABOUT $125 U.S.
SOME PUNK TRIED TO HASSLE ME DOWNTOWN, SO I SAID I WAS URAMESHI'S COUSIN.
AND HE GAVE YOU HIS WALLET? PRETTY SLICK...
FLICK

READ THIS WAY

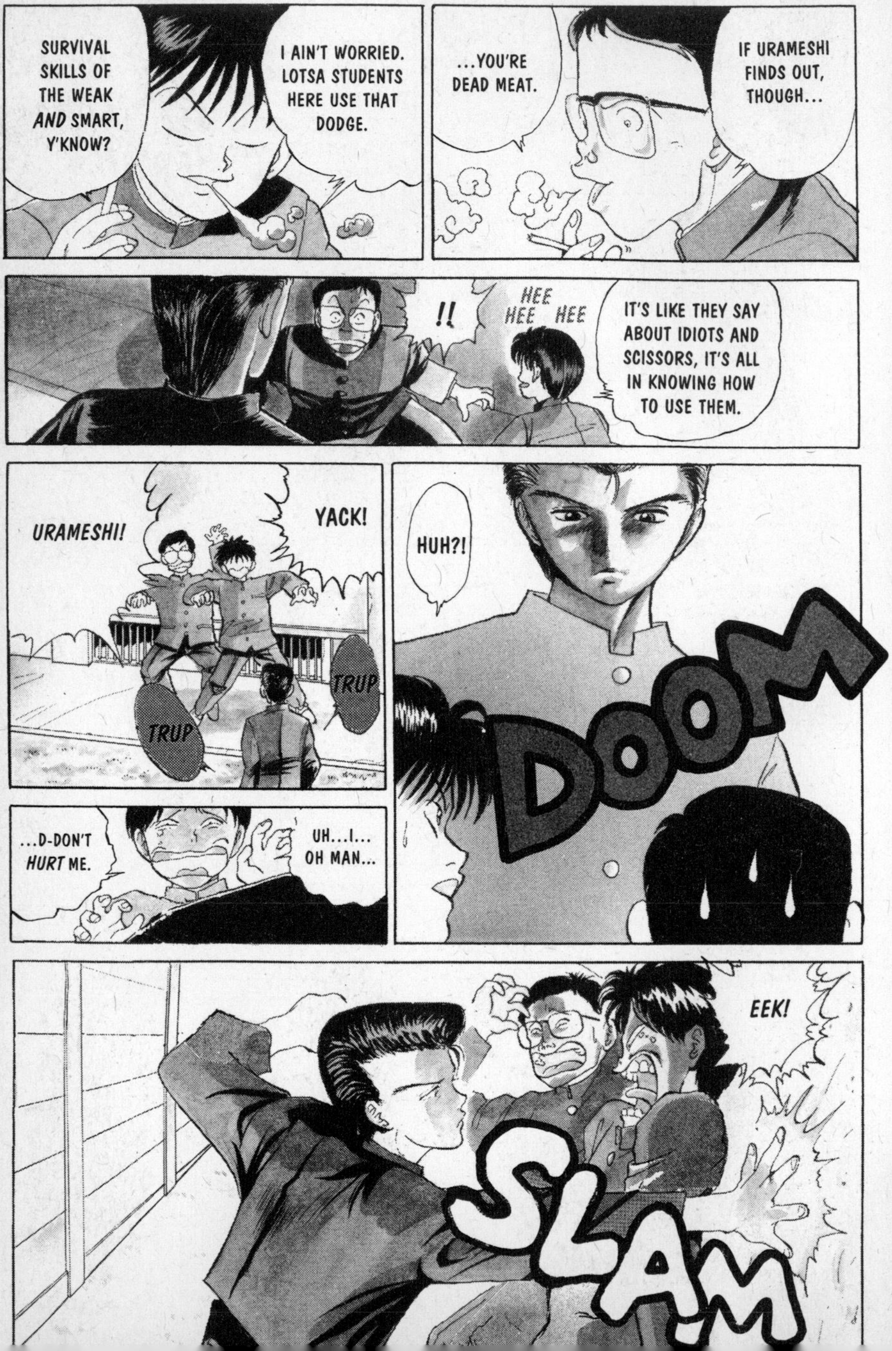
IF URAMESHI FINDS OUT, THOUGH...
...YOU'RE DEAD MEAT.
I AIN'T WORRIED. LOTSA STUDENTS HERE USE THAT DODGE.
SURVIVAL SKILLS OF THE WEAK *AND* SMART, Y'KNOW?
IT'S LIKE THEY SAY ABOUT IDIOTS AND SCISSORS, IT'S ALL IN KNOWING HOW TO USE THEM.
HEE HEE HEE
!!
HUH?!
DOOM
YACK!
URAMESHI!
TRUP
TRUP
UH...I... OH MAN...
...D-DON'T *HURT* ME.
EEK!
SLAM

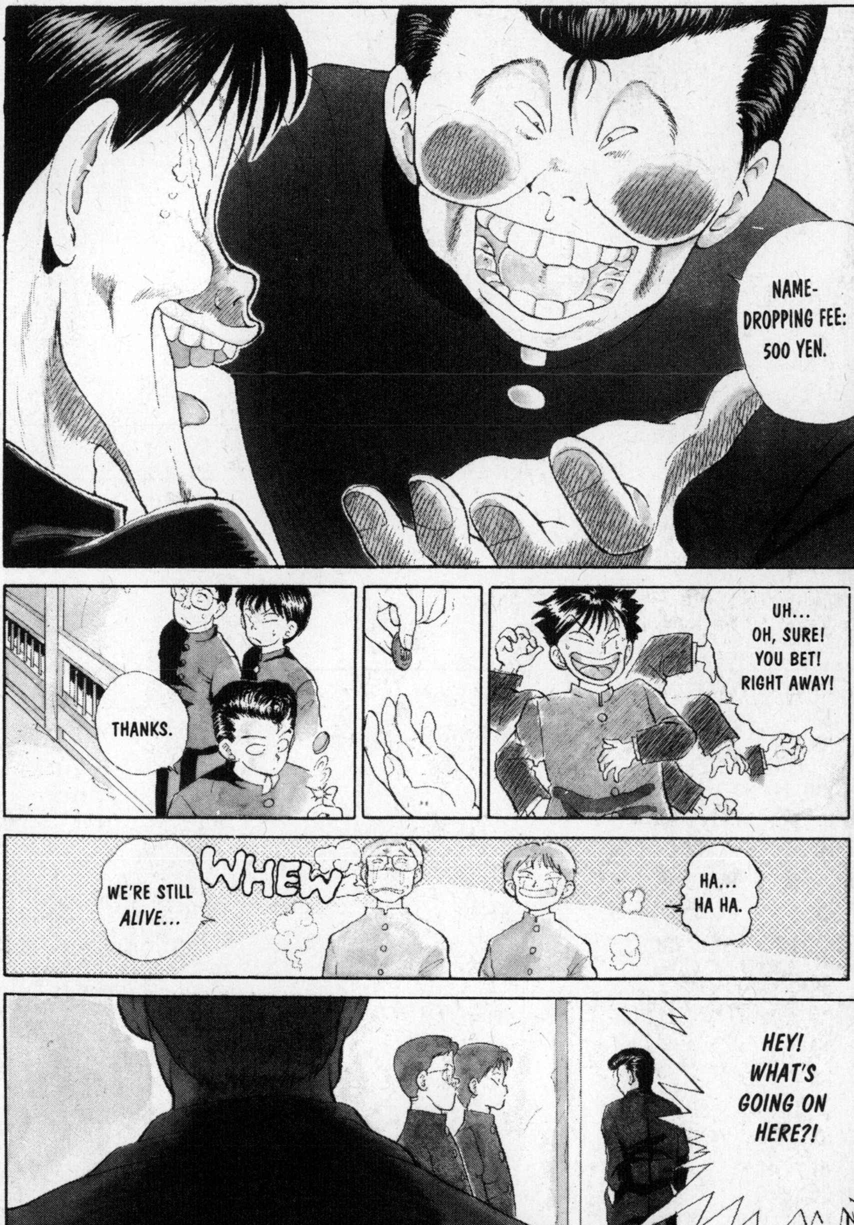
NAME-DROPPING FEE: 500 YEN.
UH... OH, SURE! YOU BET! RIGHT AWAY!
THANKS.
HA... HA HA.
WHEW
WE'RE STILL ALIVE...
HEY! WHAT'S GOING ON HERE?!

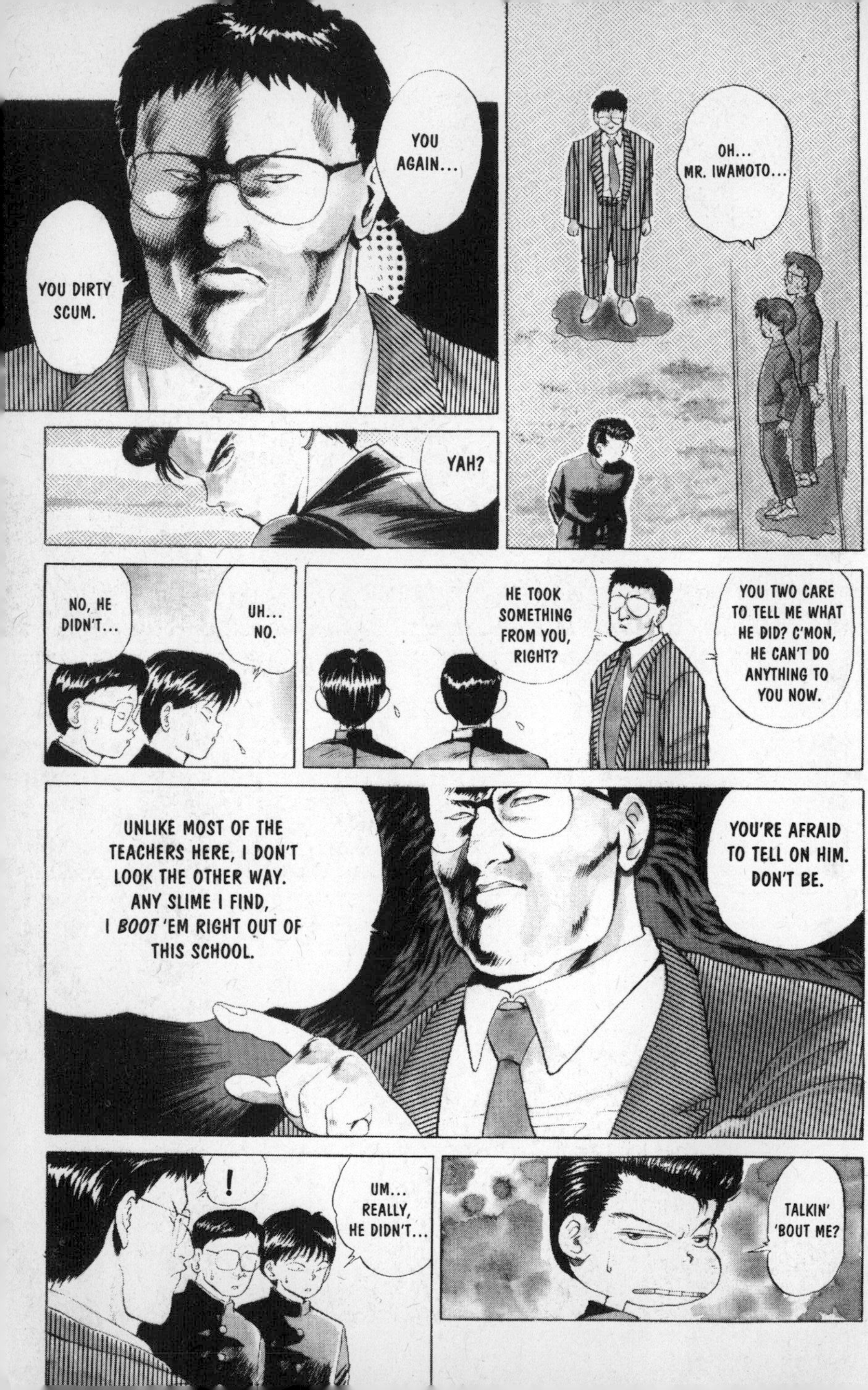

OH...
MR. IWAMOTO...
YOU AGAIN...
YOU DIRTY SCUM.
YAH?
YOU TWO CARE TO TELL ME WHAT HE DID? C'MON, HE CAN'T DO ANYTHING TO YOU NOW.
HE TOOK SOMETHING FROM YOU, RIGHT?
UH... NO.
NO, HE DIDN'T...
YOU'RE AFRAID TO TELL ON HIM. DON'T BE.
UNLIKE MOST OF THE TEACHERS HERE, I DON'T LOOK THE OTHER WAY. ANY SLIME I FIND, I *BOOT* 'EM RIGHT OUT OF THIS SCHOOL.
TALKIN' 'BOUT ME?
UM... REALLY, HE DIDN'T...
!

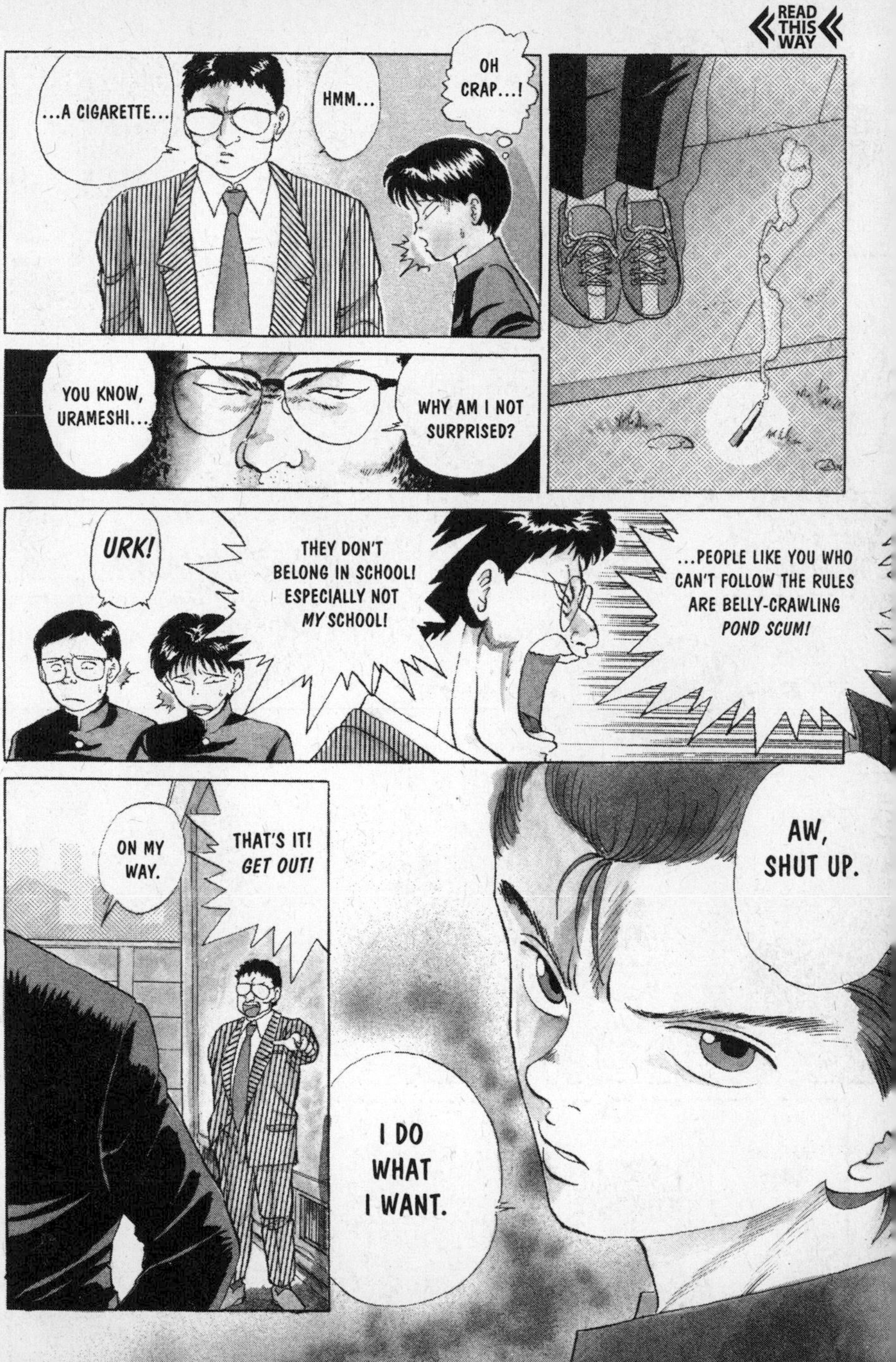
READ THIS WAY
OH CRAP...!
HMM...
...A CIGARETTE...
WHY AM I NOT SURPRISED?
YOU KNOW, URAMESHI...
...PEOPLE LIKE YOU WHO CAN'T FOLLOW THE RULES ARE BELLY-CRAWLING *POND SCUM!*
THEY DON'T BELONG IN SCHOOL! ESPECIALLY NOT *MY* SCHOOL!
URK!
AW, SHUT UP.
I DO WHAT I WANT.
THAT'S IT! *GET OUT!*
ON MY WAY.

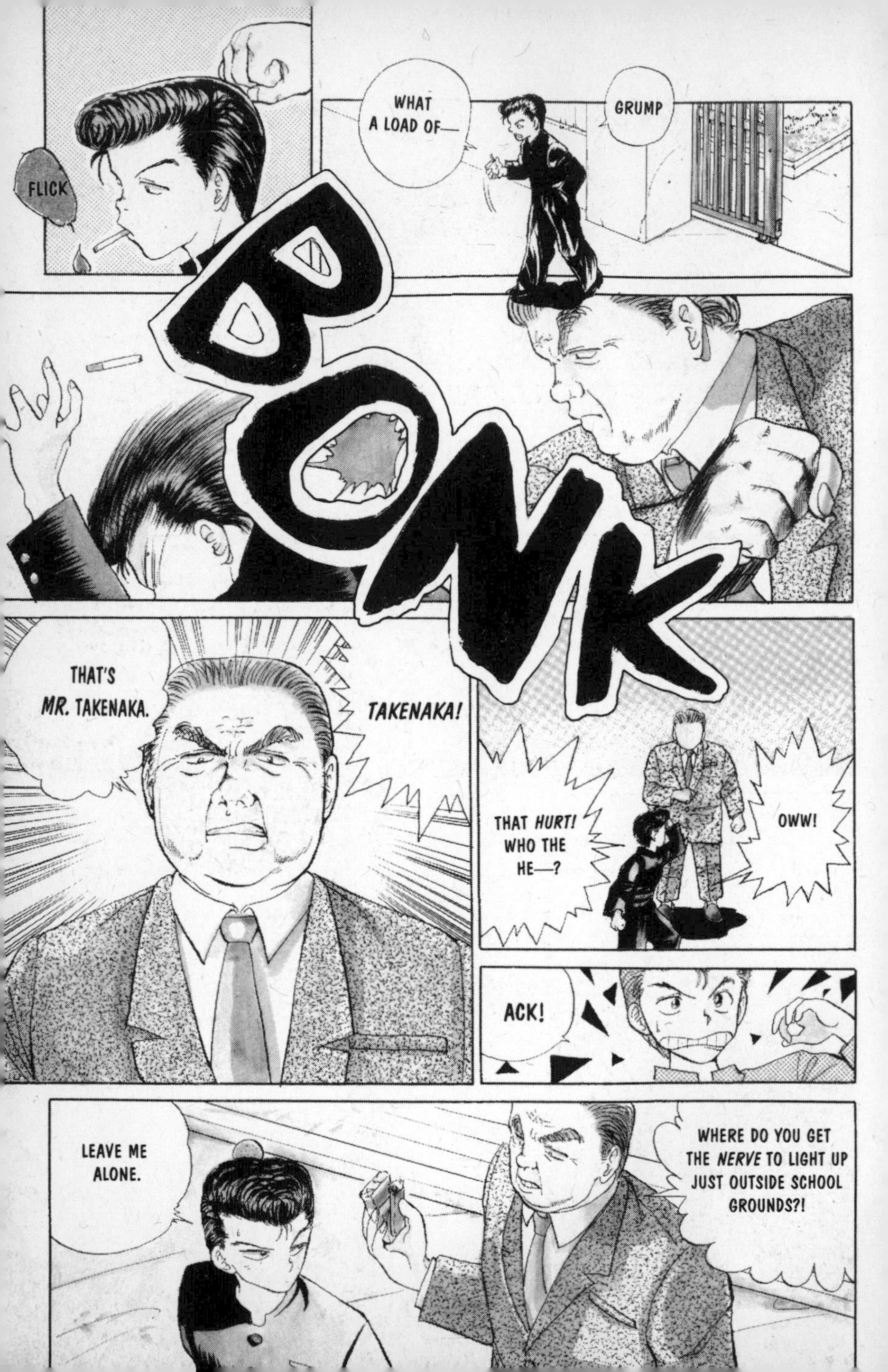
GRUMP
WHAT A LOAD OF—
FLICK
BONK
OWW!
THAT HURT! WHO THE HE—?
ACK!
TAKENAKA!
THAT'S MR. TAKENAKA.
WHERE DO YOU GET THE NERVE TO LIGHT UP JUST OUTSIDE SCHOOL GROUNDS?!
LEAVE ME ALONE.

READ THIS WAY

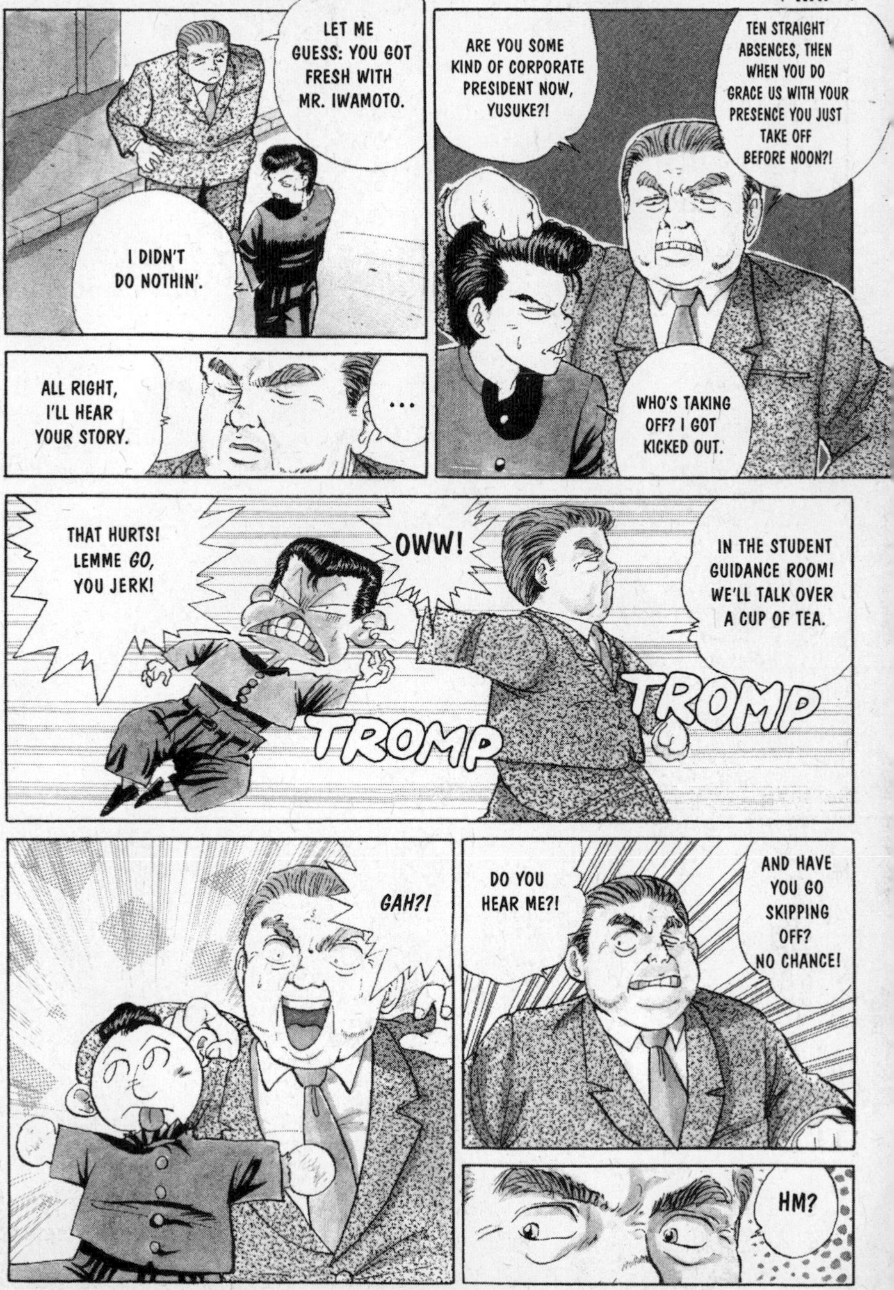

TEN STRAIGHT ABSENCES, THEN WHEN YOU DO GRACE US WITH YOUR PRESENCE YOU JUST TAKE OFF BEFORE NOON?!
ARE YOU SOME KIND OF CORPORATE PRESIDENT NOW, YUSUKE?!
WHO'S TAKING OFF? I GOT KICKED OUT.
LET ME GUESS: YOU GOT FRESH WITH MR. IWAMOTO.
I DIDN'T DO NOTHIN'.
...
ALL RIGHT, I'LL HEAR YOUR STORY.
IN THE STUDENT GUIDANCE ROOM! WE'LL TALK OVER A CUP OF TEA.
TROMP
TROMP
OWW!
THAT HURTS! LEMME *GO*, YOU JERK!
AND HAVE YOU GO SKIPPING OFF? NO CHANCE!
DO YOU HEAR ME?!
HM?
GAH?!

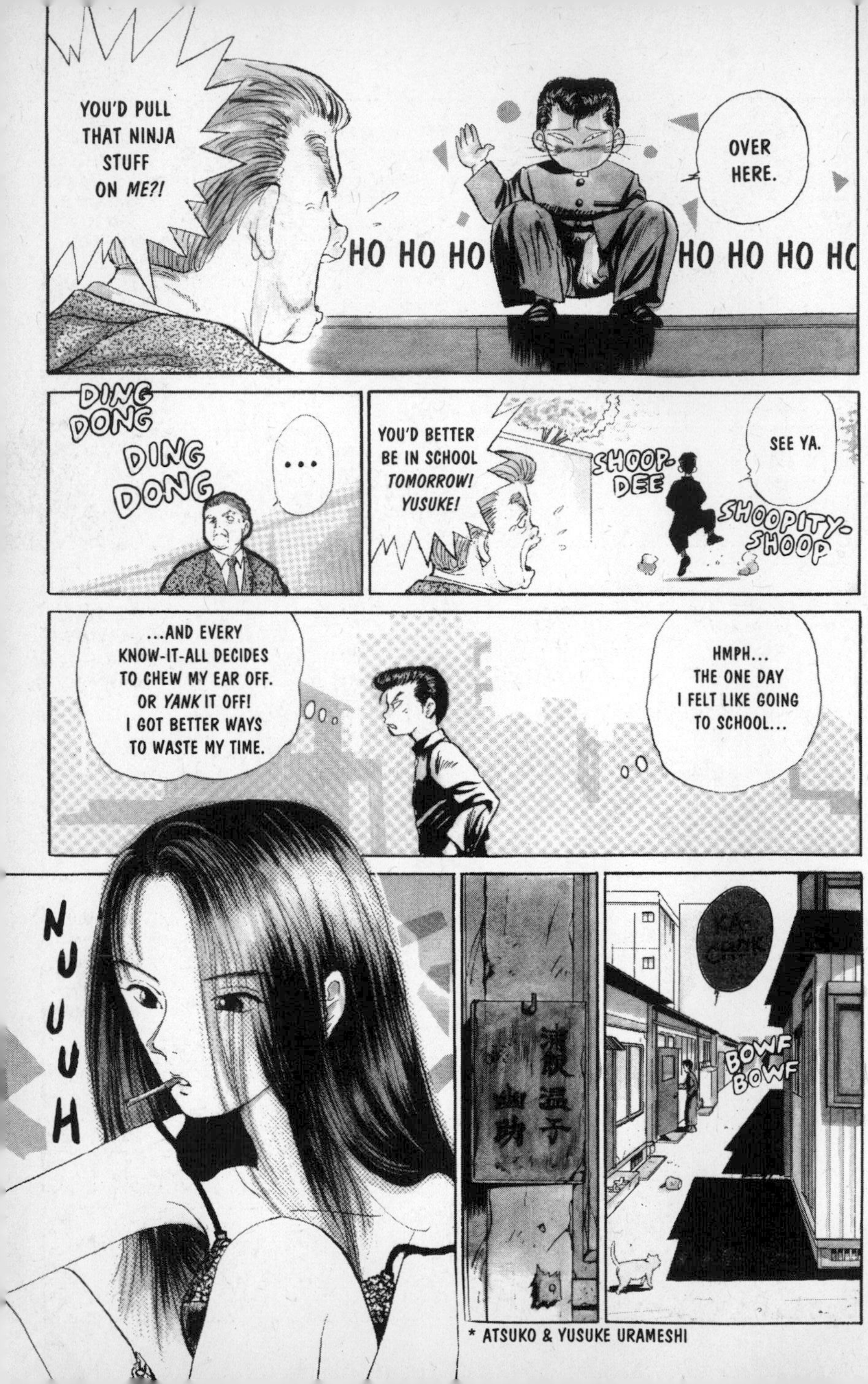
OVER HERE.
HO HO HO HO HO HO HO
YOU'D PULL THAT NINJA STUFF ON *ME?!*
SEE YA.
SHOOP-DEE
SHOOPITY-SHOOP
YOU'D BETTER BE IN SCHOOL *TOMORROW! YUSUKE!*
DING DONG
DING DONG
...
HMPH... THE ONE DAY I FELT LIKE GOING TO SCHOOL...
...AND EVERY KNOW-IT-ALL DECIDES TO CHEW MY EAR OFF. OR *YANK* IT OFF! I GOT BETTER WAYS TO WASTE MY TIME.
BOWF BOWF
浦飯温子
幽助
NUUUH

* ATSUKO & YUSUKE URAMESHI

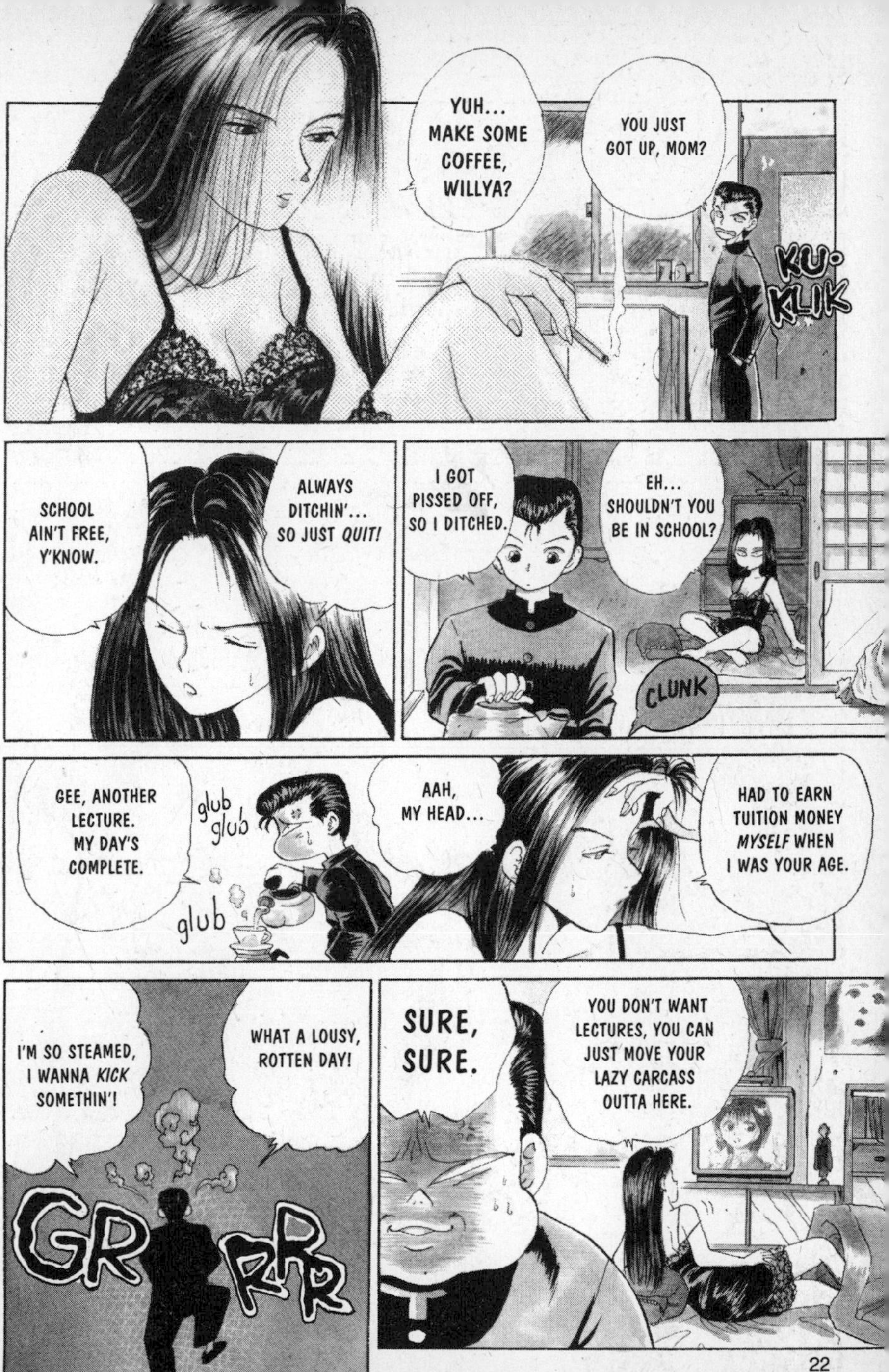
KU-KLIK
YOU JUST GOT UP, MOM?
YUH... MAKE SOME COFFEE, WILLYA?
EH... SHOULDN'T YOU BE IN SCHOOL?
I GOT PISSED OFF, SO I DITCHED.
CLUNK
ALWAYS DITCHIN'... SO JUST *QUIT!*
SCHOOL AIN'T FREE, Y'KNOW.
HAD TO EARN TUITION MONEY *MYSELF* WHEN I WAS YOUR AGE.
AAH, MY HEAD...
glub glub
GEE, ANOTHER LECTURE. MY DAY'S COMPLETE.
glub
YOU DON'T WANT LECTURES, YOU CAN JUST MOVE YOUR LAZY CARCASS OUTTA HERE.
SURE, SURE.
WHAT A LOUSY, ROTTEN DAY!
I'M SO STEAMED, I WANNA *KICK* SOMETHIN'!
GRRRR

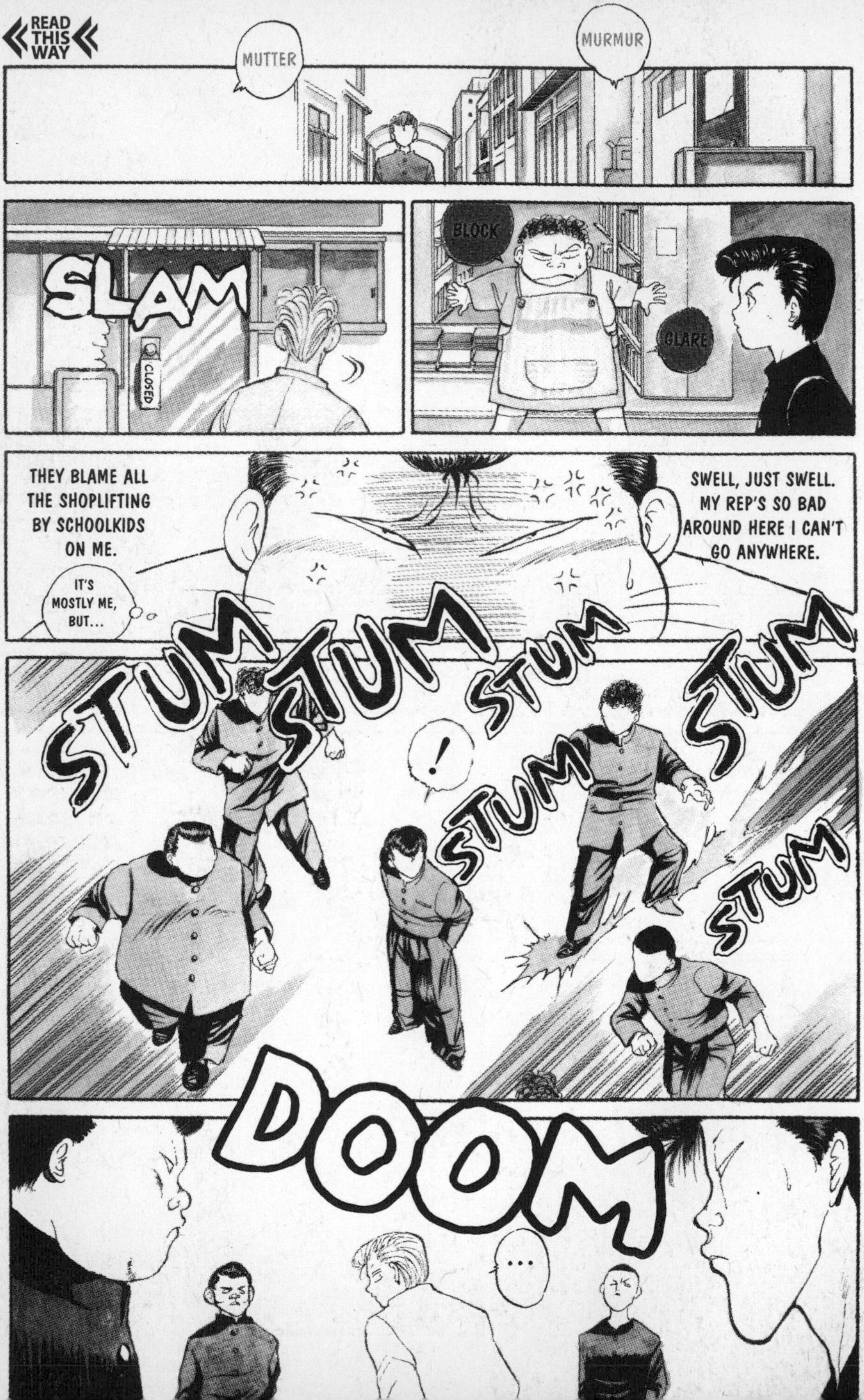

READ THIS WAY
MURMUR
MUTTER
BLOCK
GLARE
SLAM
CLOSED
SWELL, JUST SWELL. MY REP'S SO BAD AROUND HERE I CAN'T GO ANYWHERE.
THEY BLAME ALL THE SHOPLIFTING BY SCHOOLKIDS ON ME.
IT'S MOSTLY ME, BUT...
STUM STUM STUM STUM STUM STUM STUM STUM
!
DOOM
...

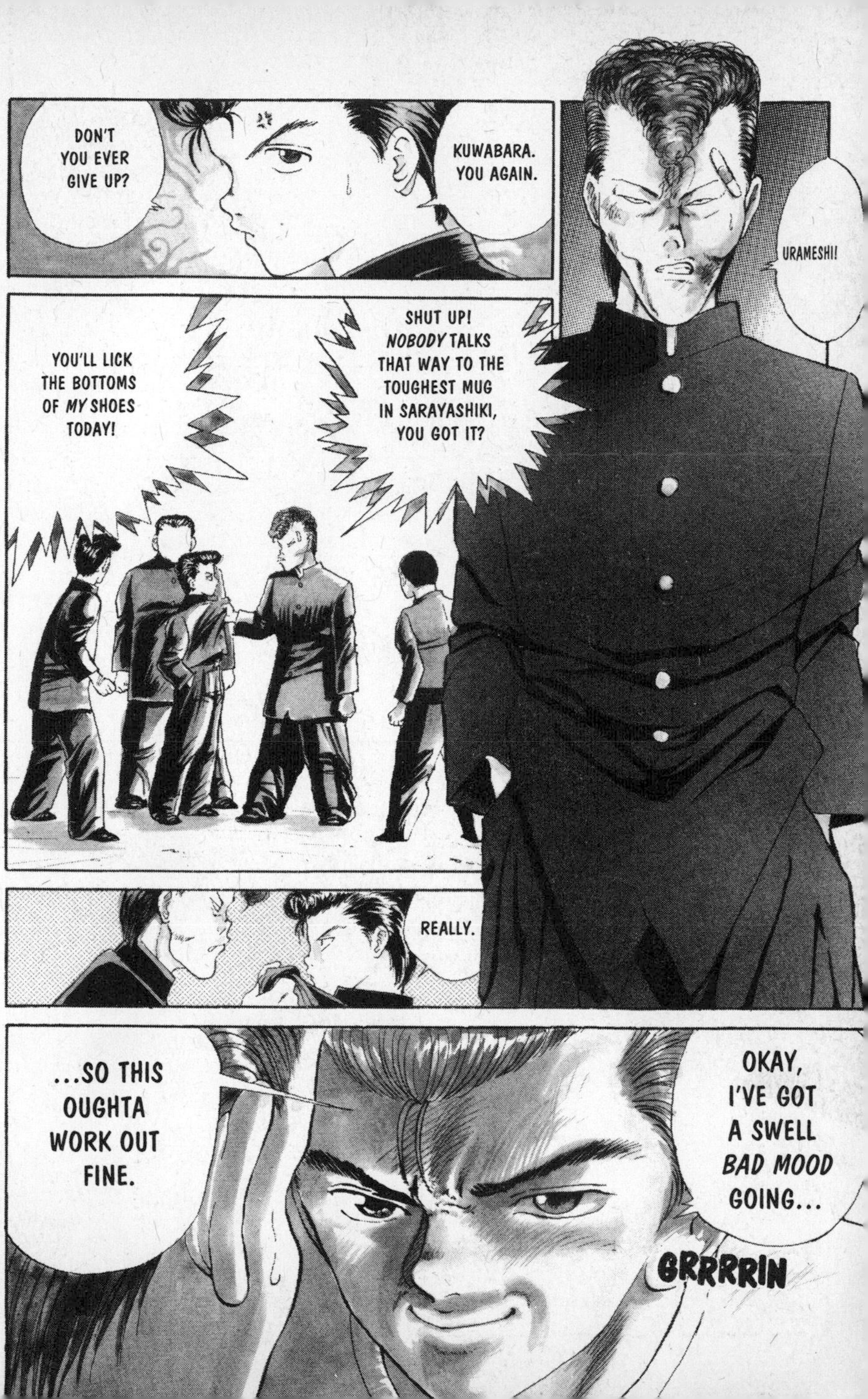
URAMESHI!
KUWABARA. YOU AGAIN.
DON'T YOU EVER GIVE UP?
SHUT UP! *NOBODY* TALKS THAT WAY TO THE TOUGHEST MUG IN SARAYASHIKI, YOU GOT IT?
YOU'LL LICK THE BOTTOMS OF *MY* SHOES TODAY!
REALLY.
OKAY, I'VE GOT A SWELL *BAD MOOD* GOING...
GRRRRIN
...SO THIS OUGHTA WORK OUT FINE.

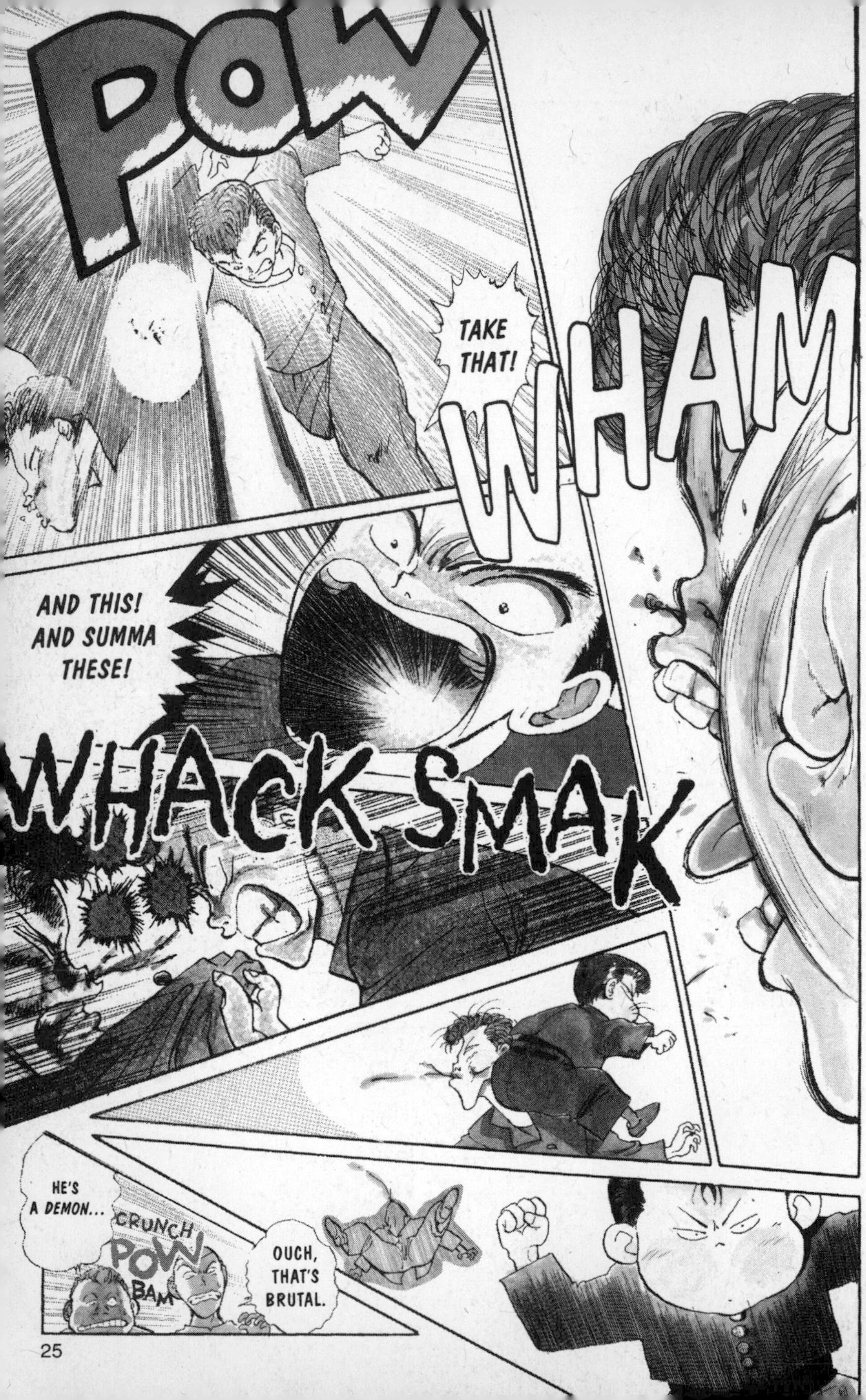
WHAM
POW
TAKE THAT!
AND THIS! AND SUMMA THESE!
WHACK
SMAK
OUCH, THAT'S BRUTAL.
HE'S A DEMON...
CRUNCH
POW
BAM

READ THIS WAY

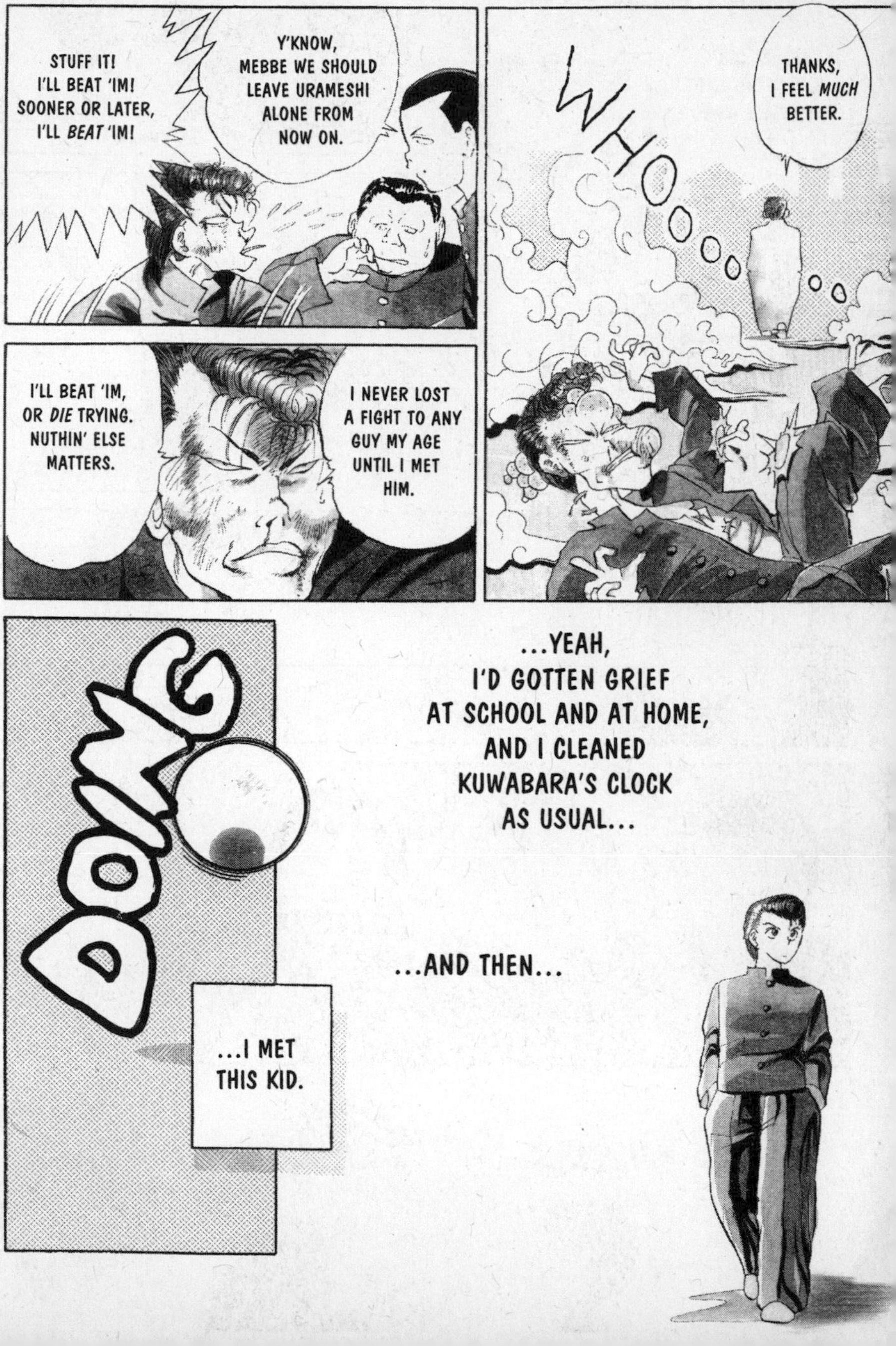
THANKS, I FEEL *MUCH* BETTER.
WHOOOOOOO
Y'KNOW, MEBBE WE SHOULD LEAVE URAMESHI ALONE FROM NOW ON.
STUFF IT! I'LL BEAT 'IM! SOONER OR LATER, I'LL *BEAT* 'IM!
I NEVER LOST A FIGHT TO ANY GUY MY AGE UNTIL I MET HIM.
I'LL BEAT 'IM, OR *DIE* TRYING. NUTHIN' ELSE MATTERS.
...YEAH, I'D GOTTEN GRIEF AT SCHOOL AND AT HOME, AND I CLEANED KUWABARA'S CLOCK AS USUAL...
...AND THEN...
DOING
...I MET THIS KID.

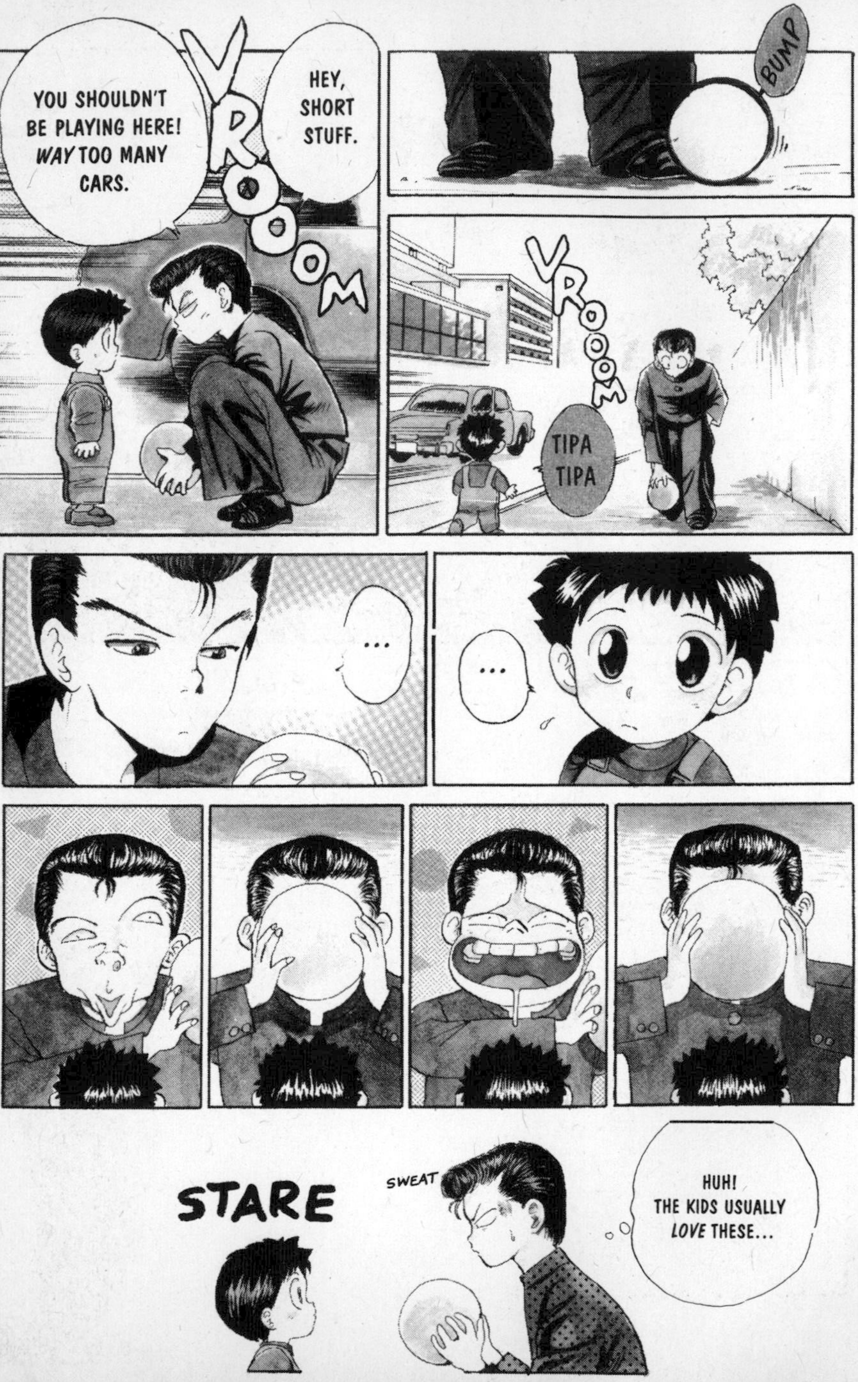
BUMP
VROOOM
TIPA TIPA
HEY, SHORT STUFF.
VROOOM
YOU SHOULDN'T BE PLAYING HERE! *WAY* TOO MANY CARS.
...
...
HUH! THE KIDS USUALLY *LOVE* THESE...
SWEAT
STARE

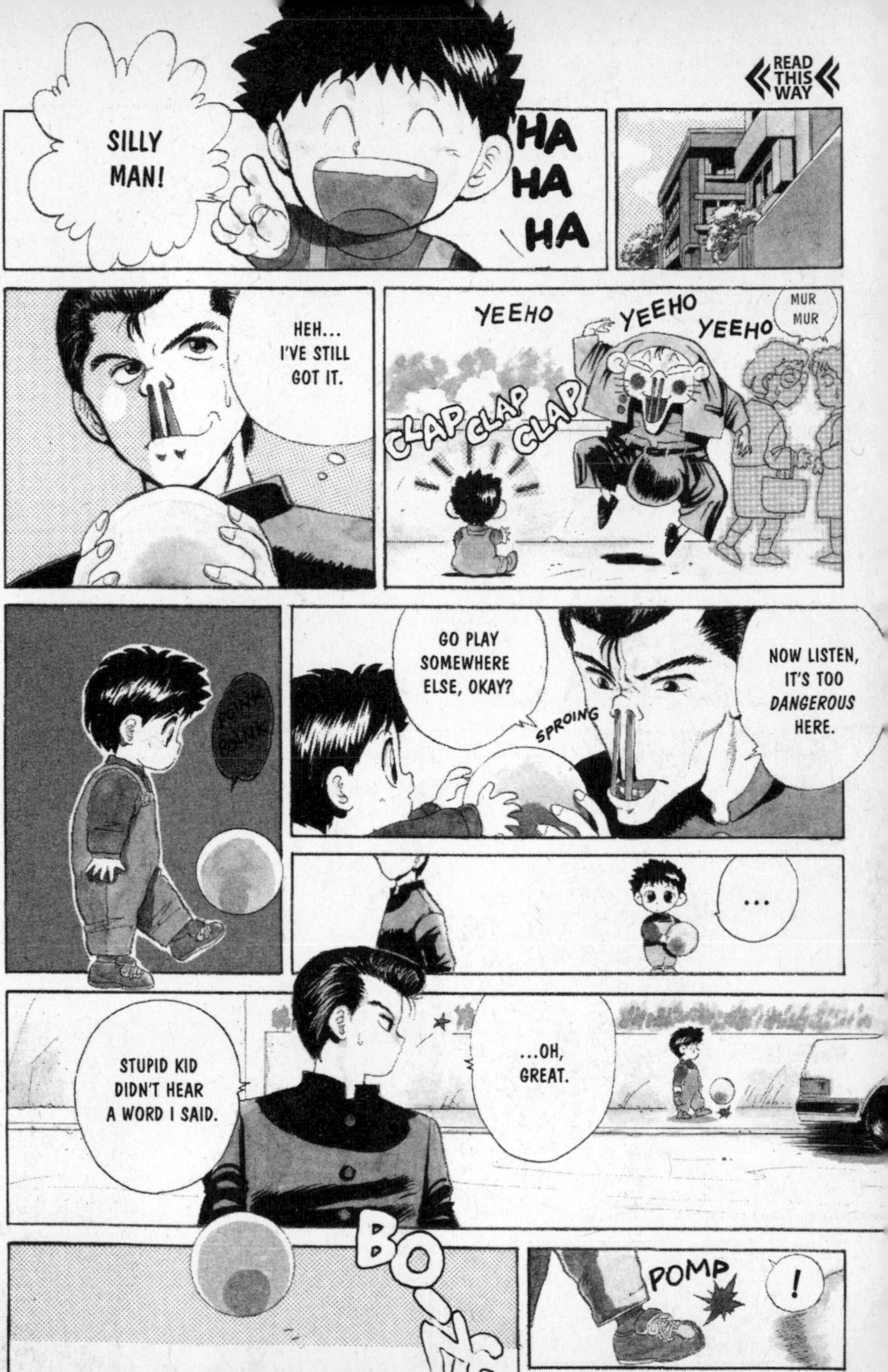
READ THIS WAY
HA HA HA
SILLY MAN!
MUR MUR
YEEHO YEEHO YEEHO
CLAP CLAP CLAP
HEH... I'VE STILL GOT IT.
NOW LISTEN, IT'S TOO *DANGEROUS* HERE.
GO PLAY SOMEWHERE ELSE, OKAY?
SPROING
...
POINK POINK
...OH, GREAT.
STUPID KID DIDN'T HEAR A WORD I SAID.
POMP
!
BOING

READ THIS WAY

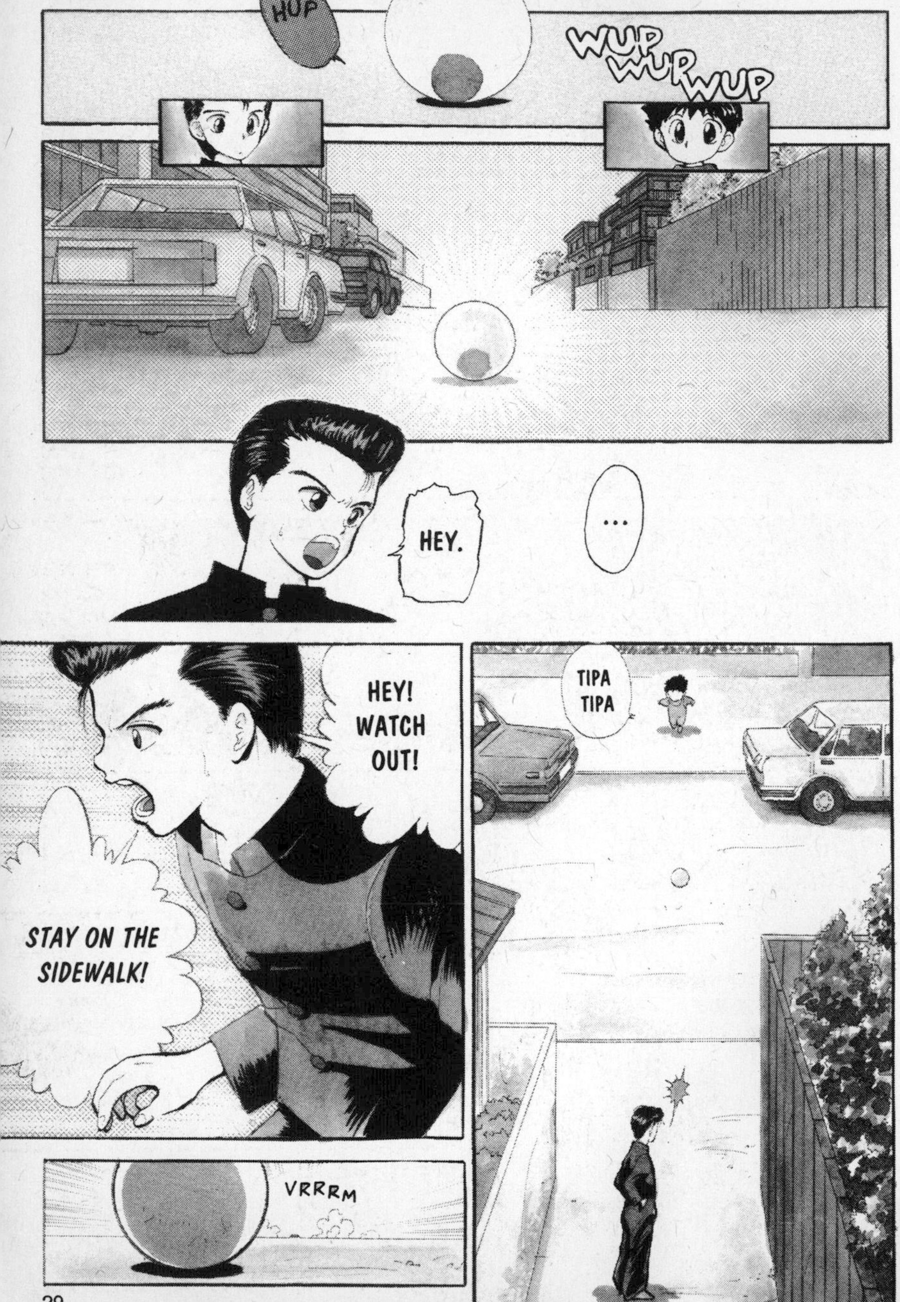
WUP WUR WUP
HUP
...
HEY.
TIPA TIPA
HEY! WATCH OUT!
STAY ON THE SIDEWALK!
VRRRM

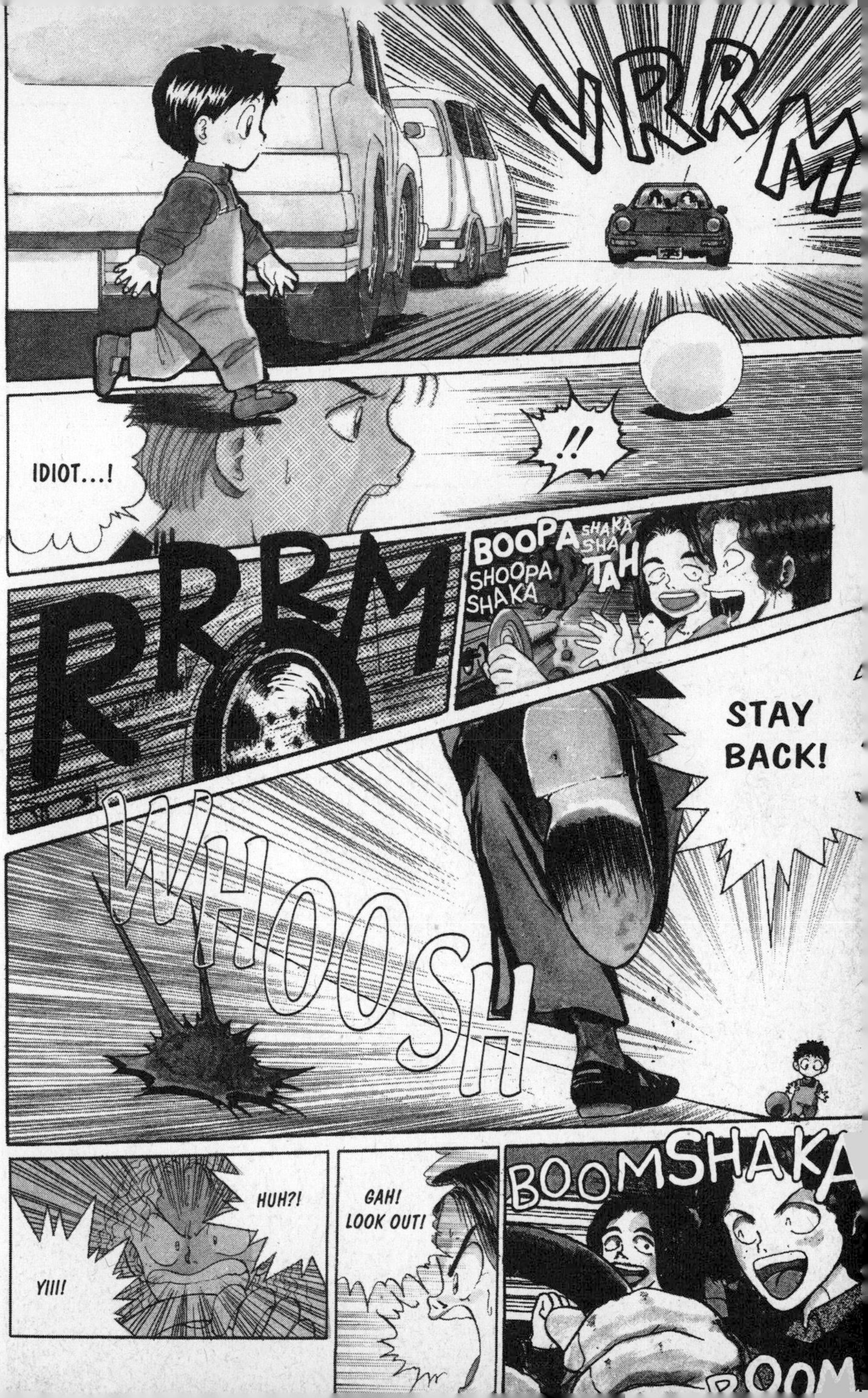
VRRM
!!
IDIOT...!
BOOPA
SHAKA SHA
TAH
SHOOPA SHAKA
RRRM
STAY BACK!
WHOOSH
BOOMSHAKA
BOOM
GAH! LOOK OUT!
HUH?!
YIII!

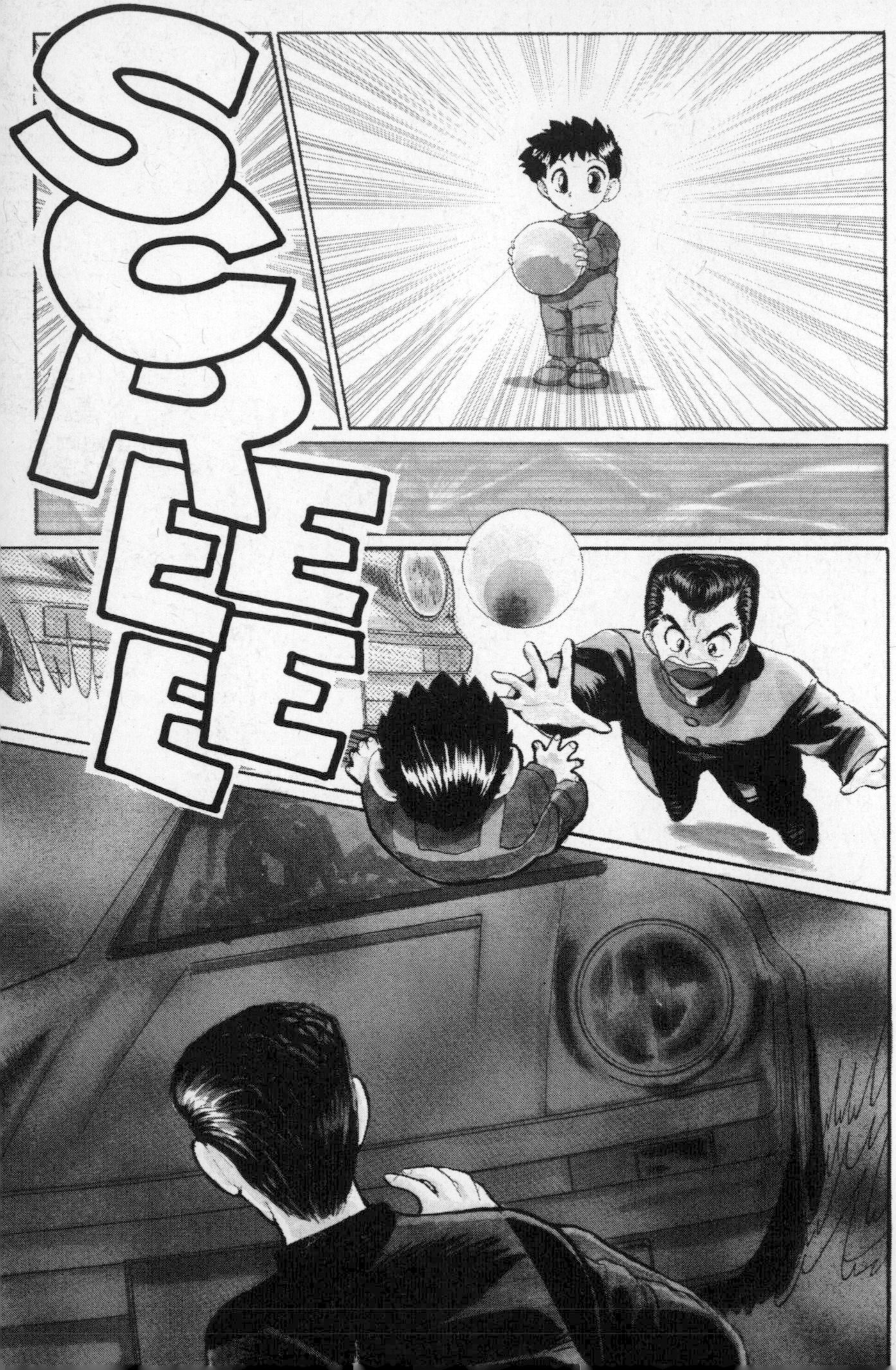
SCREEEE

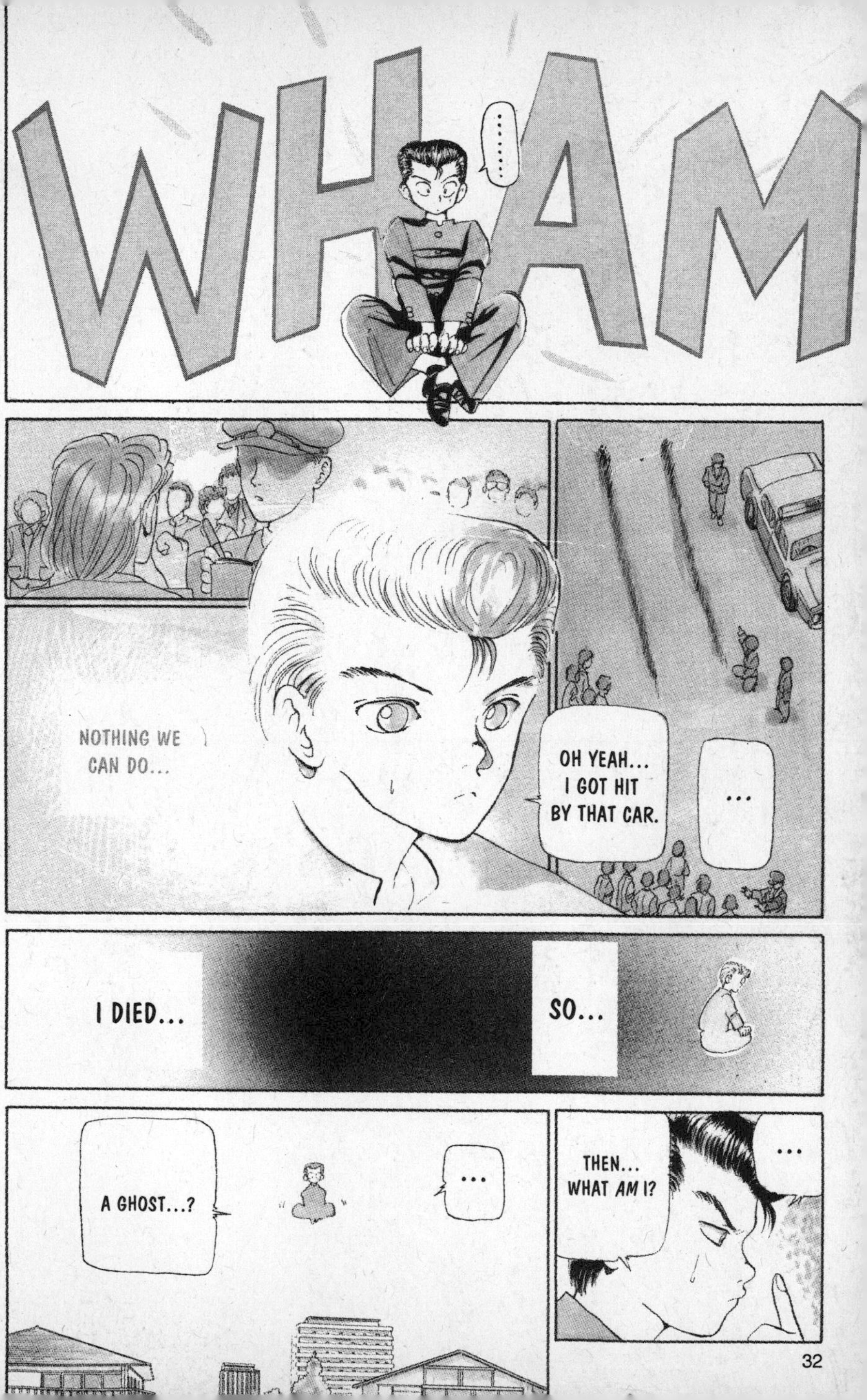
WHAM
......
...
OH YEAH... I GOT HIT BY THAT CAR.
NOTHING WE CAN DO...
SO...
I DIED...
...
THEN... WHAT *AM* I?
...
A GHOST...?

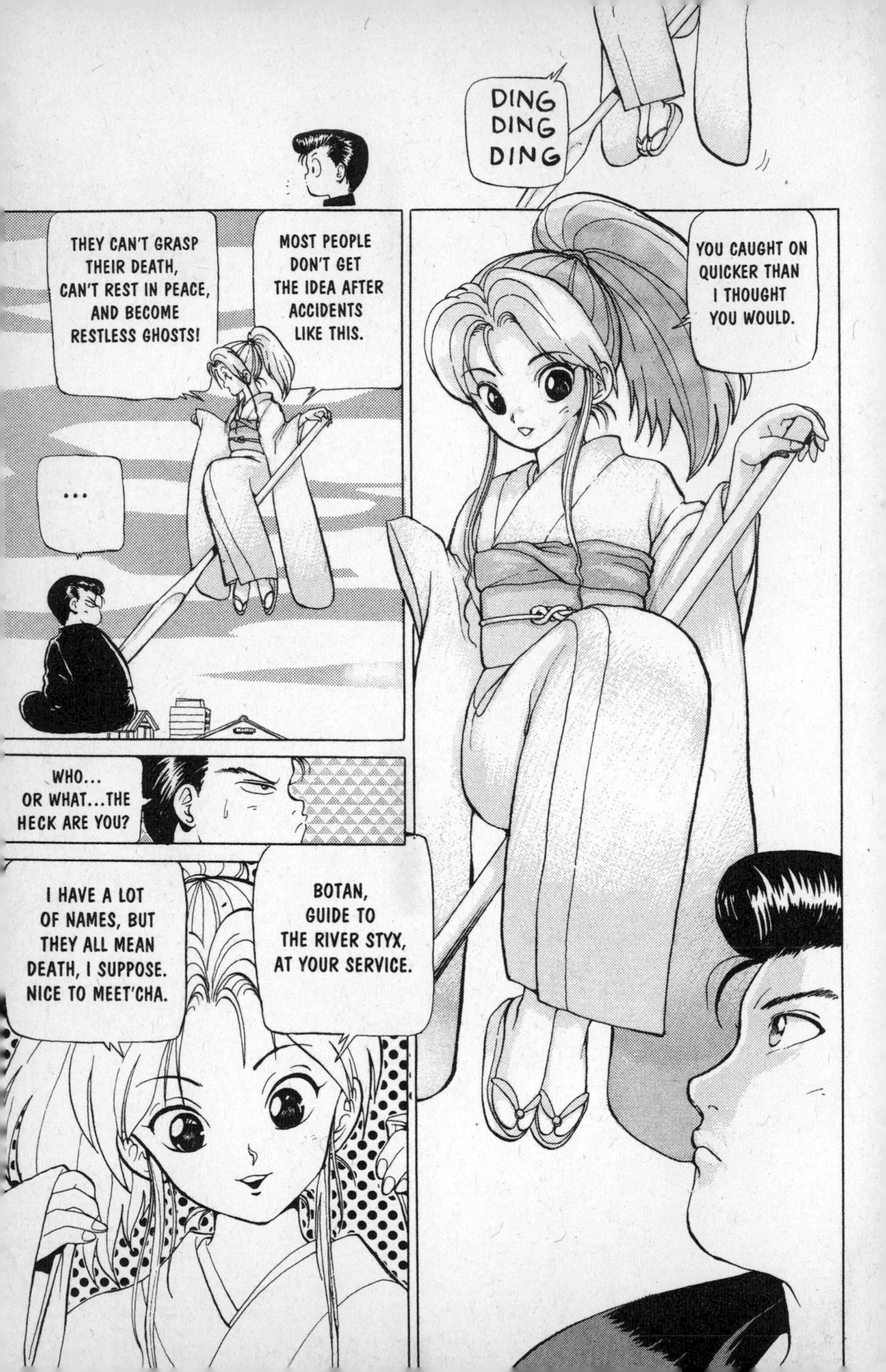
DING DING DING
YOU CAUGHT ON QUICKER THAN I THOUGHT YOU WOULD.
MOST PEOPLE DON'T GET THE IDEA AFTER ACCIDENTS LIKE THIS.
THEY CAN'T GRASP THEIR DEATH, CAN'T REST IN PEACE, AND BECOME RESTLESS GHOSTS!
...
WHO... OR WHAT...THE HECK ARE YOU?
BOTAN, GUIDE TO THE RIVER STYX, AT YOUR SERVICE.
I HAVE A LOT OF NAMES, BUT THEY ALL MEAN DEATH, I SUPPOSE. NICE TO MEET'CHA.

READ THIS WAY

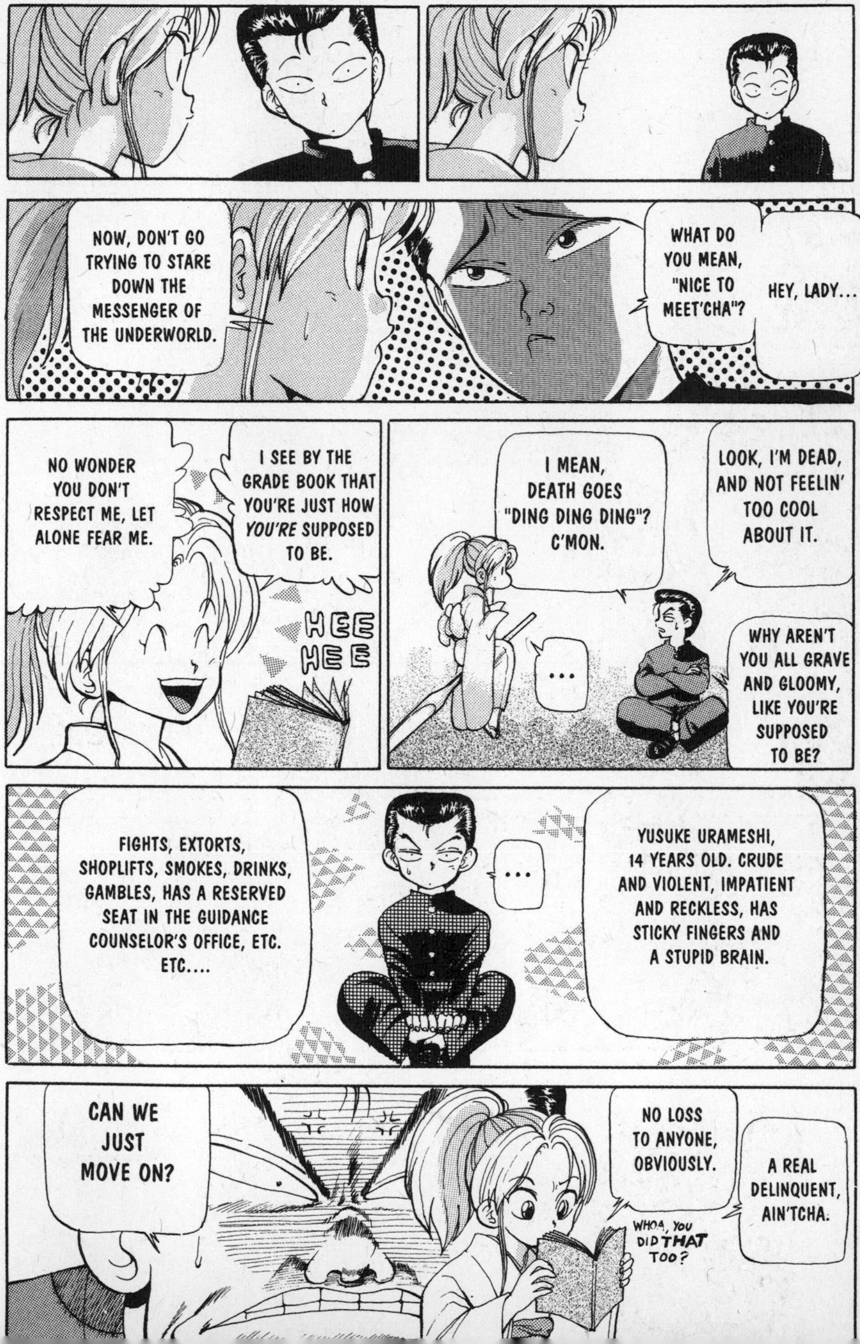
HEY, LADY...
WHAT DO YOU MEAN, "NICE TO MEET'CHA"?
NOW, DON'T GO TRYING TO STARE DOWN THE MESSENGER OF THE UNDERWORLD.
LOOK, I'M DEAD, AND NOT FEELIN' TOO COOL ABOUT IT.
I MEAN, DEATH GOES "DING DING DING"? C'MON.
WHY AREN'T YOU ALL GRAVE AND GLOOMY, LIKE YOU'RE SUPPOSED TO BE?
...
I SEE BY THE GRADE BOOK THAT YOU'RE JUST HOW *YOU'RE* SUPPOSED TO BE.
NO WONDER YOU DON'T RESPECT ME, LET ALONE FEAR ME.
HEE HEE
YUSUKE URAMESHI, 14 YEARS OLD. CRUDE AND VIOLENT, IMPATIENT AND RECKLESS, HAS STICKY FINGERS AND A STUPID BRAIN.
...
FIGHTS, EXTORTS, SHOPLIFTS, SMOKES, DRINKS, GAMBLES, HAS A RESERVED SEAT IN THE GUIDANCE COUNSELOR'S OFFICE, ETC. ETC....
A REAL DELINQUENT, AIN'TCHA.
NO LOSS TO ANYONE, OBVIOUSLY.
WHOA, YOU DID THAT TOO?
CAN WE JUST MOVE ON?

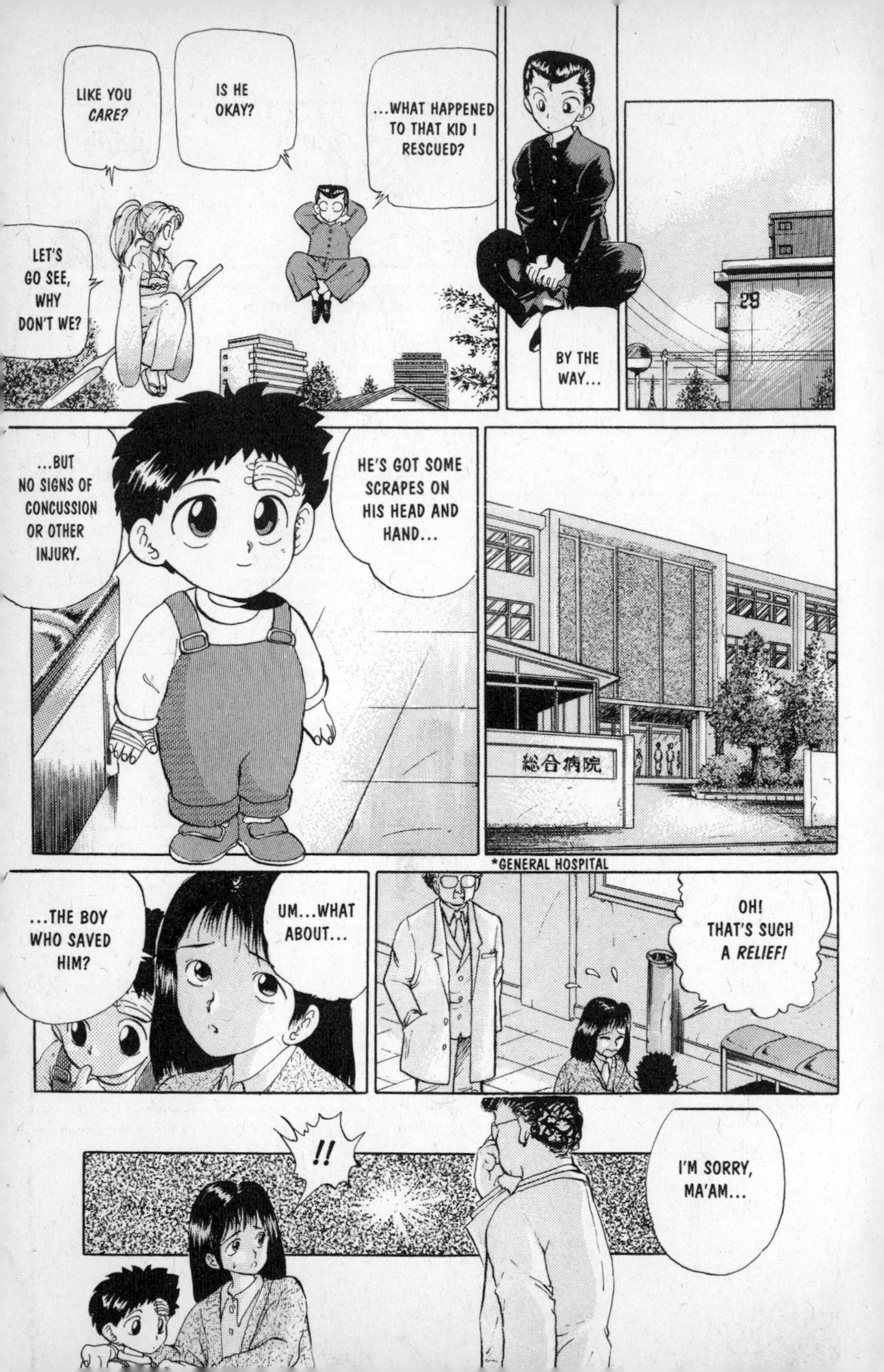
BY THE WAY...
...WHAT HAPPENED TO THAT KID I RESCUED?
IS HE OKAY?
LIKE YOU *CARE?*
LET'S GO SEE, WHY DON'T WE?
総合病院
*GENERAL HOSPITAL
HE'S GOT SOME SCRAPES ON HIS HEAD AND HAND...
...BUT NO SIGNS OF CONCUSSION OR OTHER INJURY.
OH! THAT'S SUCH A *RELIEF!*
UM...WHAT ABOUT...
...THE BOY WHO SAVED HIM?
I'M SORRY, MA'AM...
!!

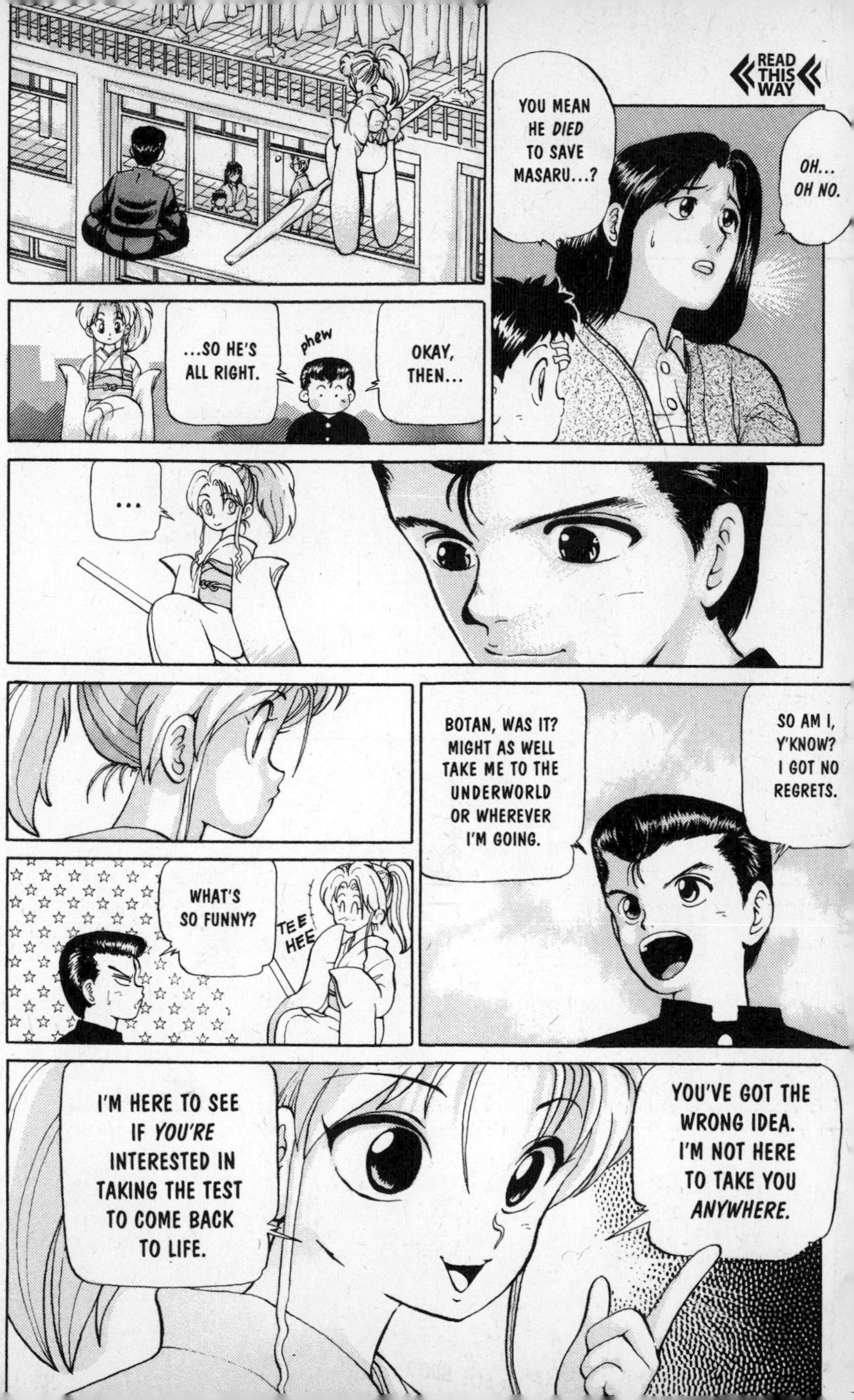
READ THIS WAY
YOU MEAN HE *DIED* TO SAVE MASARU...?
OH... OH NO.
OKAY, THEN...
phew
...SO HE'S ALL RIGHT.
...
SO AM I, Y'KNOW? I GOT NO REGRETS.
BOTAN, WAS IT? MIGHT AS WELL TAKE ME TO THE UNDERWORLD OR WHEREVER I'M GOING.
TEE HEE
WHAT'S SO FUNNY?
YOU'VE GOT THE WRONG IDEA. I'M NOT HERE TO TAKE YOU *ANYWHERE.*
I'M HERE TO SEE IF *YOU'RE* INTERESTED IN TAKING THE TEST TO COME BACK TO LIFE.

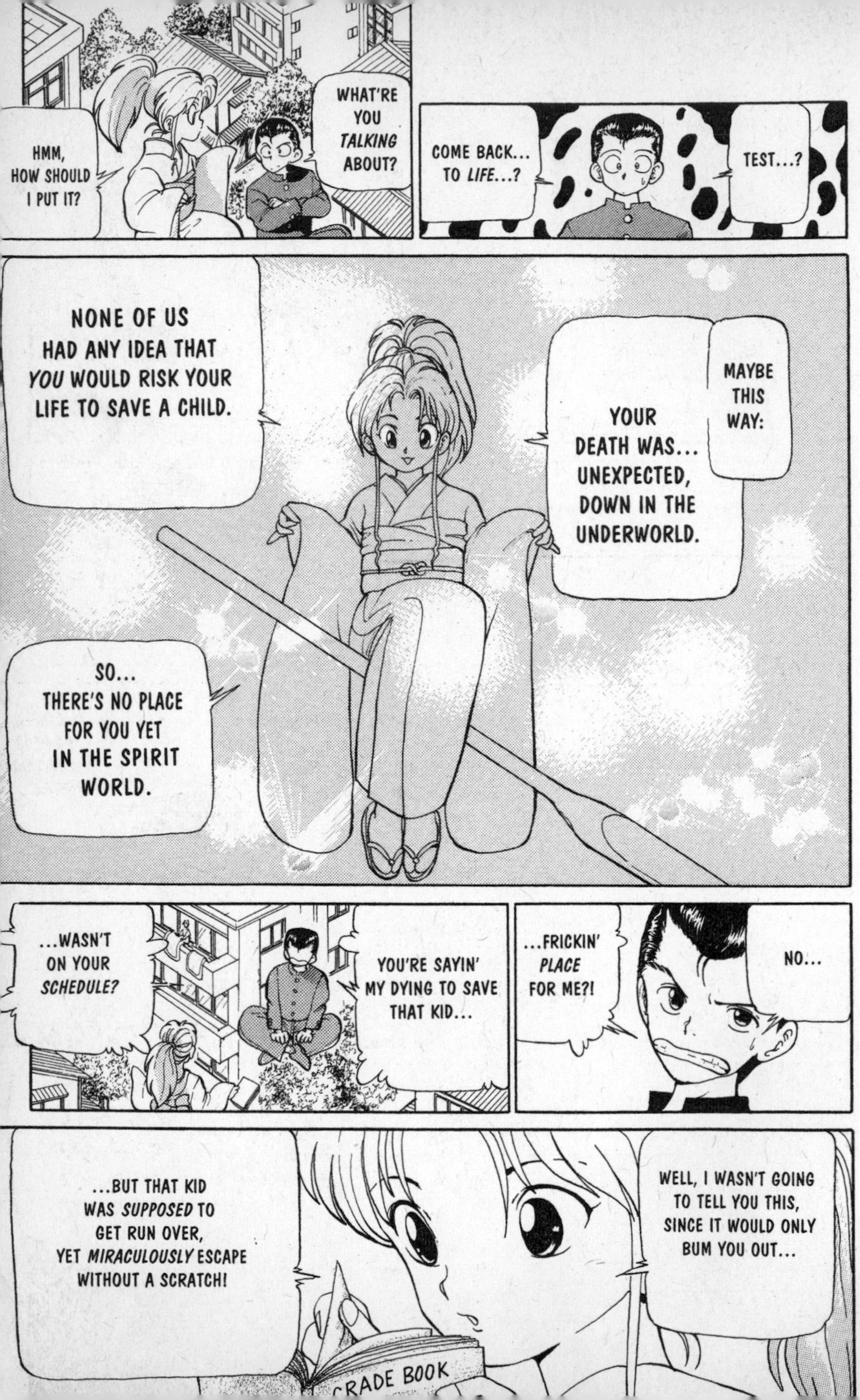
TEST...?
COME BACK... TO *LIFE*...?
WHAT'RE YOU *TALKING* ABOUT?
HMM, HOW SHOULD I PUT IT?
MAYBE THIS WAY:
YOUR DEATH WAS... UNEXPECTED, DOWN IN THE UNDERWORLD.
NONE OF US HAD ANY IDEA THAT *YOU* WOULD RISK YOUR LIFE TO SAVE A CHILD.
SO... THERE'S NO PLACE FOR YOU YET IN THE SPIRIT WORLD.
NO...
...FRICKIN' *PLACE* FOR ME?!
YOU'RE SAYIN' MY DYING TO SAVE THAT KID...
...WASN'T ON YOUR *SCHEDULE?*
WELL, I WASN'T GOING TO TELL YOU THIS, SINCE IT WOULD ONLY BUM YOU OUT...
...BUT THAT KID WAS *SUPPOSED* TO GET RUN OVER, YET *MIRACULOUSLY* ESCAPE WITHOUT A SCRATCH!
GRADE BOOK

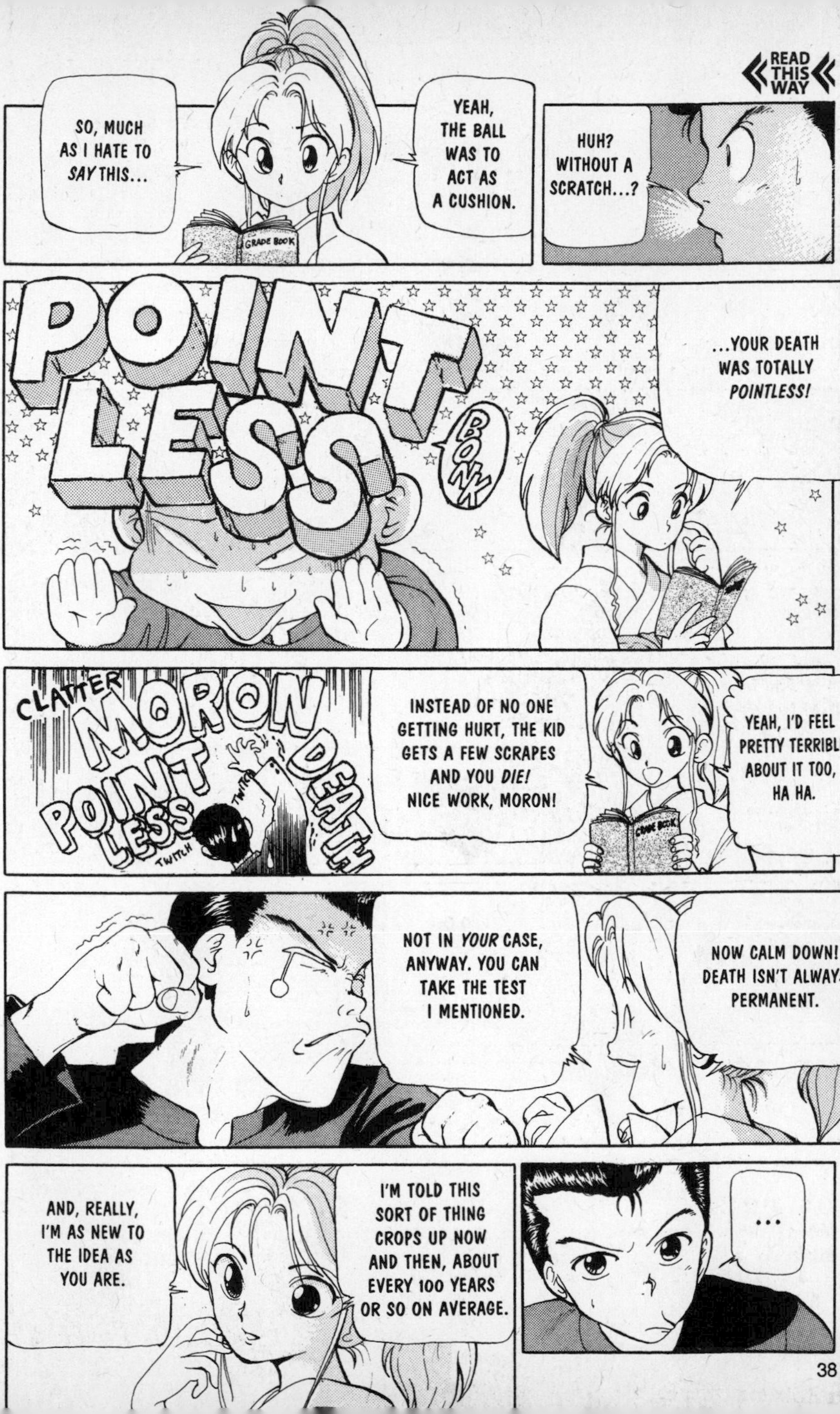
READ THIS WAY
HUH? WITHOUT A SCRATCH...?
YEAH, THE BALL WAS TO ACT AS A CUSHION.
SO, MUCH AS I HATE TO SAY THIS...
...YOUR DEATH WAS TOTALLY *POINTLESS!*
BONK
POINTLESS
YEAH, I'D FEEL PRETTY TERRIBLE ABOUT IT TOO, HA HA.
INSTEAD OF NO ONE GETTING HURT, THE KID GETS A FEW SCRAPES AND YOU *DIE!* NICE WORK, MORON!
CLATTER
MORON
DEATH
POINTLESS
TWITCH
TWITCH
NOW CALM DOWN! DEATH ISN'T ALWAYS PERMANENT.
NOT IN *YOUR* CASE, ANYWAY. YOU CAN TAKE THE TEST I MENTIONED.
...
I'M TOLD THIS SORT OF THING CROPS UP NOW AND THEN, ABOUT EVERY 100 YEARS OR SO ON AVERAGE.
AND, REALLY, I'M AS NEW TO THE IDEA AS YOU ARE.

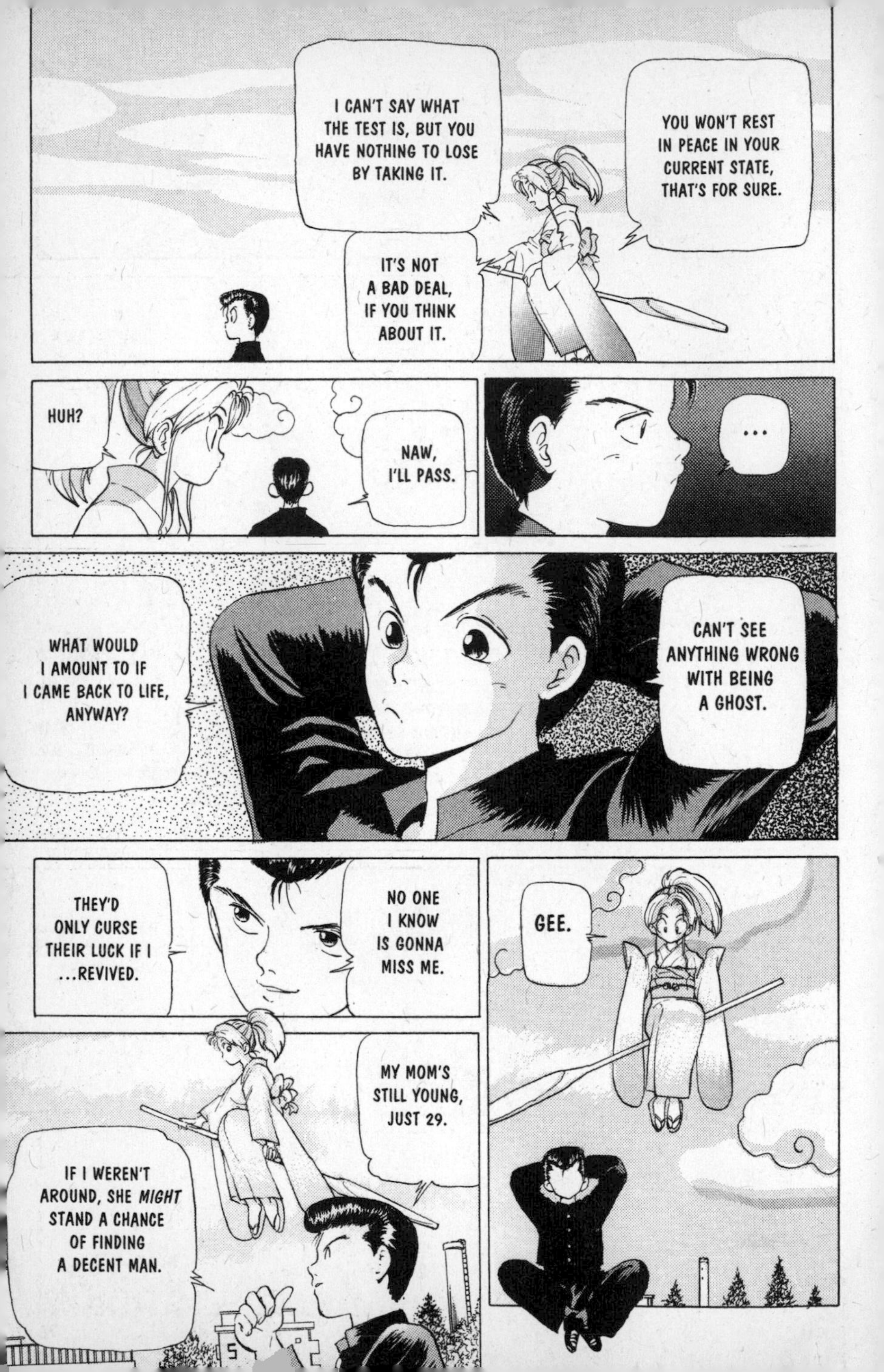
YOU WON'T REST IN PEACE IN YOUR CURRENT STATE, THAT'S FOR SURE.
I CAN'T SAY WHAT THE TEST IS, BUT YOU HAVE NOTHING TO LOSE BY TAKING IT.
IT'S NOT A BAD DEAL, IF YOU THINK ABOUT IT.
...
NAW, I'LL PASS.
HUH?
CAN'T SEE ANYTHING WRONG WITH BEING A GHOST.
WHAT WOULD I AMOUNT TO IF I CAME BACK TO LIFE, ANYWAY?
GEE.
NO ONE I KNOW IS GONNA MISS ME.
THEY'D ONLY CURSE THEIR LUCK IF I ...REVIVED.
MY MOM'S STILL YOUNG, JUST 29.
IF I WEREN'T AROUND, SHE *MIGHT* STAND A CHANCE OF FINDING A DECENT MAN.

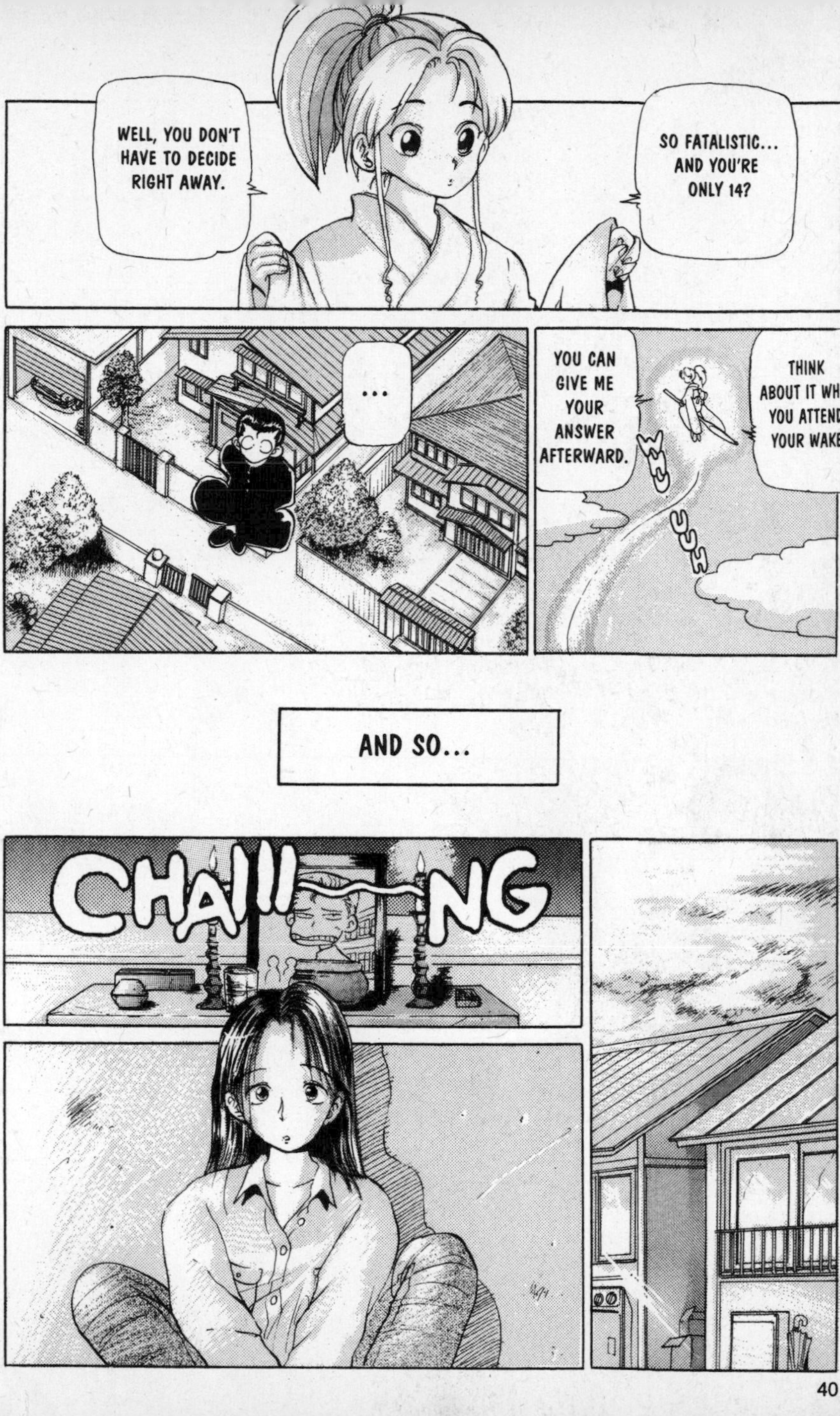
SO FATALISTIC... AND YOU'RE ONLY 14?
WELL, YOU DON'T HAVE TO DECIDE RIGHT AWAY.
THINK ABOUT IT WHILE YOU ATTEND YOUR WAKE.
YOU CAN GIVE ME YOUR ANSWER AFTERWARD.
...
AND SO...
CHAIII—NG

READ THIS WAY

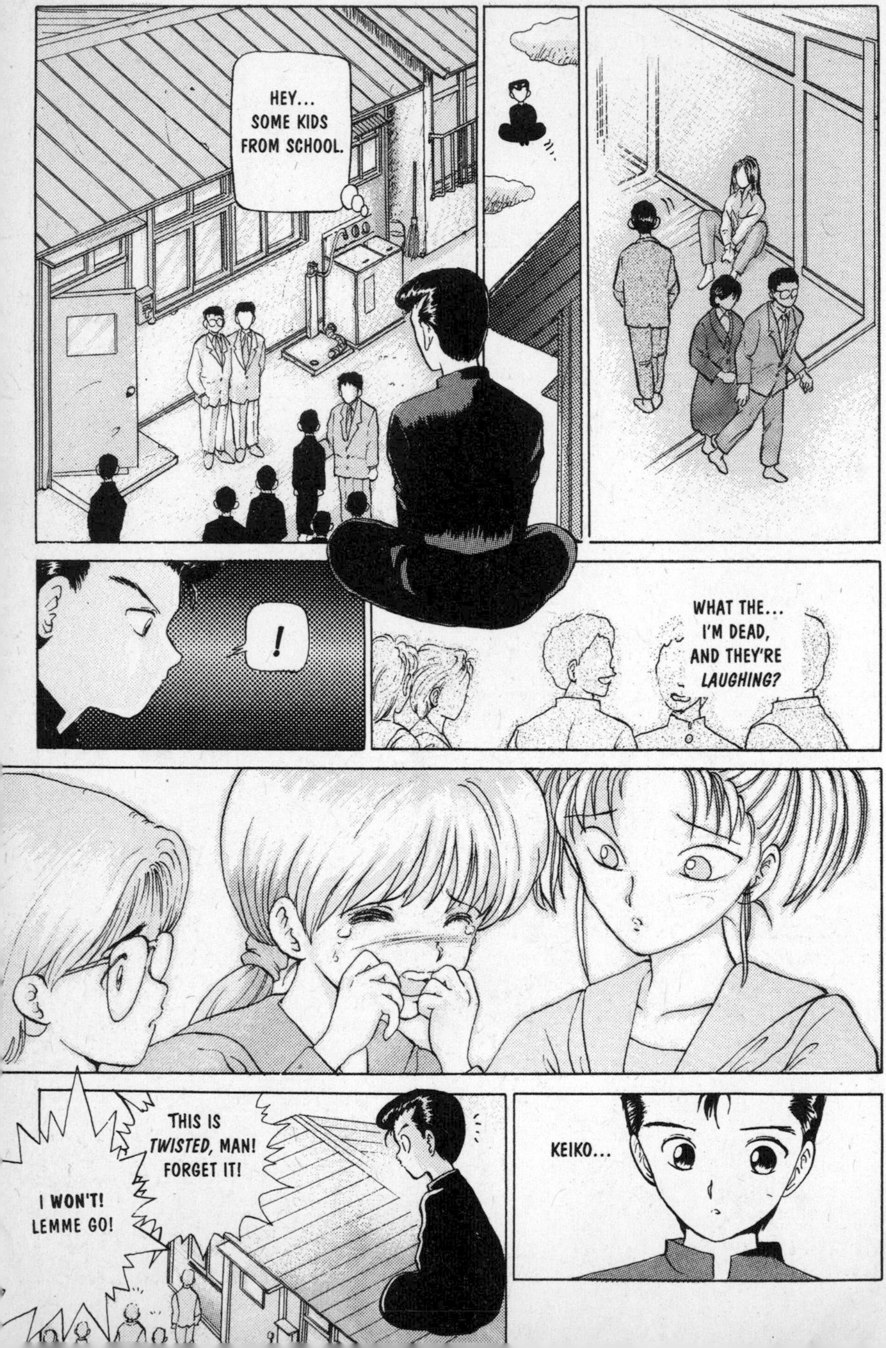
HEY... SOME KIDS FROM SCHOOL.
WHAT THE... I'M DEAD, AND THEY'RE *LAUGHING?*
!
KEIKO...
THIS IS *TWISTED,* MAN! FORGET IT!
I WON'T! LEMME GO!

READ THIS WAY

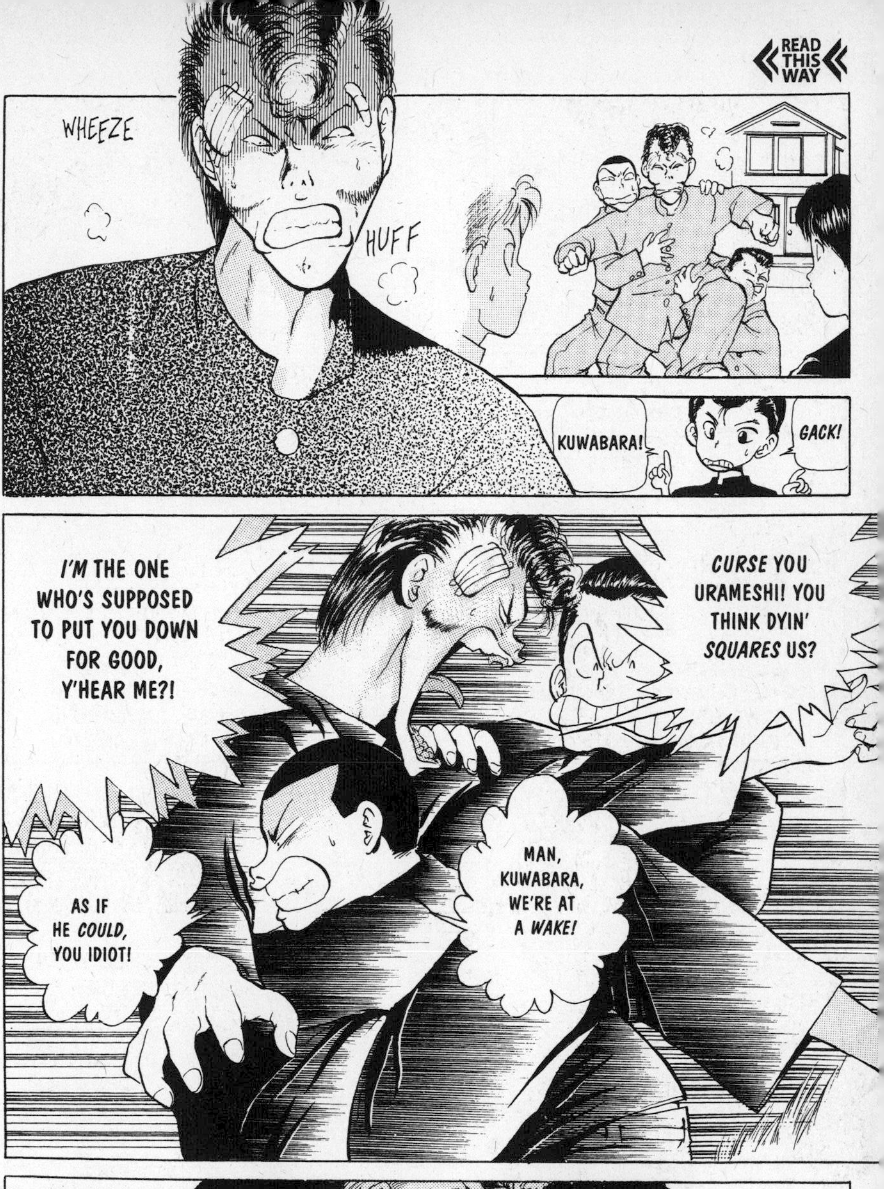
GACK!
KUWABARA!
WHEEZE
HUFF
CURSE YOU URAMESHI! YOU THINK DYIN' SQUARES US?
I'M THE ONE WHO'S SUPPOSED TO PUT YOU DOWN FOR GOOD, Y'HEAR ME?!
MAN, KUWABARA, WE'RE AT A WAKE!
AS IF HE COULD, YOU IDIOT!
NO STALLIN'! GIT OUTTA THAT COFFIN!
GIT OUT AND FIGHT ME, YOU FRICKIN' IDIOT!

READ THIS WAY

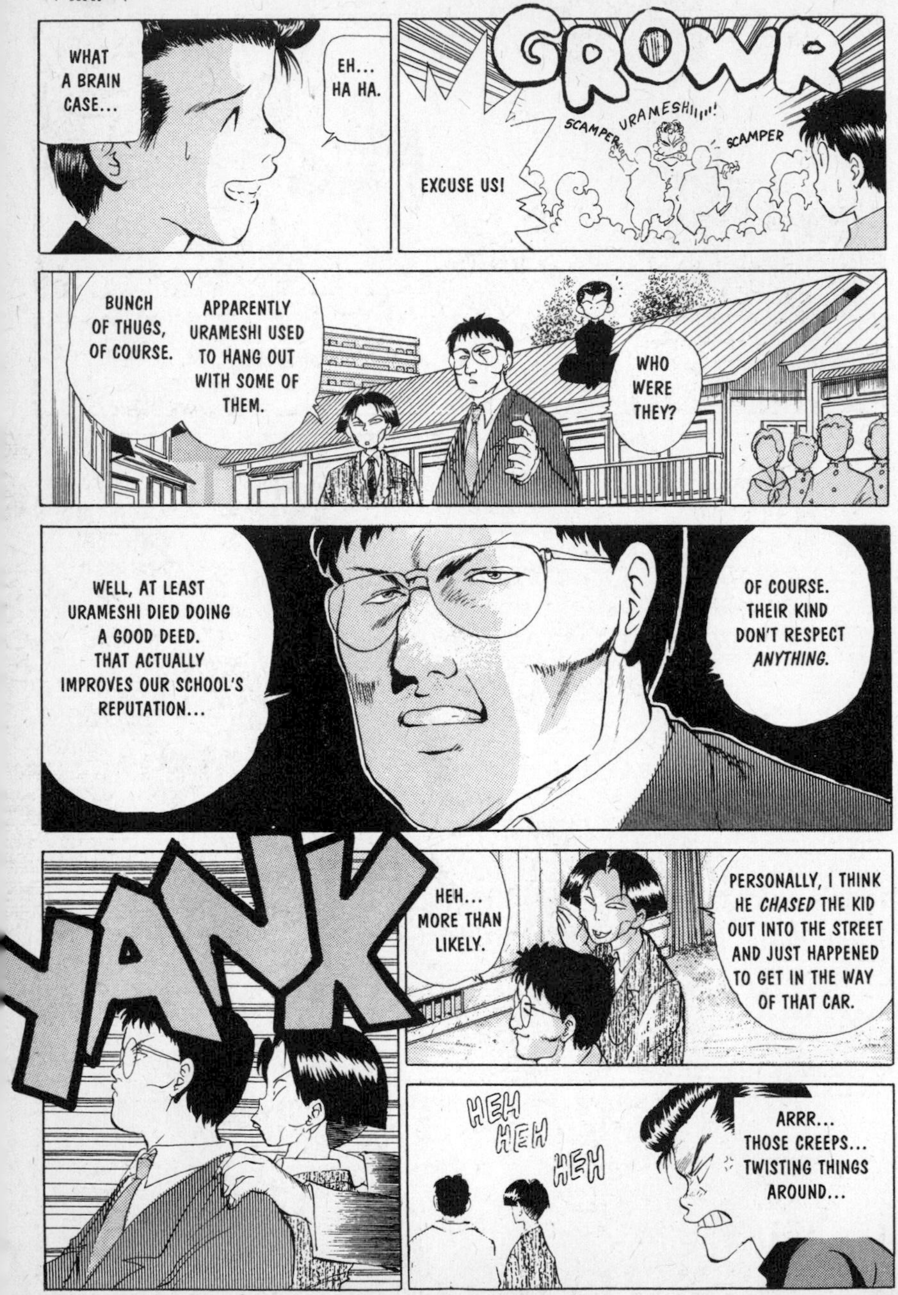
GROWR
URAMESHI!!!!
SCAMPER
SCAMPER
EXCUSE US!
EH... HA HA.
WHAT A BRAIN CASE...
WHO WERE THEY?
APPARENTLY URAMESHI USED TO HANG OUT WITH SOME OF THEM.
BUNCH OF THUGS, OF COURSE.
OF COURSE. THEIR KIND DON'T RESPECT *ANYTHING*.
WELL, AT LEAST URAMESHI DIED DOING A GOOD DEED. THAT ACTUALLY IMPROVES OUR SCHOOL'S REPUTATION...
PERSONALLY, I THINK HE *CHASED* THE KID OUT INTO THE STREET AND JUST HAPPENED TO GET IN THE WAY OF THAT CAR.
HEH... MORE THAN LIKELY.
ARRR... THOSE CREEPS... TWISTING THINGS AROUND...
HEH HEH HEH
YANK

READ THIS WAY

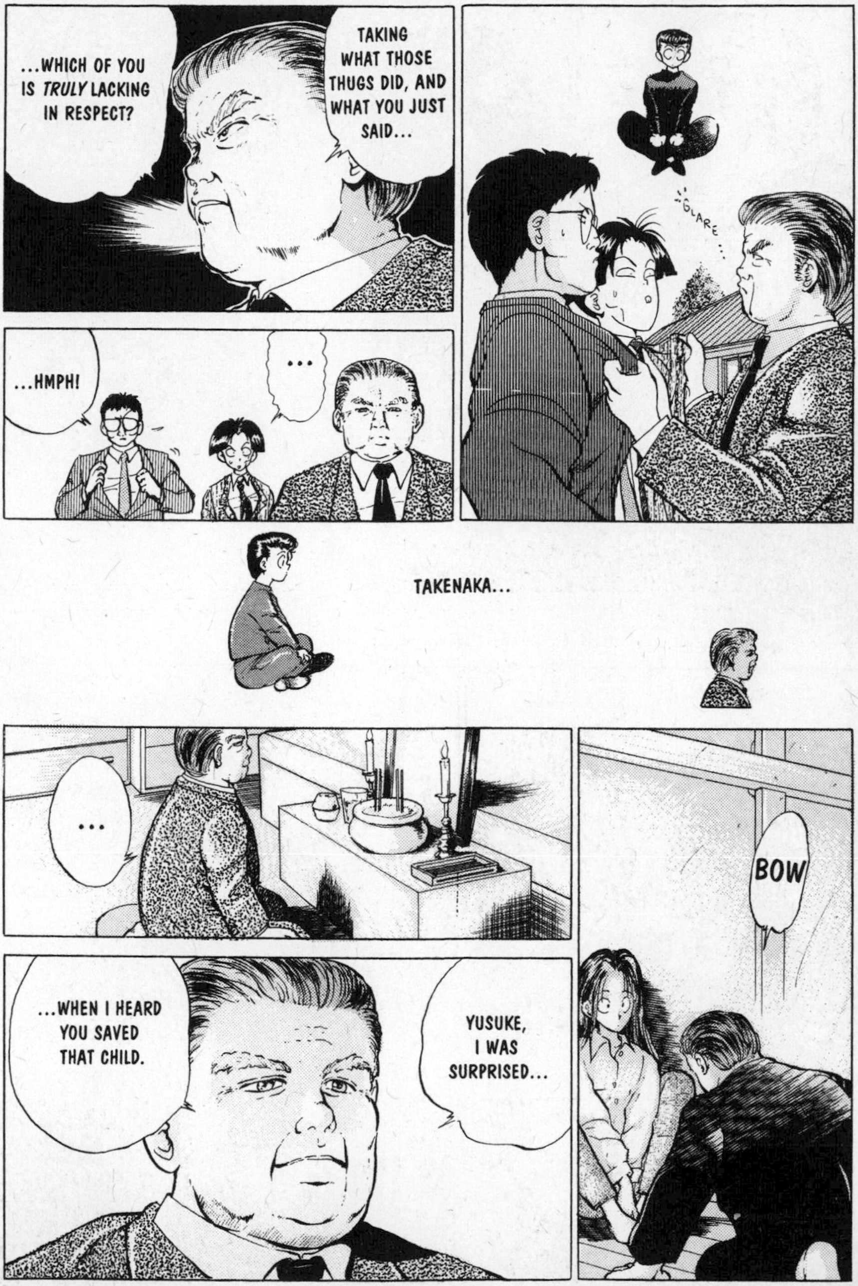
GLARE...
TAKING WHAT THOSE THUGS DID, AND WHAT YOU JUST SAID...
...WHICH OF YOU IS *TRULY* LACKING IN RESPECT?
...
...HMPH!
TAKENAKA...
BOW
...
YUSUKE, I WAS SURPRISED...
...WHEN I HEARD YOU SAVED THAT CHILD.

READ THIS WAY

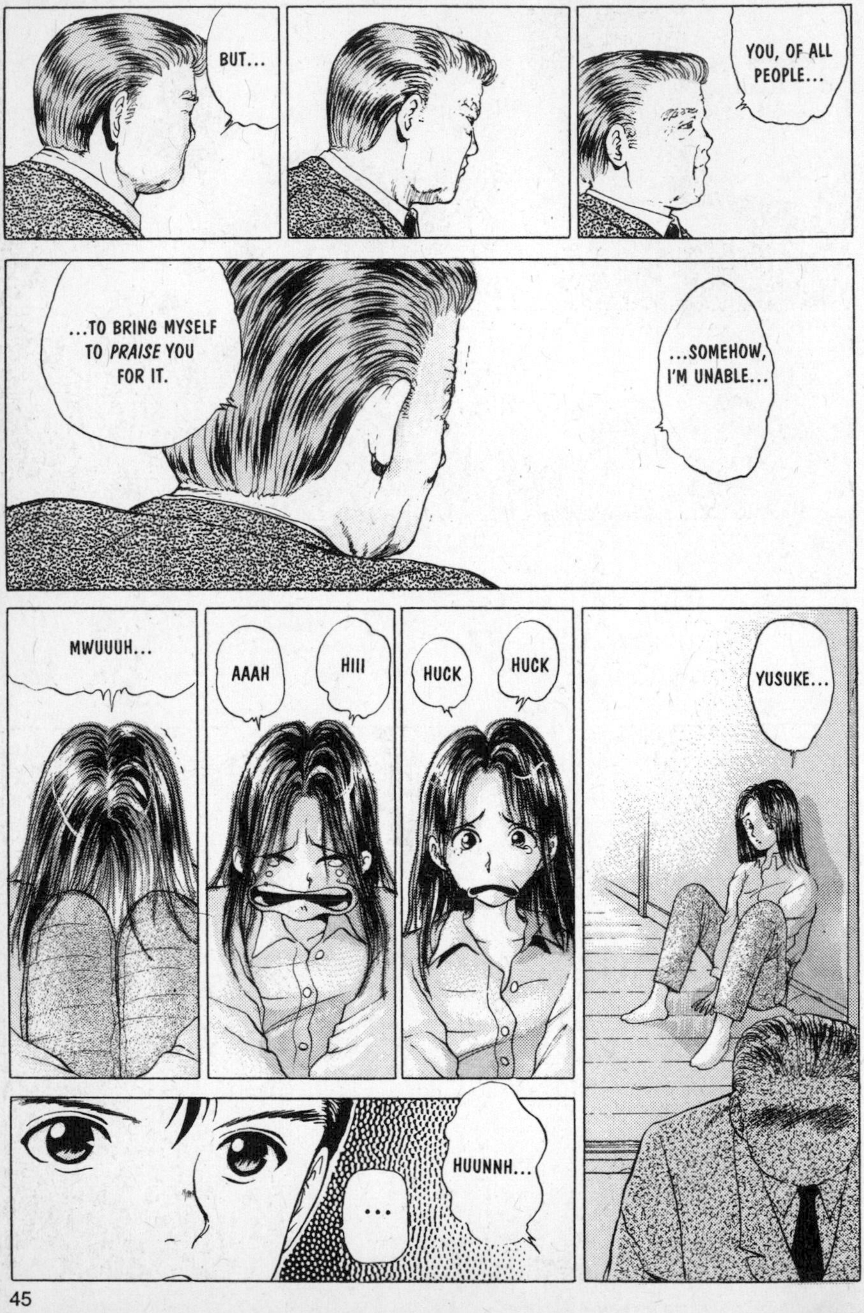
YOU, OF ALL PEOPLE...
BUT...
...SOMEHOW, I'M UNABLE...
...TO BRING MYSELF TO *PRAISE* YOU FOR IT.
YUSUKE...
HUCK
HUCK
HIII
AAAH
MWUUUH...
HUUNNH...
...

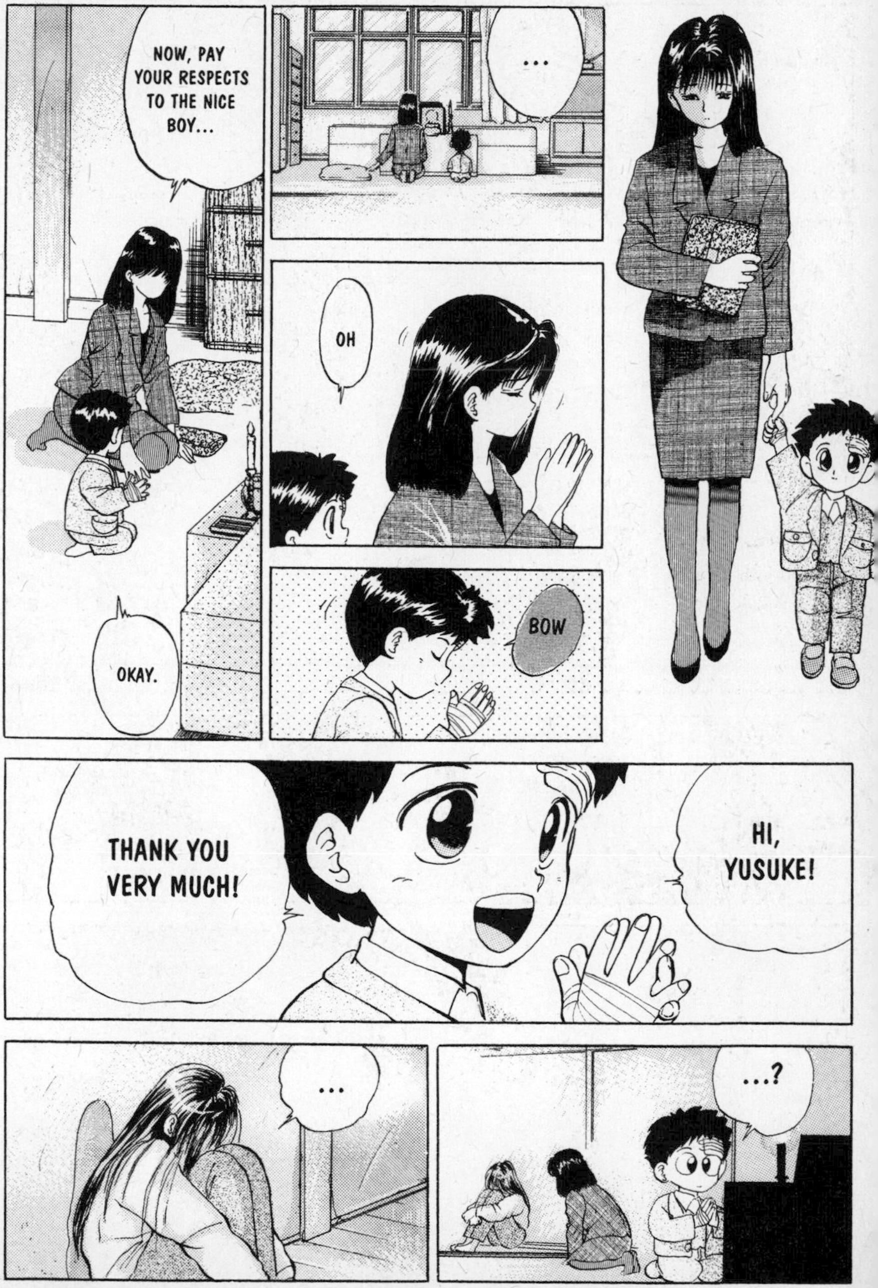
NOW, PAY YOUR RESPECTS TO THE NICE BOY...
OKAY.
...
OH
BOW
THANK YOU VERY MUCH!
HI, YUSUKE!
...
...?

READ THIS WAY

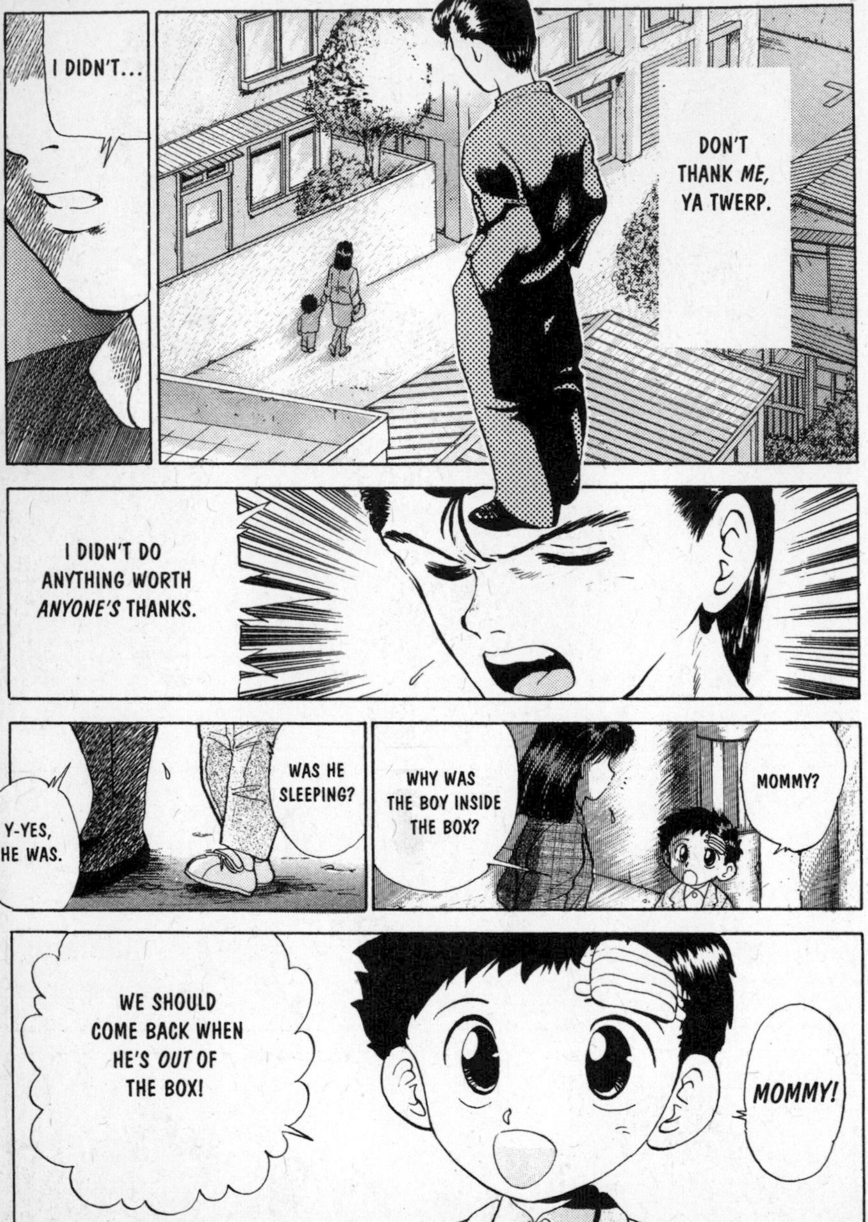
DON'T THANK *ME*, YA TWERP.
I DIDN'T...
I DIDN'T DO ANYTHING WORTH *ANYONE'S* THANKS.
MOMMY?
WHY WAS THE BOY INSIDE THE BOX?
WAS HE SLEEPING?
Y-YES, HE WAS.
MOMMY!
WE SHOULD COME BACK WHEN HE'S *OUT* OF THE BOX!

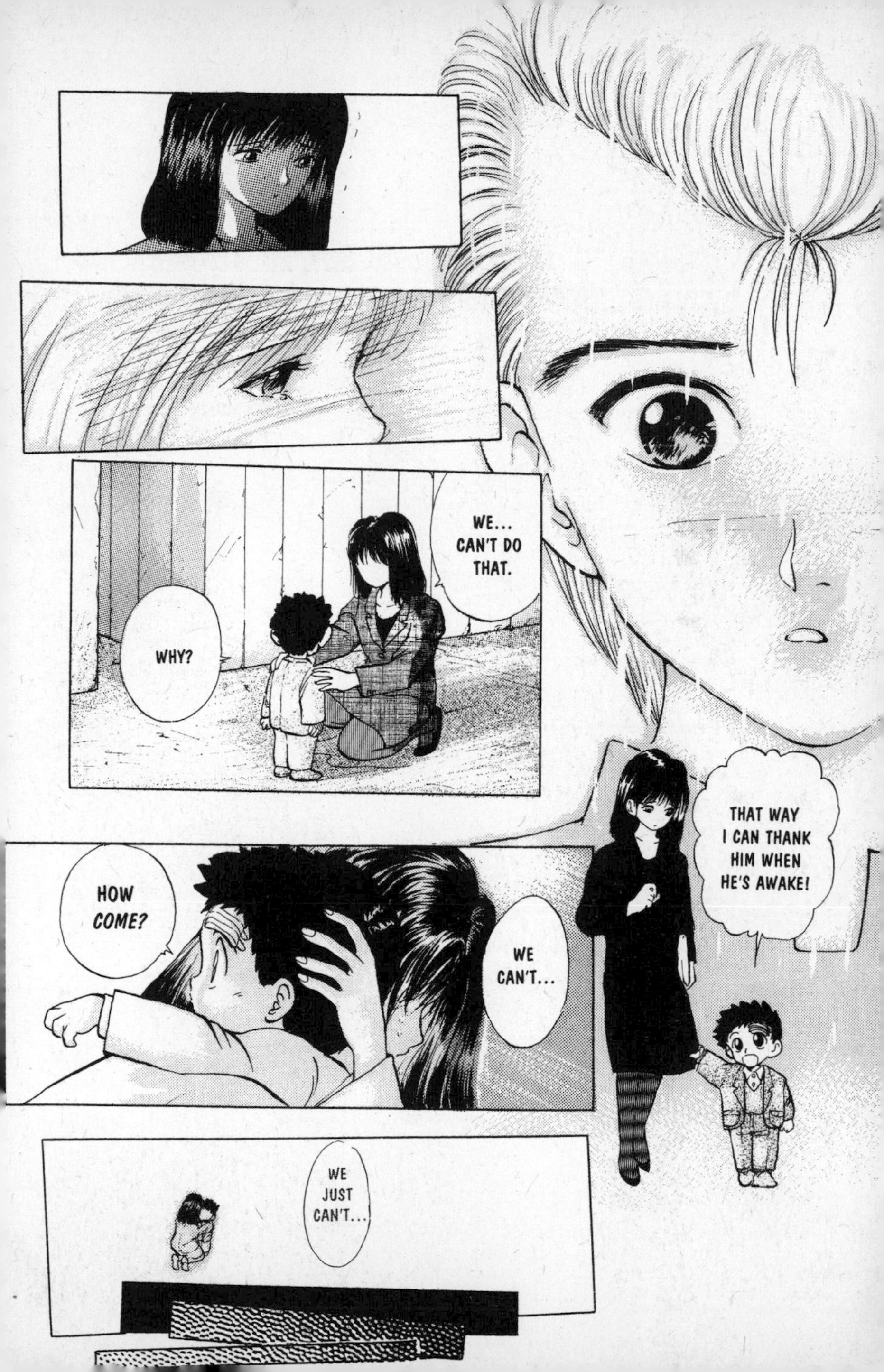
THAT WAY I CAN THANK HIM WHEN HE'S AWAKE!
WE... CAN'T DO THAT.
WHY?
HOW COME?
WE CAN'T...
WE JUST CAN'T...

READ THIS WAY

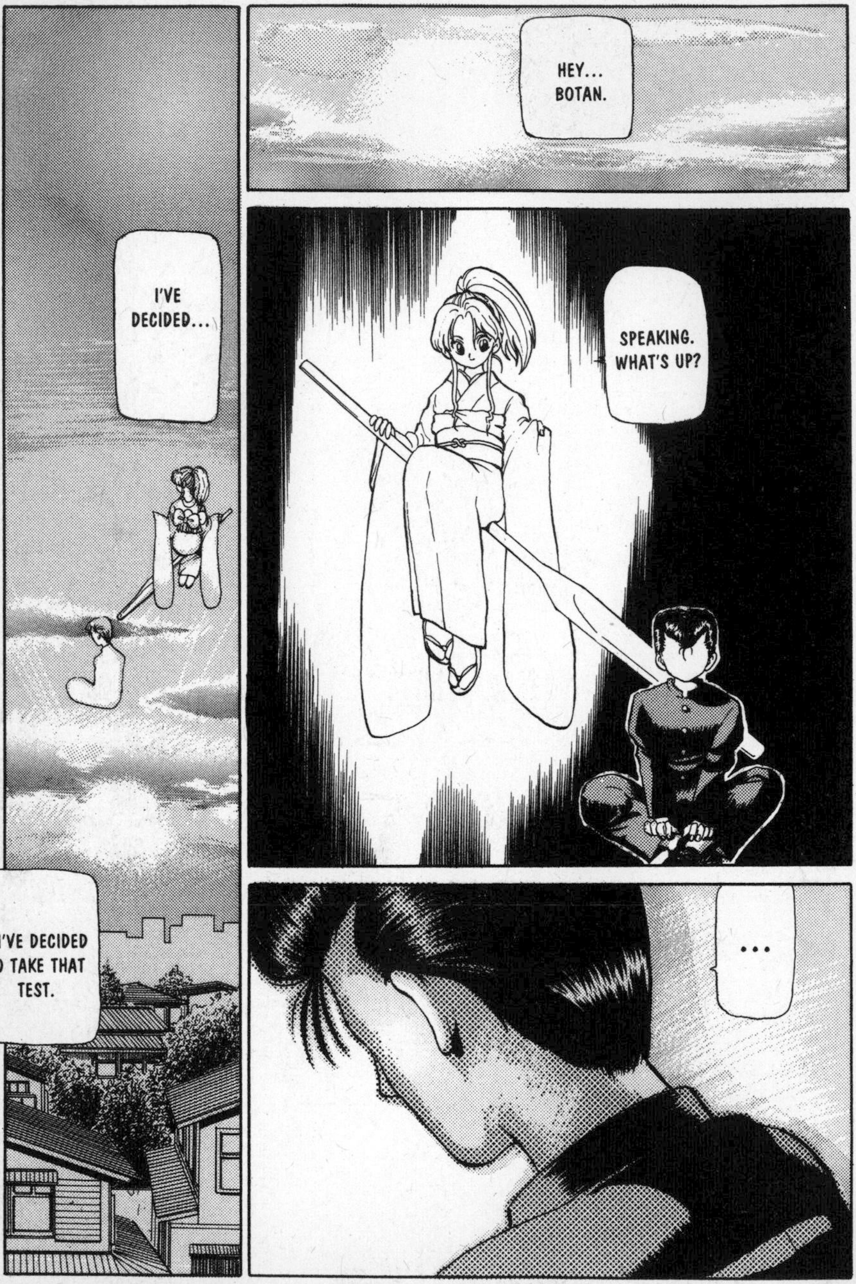
HEY... BOTAN.
SPEAKING. WHAT'S UP?
...
I'VE DECIDED...
...I'VE DECIDED TO TAKE THAT TEST.

CONGRATULATIONS ON VOLUME 1!

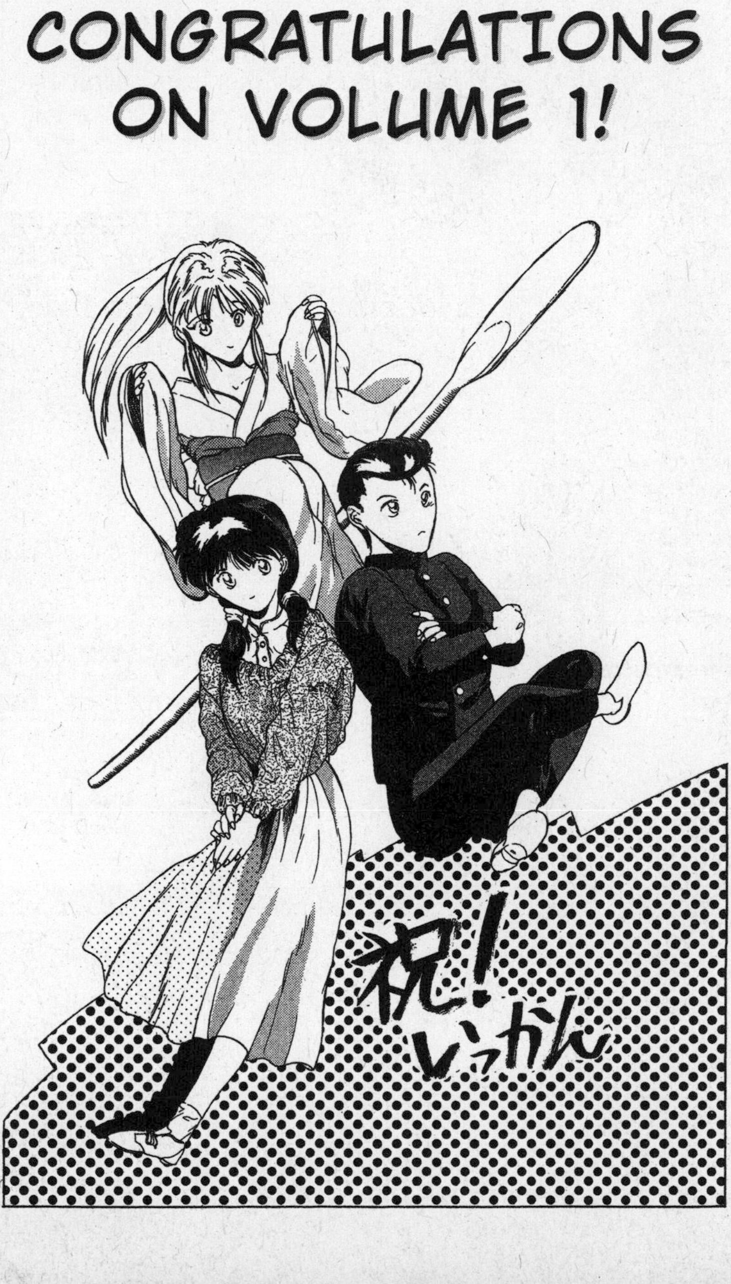
祝！
いっかん

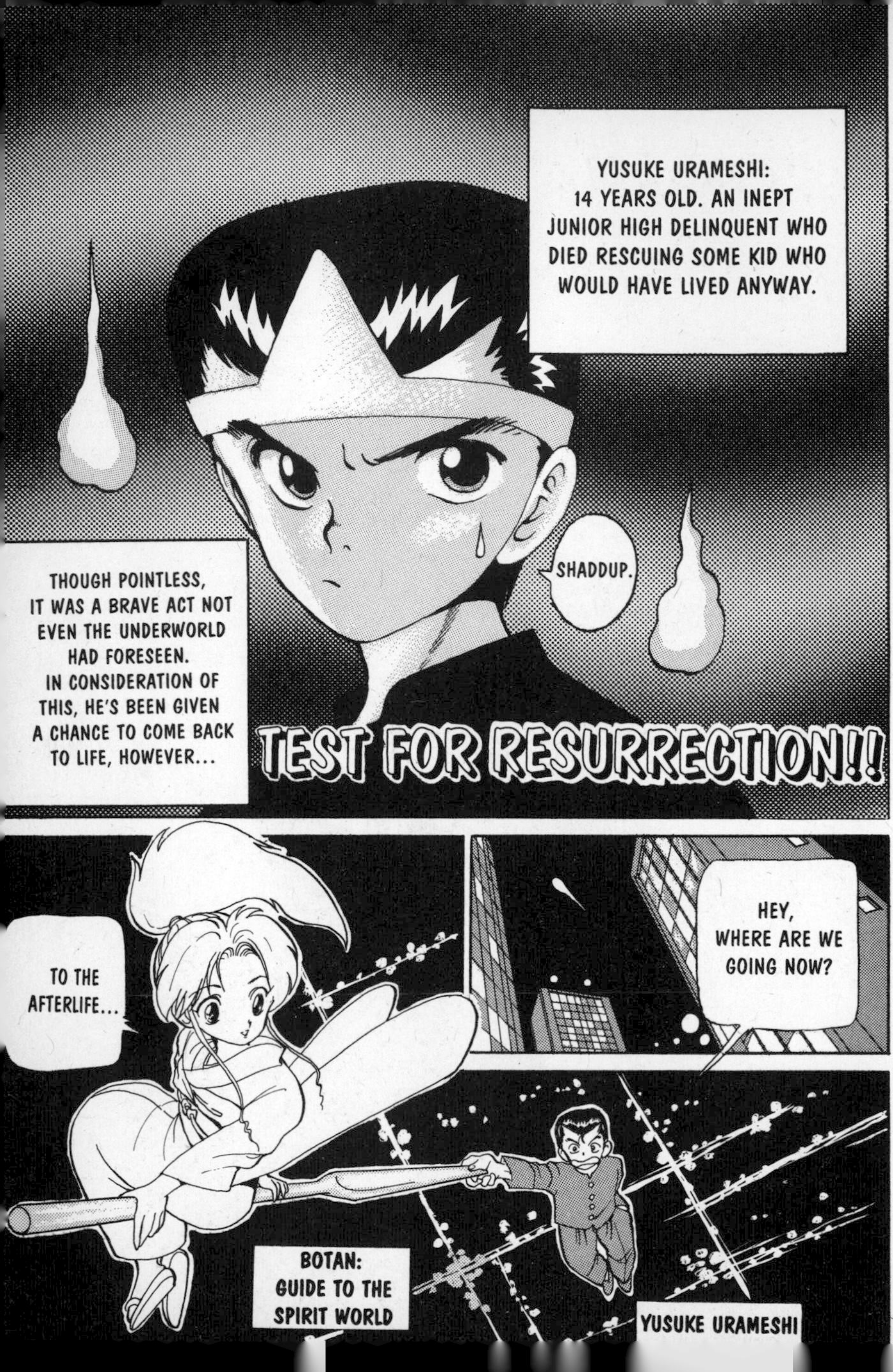
YUSUKE URAMESHI: 14 YEARS OLD. AN INEPT JUNIOR HIGH DELINQUENT WHO DIED RESCUING SOME KID WHO WOULD HAVE LIVED ANYWAY.
SHADDUP.
THOUGH POINTLESS, IT WAS A BRAVE ACT NOT EVEN THE UNDERWORLD HAD FORESEEN. IN CONSIDERATION OF THIS, HE'S BEEN GIVEN A CHANCE TO COME BACK TO LIFE, HOWEVER...
TEST FOR RESURRECTION!!
HEY, WHERE ARE WE GOING NOW?
YUSUKE URAMESHI
TO THE AFTERLIFE...
BOTAN: GUIDE TO THE SPIRIT WORLD

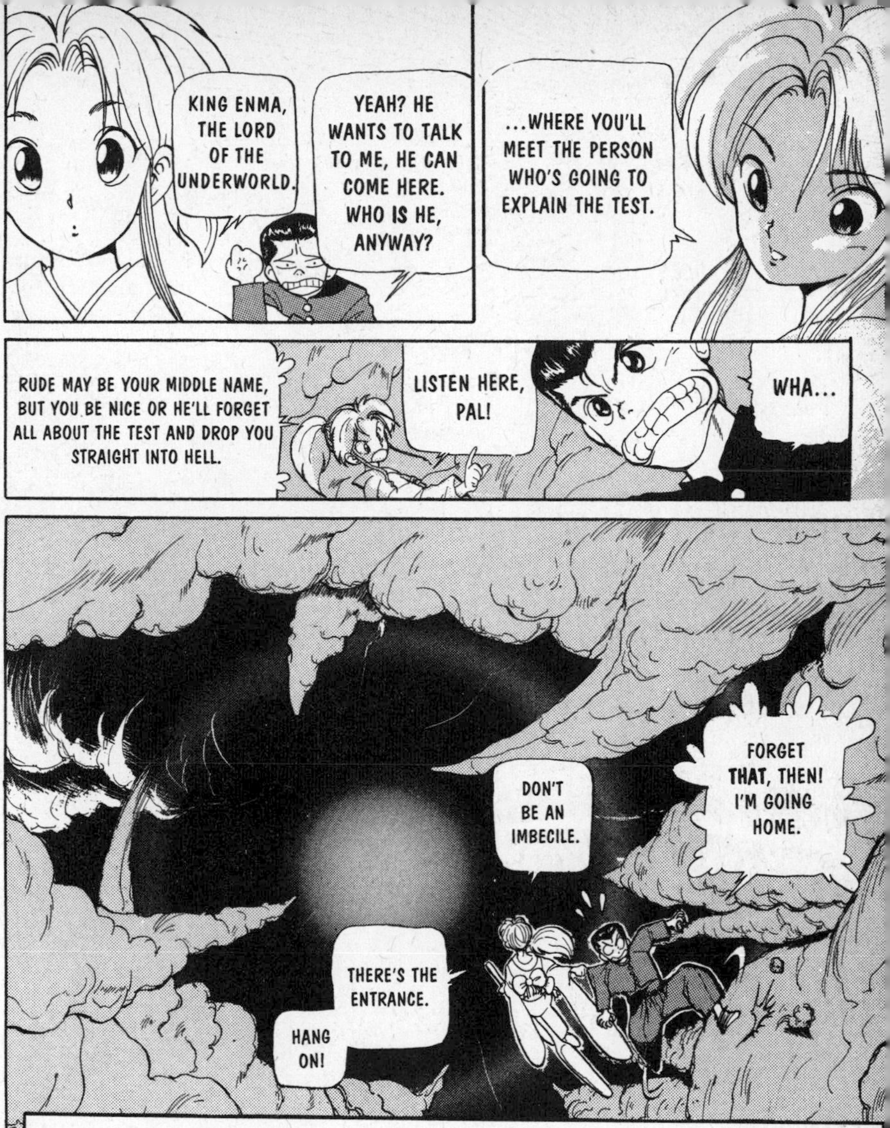
...WHERE YOU'LL MEET THE PERSON WHO'S GOING TO EXPLAIN THE TEST.
YEAH? HE WANTS TO TALK TO ME, HE CAN COME HERE. WHO IS HE, ANYWAY?
KING ENMA, THE LORD OF THE UNDERWORLD.
WHA...
LISTEN HERE, PAL!
RUDE MAY BE YOUR MIDDLE NAME, BUT YOU BE NICE OR HE'LL FORGET ALL ABOUT THE TEST AND DROP YOU STRAIGHT INTO HELL.
FORGET THAT, THEN! I'M GOING HOME.
DON'T BE AN IMBECILE.
THERE'S THE ENTRANCE.
HANG ON!

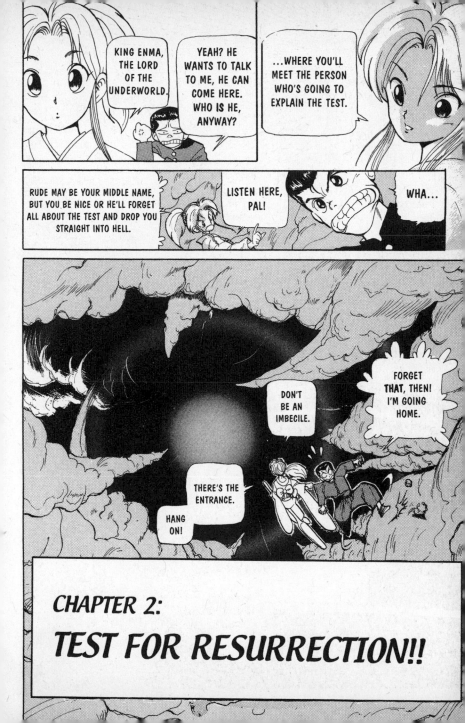

CHAPTER 2:
TEST FOR RESURRECTION!!

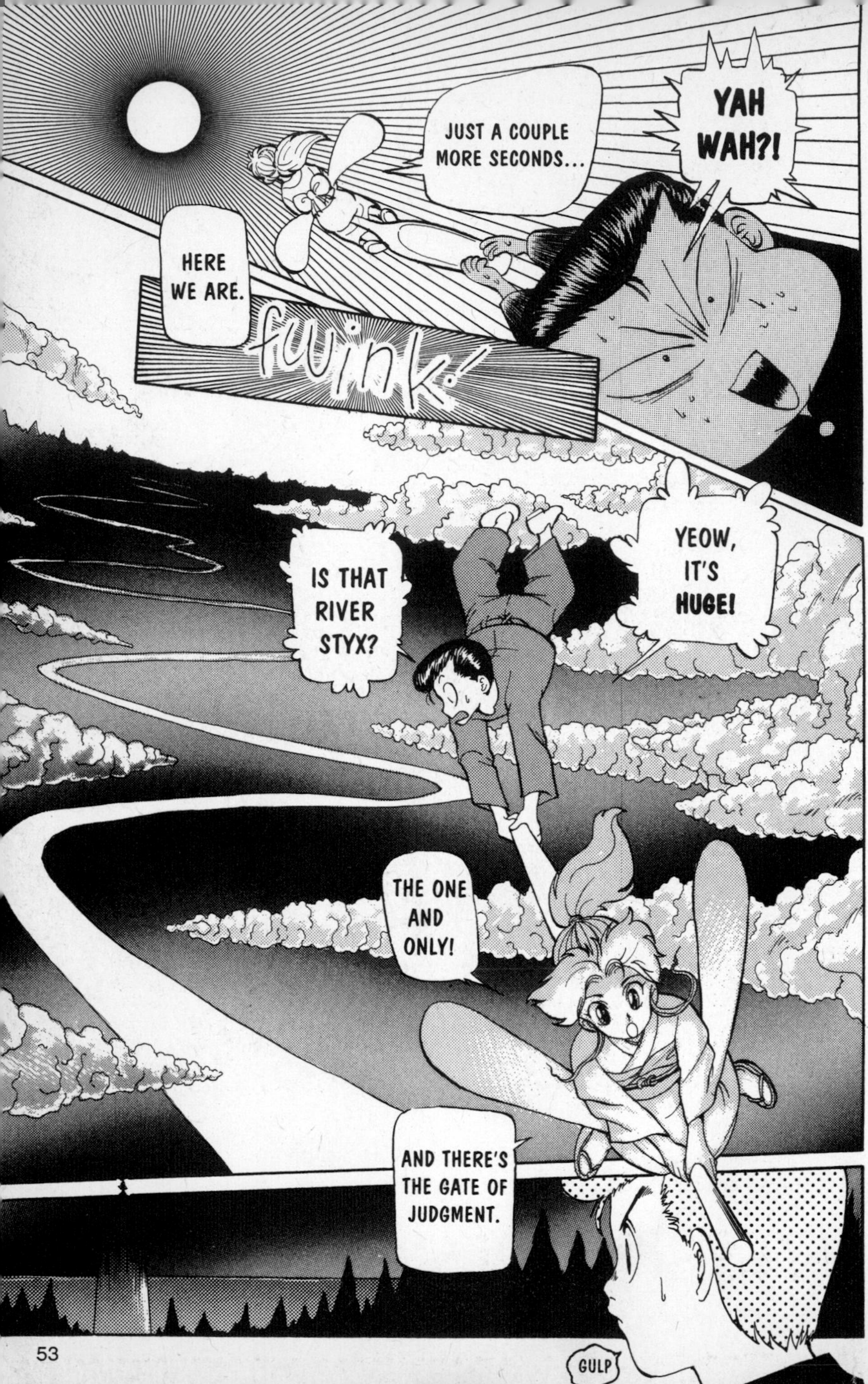
YAH WAH?!
JUST A COUPLE MORE SECONDS...
HERE WE ARE.
fwink!
YEOW, IT'S HUGE!
IS THAT RIVER STYX?
THE ONE AND ONLY!
AND THERE'S THE GATE OF JUDGMENT.
GULP

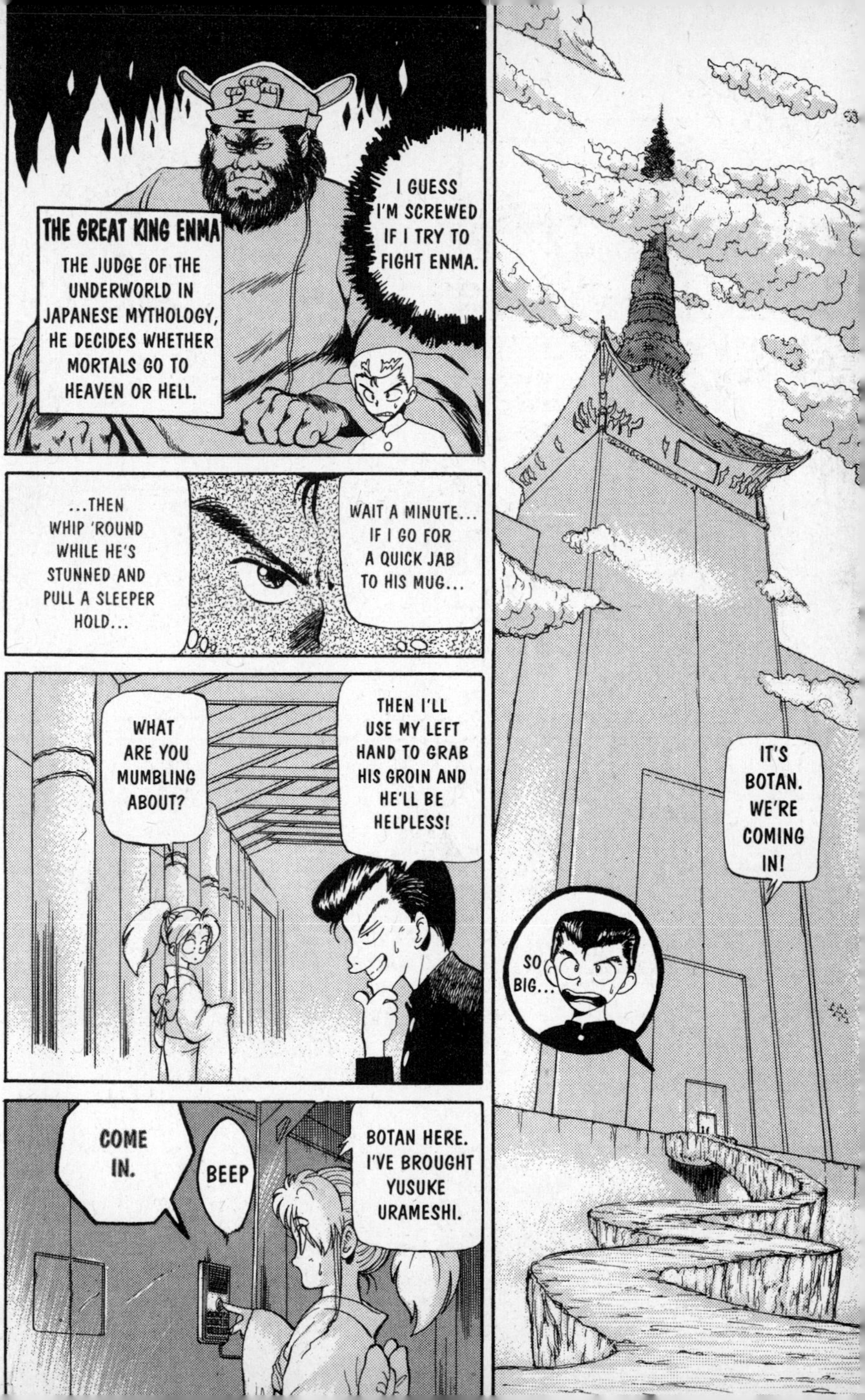
IT'S BOTAN. WE'RE COMING IN!
SO BIG...
I GUESS I'M SCREWED IF I TRY TO FIGHT ENMA.
THE GREAT KING ENMA
THE JUDGE OF THE UNDERWORLD IN JAPANESE MYTHOLOGY, HE DECIDES WHETHER MORTALS GO TO HEAVEN OR HELL.
WAIT A MINUTE... IF I GO FOR A QUICK JAB TO HIS MUG...
...THEN WHIP 'ROUND WHILE HE'S STUNNED AND PULL A SLEEPER HOLD...
THEN I'LL USE MY LEFT HAND TO GRAB HIS GROIN AND HE'LL BE HELPLESS!
WHAT ARE YOU MUMBLING ABOUT?
BOTAN HERE. I'VE BROUGHT YUSUKE URAMESHI.
BEEP
COME IN.

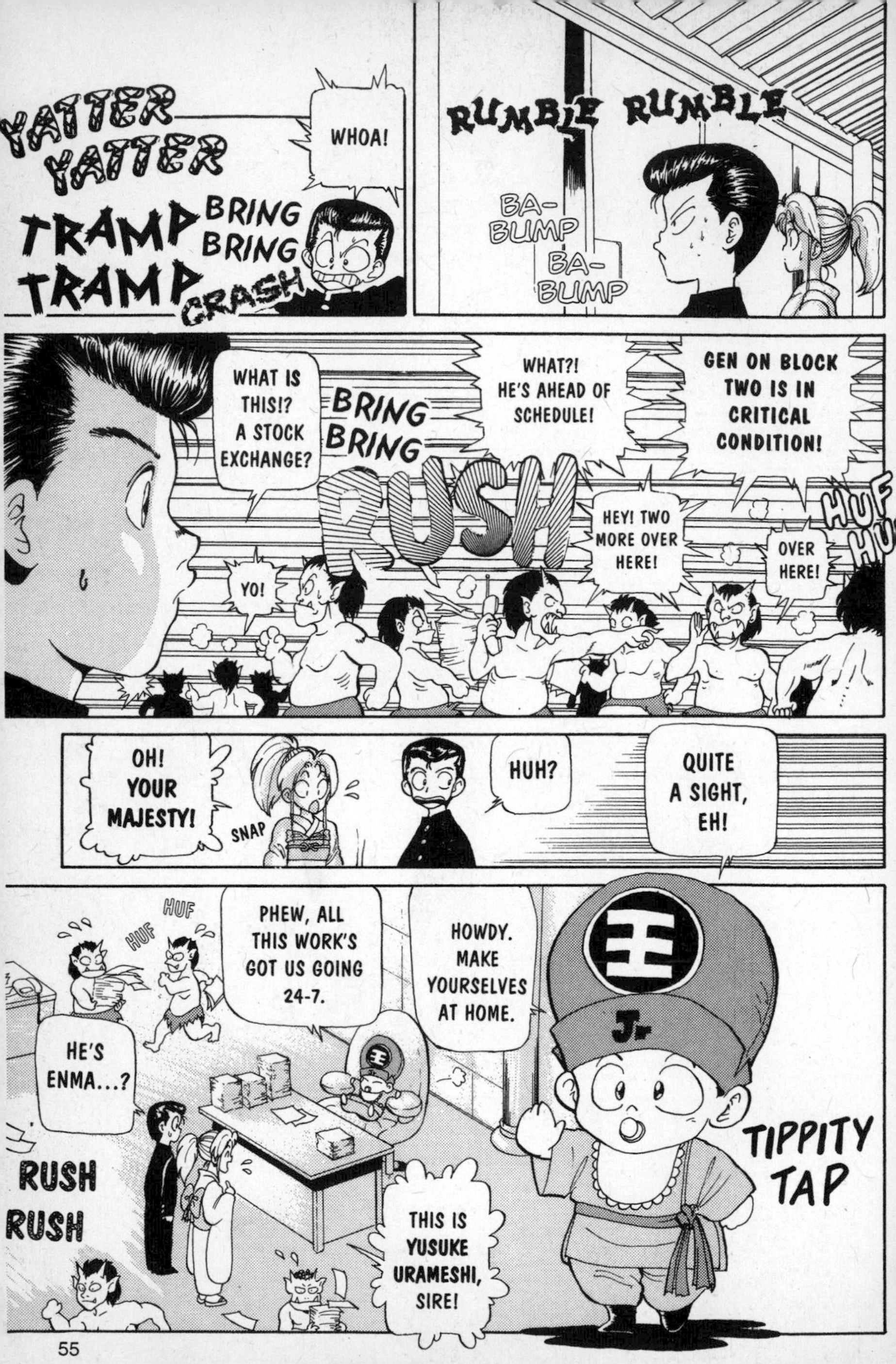
RUMBLE RUMBLE
BA-BUMP
BA-BUMP
WHOA!
YATTER YATTER
TRAMP TRAMP
BRING BRING
CRASH
GEN ON BLOCK TWO IS IN CRITICAL CONDITION!
HUF HU
OVER HERE!
WHAT?! HE'S AHEAD OF SCHEDULE!
HEY! TWO MORE OVER HERE!
RUSH
BRING BRING
WHAT IS THIS!? A STOCK EXCHANGE?
YO!
QUITE A SIGHT, EH!
HUH?
OH! YOUR MAJESTY!
SNAP
Jr
TIPPITY TAP
HOWDY. MAKE YOURSELVES AT HOME.
THIS IS YUSUKE URAMESHI, SIRE!
PHEW, ALL THIS WORK'S GOT US GOING 24-7.
HUF
HUF
HE'S ENMA...?
RUSH RUSH

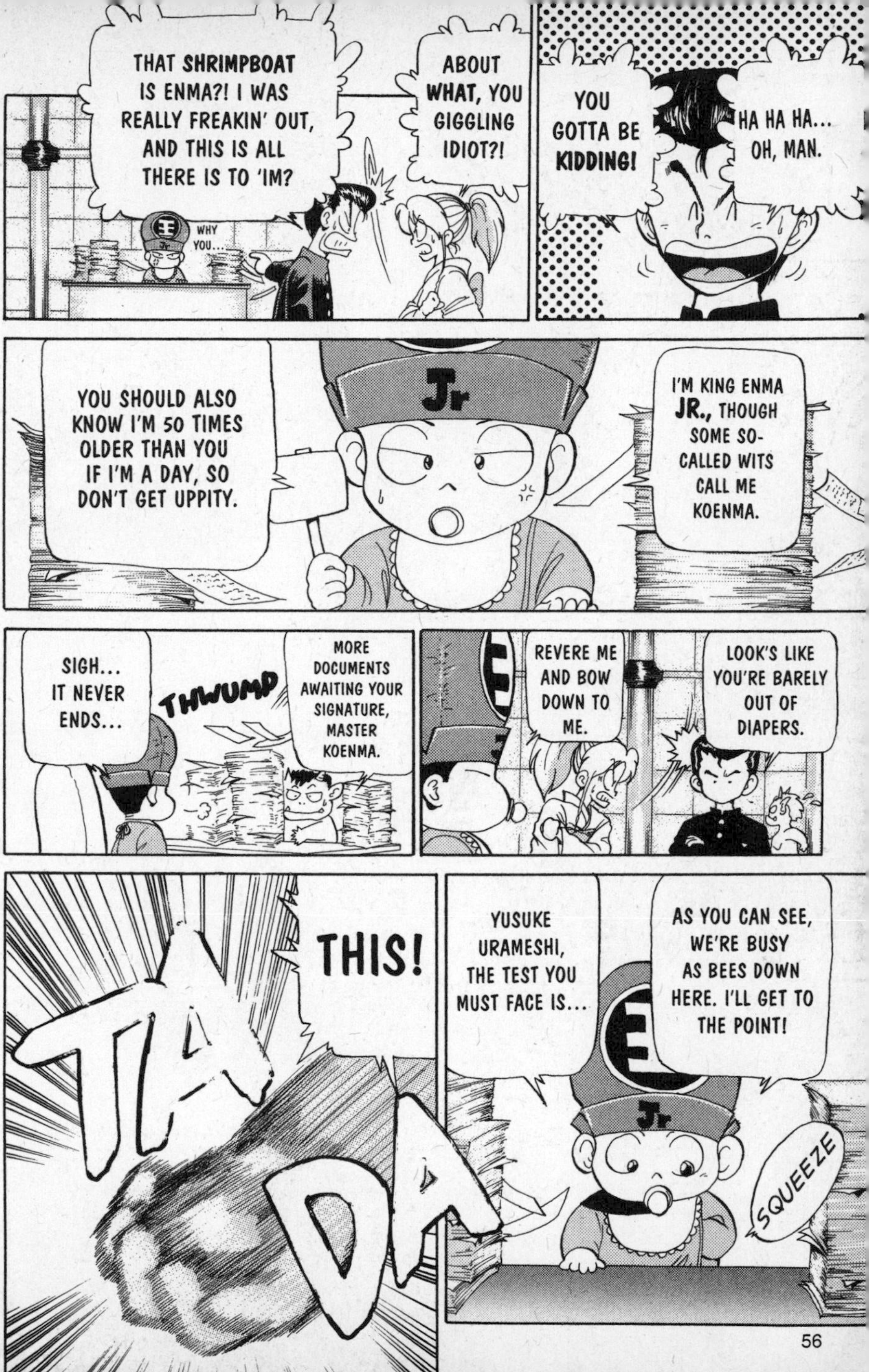
HA HA HA... OH, MAN.
YOU GOTTA BE KIDDING!
ABOUT WHAT, YOU GIGGLING IDIOT?!
THAT SHRIMPBOAT IS ENMA?! I WAS REALLY FREAKIN' OUT, AND THIS IS ALL THERE IS TO 'IM?
WHY YOU...
I'M KING ENMA JR., THOUGH SOME SO-CALLED WITS CALL ME KOENMA.
YOU SHOULD ALSO KNOW I'M 50 TIMES OLDER THAN YOU IF I'M A DAY, SO DON'T GET UPPITY.
LOOK'S LIKE YOU'RE BARELY OUT OF DIAPERS.
REVERE ME AND BOW DOWN TO ME.
MORE DOCUMENTS AWAITING YOUR SIGNATURE, MASTER KOENMA.
THWUMP
SIGH... IT NEVER ENDS...
AS YOU CAN SEE, WE'RE BUSY AS BEES DOWN HERE. I'LL GET TO THE POINT!
SQUEEZE
YUSUKE URAMESHI, THE TEST YOU MUST FACE IS...
THIS!
TA DA

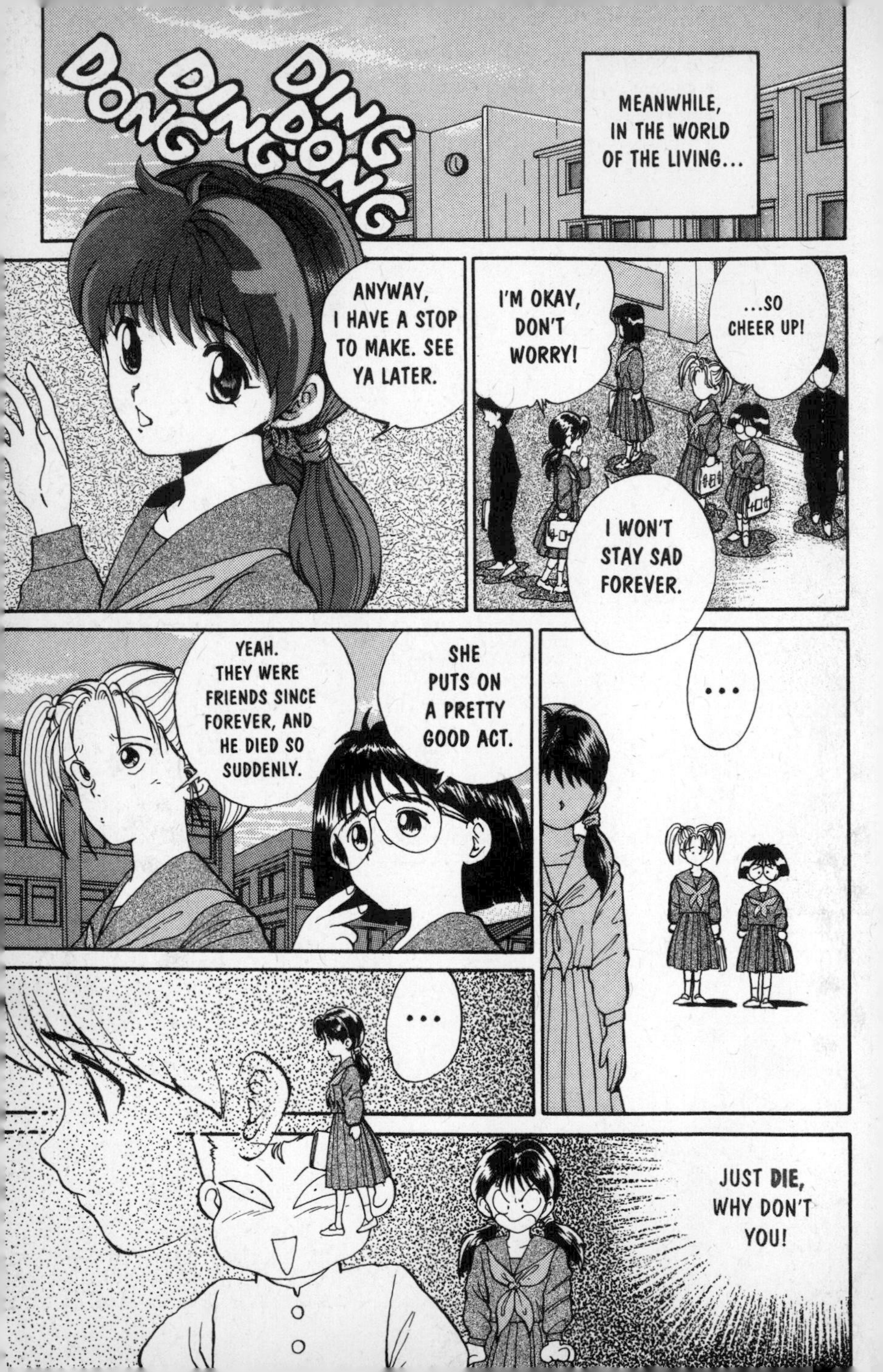
MEANWHILE, IN THE WORLD OF THE LIVING...
DING DONG DING DONG
...SO CHEER UP!
I'M OKAY, DON'T WORRY!
I WON'T STAY SAD FOREVER.
ANYWAY, I HAVE A STOP TO MAKE. SEE YA LATER.
...
SHE PUTS ON A PRETTY GOOD ACT.
YEAH. THEY WERE FRIENDS SINCE FOREVER, AND HE DIED SO SUDDENLY.
...
JUST DIE, WHY DON'T YOU!

READ THIS WAY

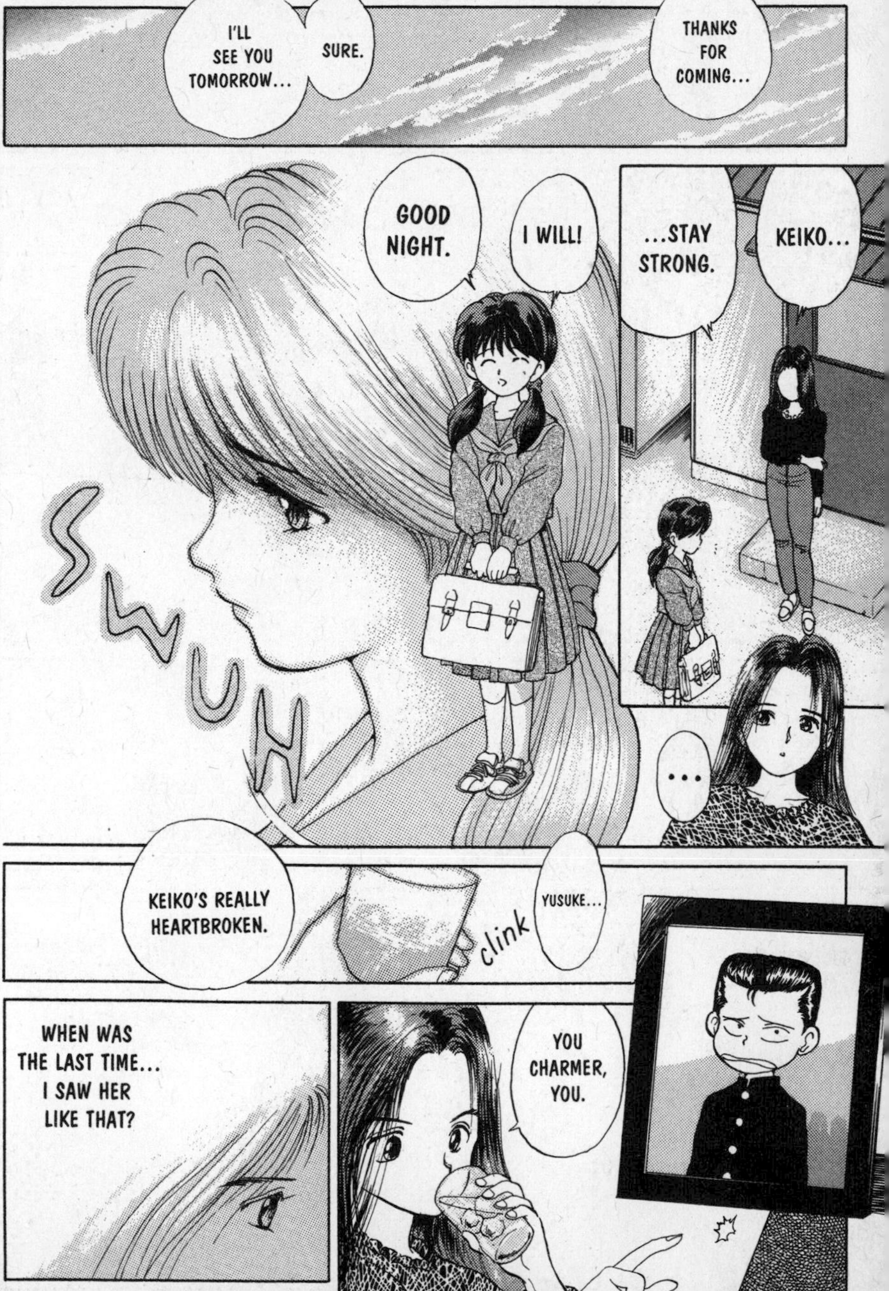

THANKS FOR COMING...
SURE.
I'LL SEE YOU TOMORROW...
KEIKO...
...STAY STRONG.
...
I WILL!
GOOD NIGHT.
SWUH
YUSUKE...
clink
KEIKO'S REALLY HEARTBROKEN.
YOU CHARMER, YOU.
WHEN WAS THE LAST TIME... I SAW HER LIKE THAT?

READ THIS WAY

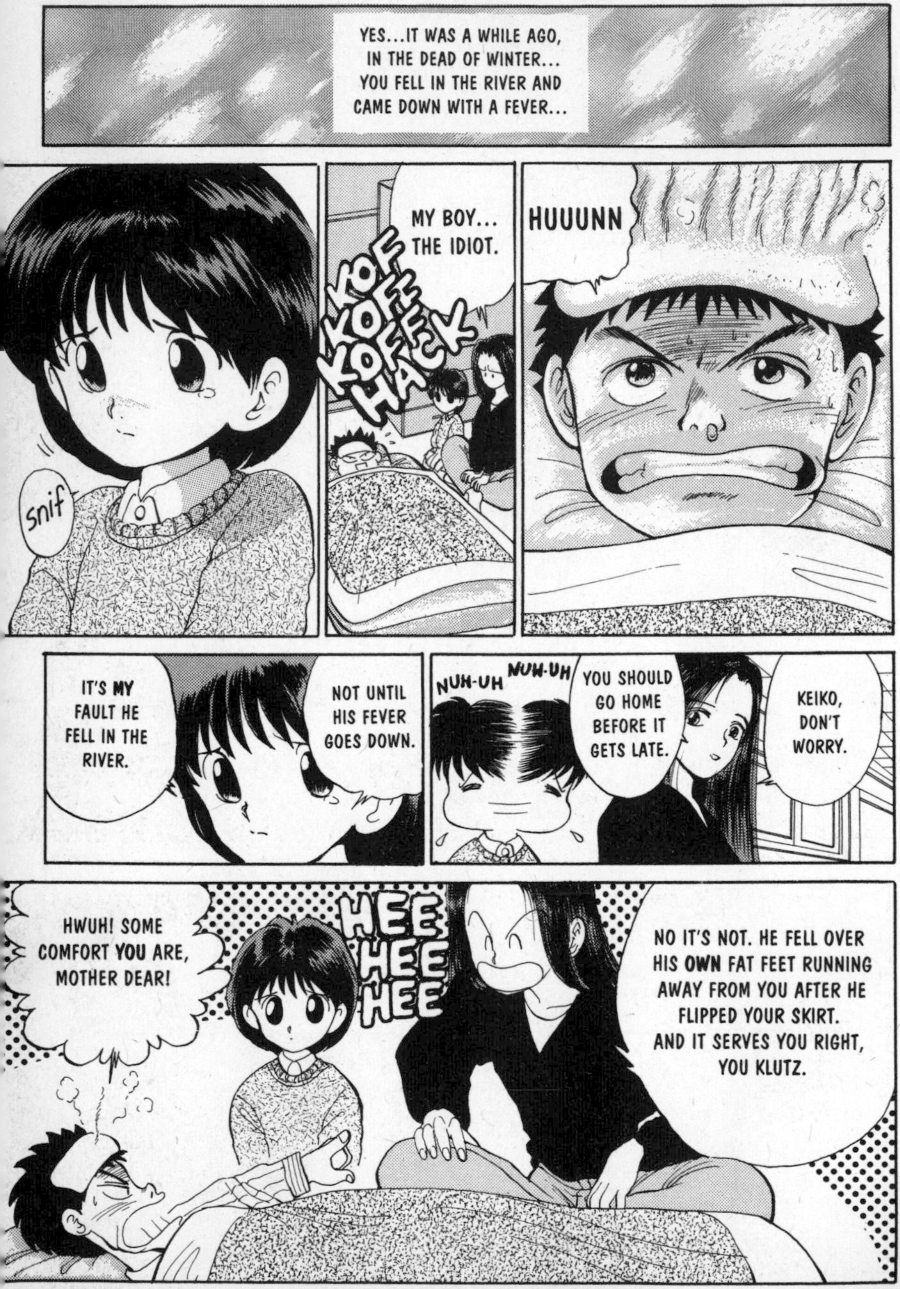
YES...IT WAS A WHILE AGO, IN THE DEAD OF WINTER... YOU FELL IN THE RIVER AND CAME DOWN WITH A FEVER...
HUUUNN
MY BOY... THE IDIOT.
KOF KOF KOFF HACK
snif
KEIKO, DON'T WORRY.
YOU SHOULD GO HOME BEFORE IT GETS LATE.
NUH-UH NUH-UH
NOT UNTIL HIS FEVER GOES DOWN.
IT'S MY FAULT HE FELL IN THE RIVER.
NO IT'S NOT. HE FELL OVER HIS OWN FAT FEET RUNNING AWAY FROM YOU AFTER HE FLIPPED YOUR SKIRT. AND IT SERVES YOU RIGHT, YOU KLUTZ.
HEE HEE HEE
HWUH! SOME COMFORT YOU ARE, MOTHER DEAR!

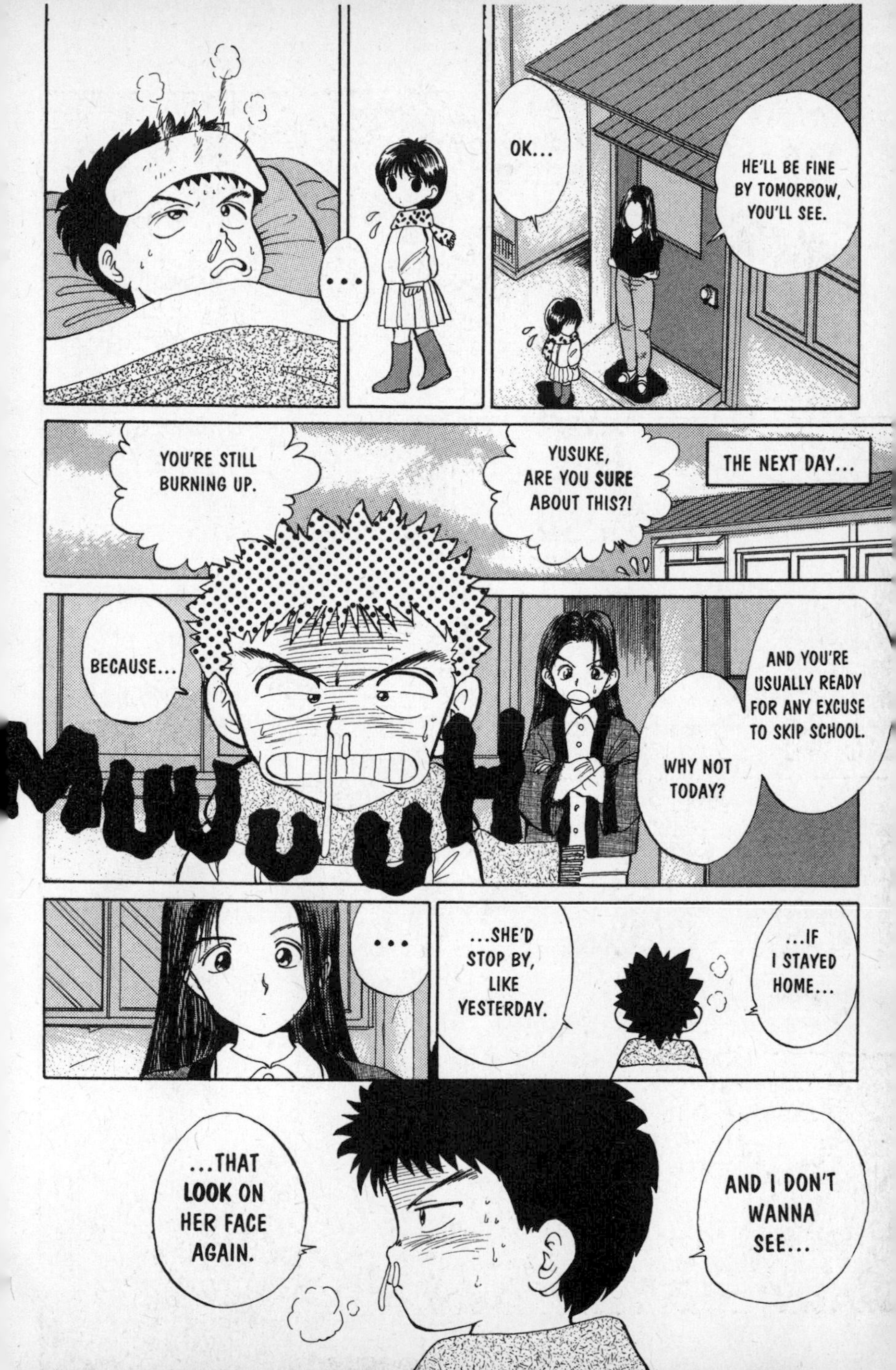
HE'LL BE FINE BY TOMORROW, YOU'LL SEE.
OK...
...
THE NEXT DAY...
YUSUKE, ARE YOU **SURE** ABOUT THIS?!
YOU'RE STILL BURNING UP.
AND YOU'RE USUALLY READY FOR ANY EXCUSE TO SKIP SCHOOL.
WHY NOT TODAY?
BECAUSE...
MUUUH
...IF I STAYED HOME...
...SHE'D STOP BY, LIKE YESTERDAY.
...
AND I DON'T WANNA SEE...
...THAT **LOOK** ON HER FACE AGAIN.

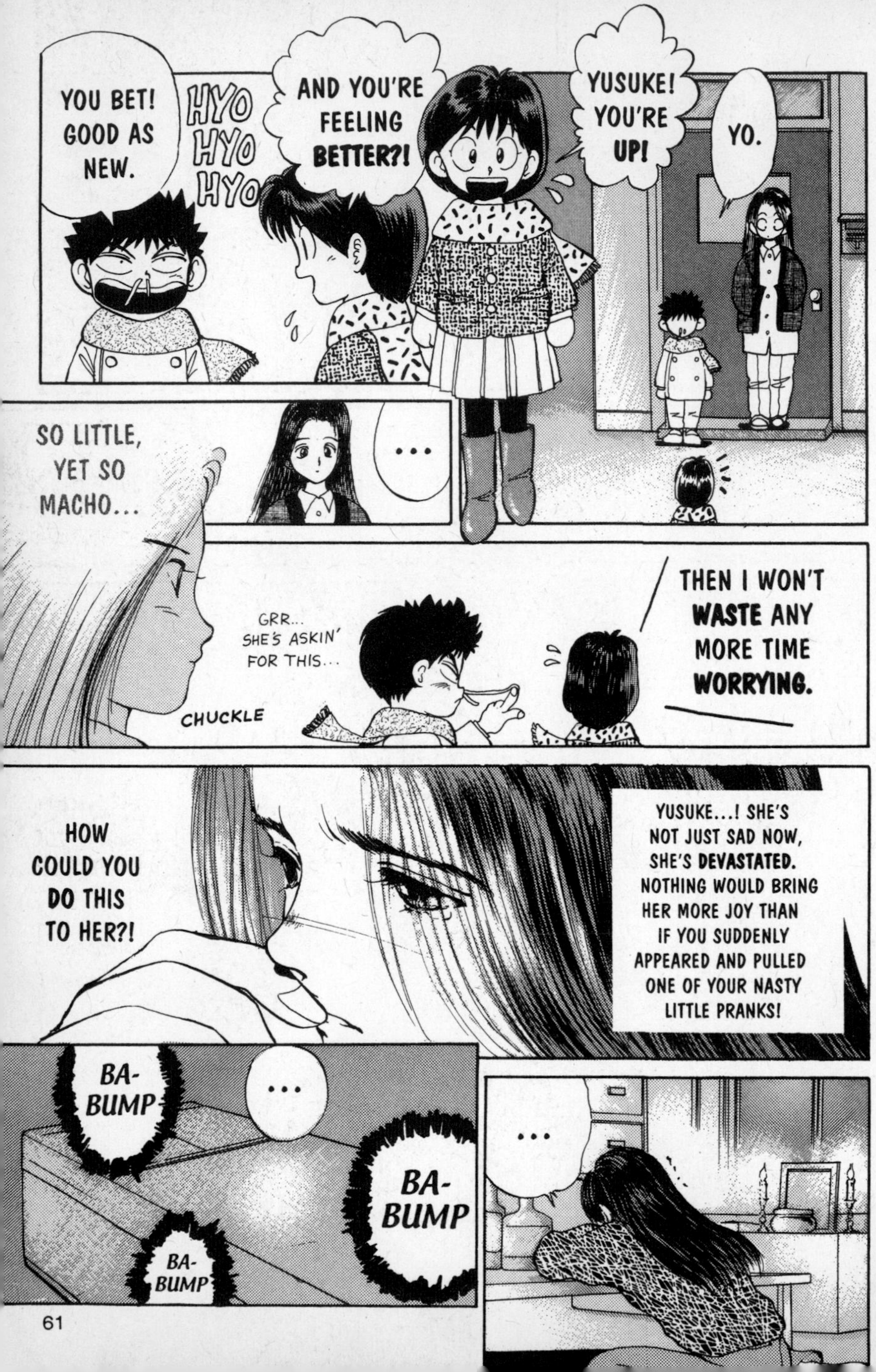
YO.
YUSUKE! YOU'RE UP!
AND YOU'RE FEELING BETTER?!
HYO HYO HYO
YOU BET! GOOD AS NEW.
...
SO LITTLE, YET SO MACHO...
THEN I WON'T WASTE ANY MORE TIME WORRYING.
GRR... SHE'S ASKIN' FOR THIS...
CHUCKLE
YUSUKE...! SHE'S NOT JUST SAD NOW, SHE'S DEVASTATED. NOTHING WOULD BRING HER MORE JOY THAN IF YOU SUDDENLY APPEARED AND PULLED ONE OF YOUR NASTY LITTLE PRANKS!
HOW COULD YOU DO THIS TO HER?!
...
BA-BUMP
...
BA-BUMP
BA-BUMP

READ THIS WAY

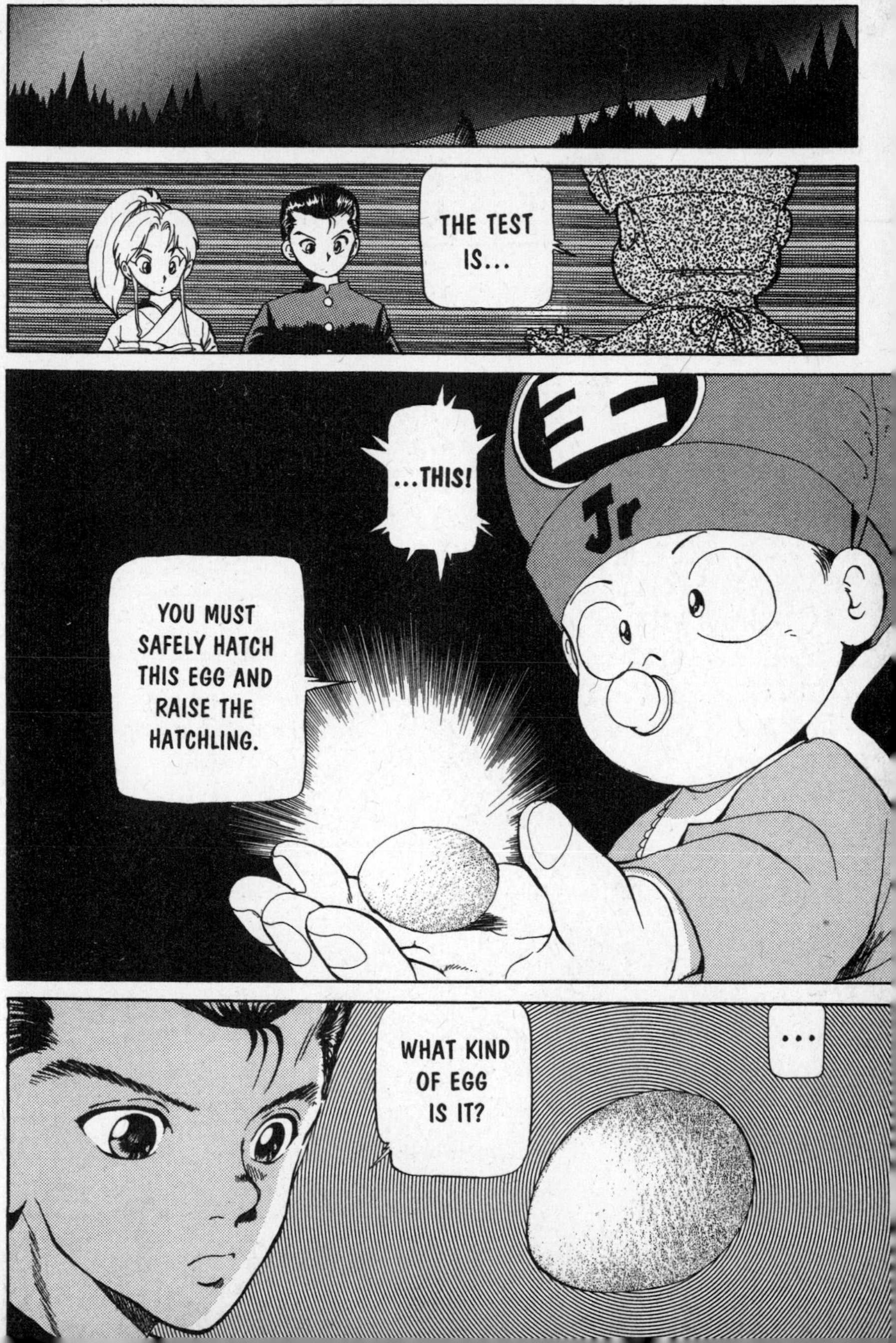
THE TEST IS...
...THIS!
YOU MUST SAFELY HATCH THIS EGG AND RAISE THE HATCHLING.
...
WHAT KIND OF EGG IS IT?

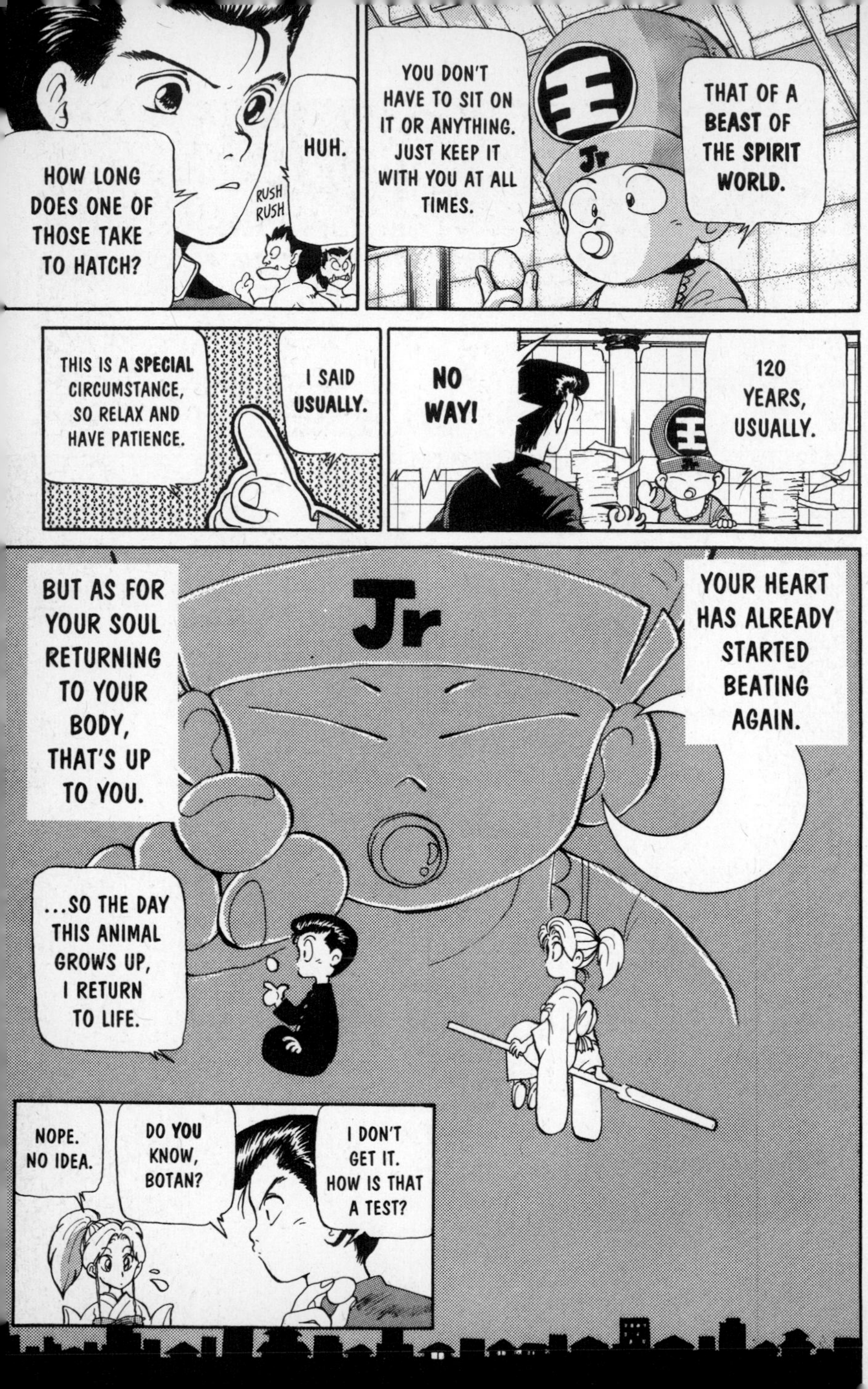
THAT OF A BEAST OF THE SPIRIT WORLD.
YOU DON'T HAVE TO SIT ON IT OR ANYTHING. JUST KEEP IT WITH YOU AT ALL TIMES.
HUH.
RUSH RUSH
HOW LONG DOES ONE OF THOSE TAKE TO HATCH?
120 YEARS, USUALLY.
NO WAY!
I SAID USUALLY.
THIS IS A SPECIAL CIRCUMSTANCE, SO RELAX AND HAVE PATIENCE.
YOUR HEART HAS ALREADY STARTED BEATING AGAIN.
BUT AS FOR YOUR SOUL RETURNING TO YOUR BODY, THAT'S UP TO YOU.
...SO THE DAY THIS ANIMAL GROWS UP, I RETURN TO LIFE.
I DON'T GET IT. HOW IS THAT A TEST?
DO YOU KNOW, BOTAN?
NOPE. NO IDEA.

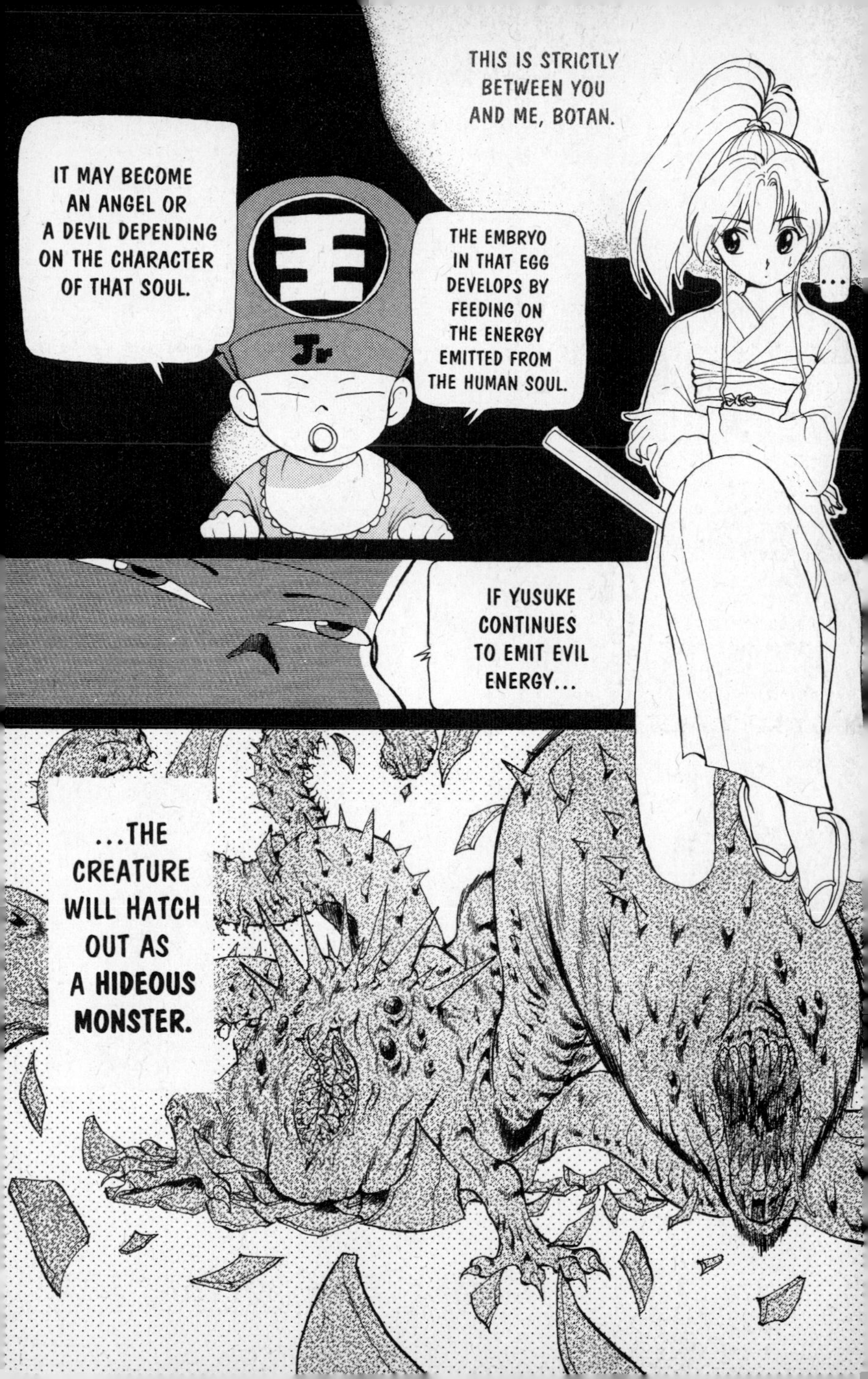

THIS IS STRICTLY BETWEEN YOU AND ME, BOTAN.
THE EMBRYO IN THAT EGG DEVELOPS BY FEEDING ON THE ENERGY EMITTED FROM THE HUMAN SOUL.
IT MAY BECOME AN ANGEL OR A DEVIL DEPENDING ON THE CHARACTER OF THAT SOUL.
...
IF YUSUKE CONTINUES TO EMIT EVIL ENERGY...
...THE CREATURE WILL HATCH OUT AS A HIDEOUS MONSTER.

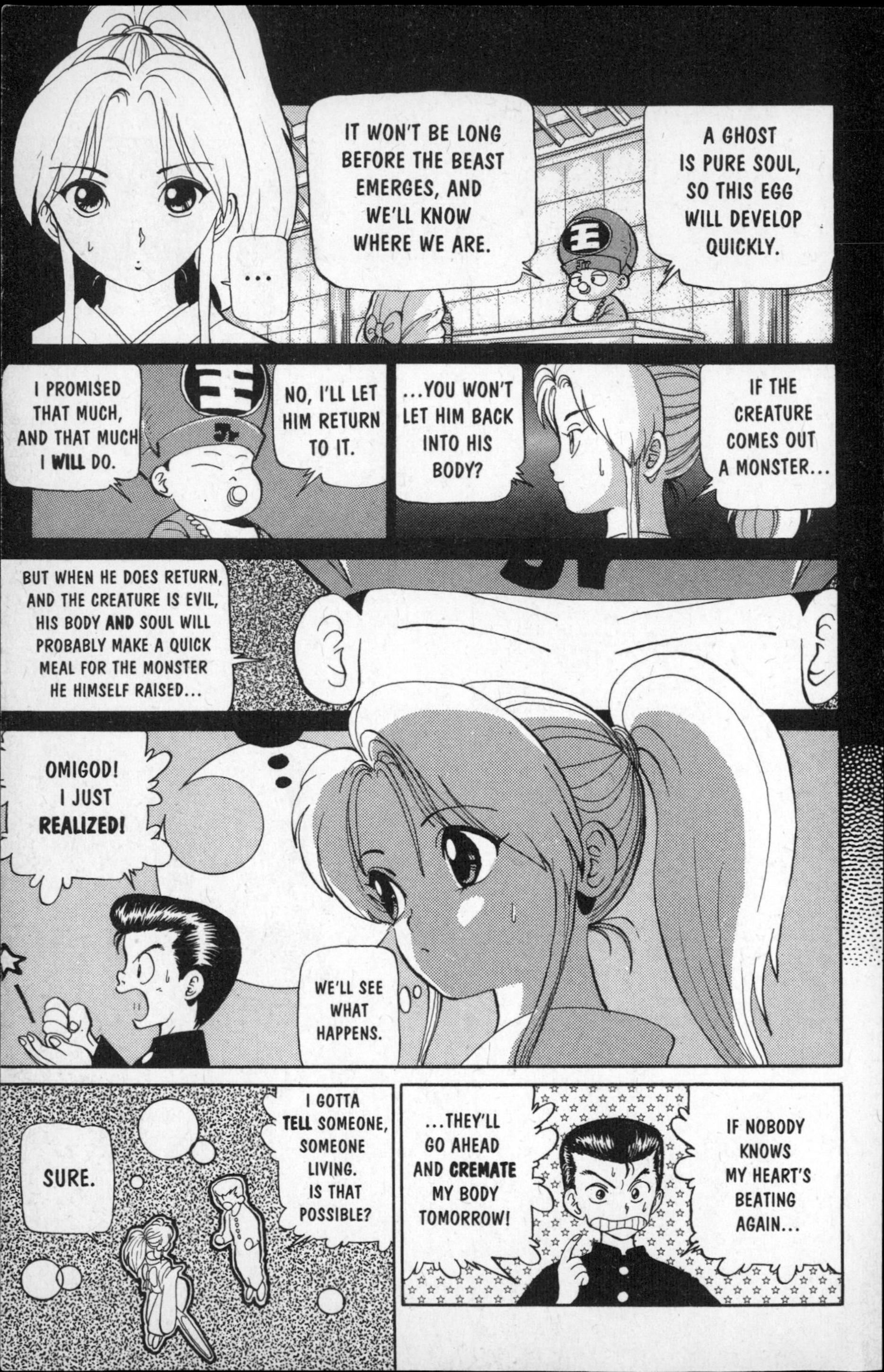
A GHOST IS PURE SOUL, SO THIS EGG WILL DEVELOP QUICKLY.
IT WON'T BE LONG BEFORE THE BEAST EMERGES, AND WE'LL KNOW WHERE WE ARE.
...
IF THE CREATURE COMES OUT A MONSTER...
...YOU WON'T LET HIM BACK INTO HIS BODY?
NO, I'LL LET HIM RETURN TO IT.
I PROMISED THAT MUCH, AND THAT MUCH I **WILL** DO.
BUT WHEN HE DOES RETURN, AND THE CREATURE IS EVIL, HIS BODY **AND** SOUL WILL PROBABLY MAKE A QUICK MEAL FOR THE MONSTER HE HIMSELF RAISED...
WE'LL SEE WHAT HAPPENS.
OMIGOD! I JUST **REALIZED!**
IF NOBODY KNOWS MY HEART'S BEATING AGAIN...
...THEY'LL GO AHEAD AND **CREMATE** MY BODY TOMORROW!
I GOTTA **TELL** SOMEONE, SOMEONE LIVING. IS THAT POSSIBLE?
SURE.

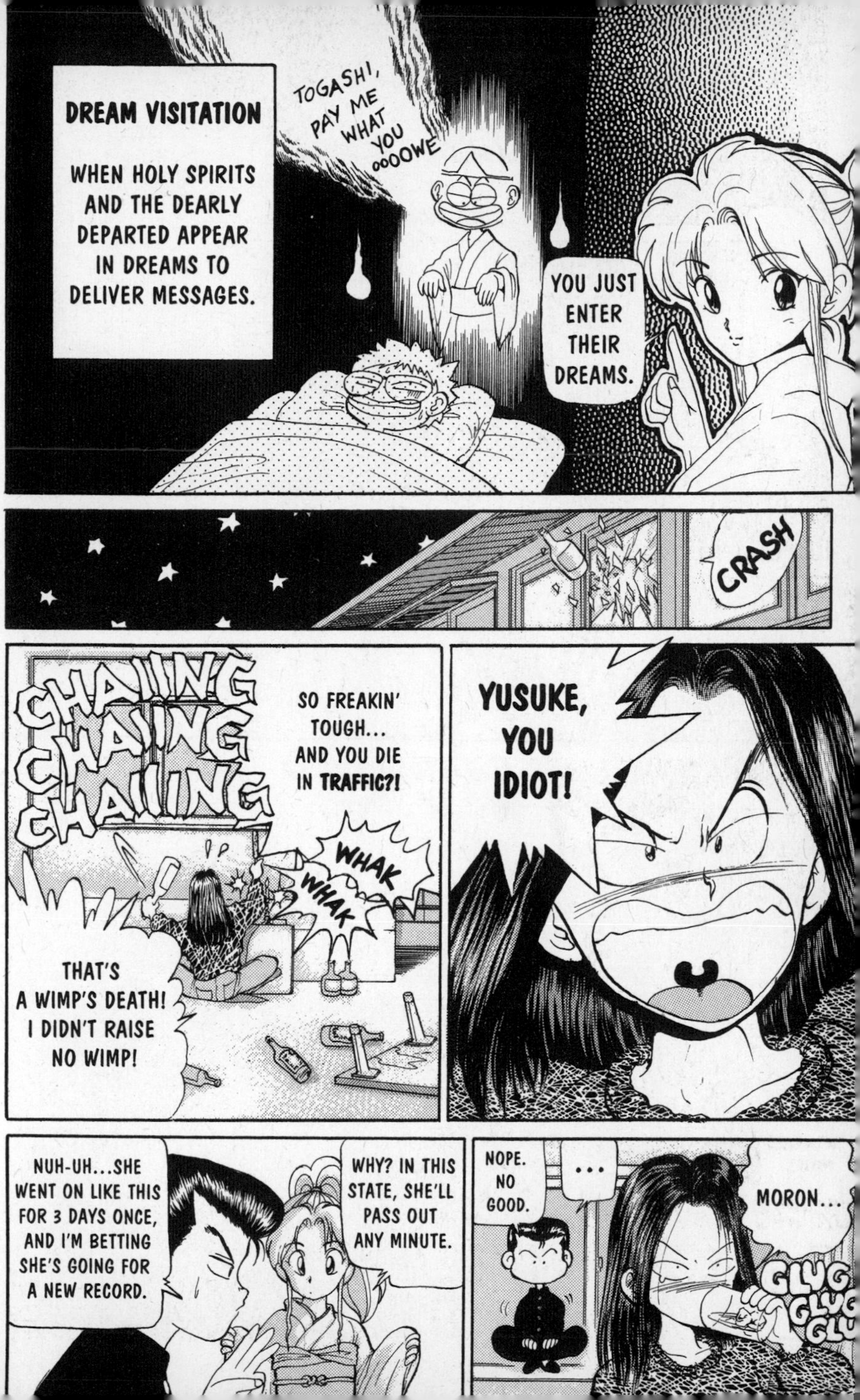
YOU JUST ENTER THEIR DREAMS.
TOGASHI, PAY ME WHAT YOU OOOOWE
DREAM VISITATION
WHEN HOLY SPIRITS AND THE DEARLY DEPARTED APPEAR IN DREAMS TO DELIVER MESSAGES.
CRASH
YUSUKE, YOU IDIOT!
SO FREAKIN' TOUGH... AND YOU DIE IN TRAFFIC?!
WHAK
WHAK
CHAIIING CHAIING CHAIIING
THAT'S A WIMP'S DEATH! I DIDN'T RAISE NO WIMP!
MORON...
...
NOPE. NO GOOD.
GLUG GLUG GLU
WHY? IN THIS STATE, SHE'LL PASS OUT ANY MINUTE.
NUH-UH...SHE WENT ON LIKE THIS FOR 3 DAYS ONCE, AND I'M BETTING SHE'S GOING FOR A NEW RECORD.

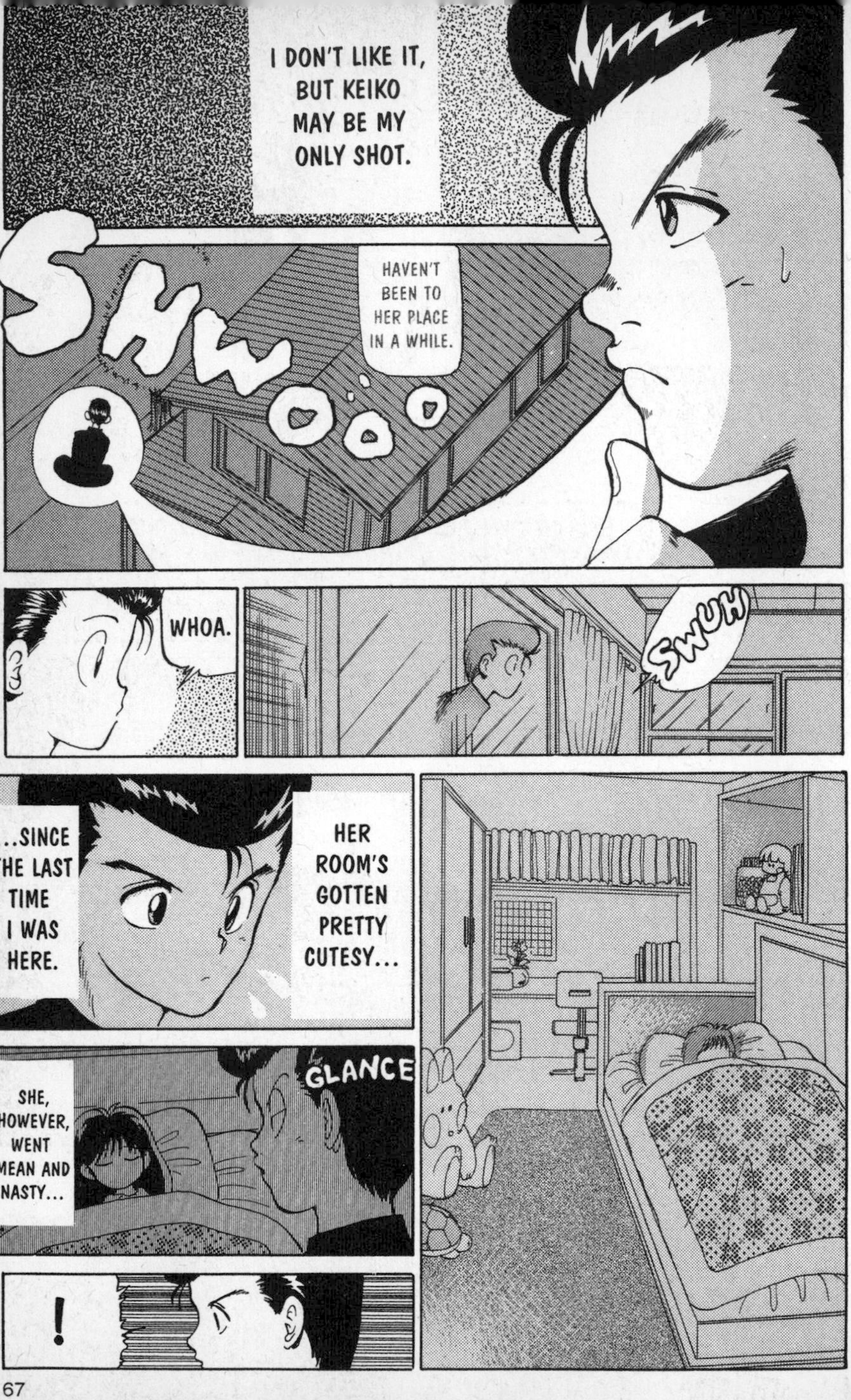
I DON'T LIKE IT, BUT KEIKO MAY BE MY ONLY SHOT.
SHWOOO
HAVEN'T BEEN TO HER PLACE IN A WHILE.
SWUH
WHOA.
HER ROOM'S GOTTEN PRETTY CUTESY...
...SINCE THE LAST TIME I WAS HERE.
GLANCE
SHE, HOWEVER, WENT MEAN AND NASTY...
!

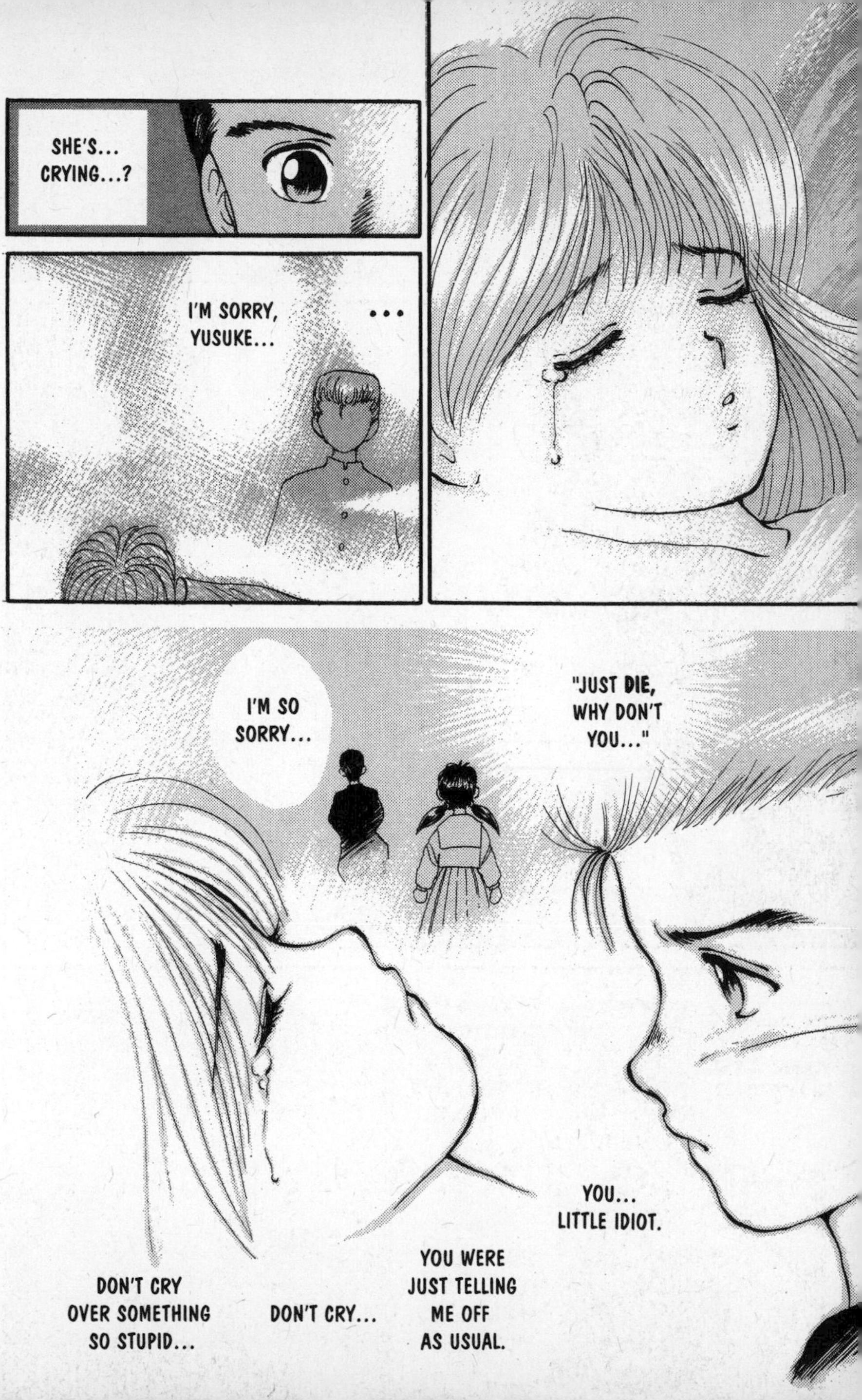
SHE'S... CRYING...?
• • •
I'M SORRY, YUSUKE...
"JUST DIE, WHY DON'T YOU..."
I'M SO SORRY...
YOU... LITTLE IDIOT.
YOU WERE JUST TELLING ME OFF AS USUAL.
DON'T CRY...
DON'T CRY OVER SOMETHING SO STUPID...

READ THIS WAY

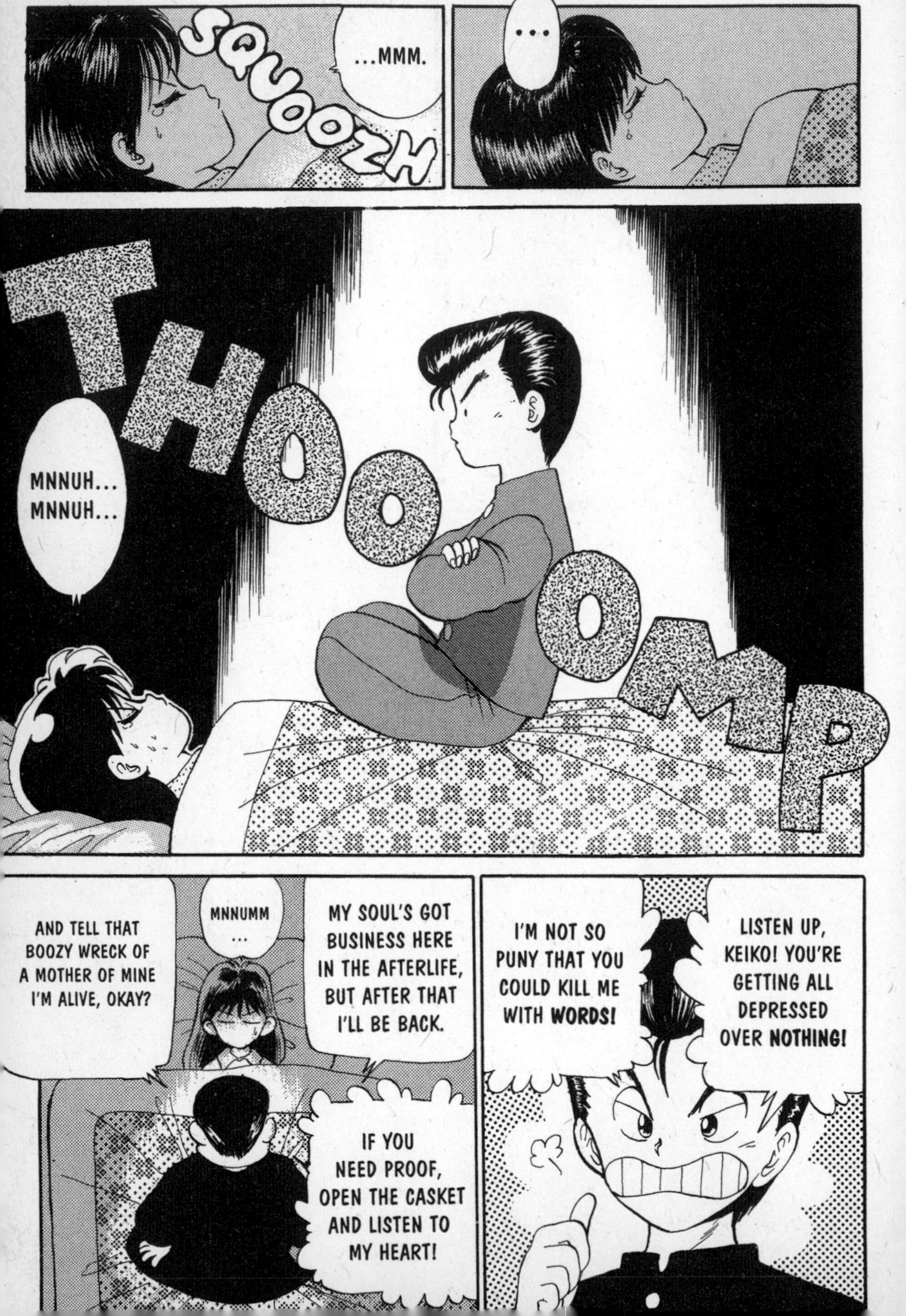
...
SQUOOZH
...MMM.
THOOOOMP
MNNUH... MNNUH...
LISTEN UP, KEIKO! YOU'RE GETTING ALL DEPRESSED OVER **NOTHING**!
I'M NOT SO PUNY THAT YOU COULD KILL ME WITH **WORDS**!
MNNUMM ...
MY SOUL'S GOT BUSINESS HERE IN THE AFTERLIFE, BUT AFTER THAT I'LL BE BACK.
AND TELL THAT BOOZY WRECK OF A MOTHER OF MINE I'M ALIVE, OKAY?
IF YOU NEED PROOF, OPEN THE CASKET AND LISTEN TO MY HEART!

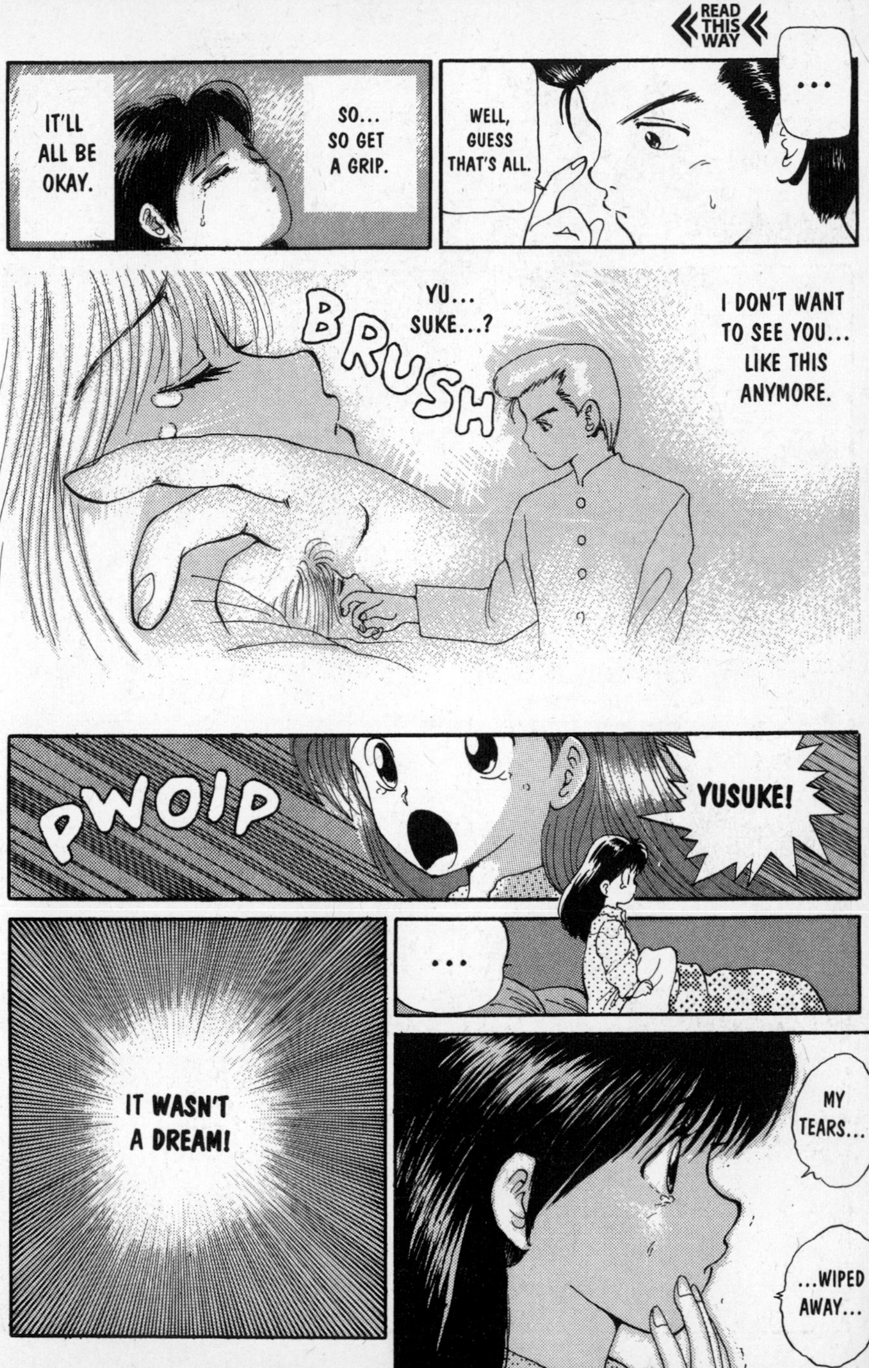
READ THIS WAY
...
WELL, GUESS THAT'S ALL.
SO... SO GET A GRIP.
IT'LL ALL BE OKAY.
I DON'T WANT TO SEE YOU... LIKE THIS ANYMORE.
YU... SUKE...?
BRUSH
YUSUKE!
PWOIP
...
IT WASN'T A DREAM!
MY TEARS...
...WIPED AWAY...

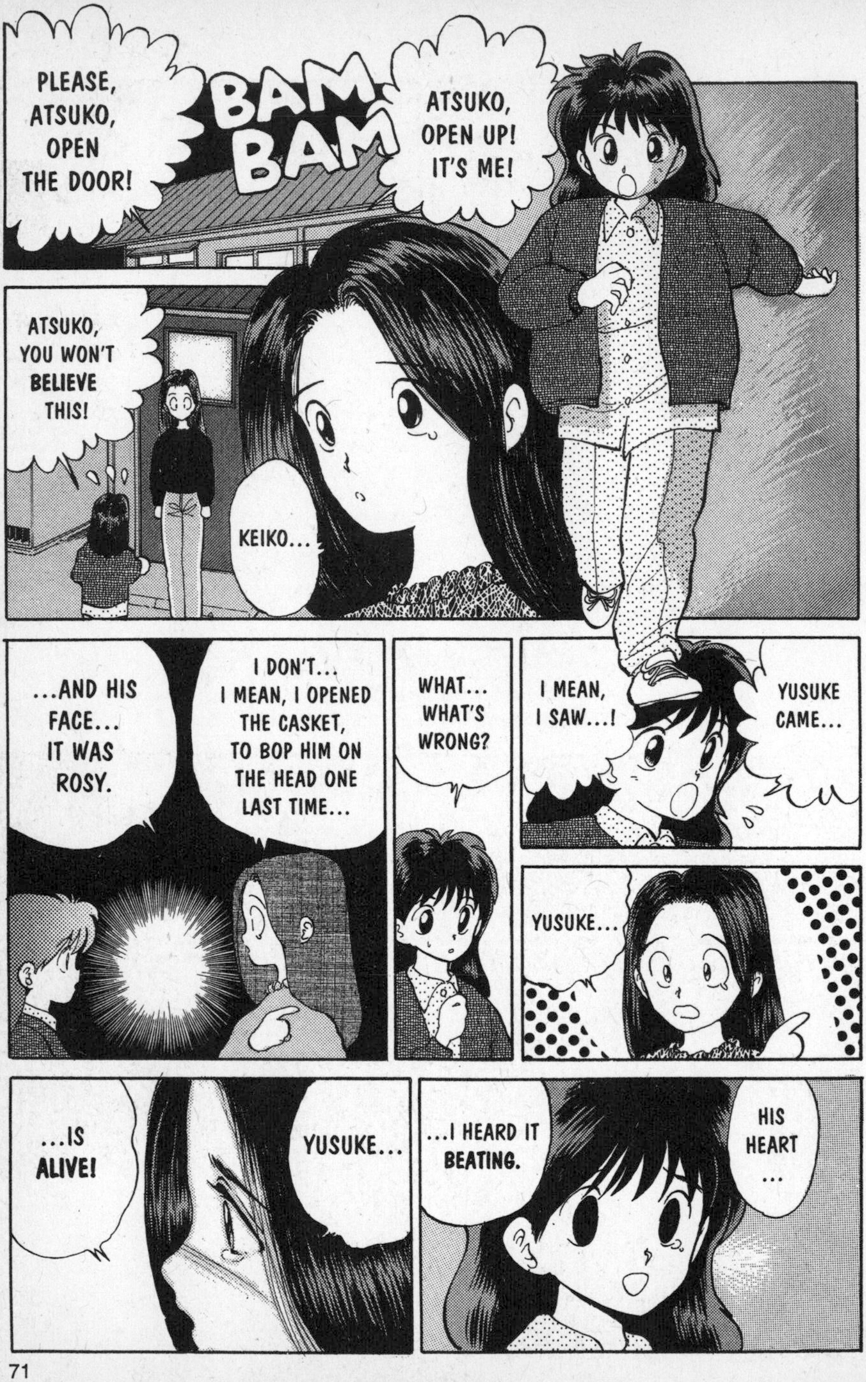
ATSUKO, OPEN UP! IT'S ME!
BAM BAM
PLEASE, ATSUKO, OPEN THE DOOR!
KEIKO...
ATSUKO, YOU WON'T BELIEVE THIS!
YUSUKE CAME...
I MEAN, I SAW...!
YUSUKE...
WHAT... WHAT'S WRONG?
I DON'T... I MEAN, I OPENED THE CASKET, TO BOP HIM ON THE HEAD ONE LAST TIME...
...AND HIS FACE... IT WAS ROSY.
HIS HEART ...
...I HEARD IT BEATING.
YUSUKE...
...IS ALIVE!

READ THIS WAY

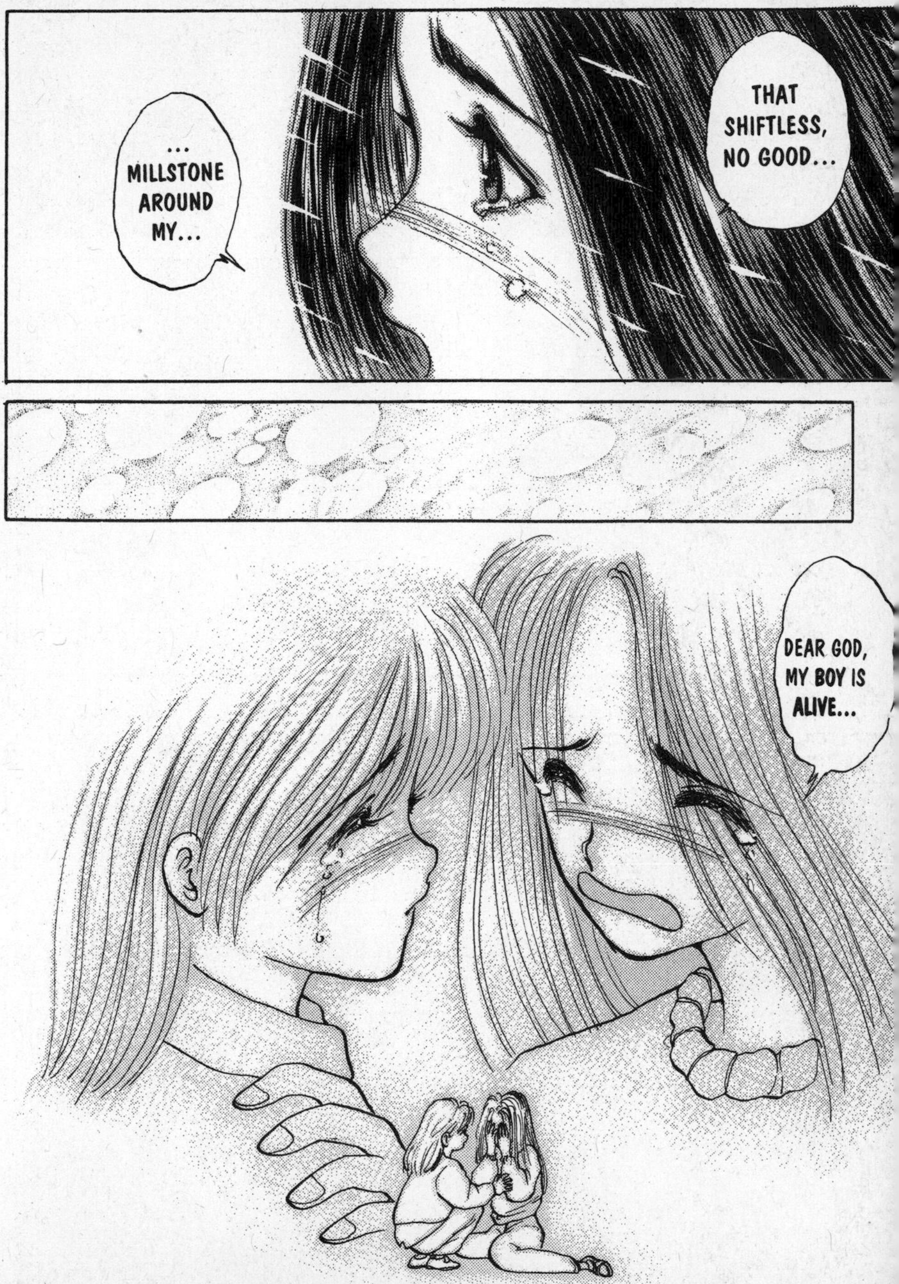
THAT SHIFTLESS, NO GOOD...
... MILLSTONE AROUND MY...
DEAR GOD, MY BOY IS ALIVE...

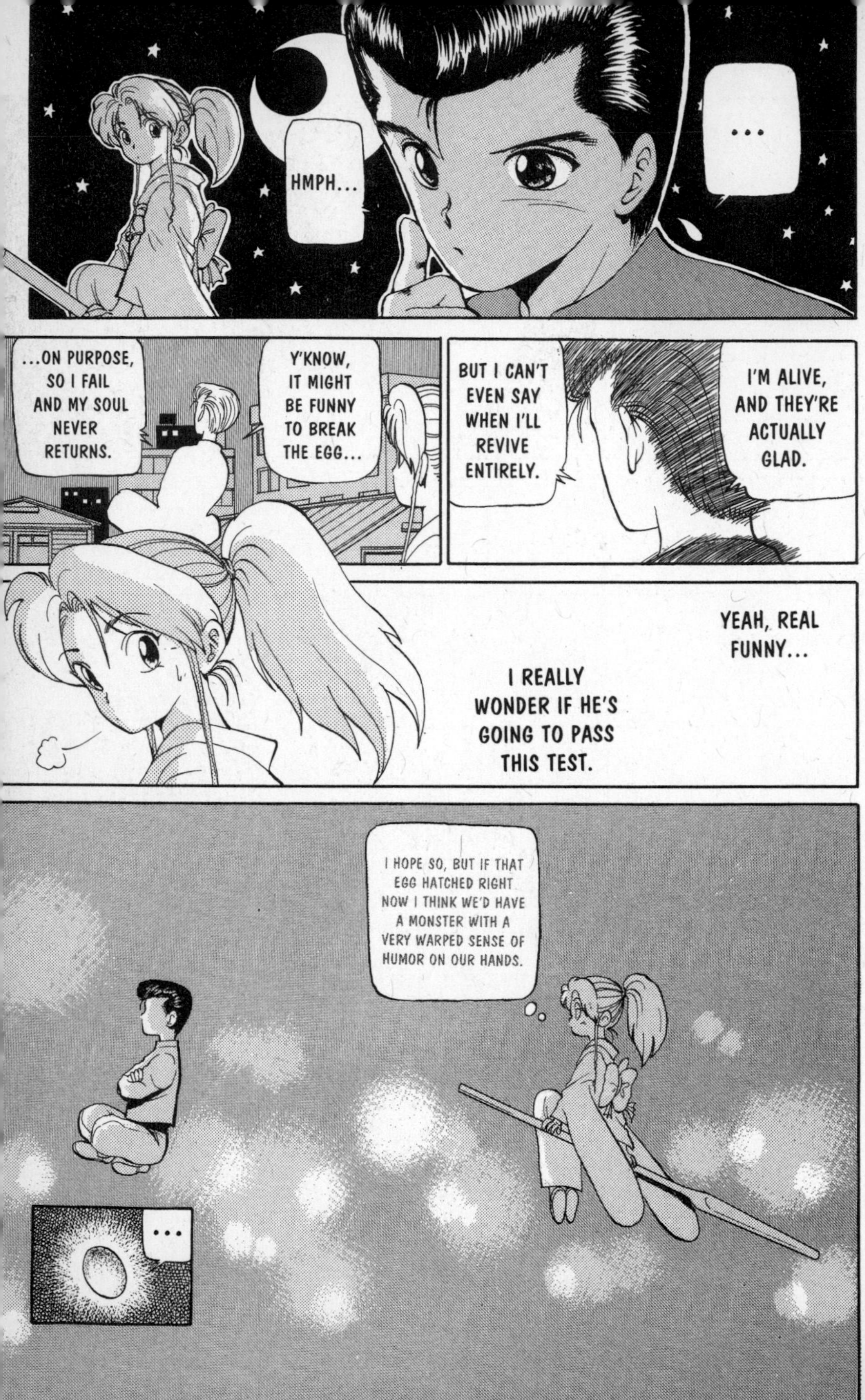
...
HMPH...
I'M ALIVE, AND THEY'RE ACTUALLY GLAD.
BUT I CAN'T EVEN SAY WHEN I'LL REVIVE ENTIRELY.
Y'KNOW, IT MIGHT BE FUNNY TO BREAK THE EGG...
...ON PURPOSE, SO I FAIL AND MY SOUL NEVER RETURNS.
YEAH, REAL FUNNY...
I REALLY WONDER IF HE'S GOING TO PASS THIS TEST.
I HOPE SO, BUT IF THAT EGG HATCHED RIGHT NOW I THINK WE'D HAVE A MONSTER WITH A VERY WARPED SENSE OF HUMOR ON OUR HANDS.
...

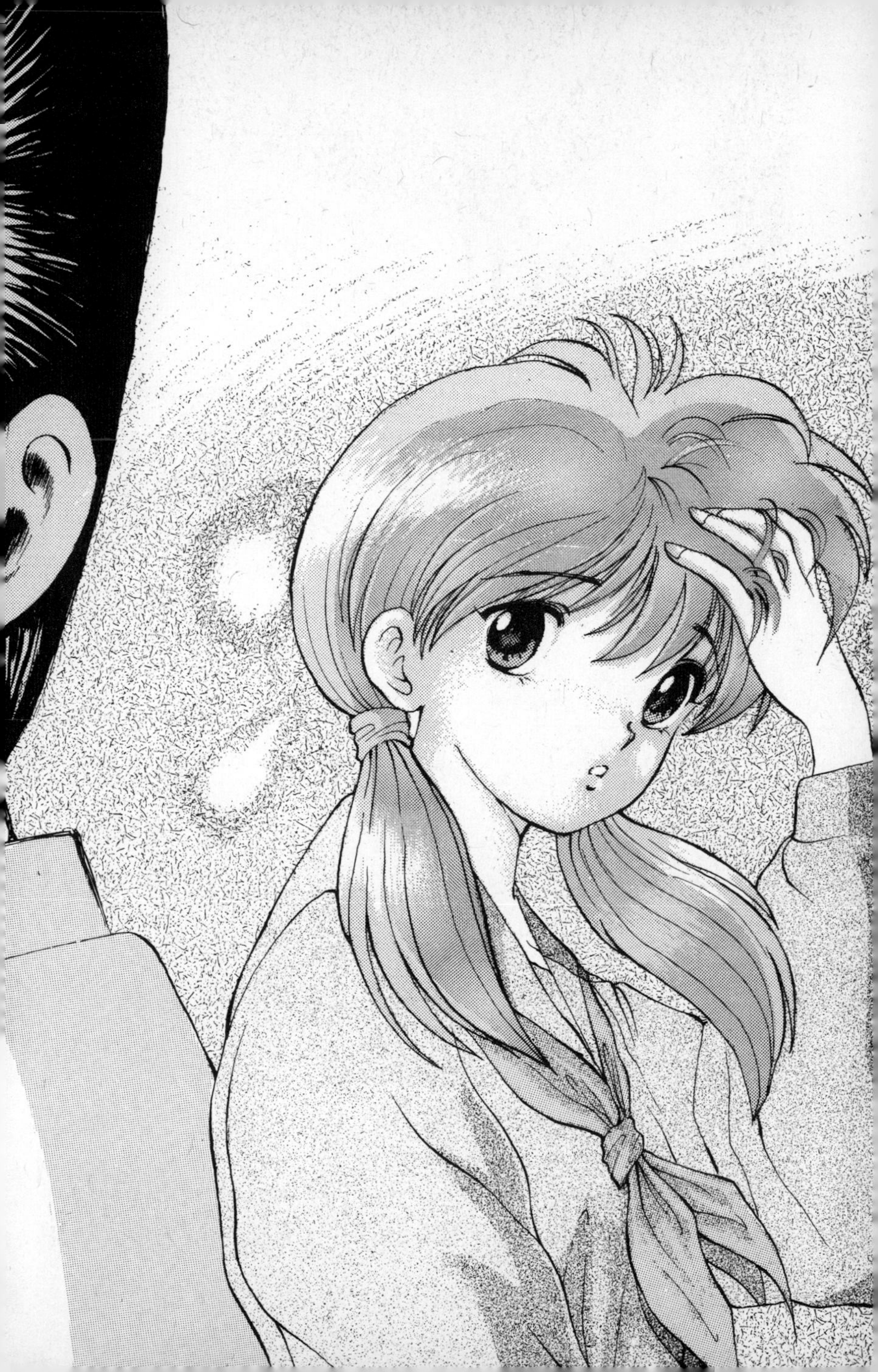

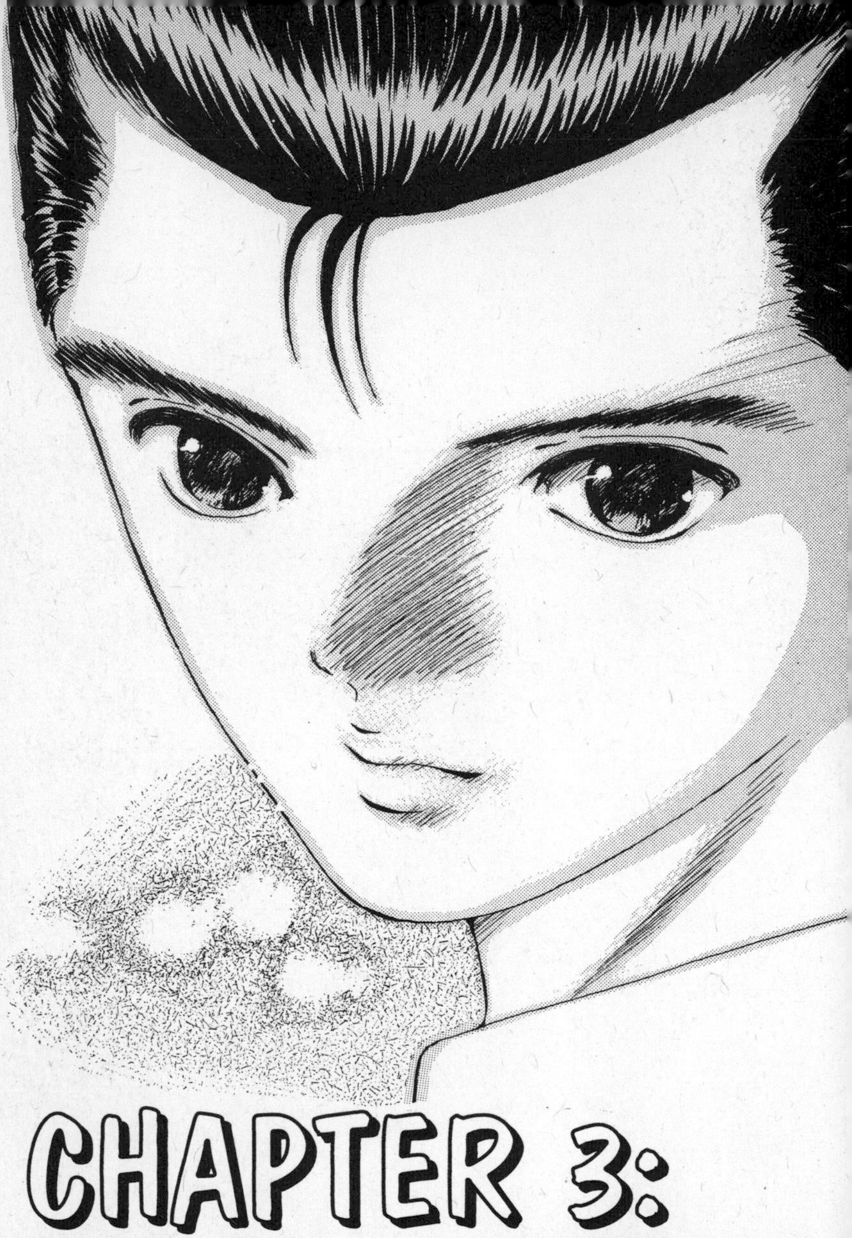

CHAPTER 3: TIME FOR DEPARTURE!!

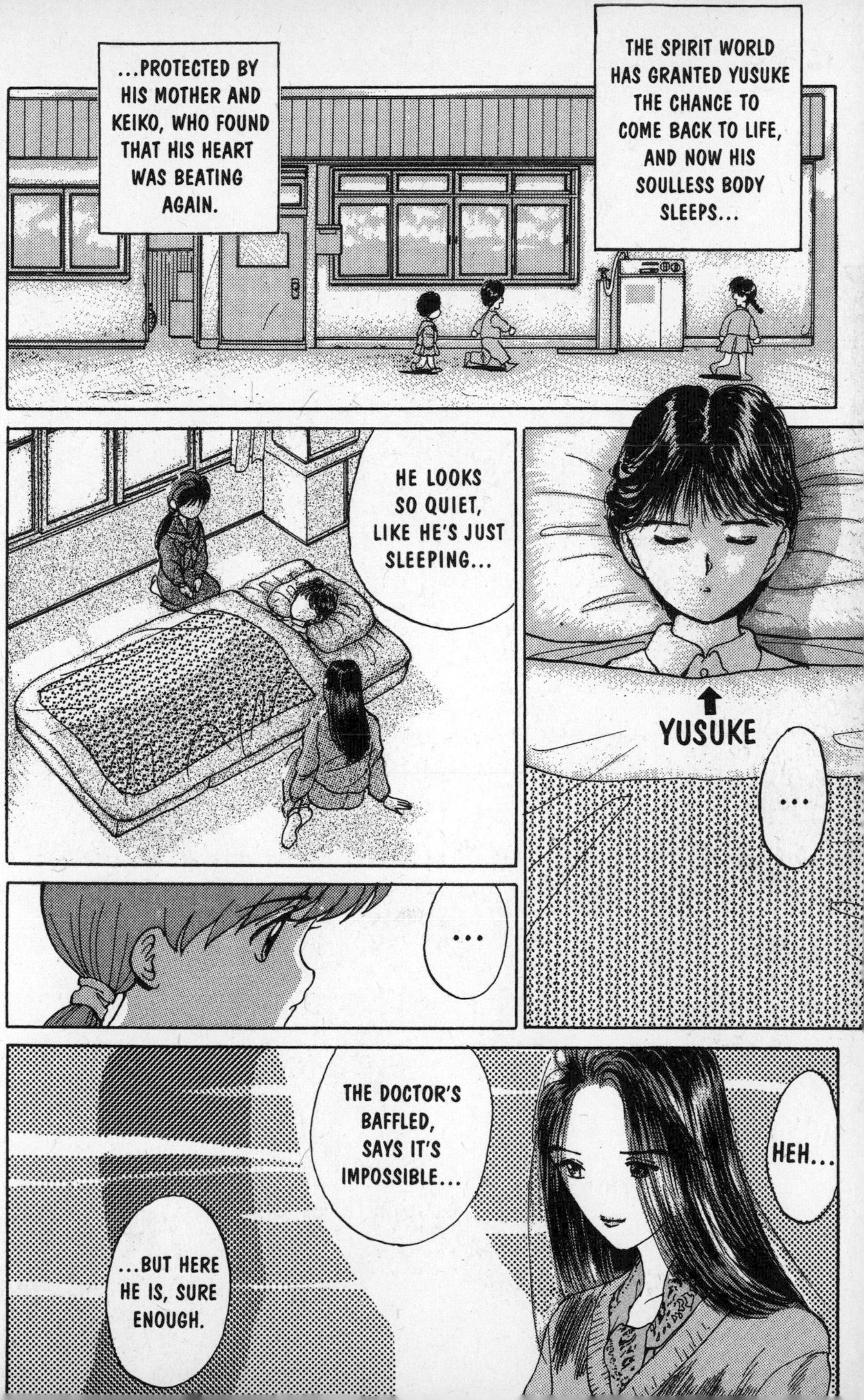
THE SPIRIT WORLD HAS GRANTED YUSUKE THE CHANCE TO COME BACK TO LIFE, AND NOW HIS SOULLESS BODY SLEEPS...
...PROTECTED BY HIS MOTHER AND KEIKO, WHO FOUND THAT HIS HEART WAS BEATING AGAIN.
YUSUKE
...
HE LOOKS SO QUIET, LIKE HE'S JUST SLEEPING...
...
HEH...
THE DOCTOR'S BAFFLED, SAYS IT'S IMPOSSIBLE...
...BUT HERE HE IS, SURE ENOUGH.

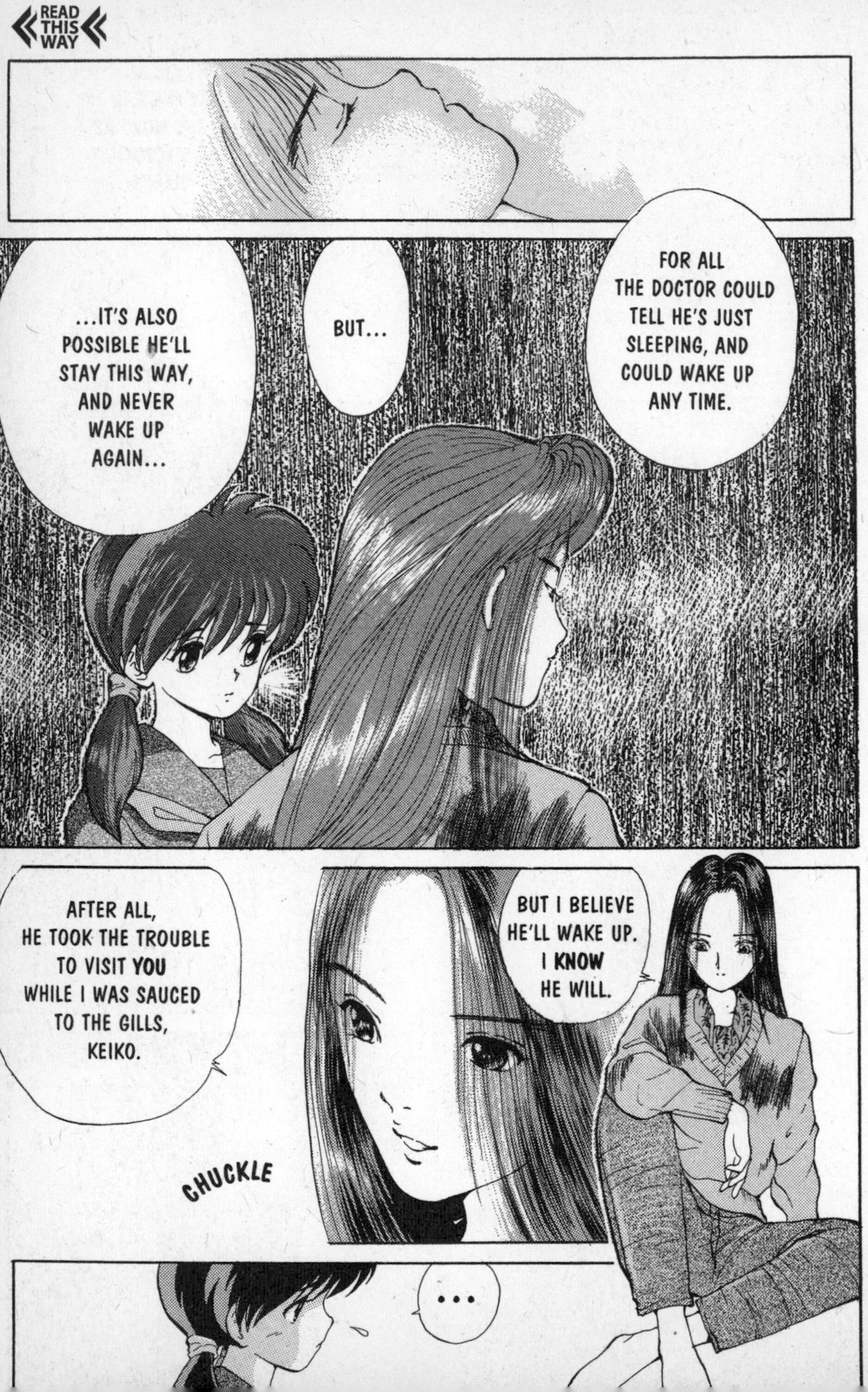

READ THIS WAY
FOR ALL THE DOCTOR COULD TELL HE'S JUST SLEEPING, AND COULD WAKE UP ANY TIME.
BUT...
...IT'S ALSO POSSIBLE HE'LL STAY THIS WAY, AND NEVER WAKE UP AGAIN...
BUT I BELIEVE HE'LL WAKE UP. I **KNOW** HE WILL.
AFTER ALL, HE TOOK THE TROUBLE TO VISIT **YOU** WHILE I WAS SAUCED TO THE GILLS, KEIKO.
CHUCKLE
...

READ THIS WAY

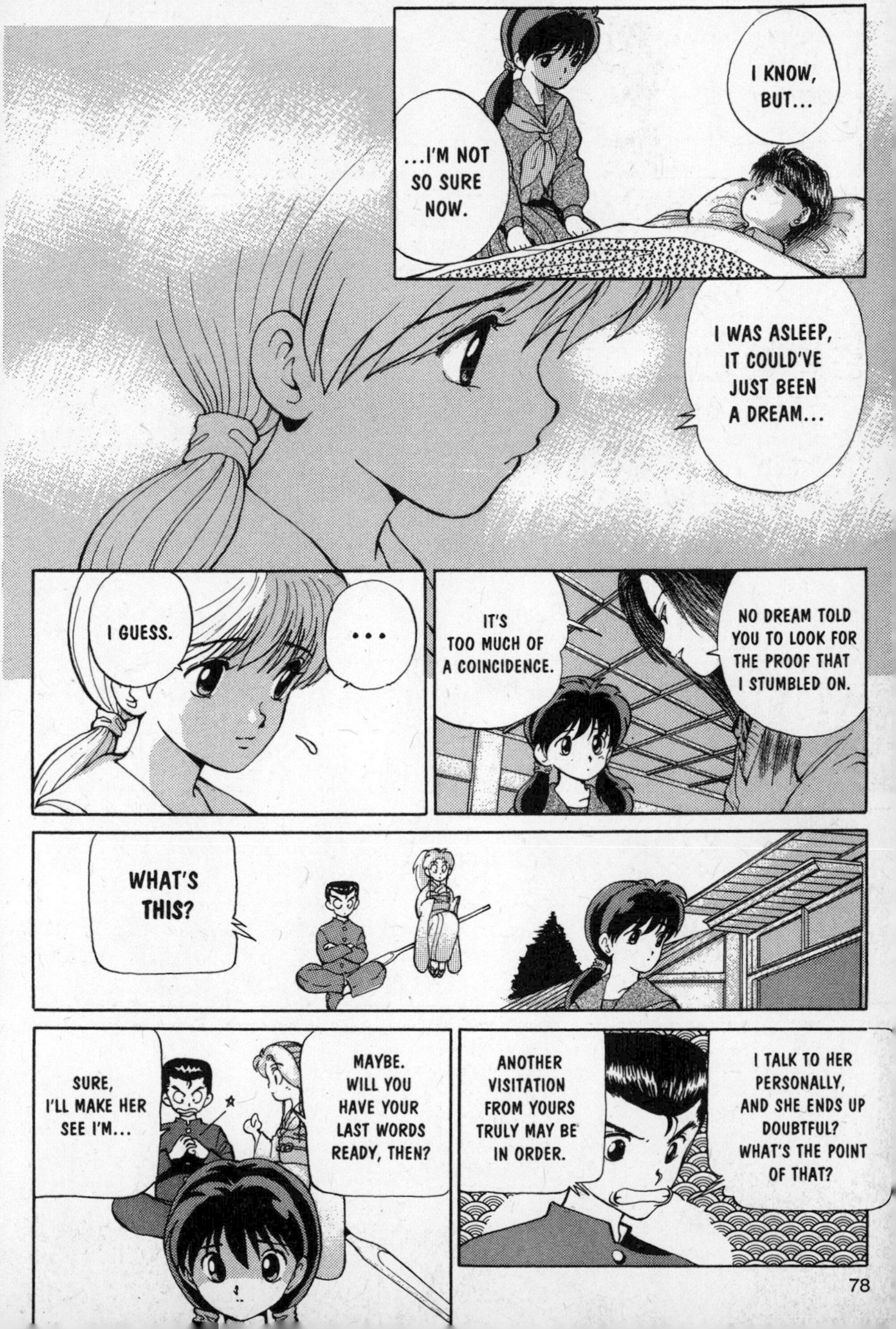
I KNOW, BUT...
...I'M NOT SO SURE NOW.
I WAS ASLEEP, IT COULD'VE JUST BEEN A DREAM...
NO DREAM TOLD YOU TO LOOK FOR THE PROOF THAT I STUMBLED ON.
IT'S TOO MUCH OF A COINCIDENCE.
...
I GUESS.
WHAT'S THIS?
I TALK TO HER PERSONALLY, AND SHE ENDS UP DOUBTFUL? WHAT'S THE POINT OF THAT?
ANOTHER VISITATION FROM YOURS TRULY MAY BE IN ORDER.
MAYBE. WILL YOU HAVE YOUR LAST WORDS READY, THEN?
SURE, I'LL MAKE HER SEE I'M...

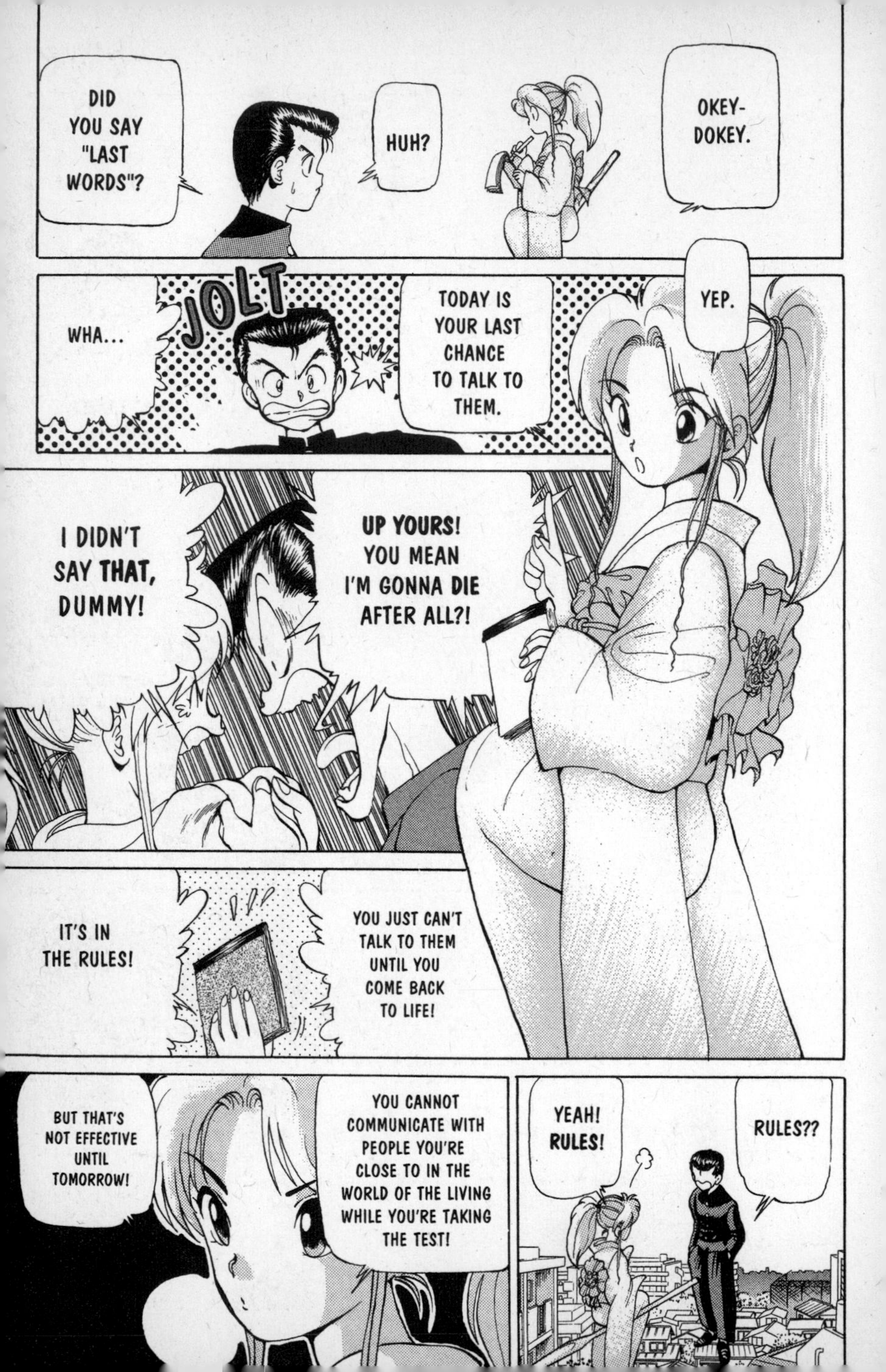
OKEY-DOKEY.
HUH?
DID YOU SAY "LAST WORDS"?
YEP.
TODAY IS YOUR LAST CHANCE TO TALK TO THEM.
JOLT
WHA...
UP YOURS! YOU MEAN I'M GONNA DIE AFTER ALL?!
I DIDN'T SAY THAT, DUMMY!
YOU JUST CAN'T TALK TO THEM UNTIL YOU COME BACK TO LIFE!
IT'S IN THE RULES!
RULES??
YEAH! RULES!
YOU CANNOT COMMUNICATE WITH PEOPLE YOU'RE CLOSE TO IN THE WORLD OF THE LIVING WHILE YOU'RE TAKING THE TEST!
BUT THAT'S NOT EFFECTIVE UNTIL TOMORROW!

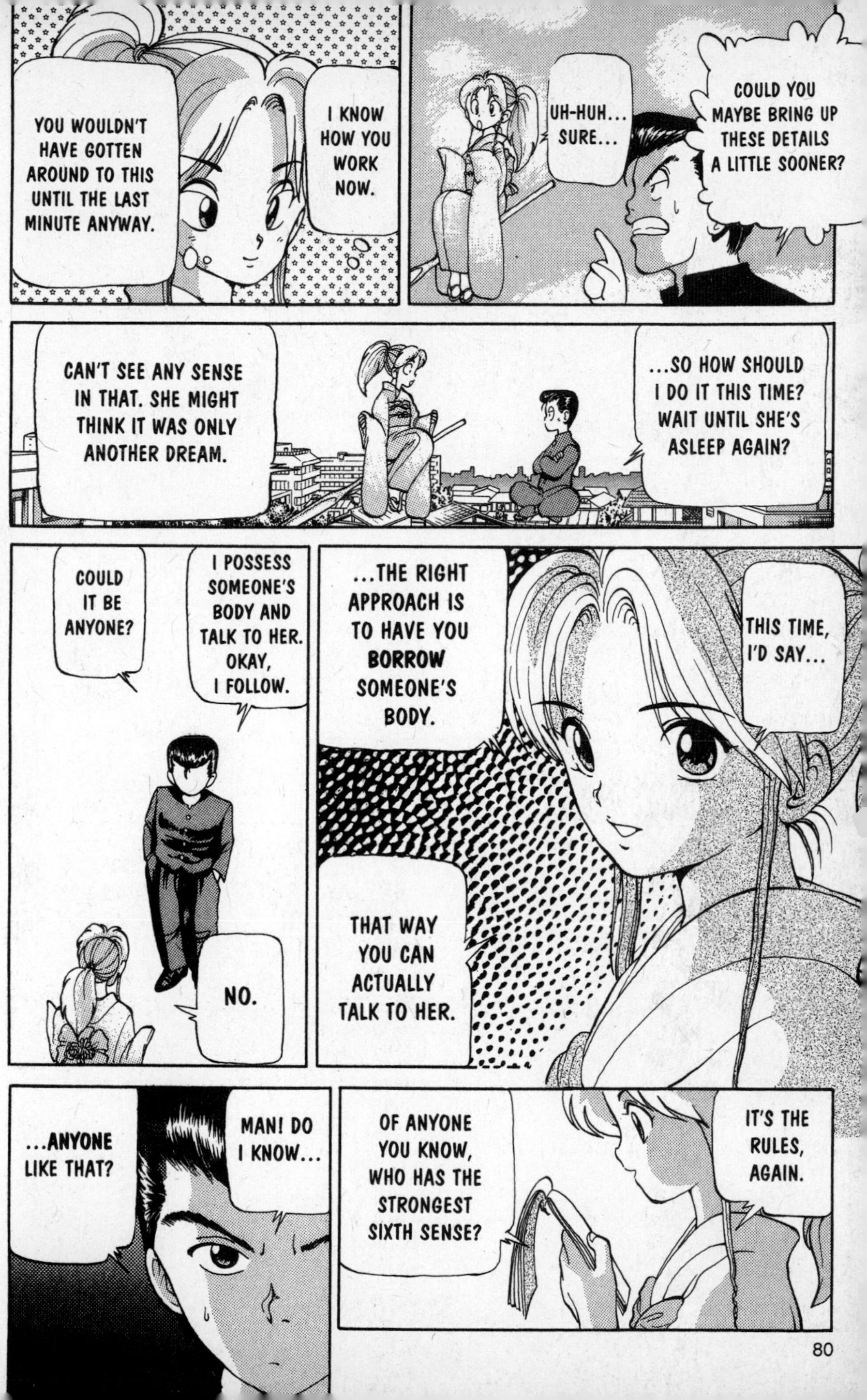
COULD YOU MAYBE BRING UP THESE DETAILS A LITTLE SOONER?
UH-HUH... SURE...
I KNOW HOW YOU WORK NOW.
YOU WOULDN'T HAVE GOTTEN AROUND TO THIS UNTIL THE LAST MINUTE ANYWAY.
...SO HOW SHOULD I DO IT THIS TIME? WAIT UNTIL SHE'S ASLEEP AGAIN?
CAN'T SEE ANY SENSE IN THAT. SHE MIGHT THINK IT WAS ONLY ANOTHER DREAM.
THIS TIME, I'D SAY...
...THE RIGHT APPROACH IS TO HAVE YOU **BORROW** SOMEONE'S BODY.
THAT WAY YOU CAN ACTUALLY TALK TO HER.
I POSSESS SOMEONE'S BODY AND TALK TO HER. OKAY, I FOLLOW.
COULD IT BE ANYONE?
NO.
IT'S THE RULES, AGAIN.
OF ANYONE YOU KNOW, WHO HAS THE STRONGEST SIXTH SENSE?
MAN! DO I KNOW...
...**ANYONE** LIKE THAT?

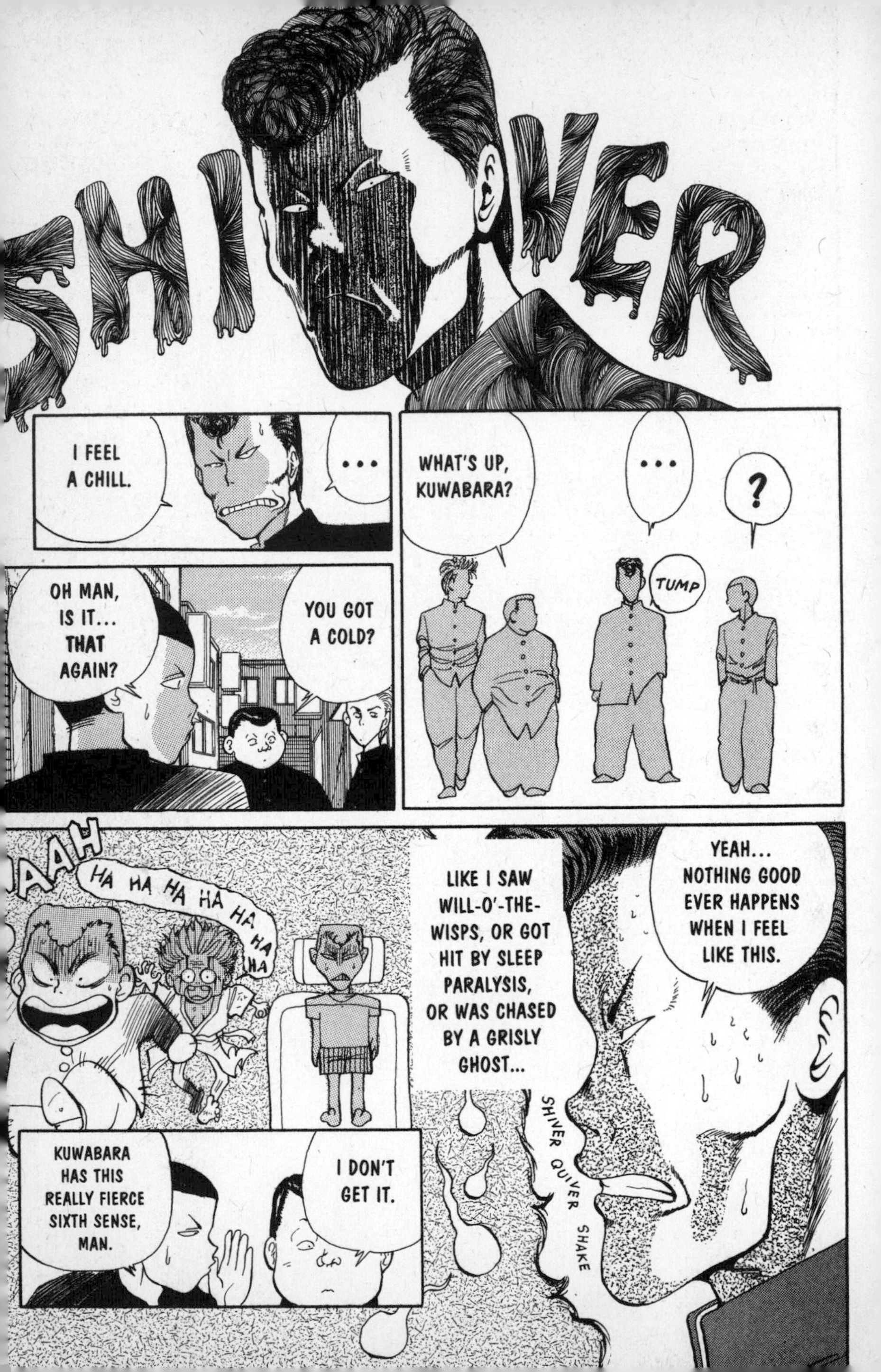
SHIVER
?
...
WHAT'S UP, KUWABARA?
TUMP
...
I FEEL A CHILL.
YOU GOT A COLD?
OH MAN, IS IT... THAT AGAIN?
YEAH... NOTHING GOOD EVER HAPPENS WHEN I FEEL LIKE THIS.
SHIVER QUIVER SHAKE
LIKE I SAW WILL-O'-THE-WISPS, OR GOT HIT BY SLEEP PARALYSIS, OR WAS CHASED BY A GRISLY GHOST...
HA HA HA HA HA HA HA
AAH
I DON'T GET IT.
KUWABARA HAS THIS REALLY FIERCE SIXTH SENSE, MAN.

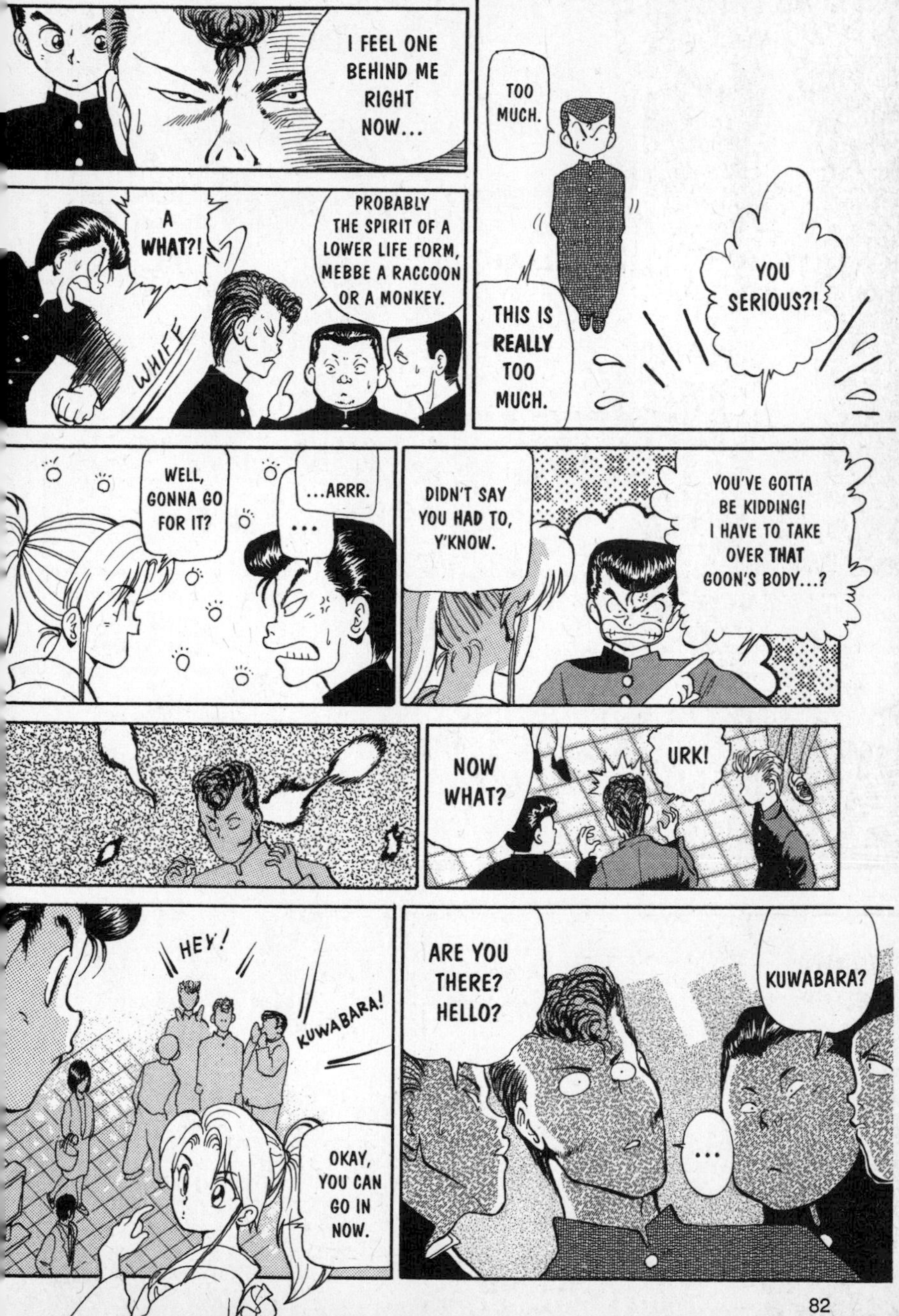
TOO MUCH.
THIS IS REALLY TOO MUCH.
YOU SERIOUS?!
I FEEL ONE BEHIND ME RIGHT NOW...
PROBABLY THE SPIRIT OF A LOWER LIFE FORM, MEBBE A RACCOON OR A MONKEY.
A WHAT?!
WHIFF
YOU'VE GOTTA BE KIDDING! I HAVE TO TAKE OVER THAT GOON'S BODY...?
DIDN'T SAY YOU HAD TO, Y'KNOW.
...ARRR.
...
WELL, GONNA GO FOR IT?
URK!
NOW WHAT?
KUWABARA?
...
ARE YOU THERE? HELLO?
KUWABARA!
HEY!
OKAY, YOU CAN GO IN NOW.

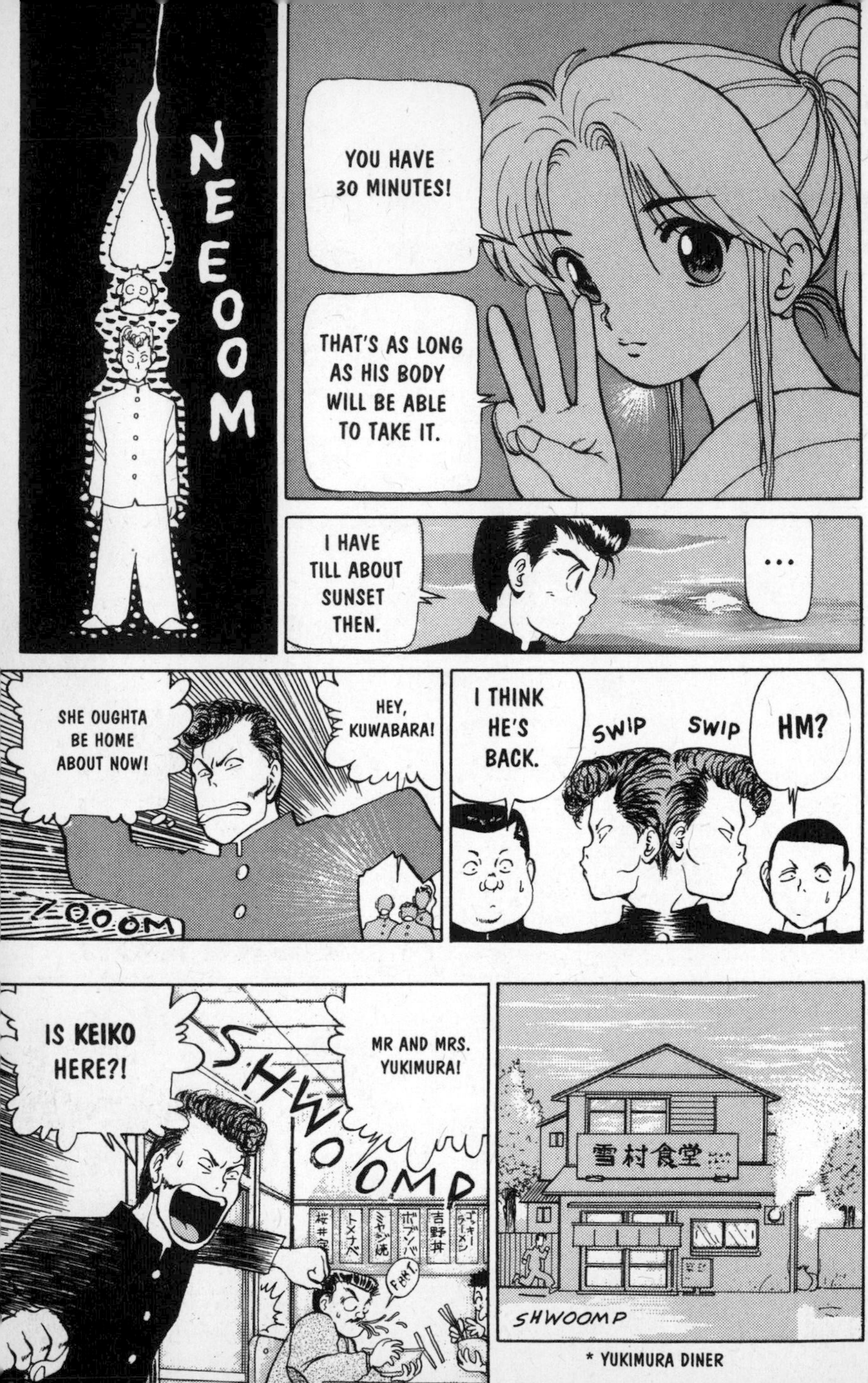
YOU HAVE 30 MINUTES!
THAT'S AS LONG AS HIS BODY WILL BE ABLE TO TAKE IT.
...
I HAVE TILL ABOUT SUNSET THEN.
NEEOOM
HM?
SWIP
SWIP
I THINK HE'S BACK.
HEY, KUWABARA!
SHE OUGHTA BE HOME ABOUT NOW!
雪村食堂
SHWOOMP
MR AND MRS. YUKIMURA!
SHWOOMP
IS KEIKO HERE?!
吉野丼
FBRT
* YUKIMURA DINER

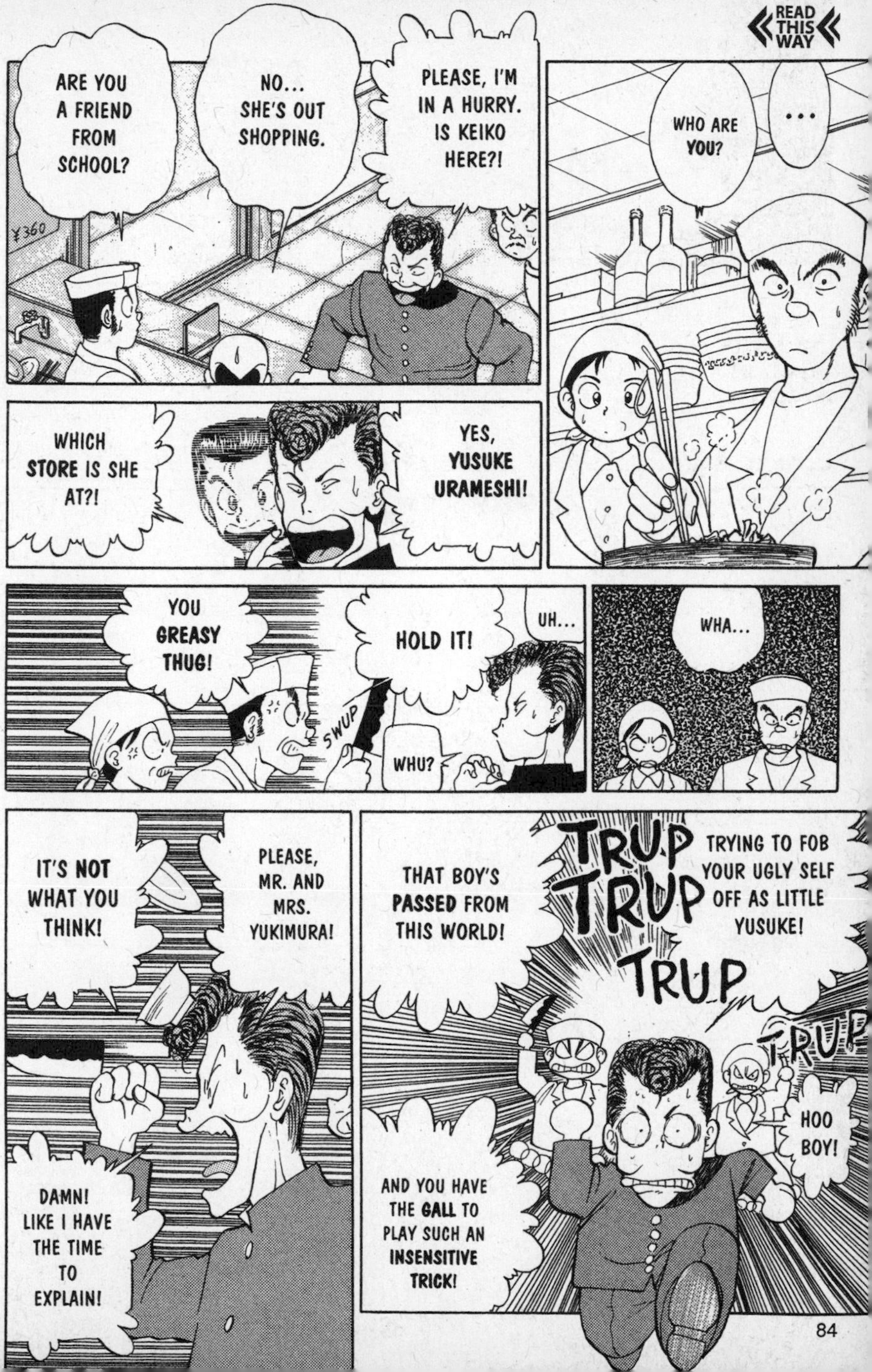
READ THIS WAY
...
WHO ARE YOU?
PLEASE, I'M IN A HURRY. IS KEIKO HERE?!
NO... SHE'S OUT SHOPPING.
ARE YOU A FRIEND FROM SCHOOL?
¥360
YES, YUSUKE URAMESHI!
WHICH STORE IS SHE AT?!
WHA...
UH...
HOLD IT!
YOU GREASY THUG!
SWUP
WHU?
TRYING TO FOB YOUR UGLY SELF OFF AS LITTLE YUSUKE!
TRUP TRUP
THAT BOY'S PASSED FROM THIS WORLD!
TRUP
TRUP
HOO BOY!
AND YOU HAVE THE GALL TO PLAY SUCH AN INSENSITIVE TRICK!
PLEASE, MR. AND MRS. YUKIMURA!
IT'S NOT WHAT YOU THINK!
DAMN! LIKE I HAVE THE TIME TO EXPLAIN!

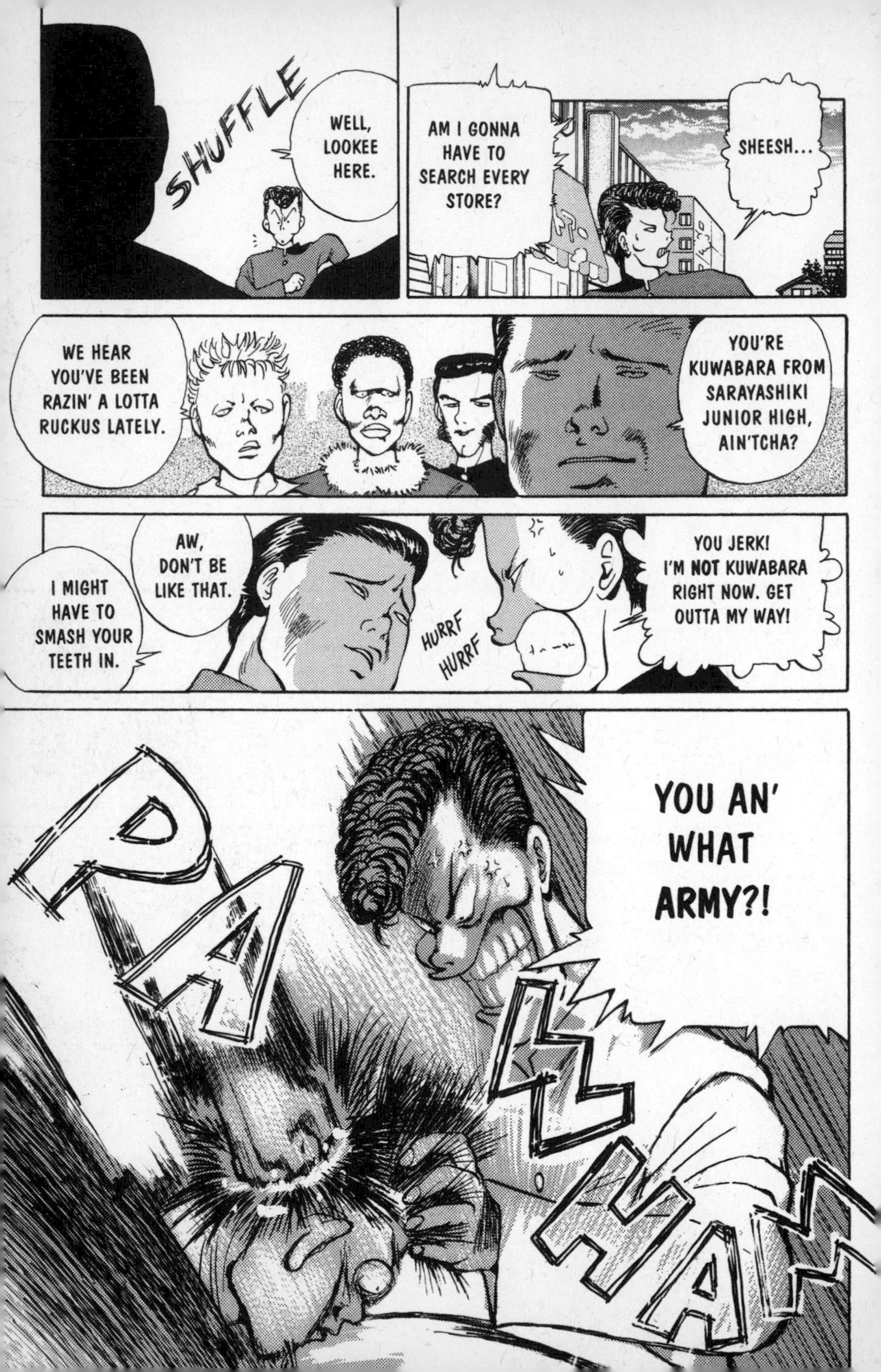
AM I GONNA HAVE TO SEARCH EVERY STORE?
SHEESH...
SHUFFLE
WELL, LOOKEE HERE.
YOU'RE KUWABARA FROM SARAYASHIKI JUNIOR HIGH, AIN'TCHA?
WE HEAR YOU'VE BEEN RAZIN' A LOTTA RUCKUS LATELY.
YOU JERK! I'M NOT KUWABARA RIGHT NOW. GET OUTTA MY WAY!
HURRF HURRF
AW, DON'T BE LIKE THAT.
I MIGHT HAVE TO SMASH YOUR TEETH IN.
YOU AN' WHAT ARMY?!

READ THIS WAY

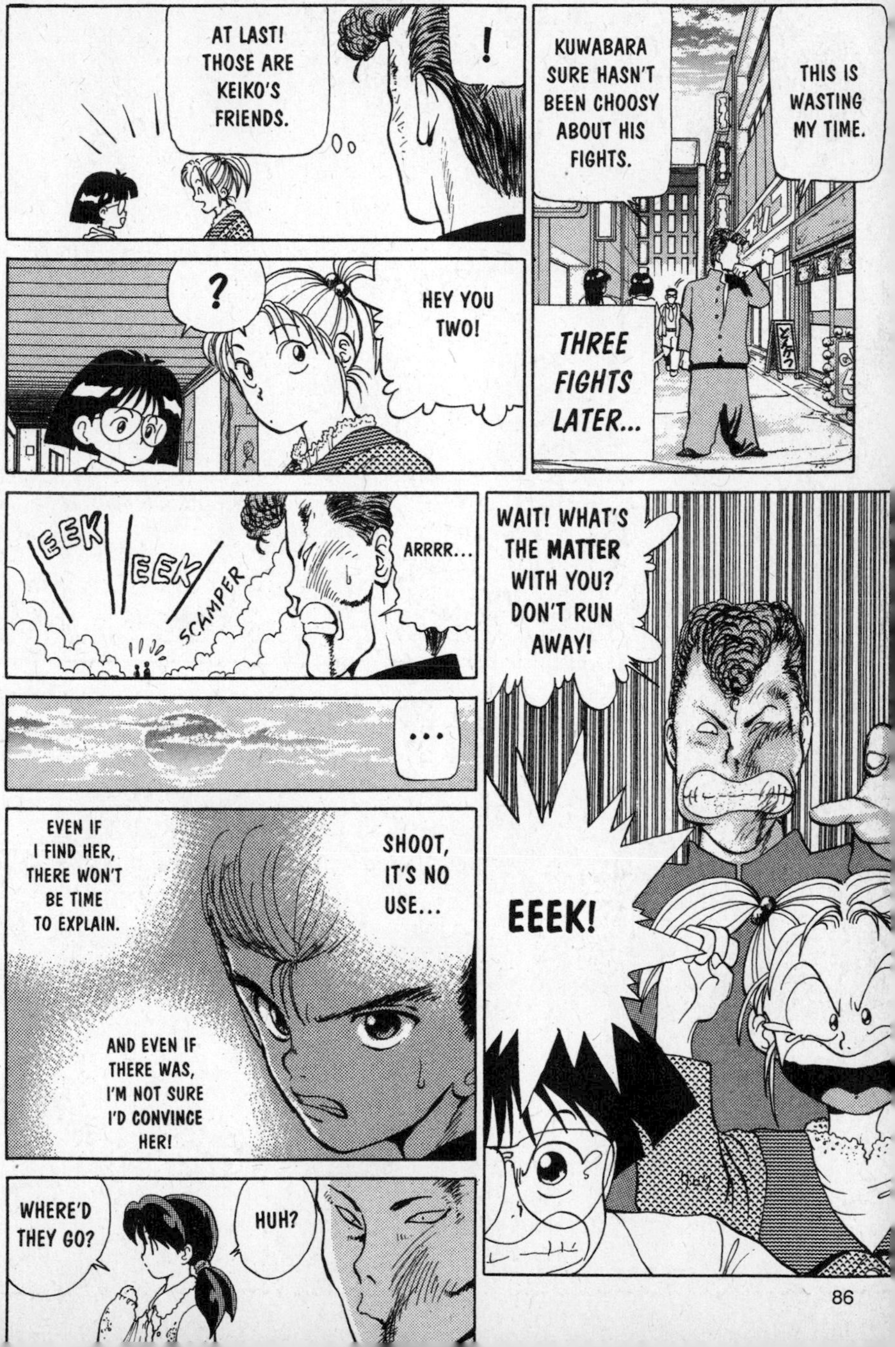
THIS IS WASTING MY TIME.
KUWABARA SURE HASN'T BEEN CHOOSY ABOUT HIS FIGHTS.
THREE FIGHTS LATER...
!
AT LAST! THOSE ARE KEIKO'S FRIENDS.
HEY YOU TWO!
?
WAIT! WHAT'S THE MATTER WITH YOU? DON'T RUN AWAY!
EEEK!
ARRRR...
EEK
EEK
SCAMPER
...
SHOOT, IT'S NO USE...
EVEN IF I FIND HER, THERE WON'T BE TIME TO EXPLAIN.
AND EVEN IF THERE WAS, I'M NOT SURE I'D CONVINCE HER!
HUH?
WHERE'D THEY GO?

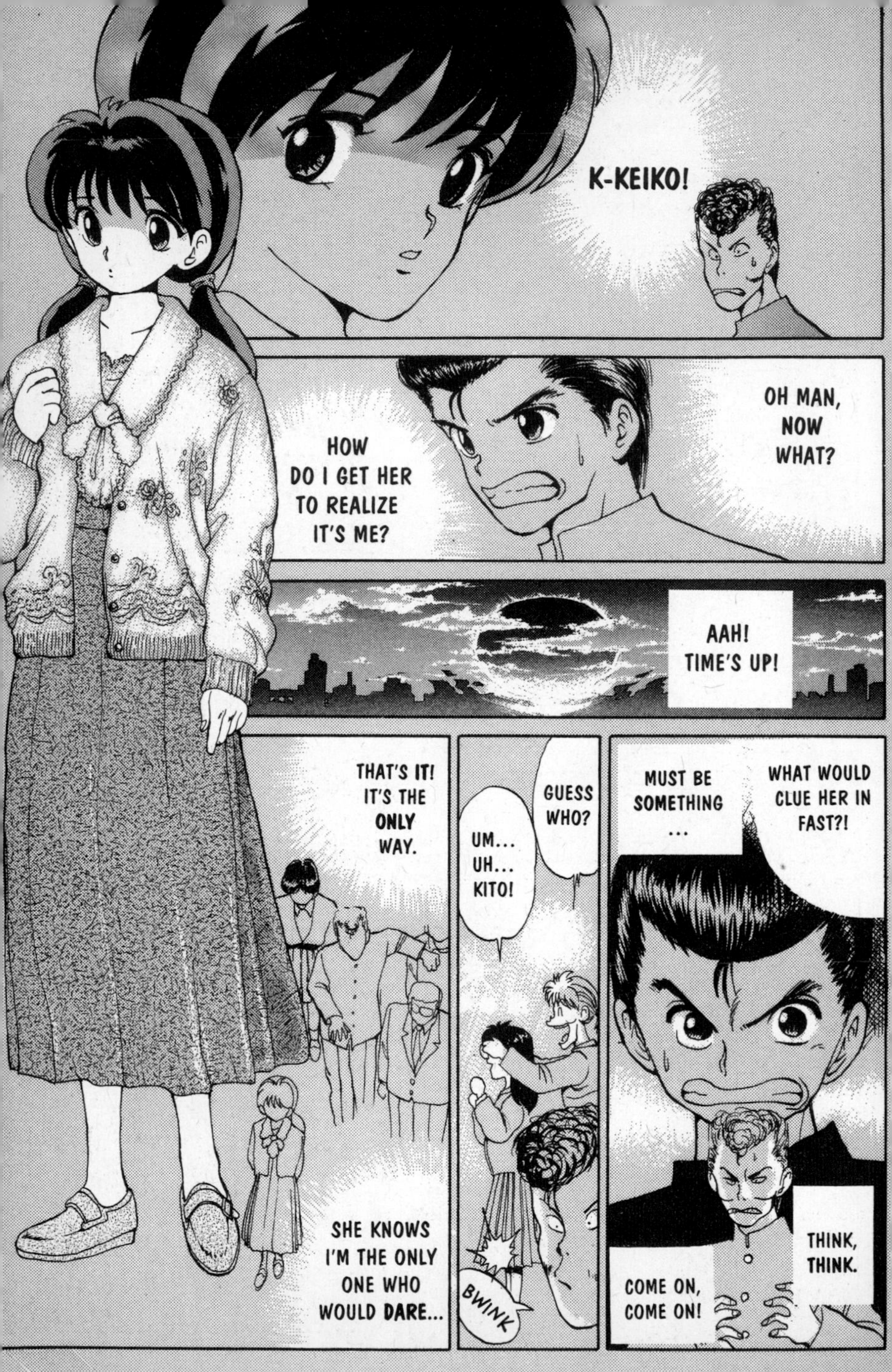
K-KEIKO!
OH MAN, NOW WHAT?
HOW DO I GET HER TO REALIZE IT'S ME?
AAH! TIME'S UP!
WHAT WOULD CLUE HER IN FAST?!
MUST BE SOMETHING ...
THINK, THINK.
COME ON, COME ON!
GUESS WHO?
UM... UH... KITO!
BWINK
THAT'S IT! IT'S THE **ONLY** WAY.
SHE KNOWS I'M THE ONLY ONE WHO WOULD **DARE**...

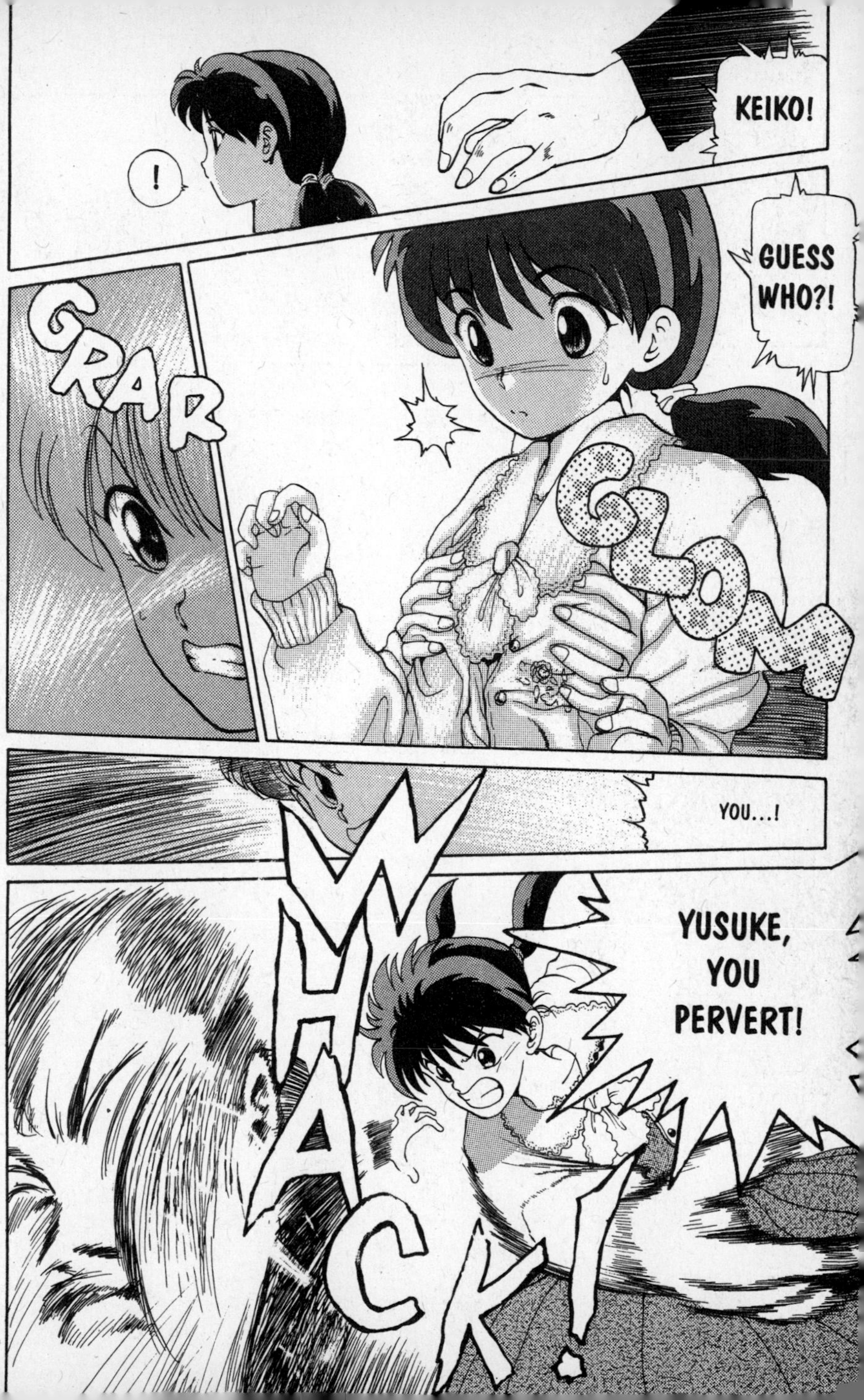
KEIKO!
!
GUESS WHO?!
GLOMP
GRAR
YOU...!
YUSUKE, YOU PERVERT!
WHACK!

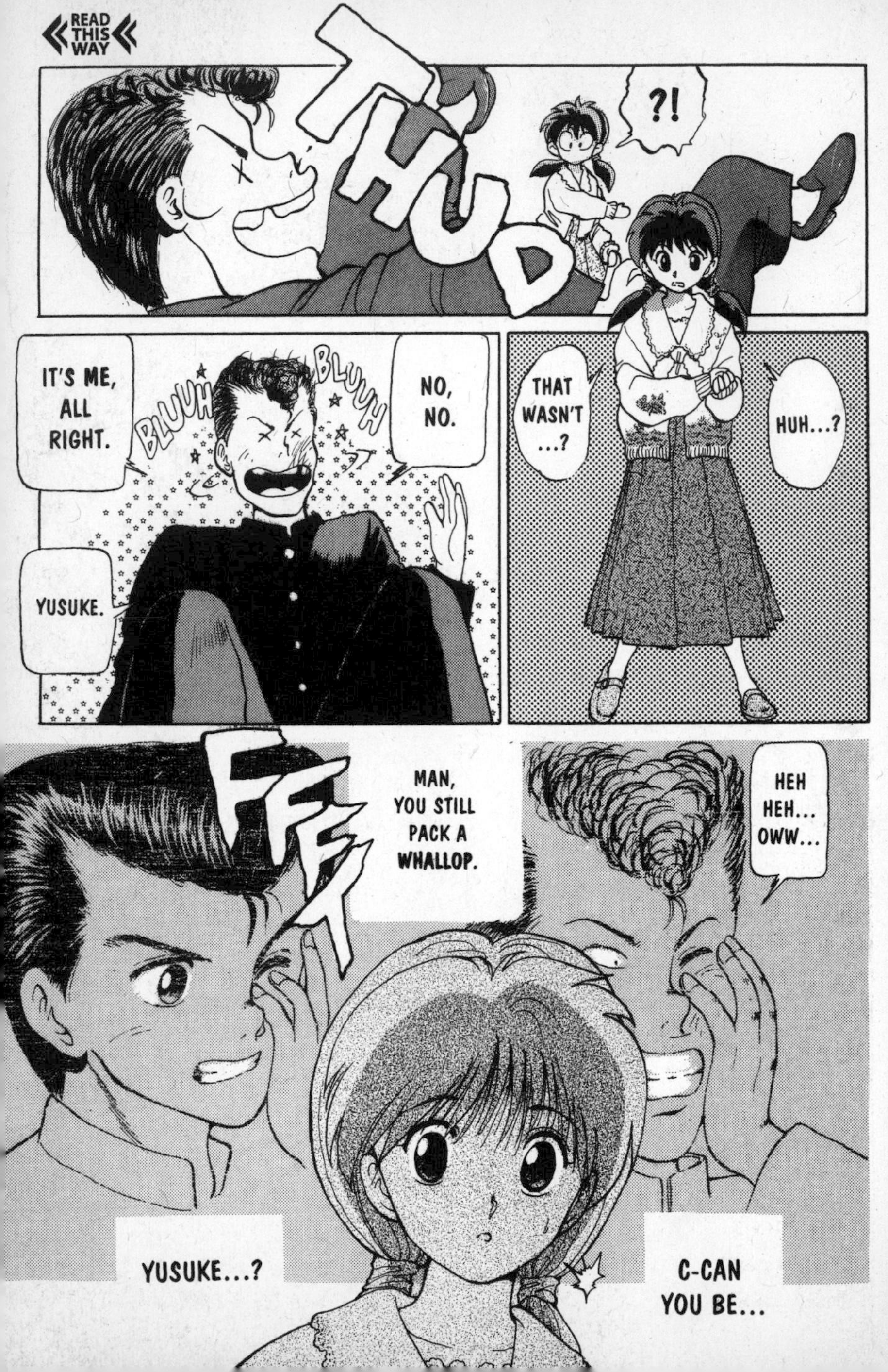
READ THIS WAY
THUD
?!
HUH...?
THAT WASN'T ...?
NO, NO.
BLUUH
BLUUH
IT'S ME, ALL RIGHT.
YUSUKE.
HEH HEH... OWW...
MAN, YOU STILL PACK A WHALLOP.
FF
C-CAN YOU BE...
YUSUKE...?

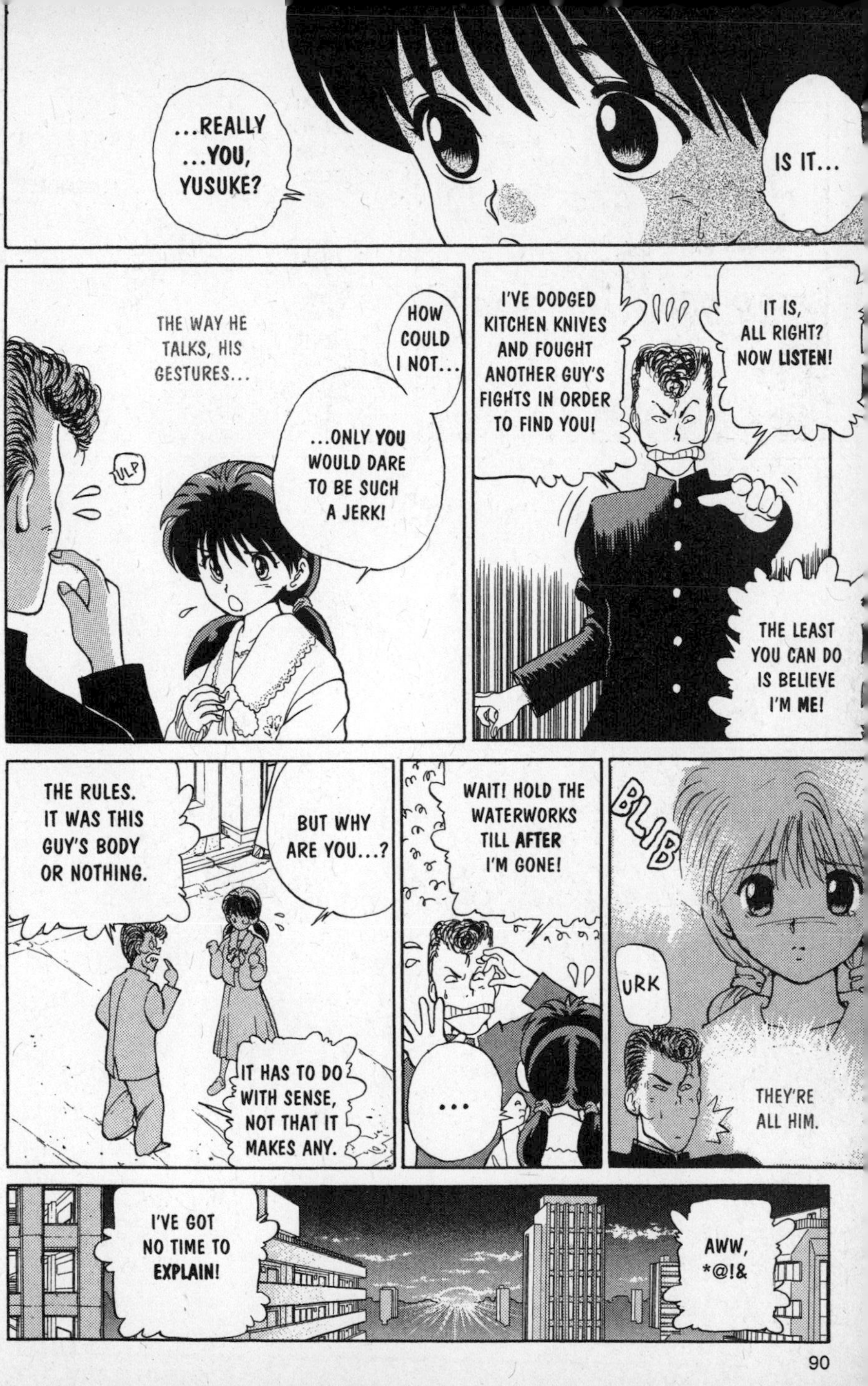
IS IT...
...REALLY ...YOU, YUSUKE?
IT IS, ALL RIGHT? NOW LISTEN!
I'VE DODGED KITCHEN KNIVES AND FOUGHT ANOTHER GUY'S FIGHTS IN ORDER TO FIND YOU!
THE LEAST YOU CAN DO IS BELIEVE I'M ME!
HOW COULD I NOT...
...ONLY YOU WOULD DARE TO BE SUCH A JERK!
THE WAY HE TALKS, HIS GESTURES...
ULP
BLIB
URK
THEY'RE ALL HIM.
WAIT! HOLD THE WATERWORKS TILL AFTER I'M GONE!
...
BUT WHY ARE YOU...?
THE RULES. IT WAS THIS GUY'S BODY OR NOTHING.
IT HAS TO DO WITH SENSE, NOT THAT IT MAKES ANY.
AWW, *@!&
I'VE GOT NO TIME TO EXPLAIN!

READ THIS WAY

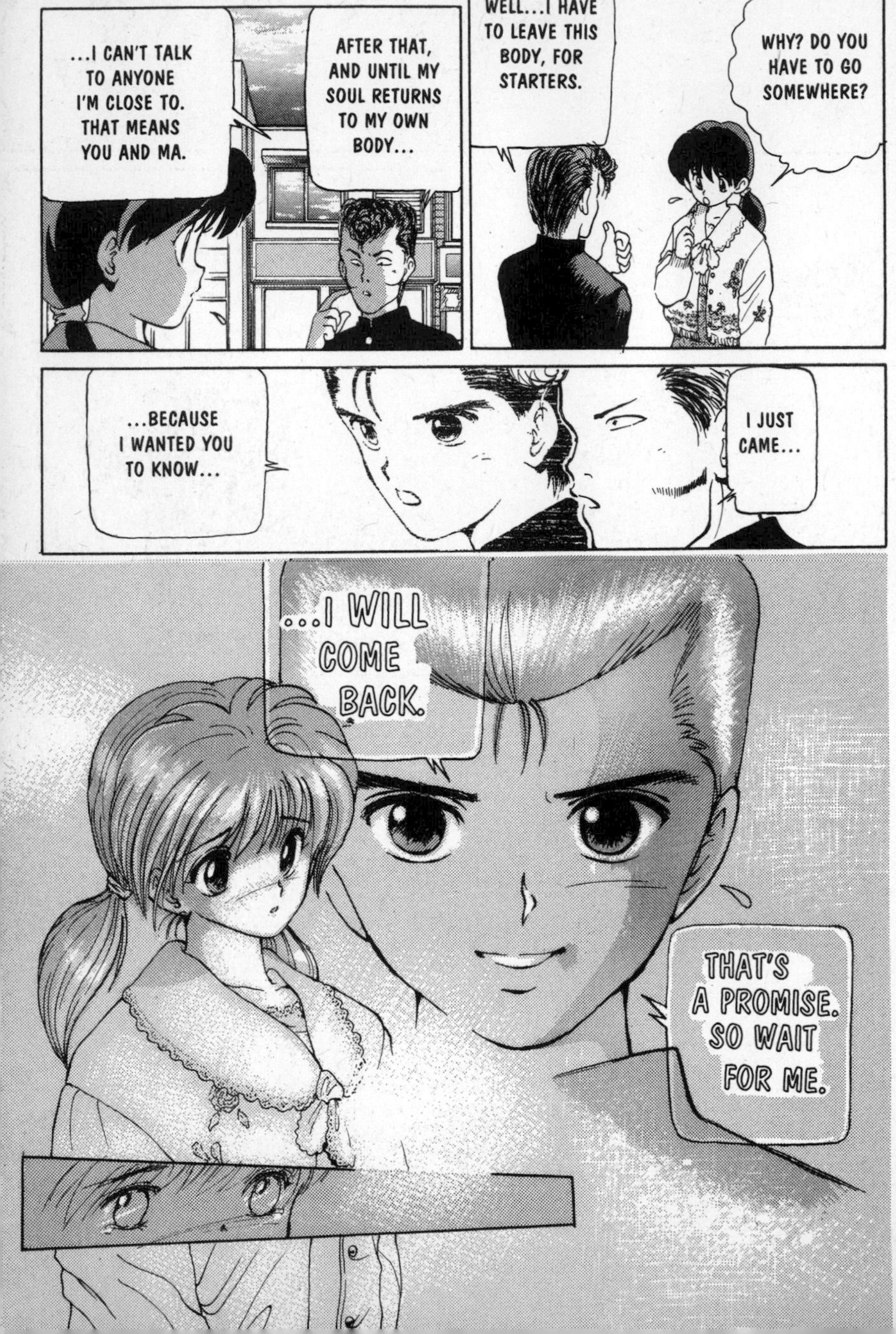

WHY? DO YOU HAVE TO GO SOMEWHERE?
WELL...I HAVE TO LEAVE THIS BODY, FOR STARTERS.
AFTER THAT, AND UNTIL MY SOUL RETURNS TO MY OWN BODY...
...I CAN'T TALK TO ANYONE I'M CLOSE TO. THAT MEANS YOU AND MA.
I JUST CAME...
...BECAUSE I WANTED YOU TO KNOW...
...I WILL COME BACK.
THAT'S A PROMISE. SO WAIT FOR ME.

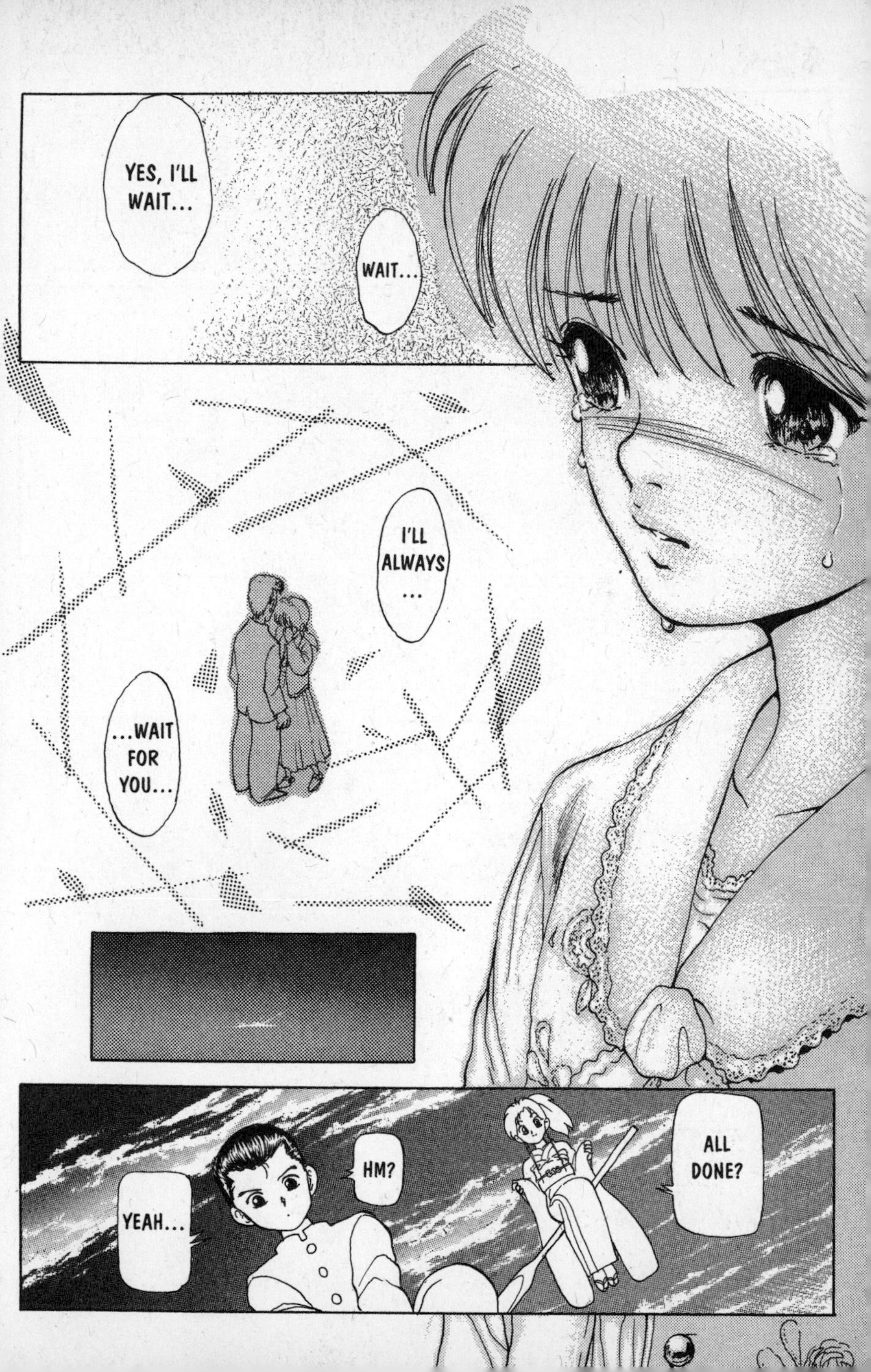
WAIT...
YES, I'LL WAIT...
I'LL ALWAYS ...
...WAIT FOR YOU...
ALL DONE?
HM?
YEAH...

READ THIS WAY

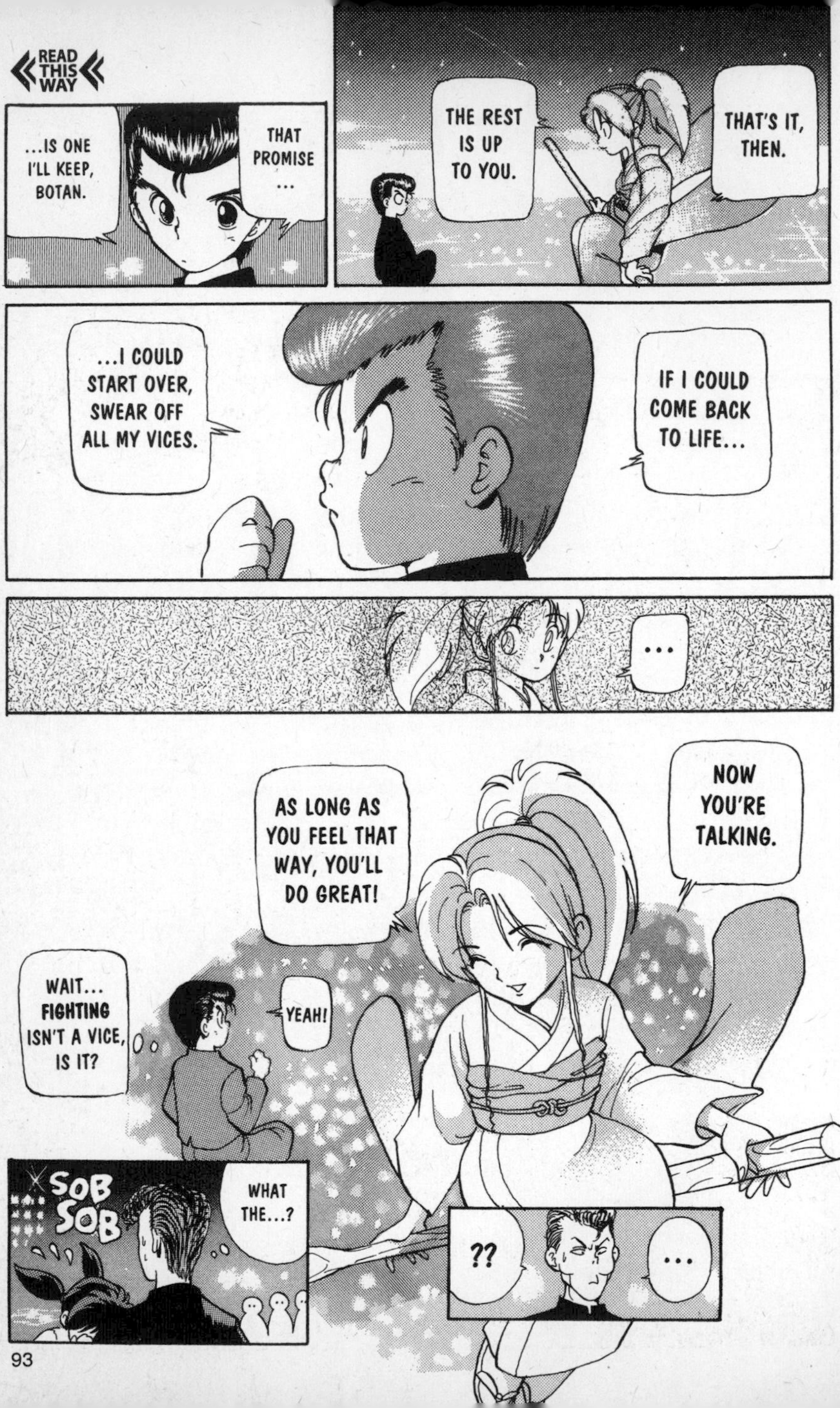

THAT'S IT, THEN.
THE REST IS UP TO YOU.
THAT PROMISE...
...IS ONE I'LL KEEP, BOTAN.
IF I COULD COME BACK TO LIFE...
...I COULD START OVER, SWEAR OFF ALL MY VICES.
...
NOW YOU'RE TALKING.
AS LONG AS YOU FEEL THAT WAY, YOU'LL DO GREAT!
YEAH!
WAIT... FIGHTING ISN'T A VICE, IS IT?
...
??
WHAT THE...?
SOB SOB

Seisaku Hakusho ("The Production Report")

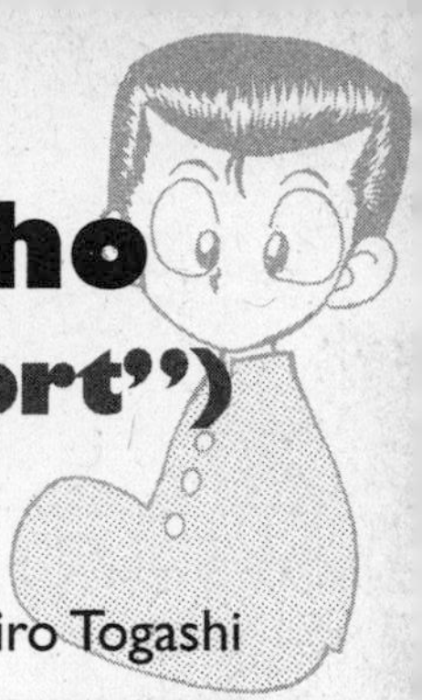

Part I

By Yoshihiro Togashi

I started **YuYu Hakusho** around November 1990. (I've already forgotten exactly when.) I'd completed my previous manga series around February 1990. (Again, I don't remember exactly.) So, you might ask, what was I doing in the nine months between the two manga? There's probably no one who wants to know, but I'll write about it anyway. (The reason is, the deadline for the next volume is coming up fast, and I'm in a state of exhaustion, so the only thing that comes to mind are these memories.)

In a previous graphic novel [which hasn't been translated to English], I faintly recall talking about the period immediately following completion of **Tende Shôwaru Cupid** [Togashi's 1989 romantic comedy manga], so let's talk about the period that followed that. Well, once again…what in the world was I doing at that time!? Actually, I wasn't doing anything. Sorry. I was having a good time. Blowing off steam.

So now, let's do a quick fast forward to the period just before the beginning of **YuYu Hakusho**. It was the summer of 1990… Actually, before beginning work on **YuYu Hakusho**, I worked on another series. (Even before that, I did a few one-shot stories that never made the cut.) In the next installment, I'll talk about one of these "yet to be seen" stories.

To be continued on page 116!

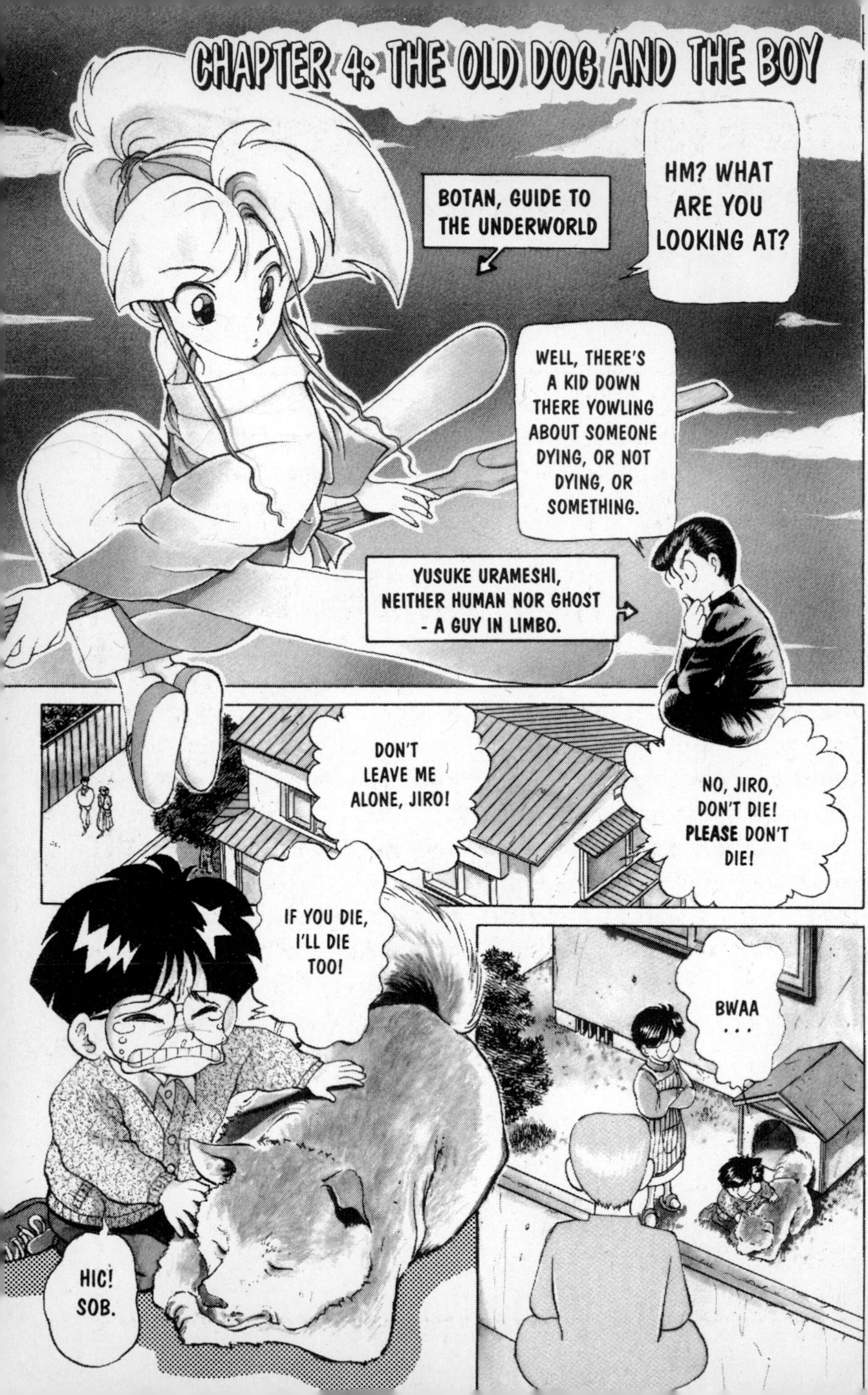
CHAPTER 4: THE OLD DOG AND THE BOY
HM? WHAT ARE YOU LOOKING AT?
BOTAN, GUIDE TO THE UNDERWORLD
WELL, THERE'S A KID DOWN THERE YOWLING ABOUT SOMEONE DYING, OR NOT DYING, OR SOMETHING.
YUSUKE URAMESHI, NEITHER HUMAN NOR GHOST - A GUY IN LIMBO.
NO, JIRO, DON'T DIE! PLEASE DON'T DIE!
DON'T LEAVE ME ALONE, JIRO!
BWAA . . .
IF YOU DIE, I'LL DIE TOO!
HIC! SOB.

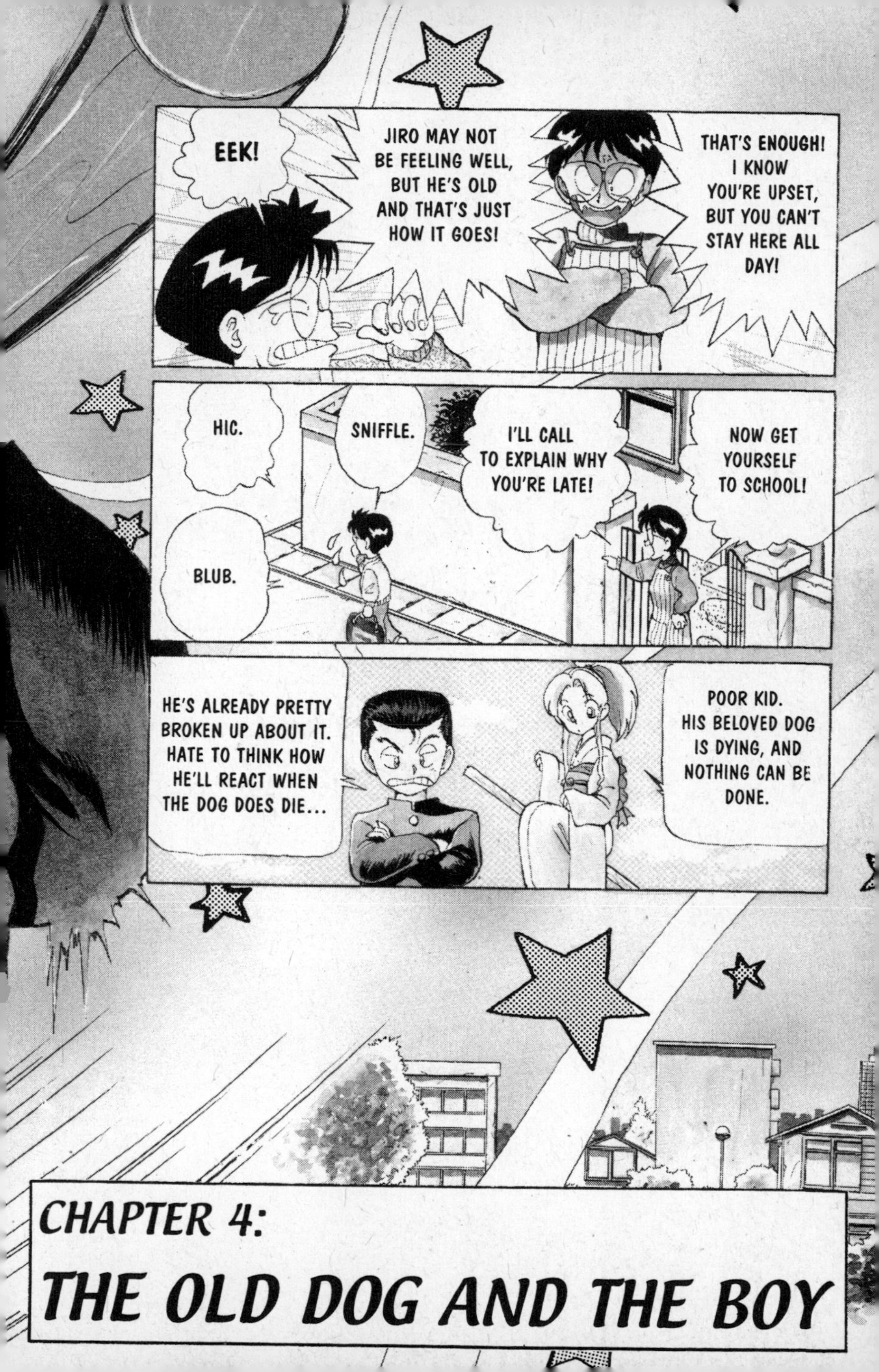
THAT'S ENOUGH! I KNOW YOU'RE UPSET, BUT YOU CAN'T STAY HERE ALL DAY!
JIRO MAY NOT BE FEELING WELL, BUT HE'S OLD AND THAT'S JUST HOW IT GOES!
EEK!
NOW GET YOURSELF TO SCHOOL!
I'LL CALL TO EXPLAIN WHY YOU'RE LATE!
SNIFFLE.
HIC.
BLUB.
POOR KID. HIS BELOVED DOG IS DYING, AND NOTHING CAN BE DONE.
HE'S ALREADY PRETTY BROKEN UP ABOUT IT. HATE TO THINK HOW HE'LL REACT WHEN THE DOG DOES DIE...
CHAPTER 4:
THE OLD DOG AND THE BOY

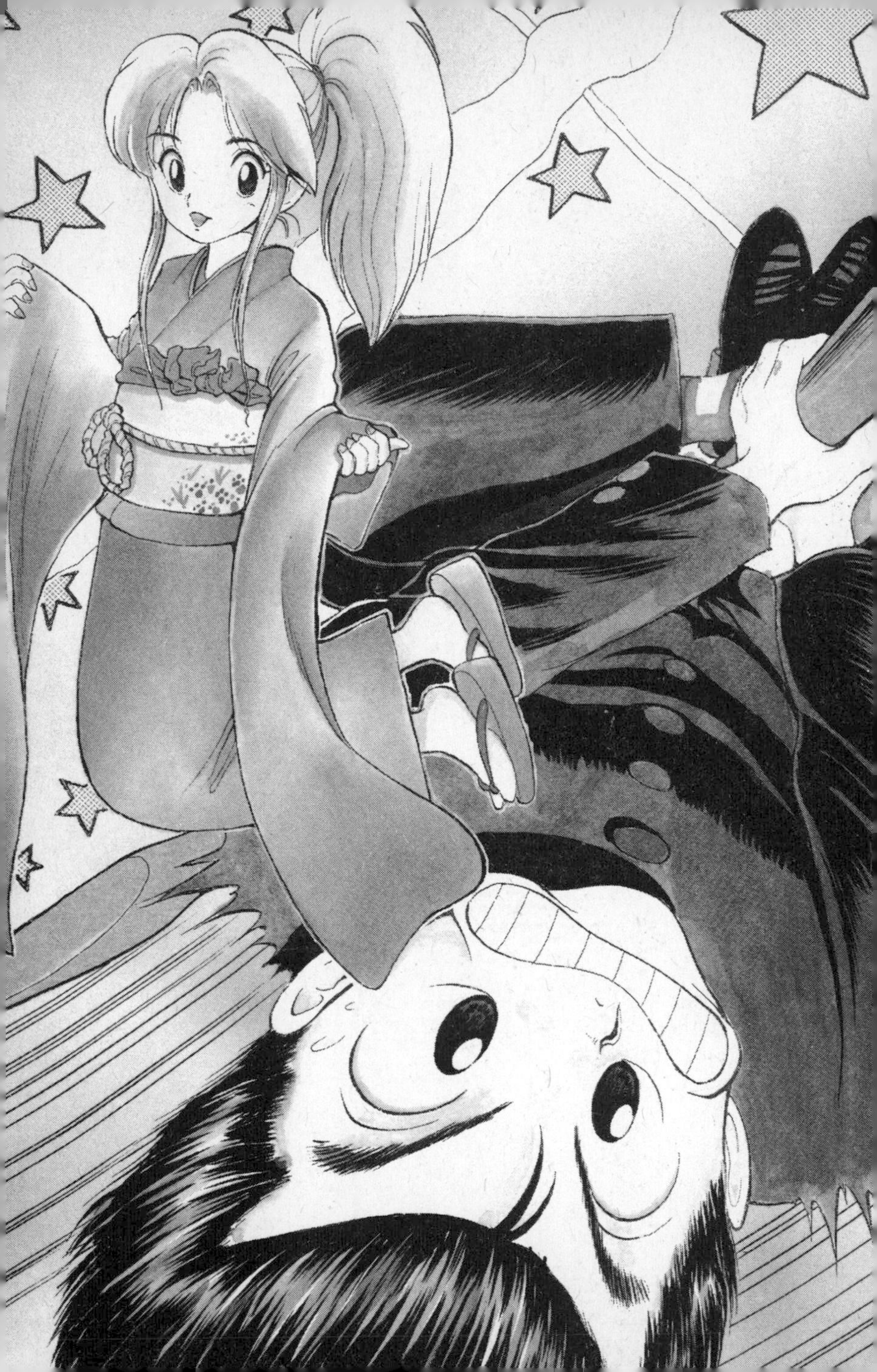

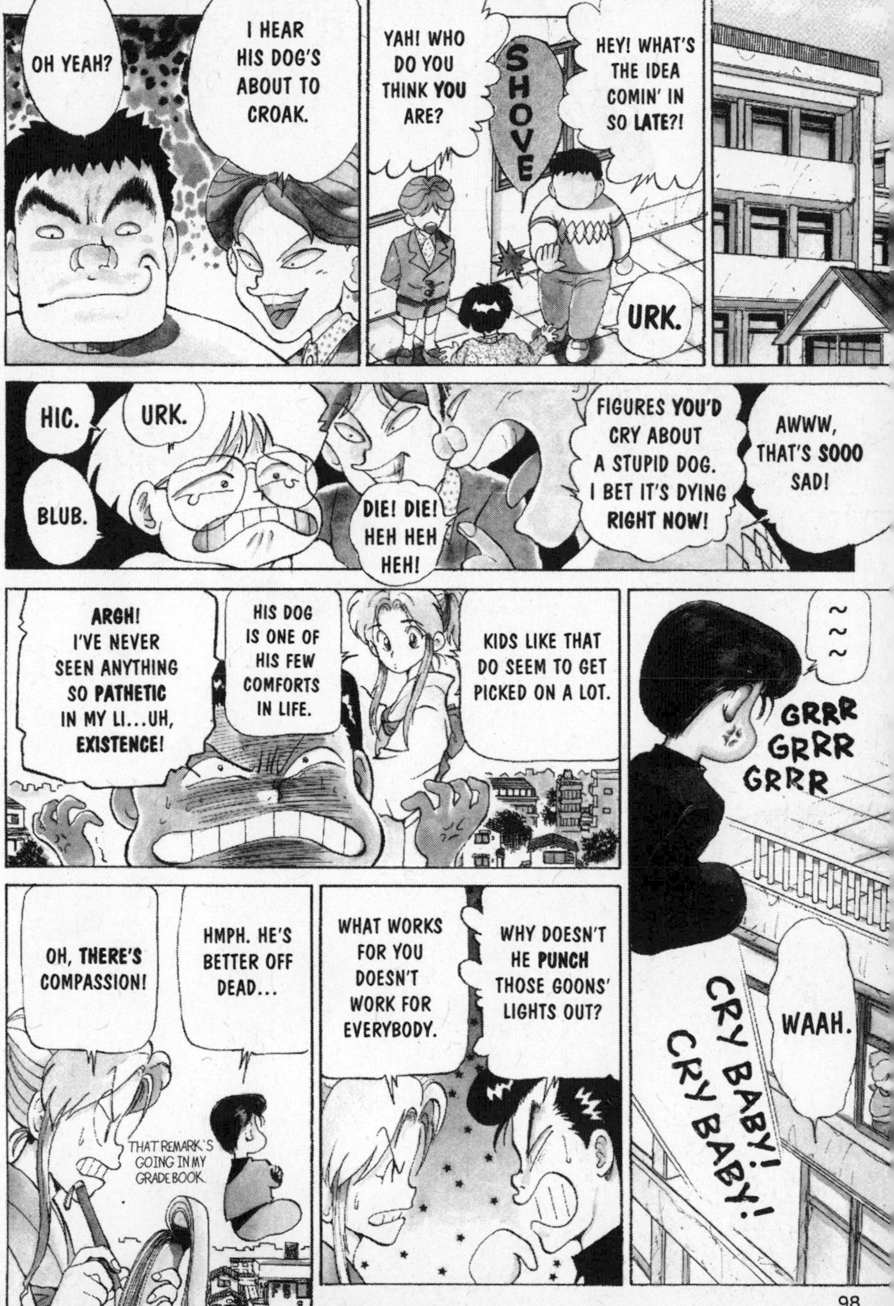
HEY! WHAT'S THE IDEA COMIN' IN SO LATE?!
SHOVE
YAH! WHO DO YOU THINK YOU ARE?
URK.
I HEAR HIS DOG'S ABOUT TO CROAK.
OH YEAH?
AWWW, THAT'S SOOO SAD!
FIGURES YOU'D CRY ABOUT A STUPID DOG. I BET IT'S DYING RIGHT NOW!
DIE! DIE! HEH HEH HEH!
URK.
HIC.
BLUB.
~ ~ ~
GRRR GRRR GRRR
WAAH.
CRY BABY! CRY BABY!
KIDS LIKE THAT DO SEEM TO GET PICKED ON A LOT.
HIS DOG IS ONE OF HIS FEW COMFORTS IN LIFE.
ARGH! I'VE NEVER SEEN ANYTHING SO PATHETIC IN MY LI...UH, EXISTENCE!
WHY DOESN'T HE PUNCH THOSE GOONS' LIGHTS OUT?
WHAT WORKS FOR YOU DOESN'T WORK FOR EVERYBODY.
HMPH. HE'S BETTER OFF DEAD...
OH, THERE'S COMPASSION!
THAT REMARK'S GOING IN MY GRADE BOOK.

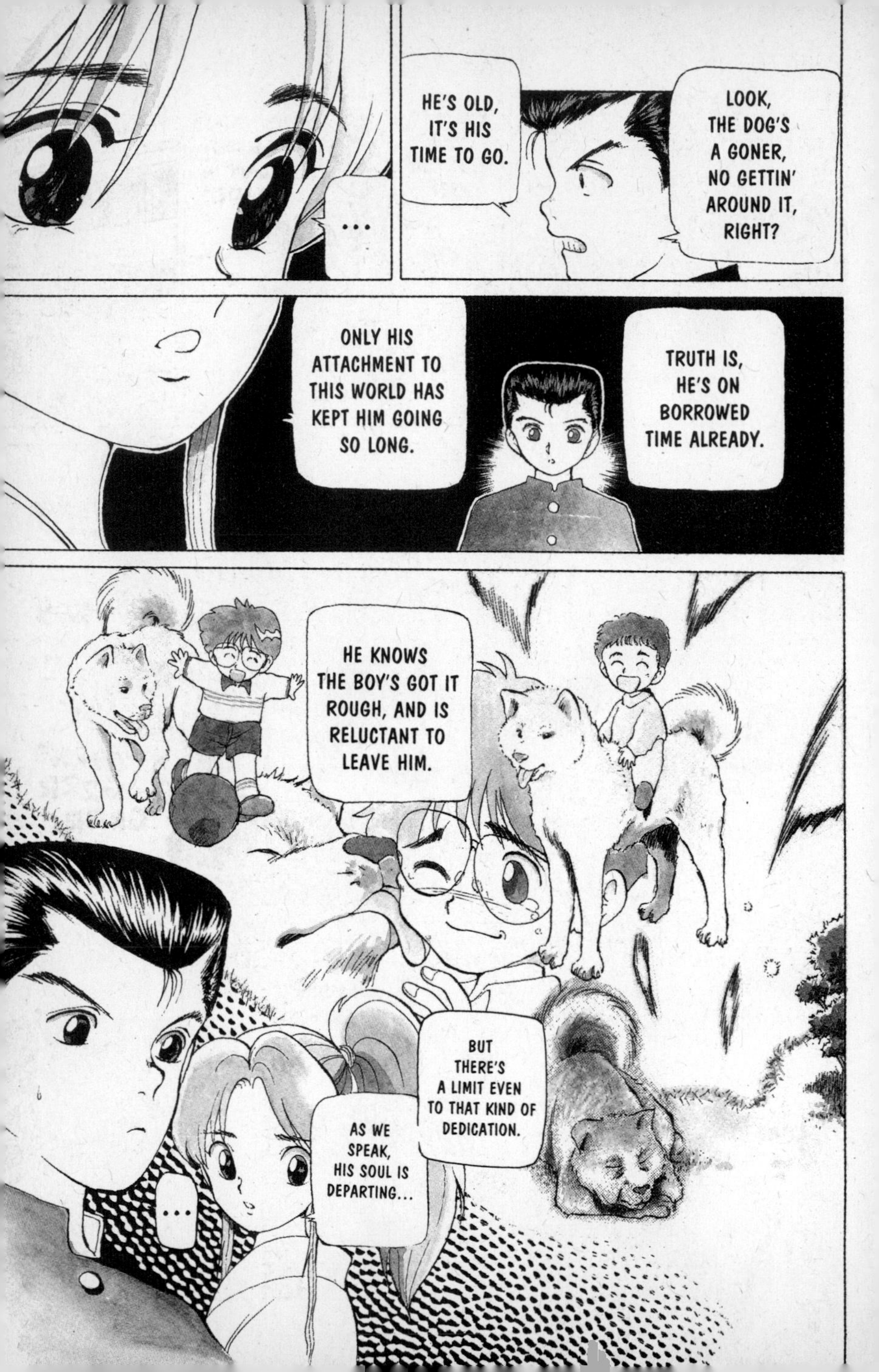
LOOK, THE DOG'S A GONER, NO GETTIN' AROUND IT, RIGHT?
HE'S OLD, IT'S HIS TIME TO GO.
...
TRUTH IS, HE'S ON BORROWED TIME ALREADY.
ONLY HIS ATTACHMENT TO THIS WORLD HAS KEPT HIM GOING SO LONG.
HE KNOWS THE BOY'S GOT IT ROUGH, AND IS RELUCTANT TO LEAVE HIM.
BUT THERE'S A LIMIT EVEN TO THAT KIND OF DEDICATION.
AS WE SPEAK, HIS SOUL IS DEPARTING...
...

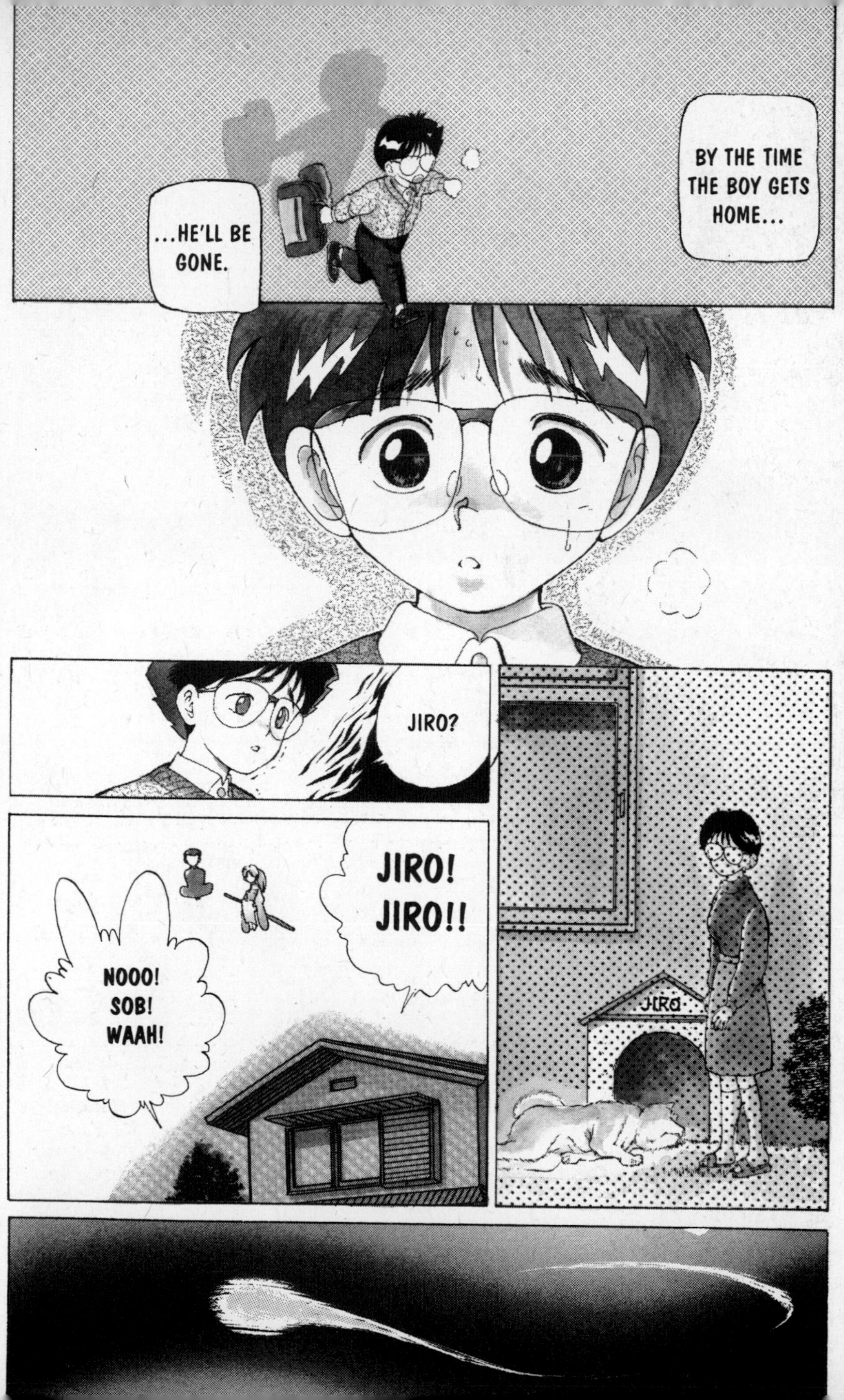
BY THE TIME THE BOY GETS HOME...
...HE'LL BE GONE.
JIRO
JIRO?
JIRO! JIRO!!
NOOO! SOB! WAAH!

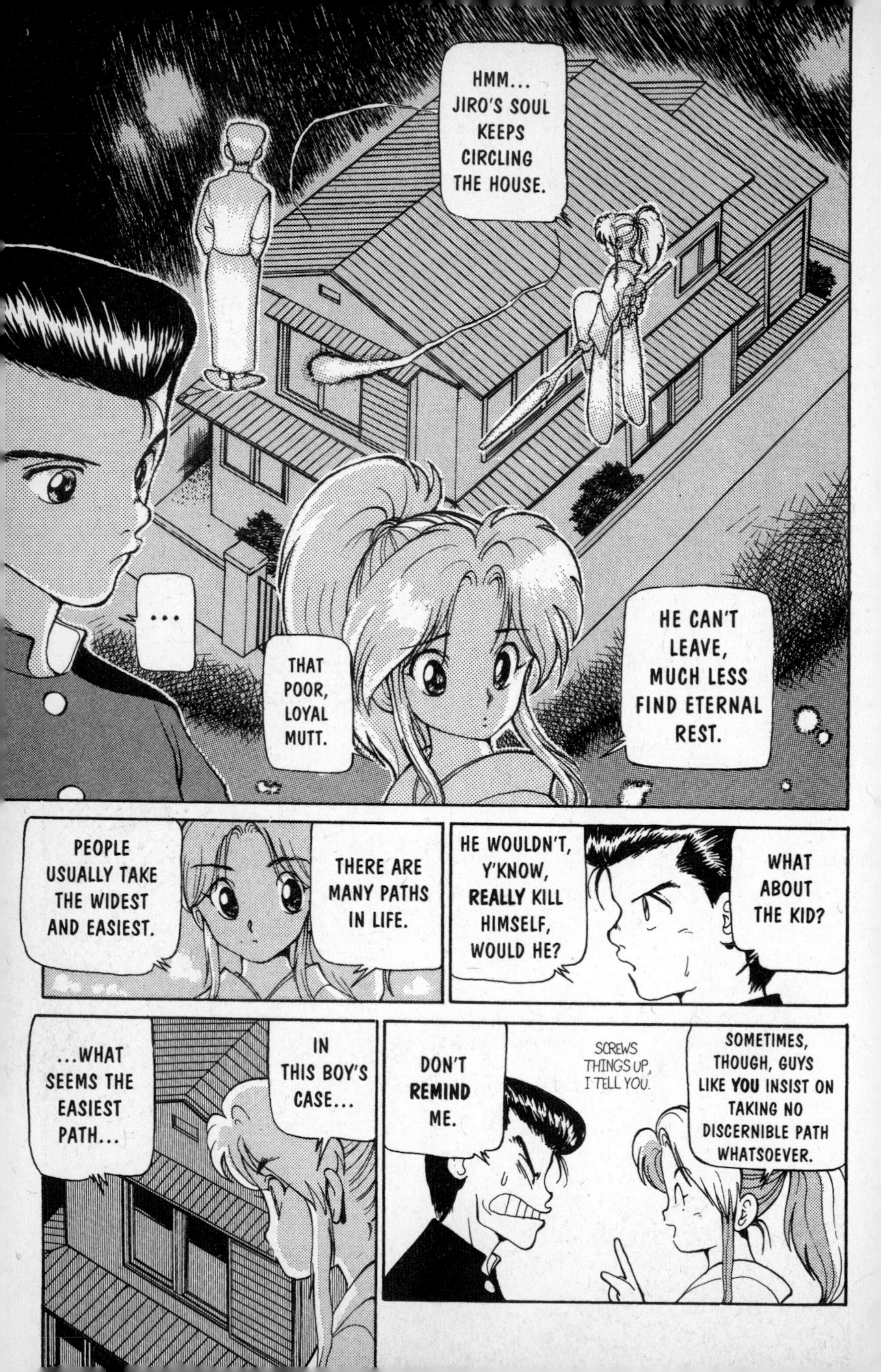
HMM... JIRO'S SOUL KEEPS CIRCLING THE HOUSE.
HE CAN'T LEAVE, MUCH LESS FIND ETERNAL REST.
THAT POOR, LOYAL MUTT.
...
WHAT ABOUT THE KID?
HE WOULDN'T, Y'KNOW, **REALLY** KILL HIMSELF, WOULD HE?
THERE ARE MANY PATHS IN LIFE.
PEOPLE USUALLY TAKE THE WIDEST AND EASIEST.
SOMETIMES, THOUGH, GUYS LIKE **YOU** INSIST ON TAKING NO DISCERNIBLE PATH WHATSOEVER.
SCREWS THINGS UP, I TELL YOU.
DON'T **REMIND** ME.
IN THIS BOY'S CASE...
...WHAT SEEMS THE EASIEST PATH...

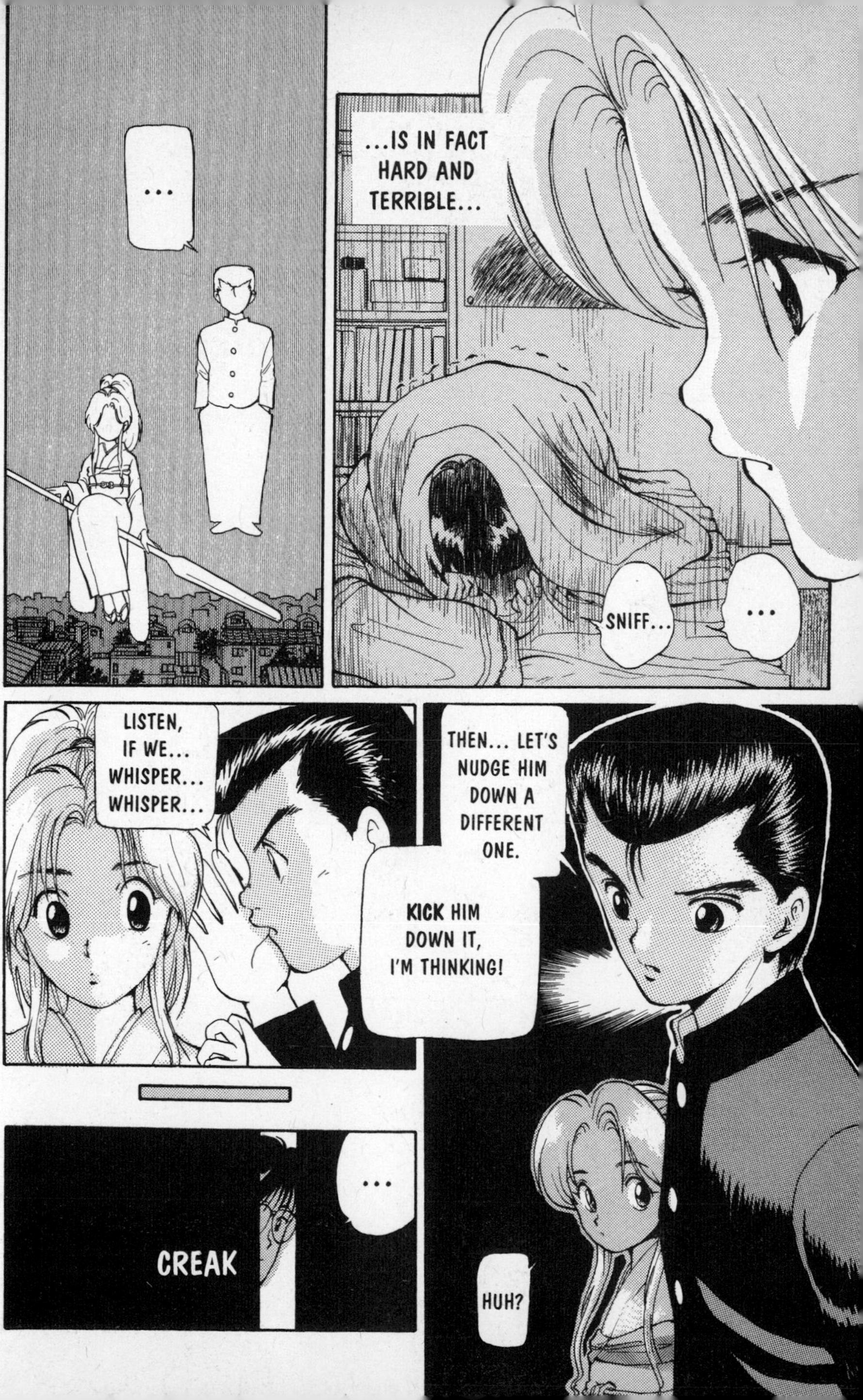
...IS IN FACT HARD AND TERRIBLE...
...
SNIFF...
...
THEN... LET'S NUDGE HIM DOWN A DIFFERENT ONE.
HUH?
LISTEN, IF WE... WHISPER... WHISPER...
KICK HIM DOWN IT, I'M THINKING!
...
CREAK

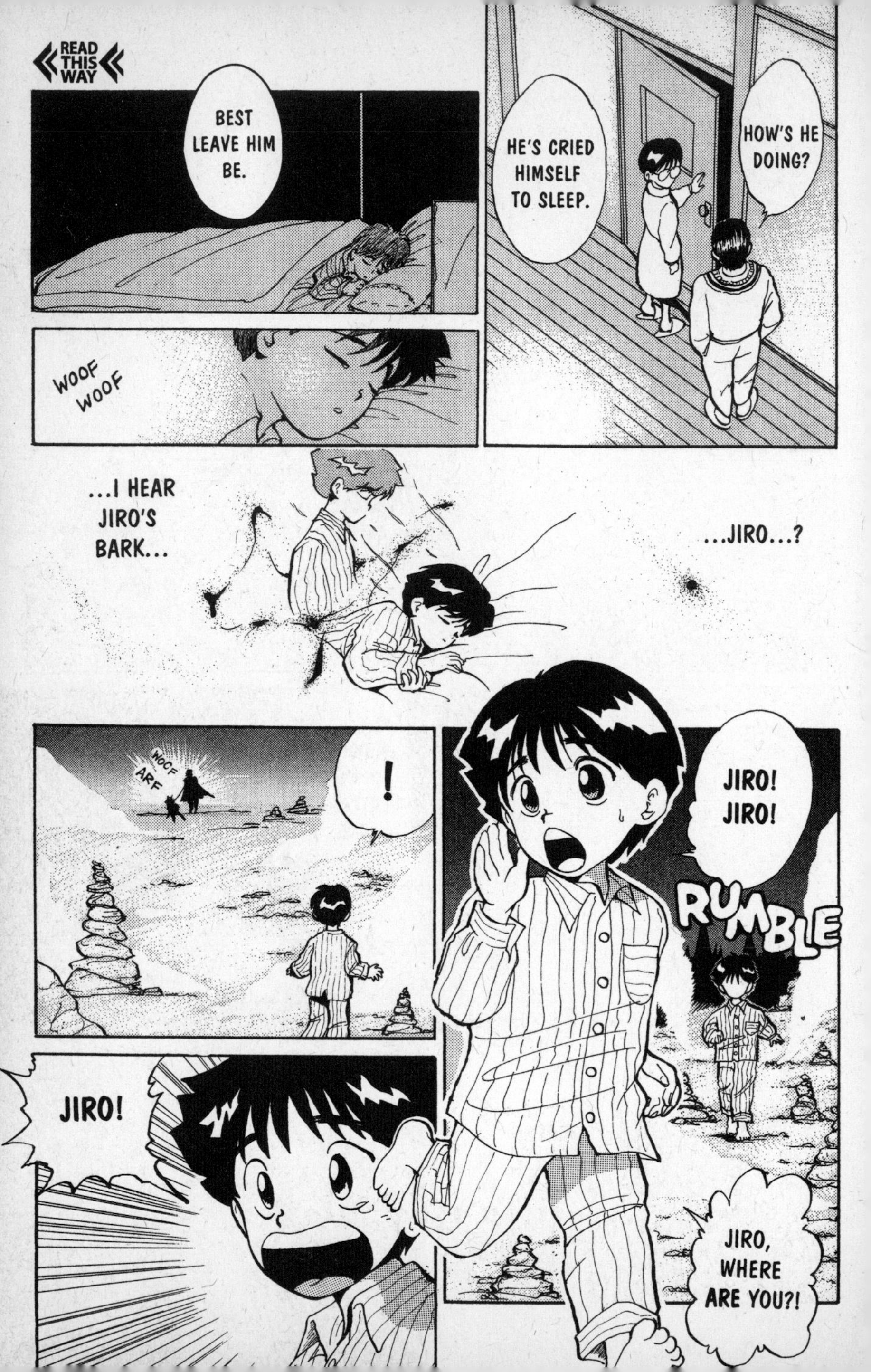
READ THIS WAY
HOW'S HE DOING?
HE'S CRIED HIMSELF TO SLEEP.
BEST LEAVE HIM BE.
WOOF WOOF
...I HEAR JIRO'S BARK...
...JIRO...?
JIRO! JIRO!
RUMBLE
JIRO, WHERE ARE YOU?!
WOOF
ARF
!
JIRO!

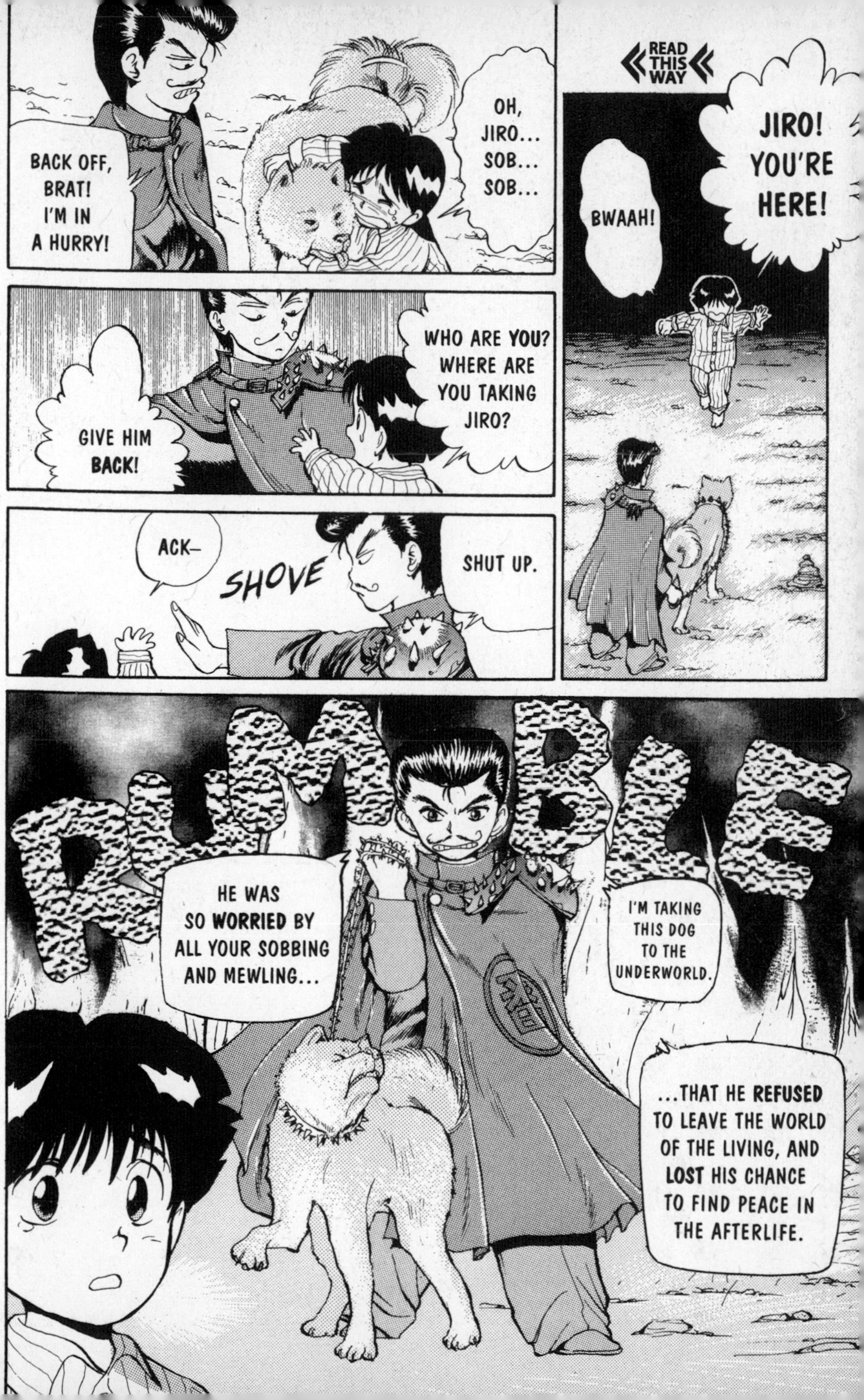
READ THIS WAY
JIRO! YOU'RE HERE!
BWAAH!
OH, JIRO... SOB... SOB...
BACK OFF, BRAT! I'M IN A HURRY!
WHO ARE YOU? WHERE ARE YOU TAKING JIRO?
GIVE HIM BACK!
SHUT UP.
SHOVE
ACK—
RUMBLE
I'M TAKING THIS DOG TO THE UNDERWORLD.
HE WAS SO WORRIED BY ALL YOUR SOBBING AND MEWLING...
...THAT HE REFUSED TO LEAVE THE WORLD OF THE LIVING, AND LOST HIS CHANCE TO FIND PEACE IN THE AFTERLIFE.

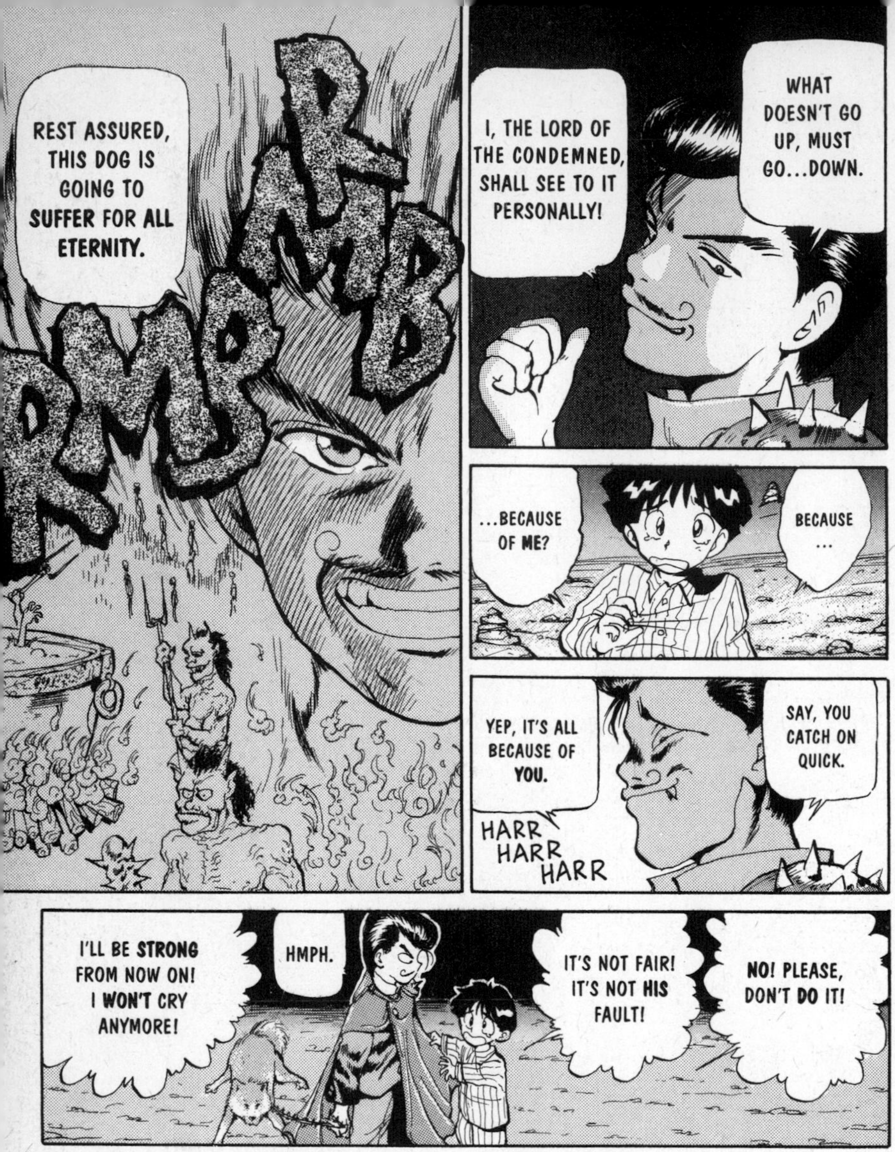
WHAT DOESN'T GO UP, MUST GO...DOWN.
I, THE LORD OF THE CONDEMNED, SHALL SEE TO IT PERSONALLY!
BECAUSE ...
...BECAUSE OF ME?
SAY, YOU CATCH ON QUICK.
YEP, IT'S ALL BECAUSE OF YOU.
HARR HARR HARR
REST ASSURED, THIS DOG IS GOING TO SUFFER FOR ALL ETERNITY.
NO! PLEASE, DON'T DO IT!
IT'S NOT FAIR! IT'S NOT HIS FAULT!
HMPH.
I'LL BE STRONG FROM NOW ON! I WON'T CRY ANYMORE!
YEAH RIGHT!
SHOVE
ACK!

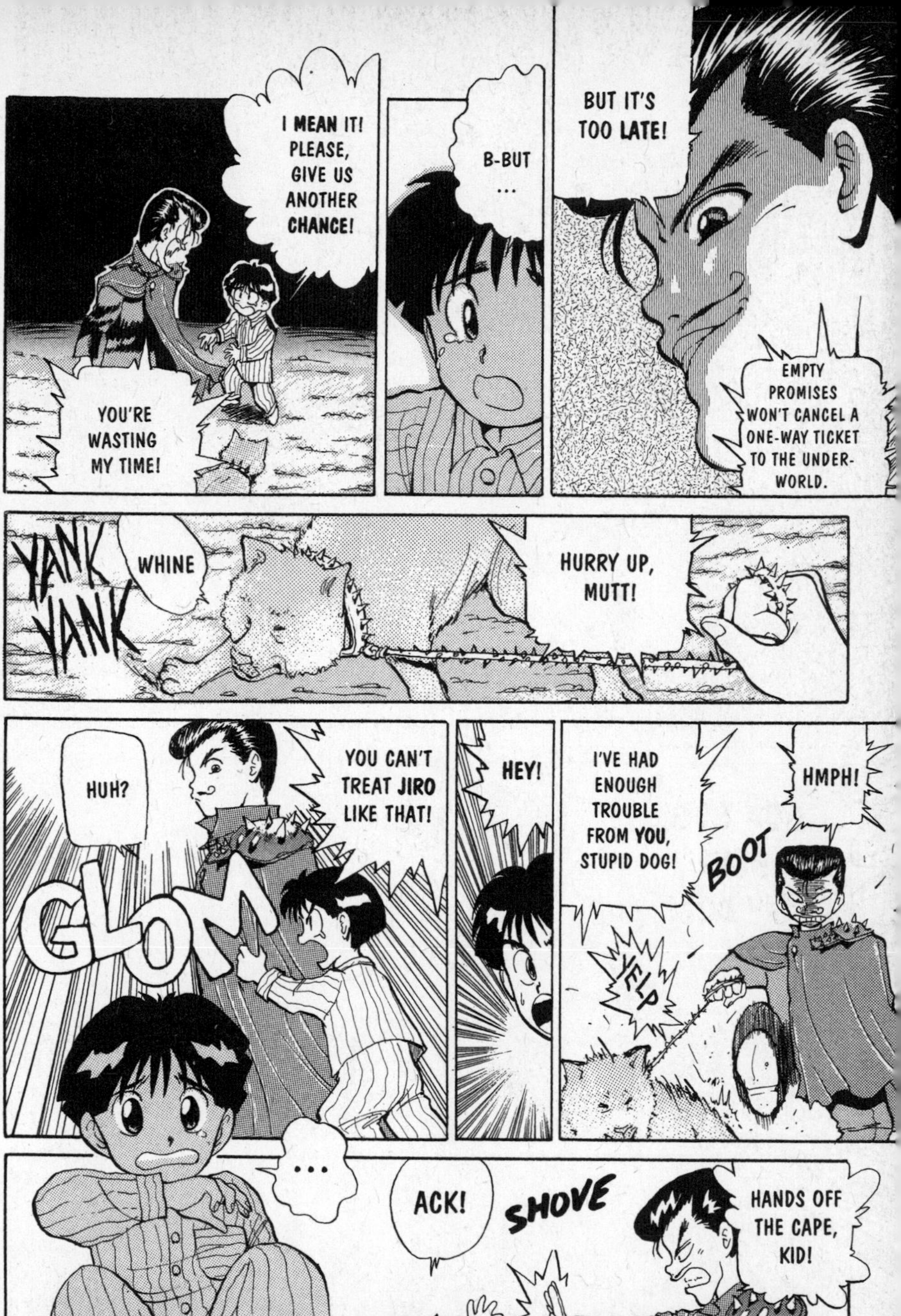
BUT IT'S TOO LATE!
EMPTY PROMISES WON'T CANCEL A ONE-WAY TICKET TO THE UNDER-WORLD.
B-BUT ...
I MEAN IT! PLEASE, GIVE US ANOTHER CHANCE!
YOU'RE WASTING MY TIME!
HURRY UP, MUTT!
WHINE
YANK YANK
HMPH!
I'VE HAD ENOUGH TROUBLE FROM YOU, STUPID DOG!
BOOT
YELP
HEY!
YOU CAN'T TREAT JIRO LIKE THAT!
HUH?
GLOM
HANDS OFF THE CAPE, KID!
SHOVE
ACK!
...

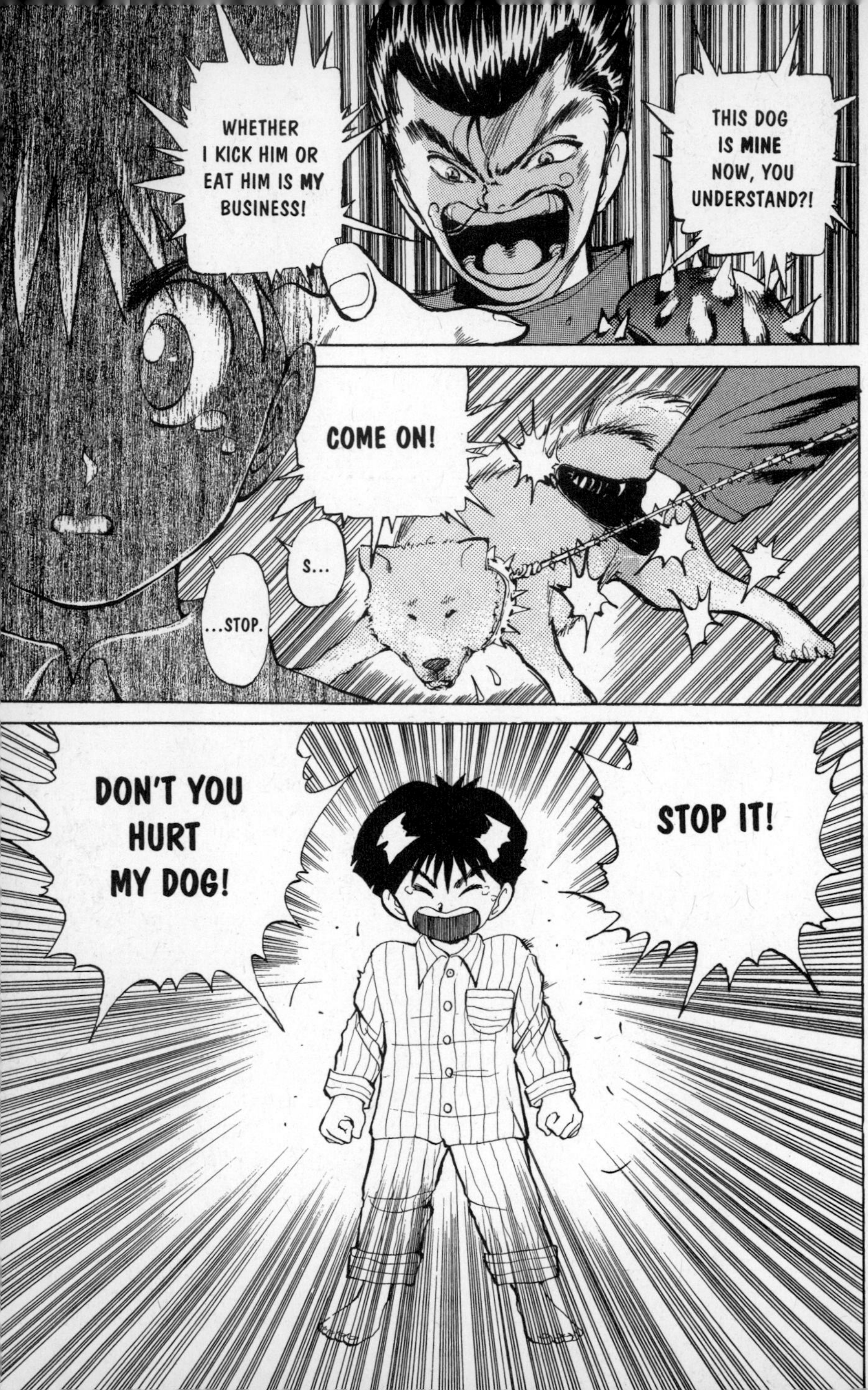
THIS DOG IS MINE NOW, YOU UNDERSTAND?!
WHETHER I KICK HIM OR EAT HIM IS MY BUSINESS!
COME ON!
S...
...STOP.
STOP IT!
DON'T YOU HURT MY DOG!

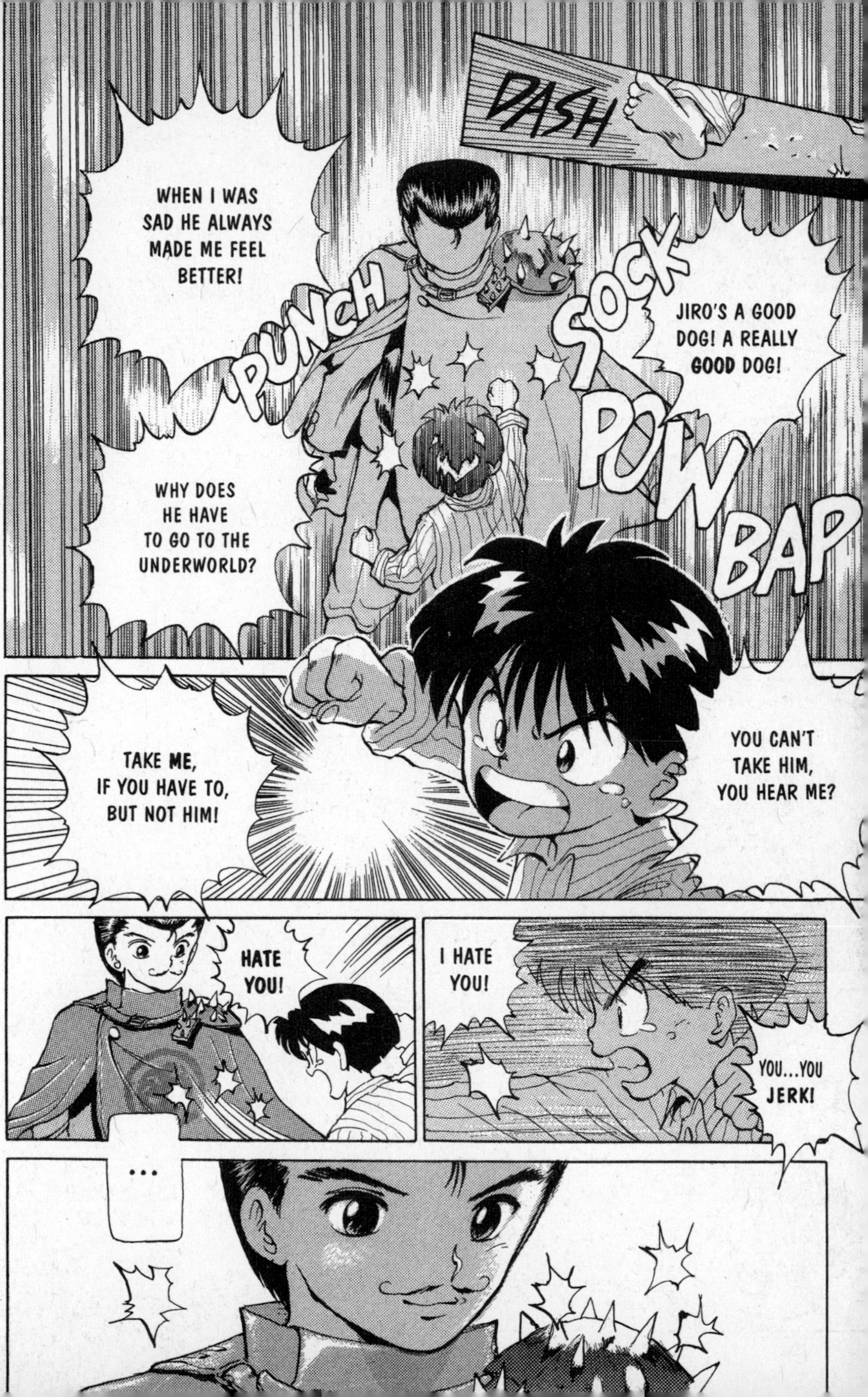
DASH
JIRO'S A GOOD DOG! A REALLY GOOD DOG!
WHEN I WAS SAD HE ALWAYS MADE ME FEEL BETTER!
SOCK
PUNCH
POW
BAP
WHY DOES HE HAVE TO GO TO THE UNDERWORLD?
YOU CAN'T TAKE HIM, YOU HEAR ME?
TAKE ME, IF YOU HAVE TO, BUT NOT HIM!
YOU...YOU JERK!
I HATE YOU!
HATE YOU!
...

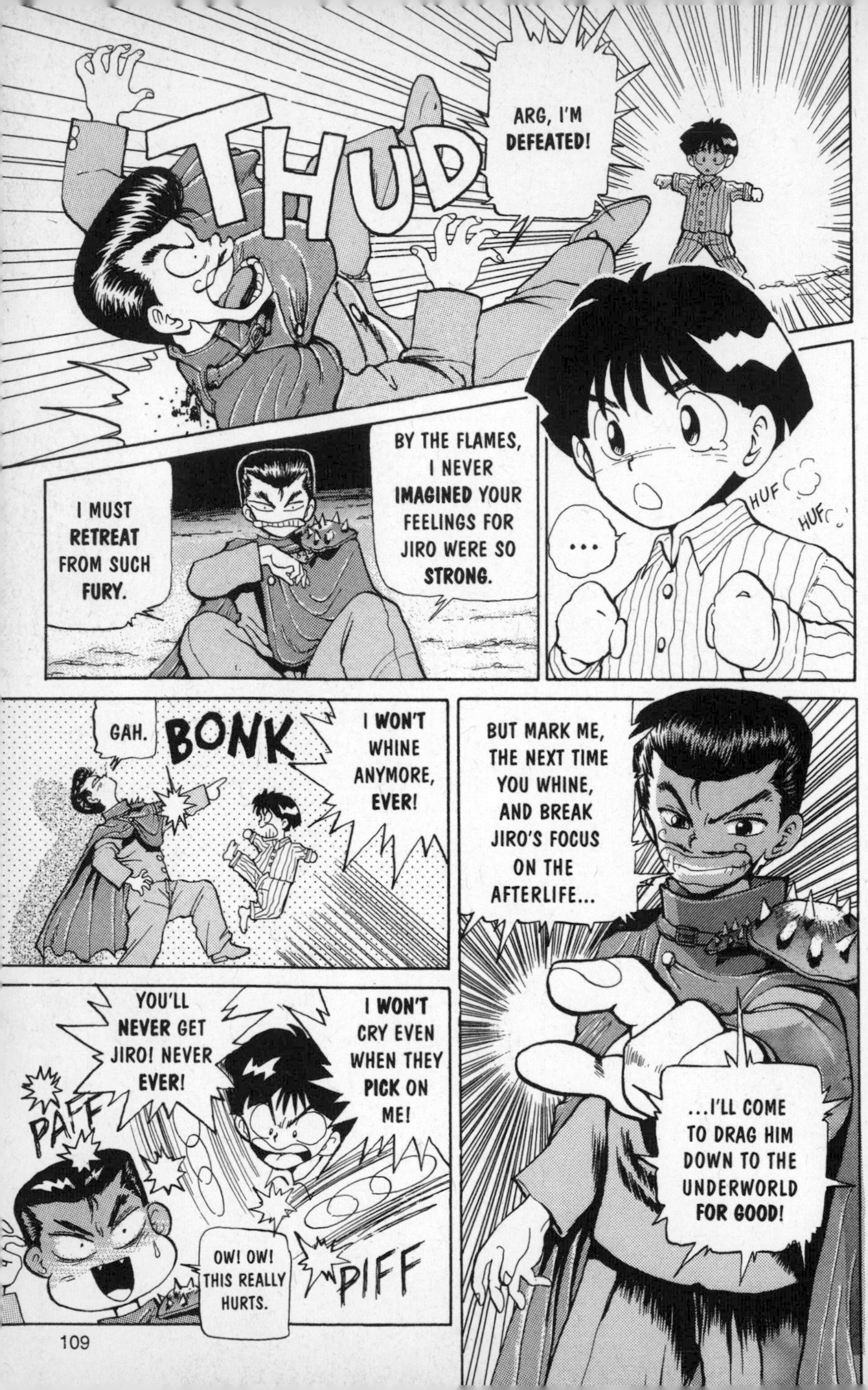

ARG, I'M DEFEATED!
THUD
...
HUF HUF
BY THE FLAMES, I NEVER IMAGINED YOUR FEELINGS FOR JIRO WERE SO STRONG.
I MUST RETREAT FROM SUCH FURY.
BUT MARK ME, THE NEXT TIME YOU WHINE, AND BREAK JIRO'S FOCUS ON THE AFTERLIFE...
...I'LL COME TO DRAG HIM DOWN TO THE UNDERWORLD FOR GOOD!
I WON'T WHINE ANYMORE, EVER!
BONK
GAH.
I WON'T CRY EVEN WHEN THEY PICK ON ME!
YOU'LL NEVER GET JIRO! NEVER EVER!
PAFF
OW! OW! THIS REALLY HURTS.
PIFF

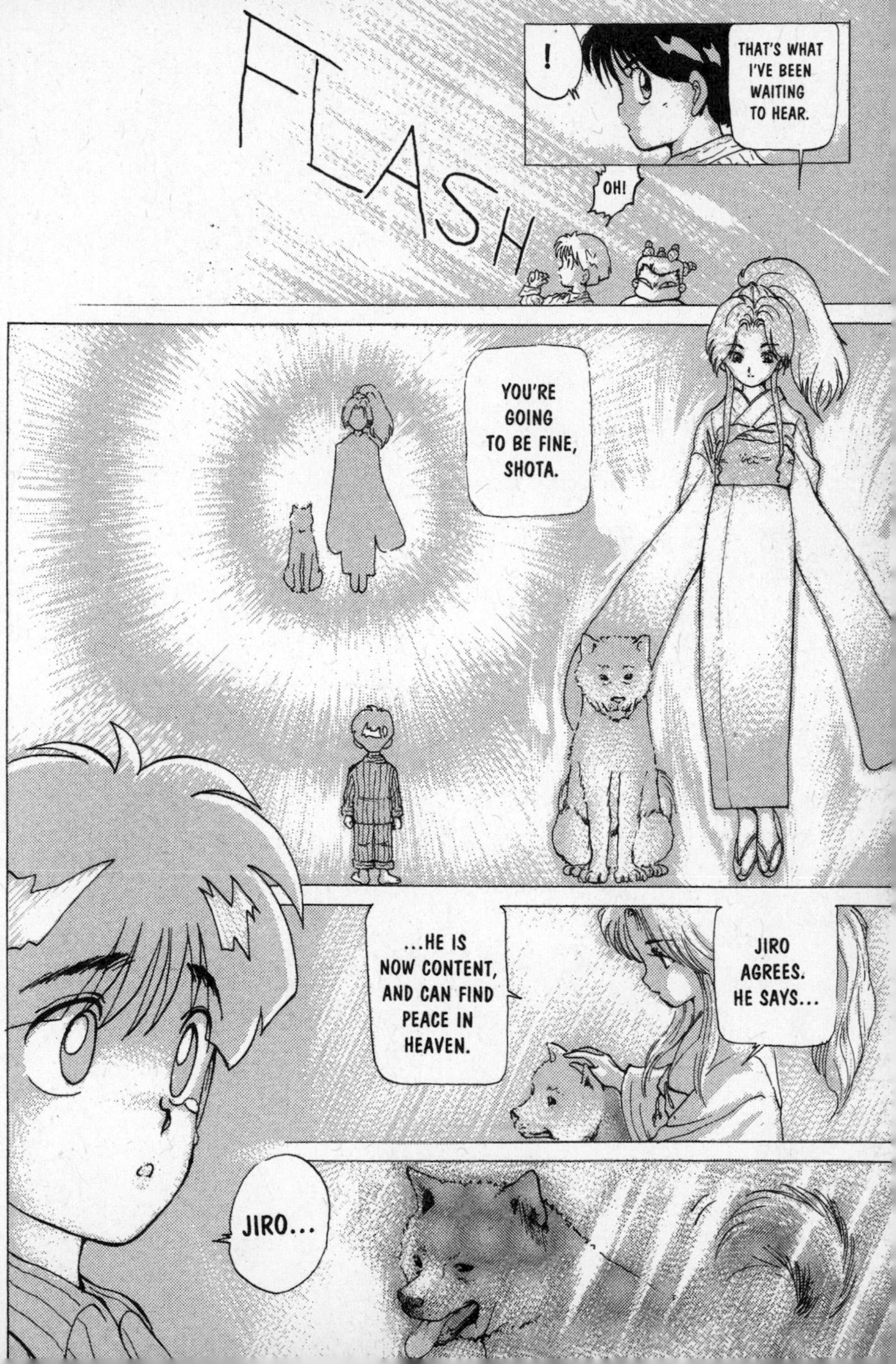
THAT'S WHAT I'VE BEEN WAITING TO HEAR.
!
FLASH
OH!
YOU'RE GOING TO BE FINE, SHOTA.
JIRO AGREES. HE SAYS...
...HE IS NOW CONTENT, AND CAN FIND PEACE IN HEAVEN.
JIRO...

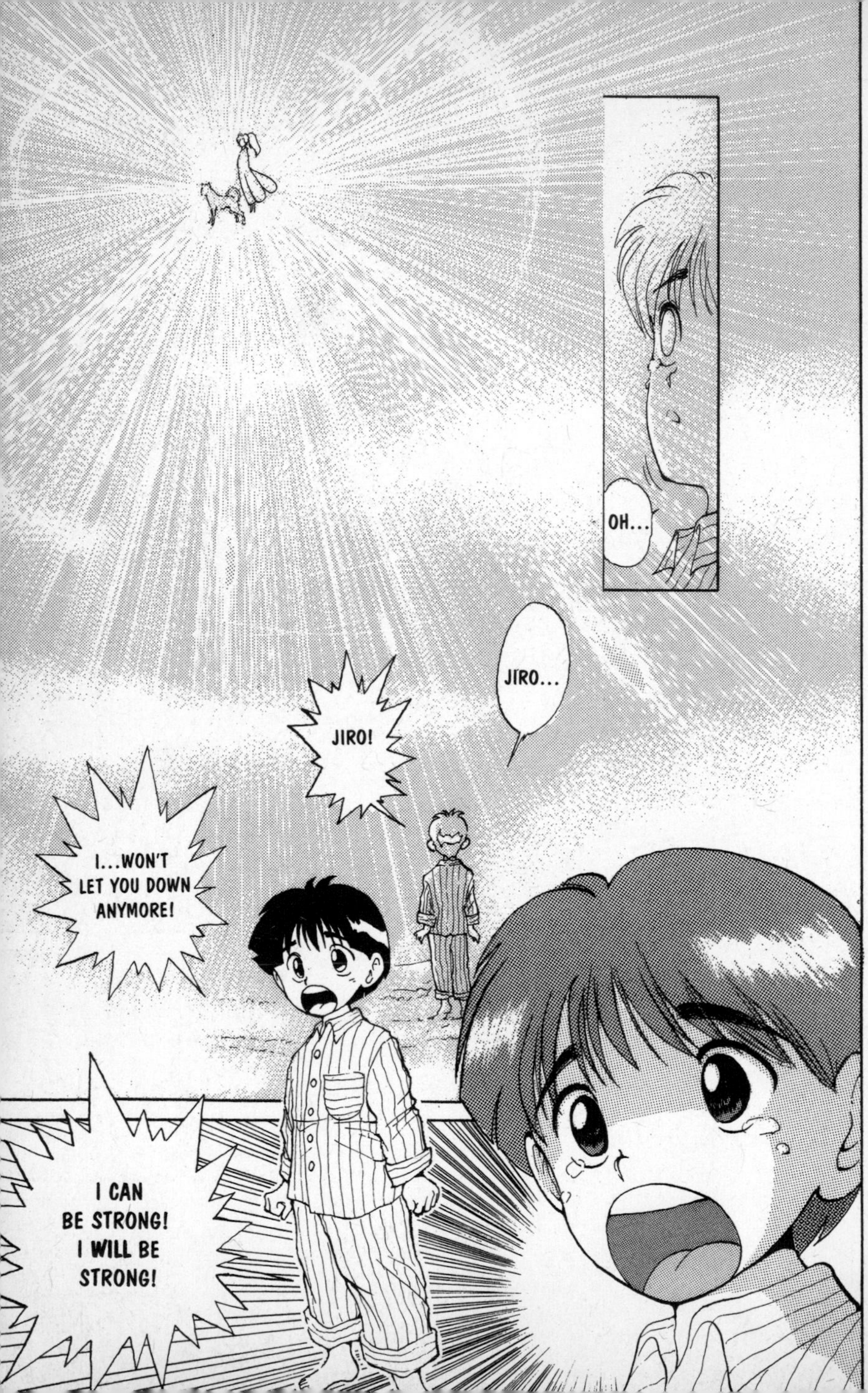
OH...
JIRO...
JIRO!
I...WON'T LET YOU DOWN ANYMORE!
I CAN BE STRONG! I WILL BE STRONG!

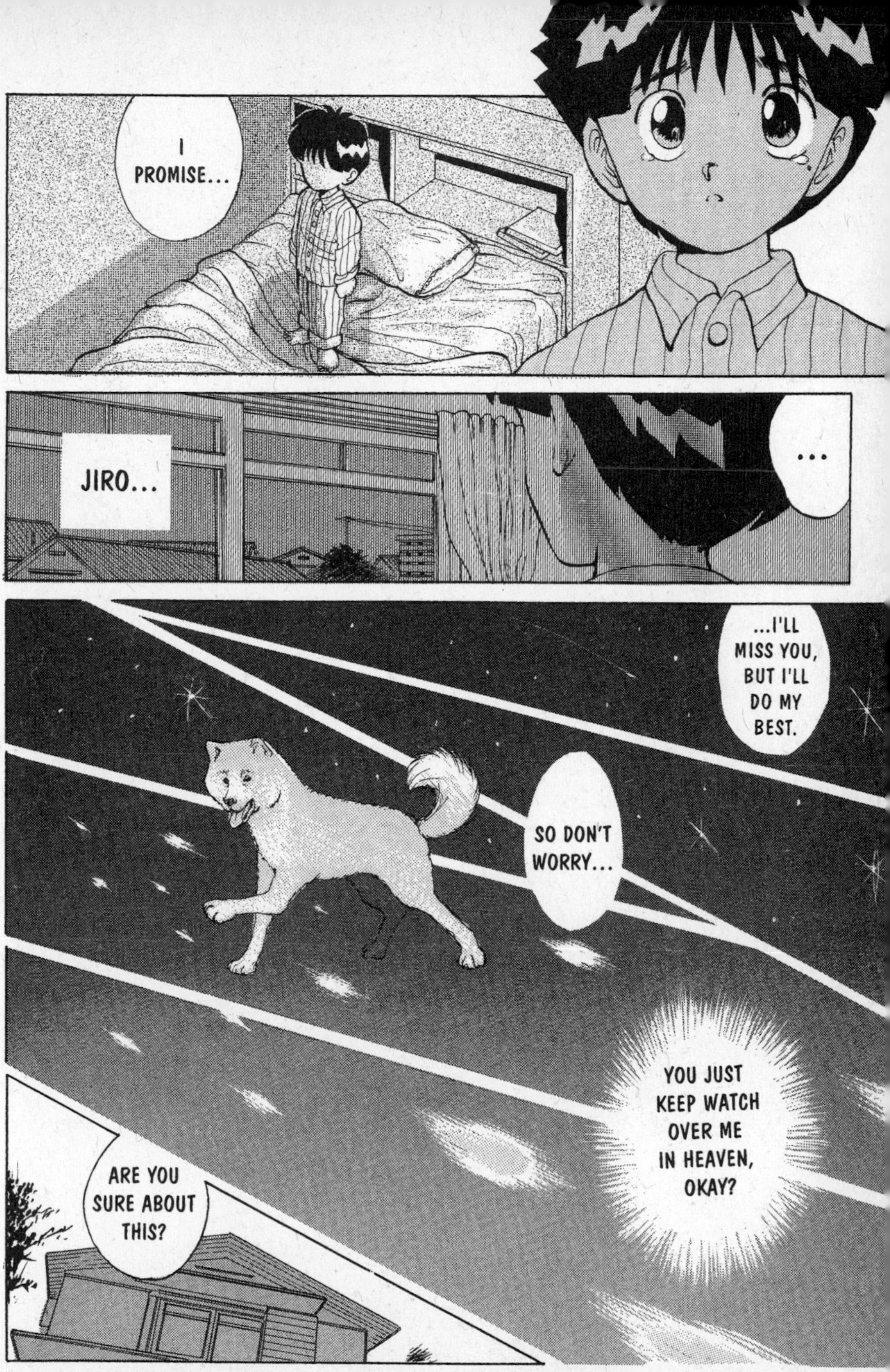
I PROMISE...
...
JIRO...
...I'LL MISS YOU, BUT I'LL DO MY BEST.
SO DON'T WORRY...
YOU JUST KEEP WATCH OVER ME IN HEAVEN, OKAY?
ARE YOU SURE ABOUT THIS?

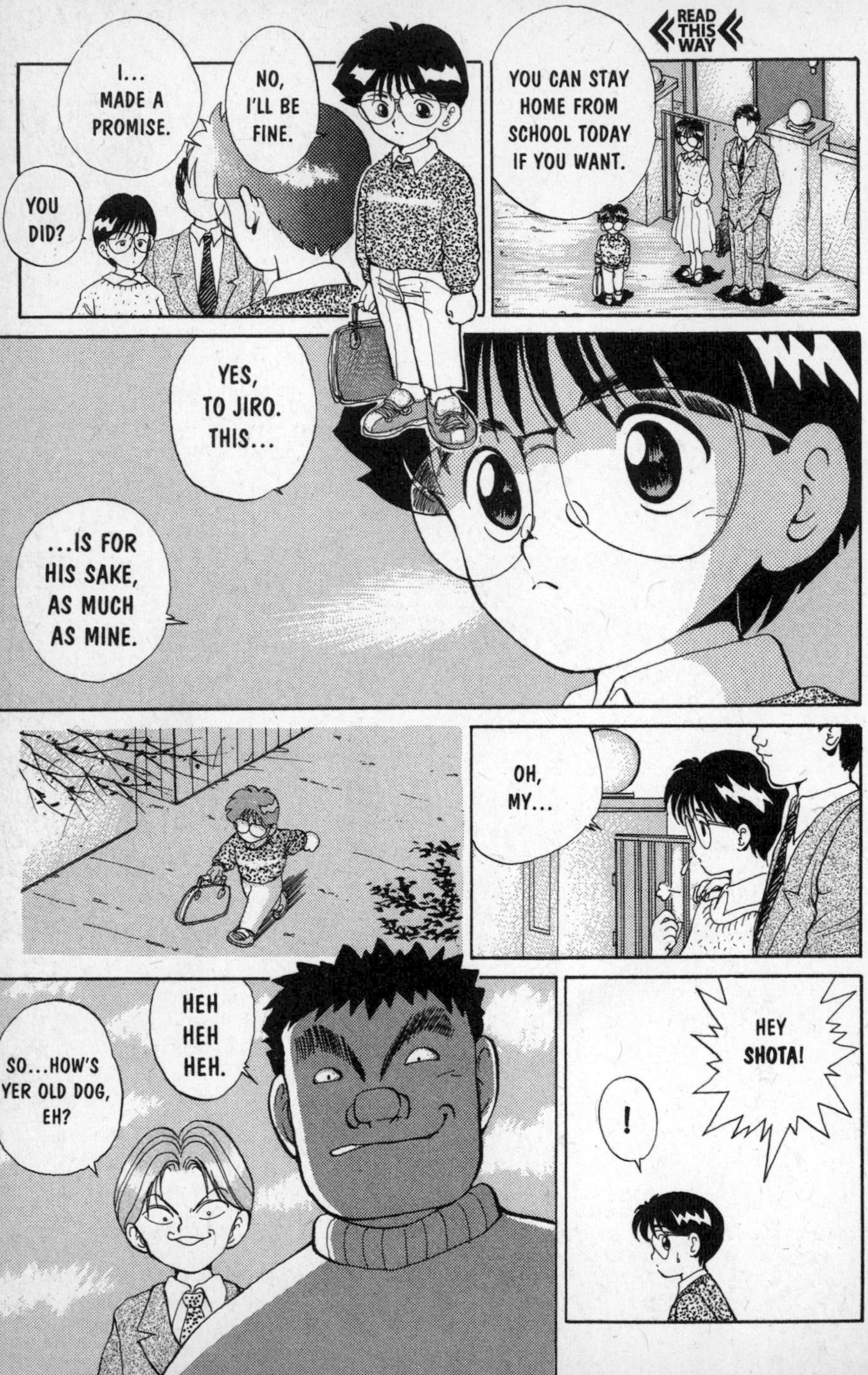
READ THIS WAY
YOU CAN STAY HOME FROM SCHOOL TODAY IF YOU WANT.
NO, I'LL BE FINE.
I... MADE A PROMISE.
YOU DID?
YES, TO JIRO. THIS...
...IS FOR HIS SAKE, AS MUCH AS MINE.
OH, MY...
HEY SHOTA!
!
HEH HEH HEH.
SO...HOW'S YER OLD DOG, EH?

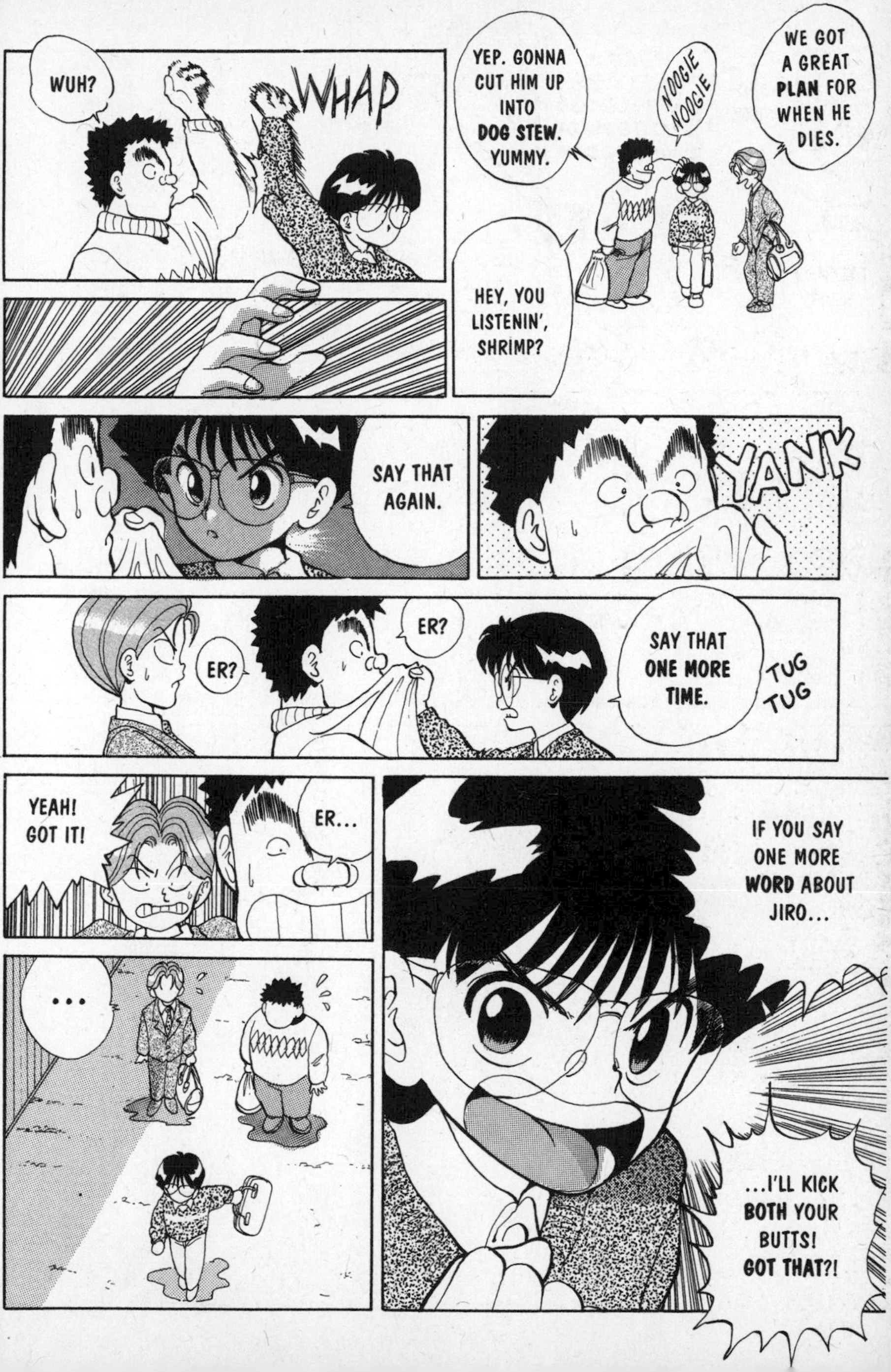
WE GOT A GREAT PLAN FOR WHEN HE DIES.
NOOGIE NOOGIE
YEP. GONNA CUT HIM UP INTO DOG STEW. YUMMY.
HEY, YOU LISTENIN', SHRIMP?
WHAP
WUH?
YANK
SAY THAT AGAIN.
TUG TUG
SAY THAT ONE MORE TIME.
ER?
ER?
IF YOU SAY ONE MORE WORD ABOUT JIRO...
...I'LL KICK BOTH YOUR BUTTS! GOT THAT?!
ER...
YEAH! GOT IT!
...

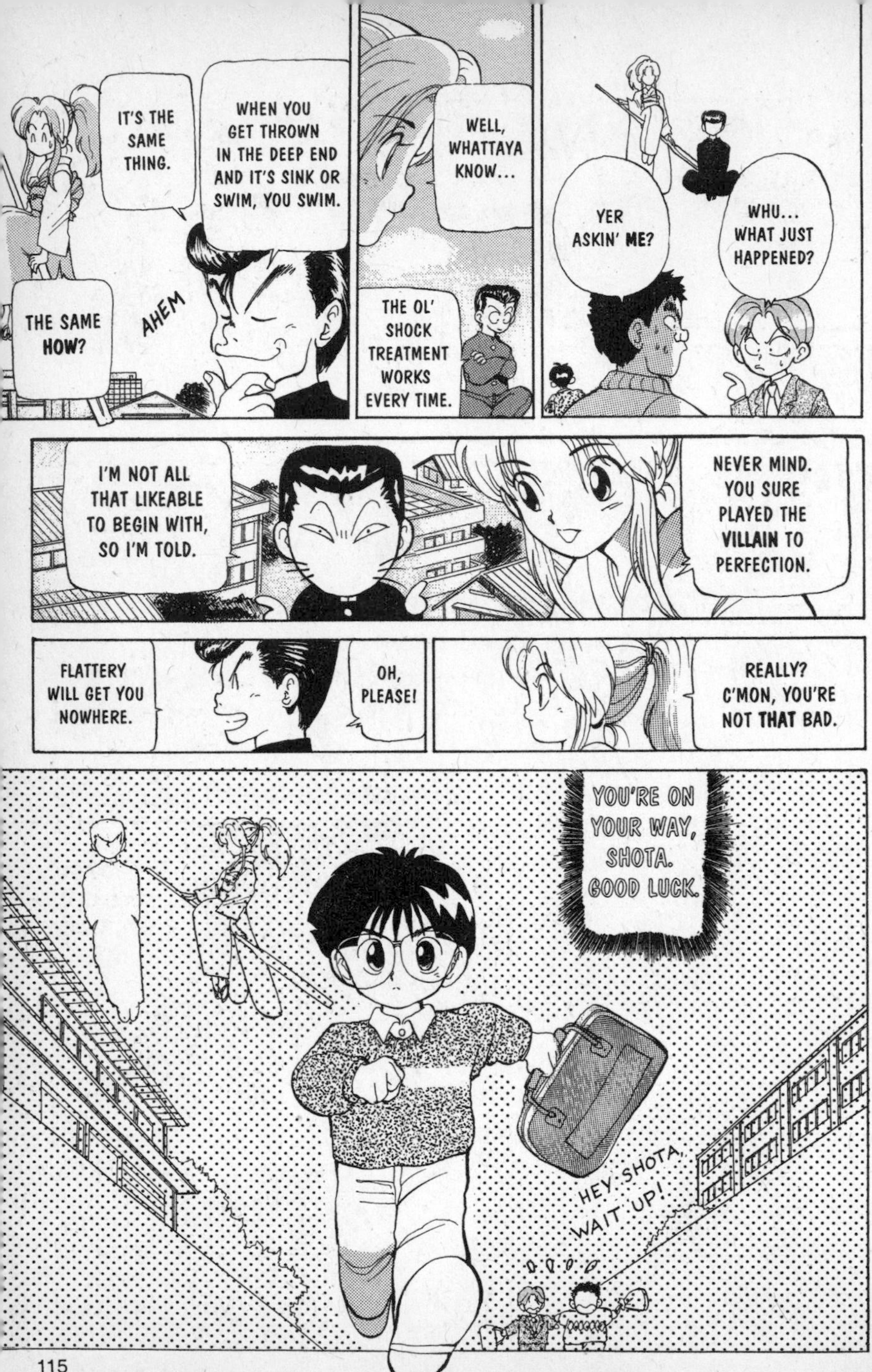
WHU... WHAT JUST HAPPENED?
YER ASKIN' ME?
WELL, WHATTAYA KNOW...
THE OL' SHOCK TREATMENT WORKS EVERY TIME.
WHEN YOU GET THROWN IN THE DEEP END AND IT'S SINK OR SWIM, YOU SWIM.
IT'S THE SAME THING.
AHEM
THE SAME HOW?
NEVER MIND. YOU SURE PLAYED THE VILLAIN TO PERFECTION.
I'M NOT ALL THAT LIKEABLE TO BEGIN WITH, SO I'M TOLD.
REALLY? C'MON, YOU'RE NOT THAT BAD.
OH, PLEASE!
FLATTERY WILL GET YOU NOWHERE.
YOU'RE ON YOUR WAY, SHOTA. GOOD LUCK.
HEY SHOTA, WAIT UP!

Seisaku Hakusho
("The Production Report")
Part 2

By Yoshihiro Togashi

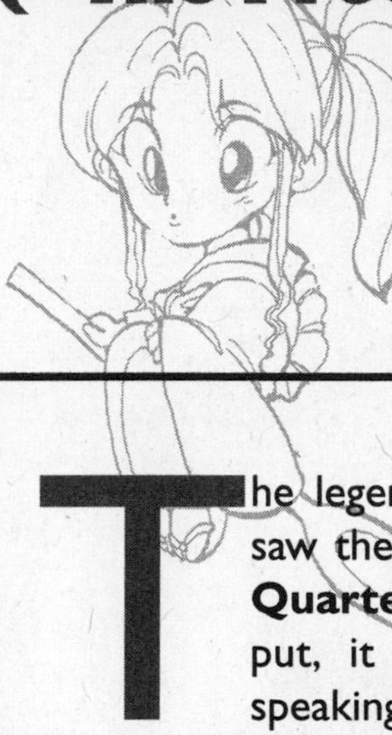

The legendary manga of mine that never saw the light of day was called **Trouble Quartet**. It got rejected because, simply put, it wasn't interesting. Objectively speaking, that is. Personally, I really liked it. It was a weird sports manga with homosexual characters and cross-dressing (I may have turned off a lot of **Weekly Shonen Jump** readers just by explaining this much of the story).

I wrote the script based on my own personal interest, and was satisfied with it, but I couldn't work it up to a level where it would be commercially successful. Still, I grew deeply attached to it. I hope that one day, once I built a name for myself as a writer, I will see the day when this title is published in a different form.

To be continued on page 136! I'll unveil the main character of **Trouble Quartet**, Gen Otoda!

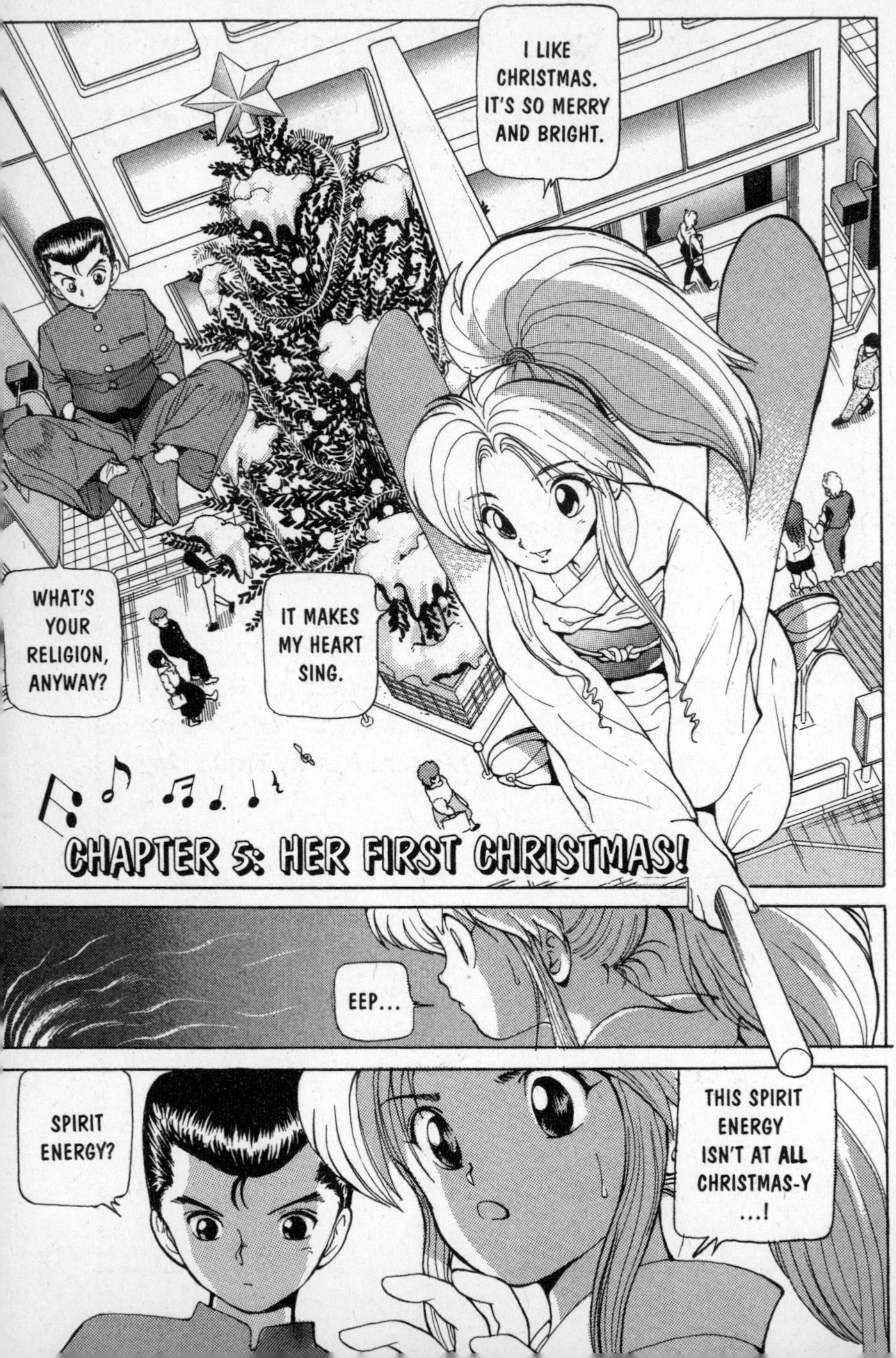
I LIKE CHRISTMAS. IT'S SO MERRY AND BRIGHT.
IT MAKES MY HEART SING.
WHAT'S YOUR RELIGION, ANYWAY?
CHAPTER 5: HER FIRST CHRISTMAS!
EEP...
THIS SPIRIT ENERGY ISN'T AT ALL CHRISTMAS-Y ...!
SPIRIT ENERGY?

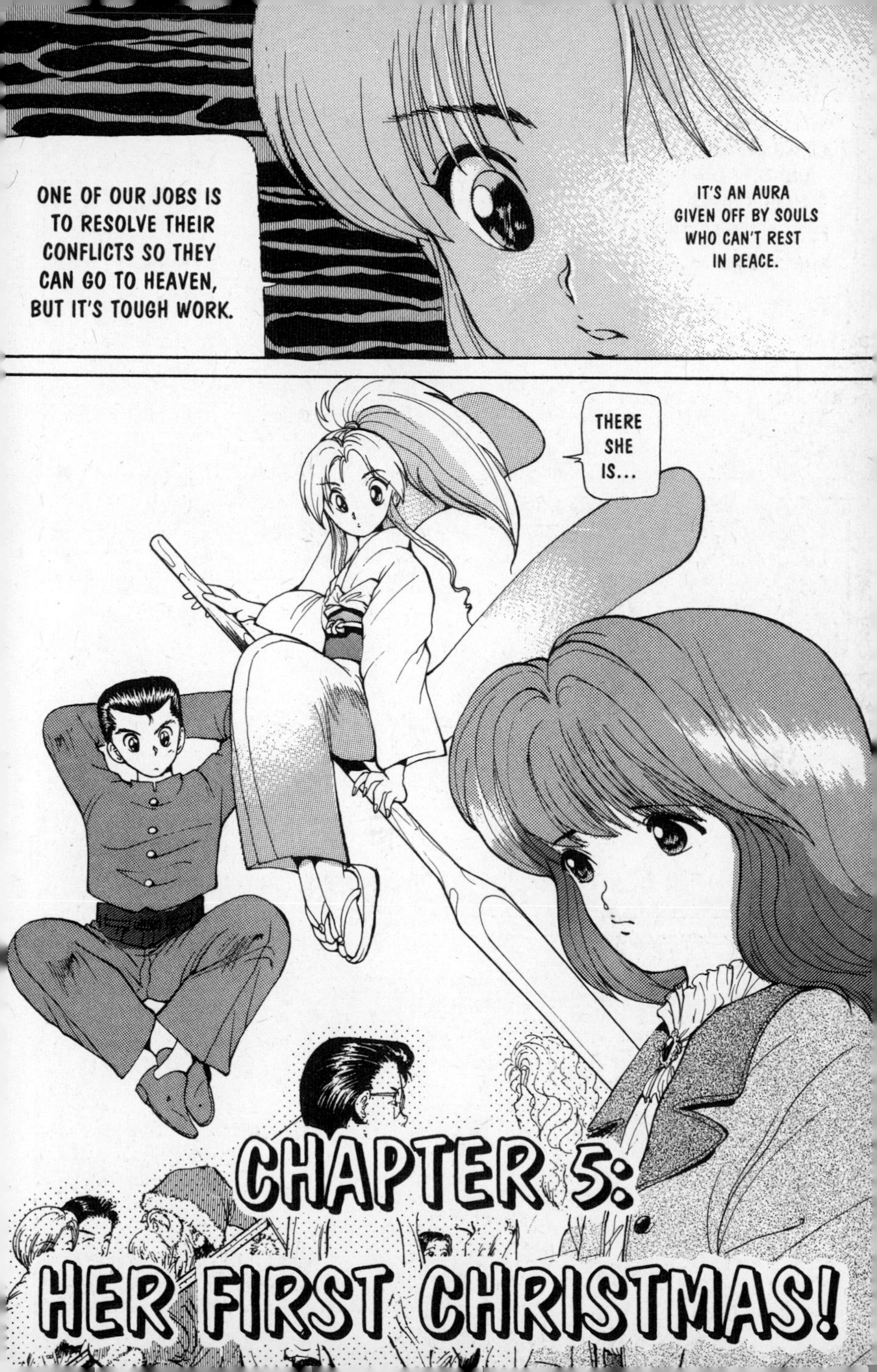
IT'S AN AURA GIVEN OFF BY SOULS WHO CAN'T REST IN PEACE.
ONE OF OUR JOBS IS TO RESOLVE THEIR CONFLICTS SO THEY CAN GO TO HEAVEN, BUT IT'S TOUGH WORK.
THERE SHE IS...
CHAPTER 5:
HER FIRST CHRISTMAS!

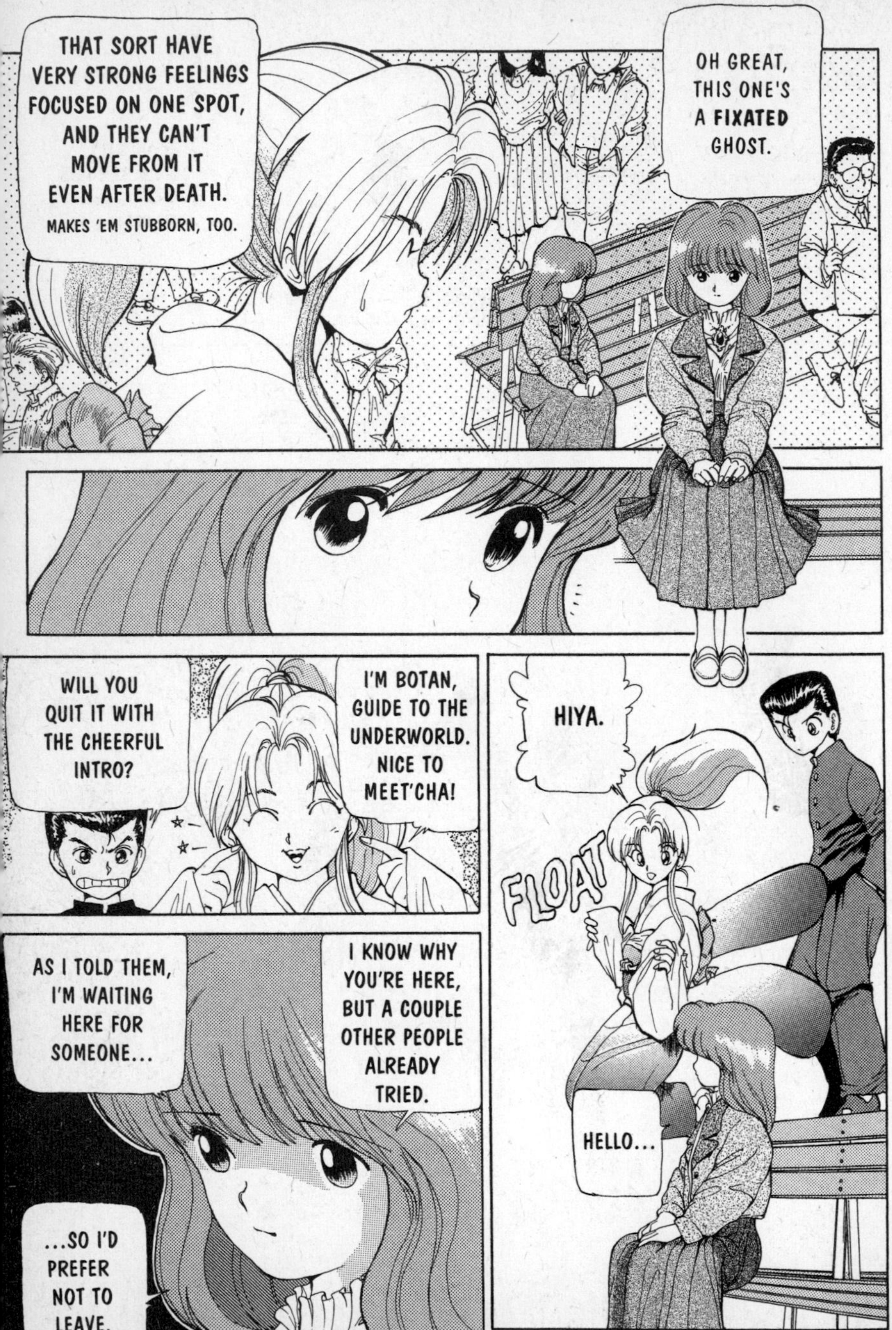
OH GREAT, THIS ONE'S A **FIXATED** GHOST.
THAT SORT HAVE VERY STRONG FEELINGS FOCUSED ON ONE SPOT, AND THEY CAN'T MOVE FROM IT EVEN AFTER DEATH.
MAKES 'EM STUBBORN, TOO.
HIYA.
FLOAT
HELLO...
I'M BOTAN, GUIDE TO THE UNDERWORLD. NICE TO MEET'CHA!
WILL YOU QUIT IT WITH THE CHEERFUL INTRO?
I KNOW WHY YOU'RE HERE, BUT A COUPLE OTHER PEOPLE ALREADY TRIED.
AS I TOLD THEM, I'M WAITING HERE FOR SOMEONE...
...SO I'D PREFER NOT TO LEAVE.

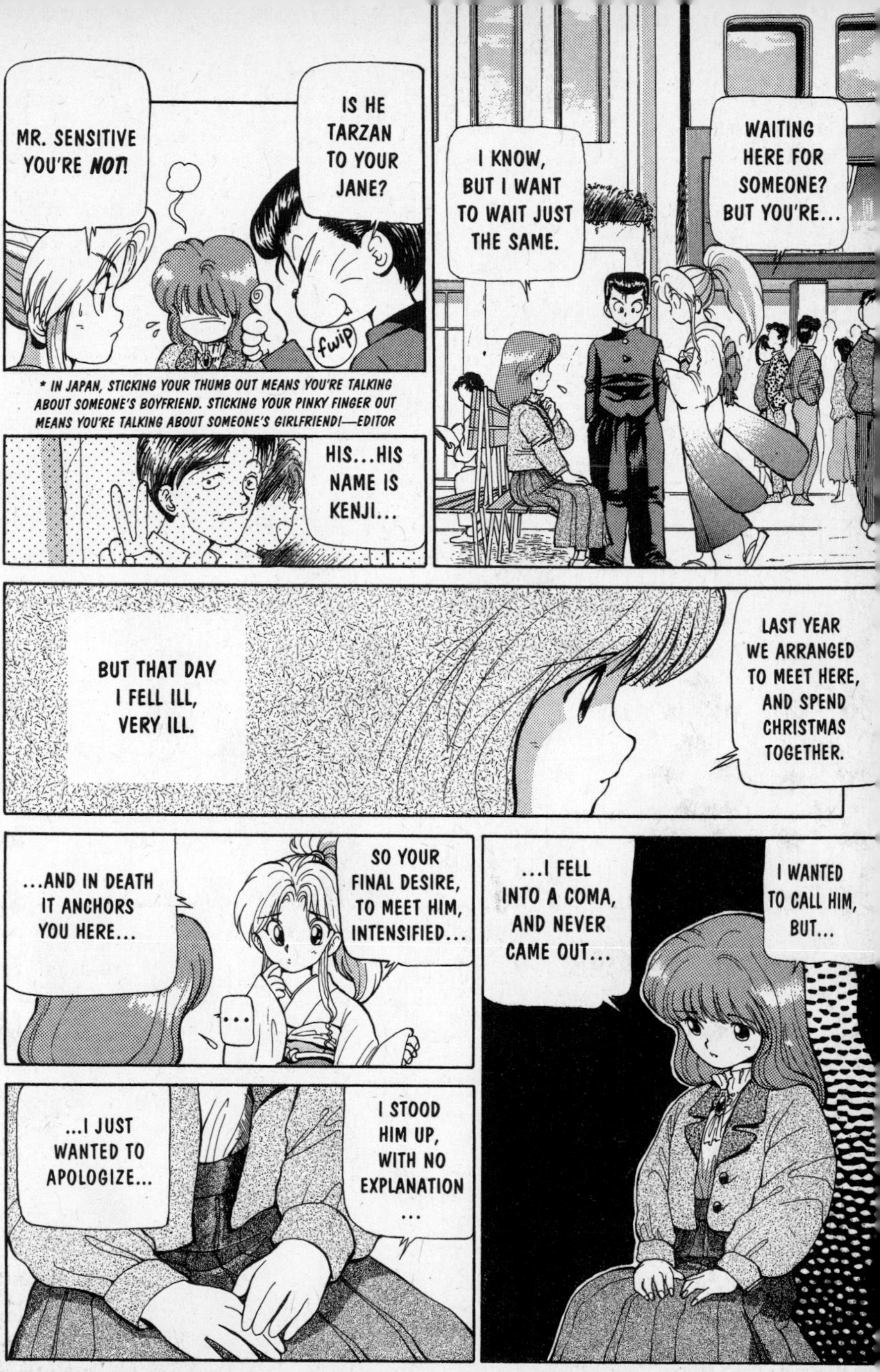
WAITING HERE FOR SOMEONE? BUT YOU'RE...
I KNOW, BUT I WANT TO WAIT JUST THE SAME.
IS HE TARZAN TO YOUR JANE?
fwip
MR. SENSITIVE YOU'RE NOT!
HIS...HIS NAME IS KENJI...
LAST YEAR WE ARRANGED TO MEET HERE, AND SPEND CHRISTMAS TOGETHER.
BUT THAT DAY I FELL ILL, VERY ILL.
I WANTED TO CALL HIM, BUT...
...I FELL INTO A COMA, AND NEVER CAME OUT...
SO YOUR FINAL DESIRE, TO MEET HIM, INTENSIFIED...
...AND IN DEATH IT ANCHORS YOU HERE...
...
I STOOD HIM UP, WITH NO EXPLANATION ...
...I JUST WANTED TO APOLOGIZE...

* IN JAPAN, STICKING YOUR THUMB OUT MEANS YOU'RE TALKING ABOUT SOMEONE'S BOYFRIEND. STICKING YOUR PINKY FINGER OUT MEANS YOU'RE TALKING ABOUT SOMEONE'S GIRLFRIEND!—EDITOR

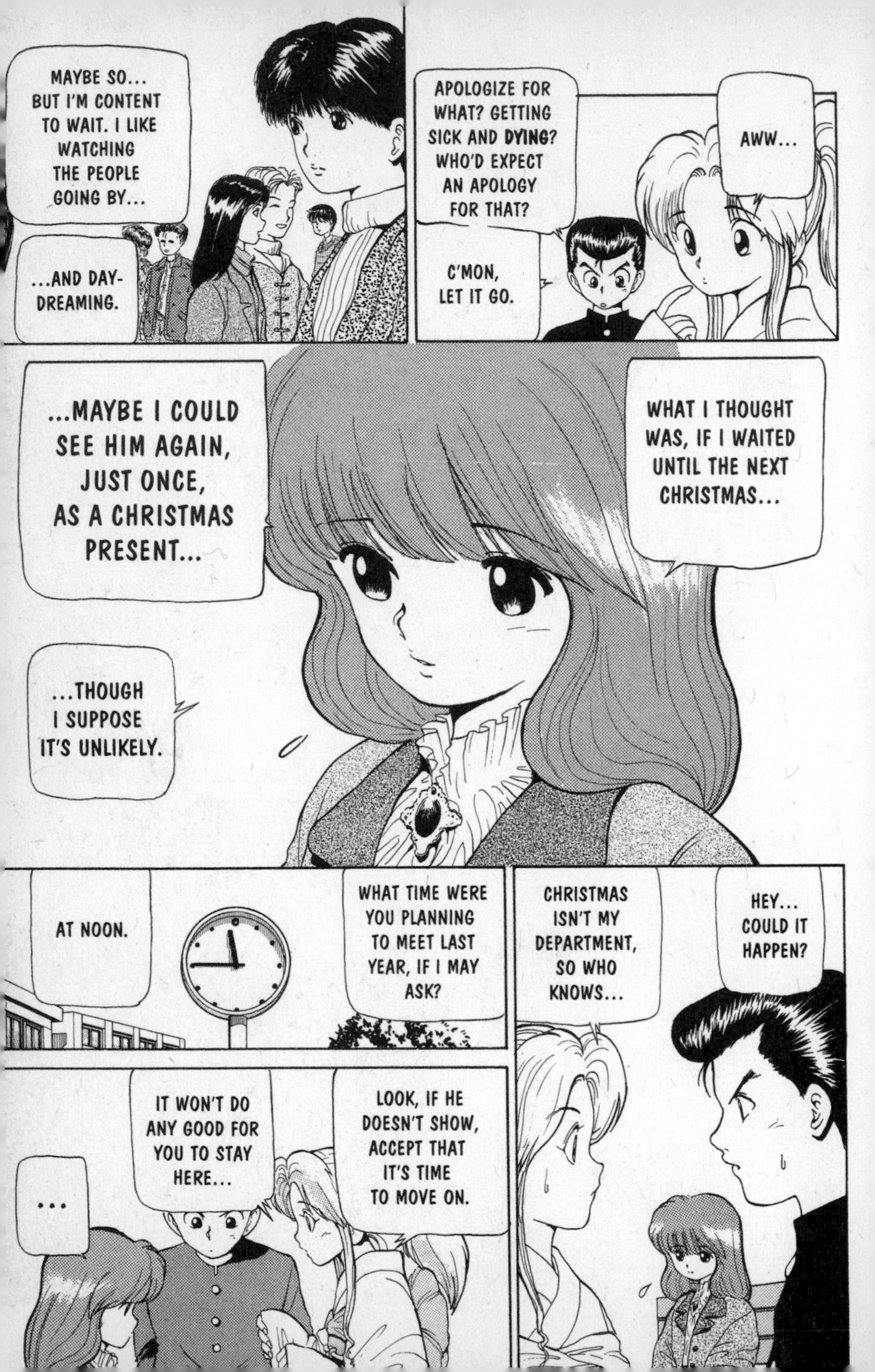
AWW...
APOLOGIZE FOR WHAT? GETTING SICK AND DYING? WHO'D EXPECT AN APOLOGY FOR THAT?
C'MON, LET IT GO.
MAYBE SO... BUT I'M CONTENT TO WAIT. I LIKE WATCHING THE PEOPLE GOING BY...
...AND DAY-DREAMING.
WHAT I THOUGHT WAS, IF I WAITED UNTIL THE NEXT CHRISTMAS...
...MAYBE I COULD SEE HIM AGAIN, JUST ONCE, AS A CHRISTMAS PRESENT...
...THOUGH I SUPPOSE IT'S UNLIKELY.
HEY... COULD IT HAPPEN?
CHRISTMAS ISN'T MY DEPARTMENT, SO WHO KNOWS...
WHAT TIME WERE YOU PLANNING TO MEET LAST YEAR, IF I MAY ASK?
AT NOON.
LOOK, IF HE DOESN'T SHOW, ACCEPT THAT IT'S TIME TO MOVE ON.
IT WON'T DO ANY GOOD FOR YOU TO STAY HERE...
...

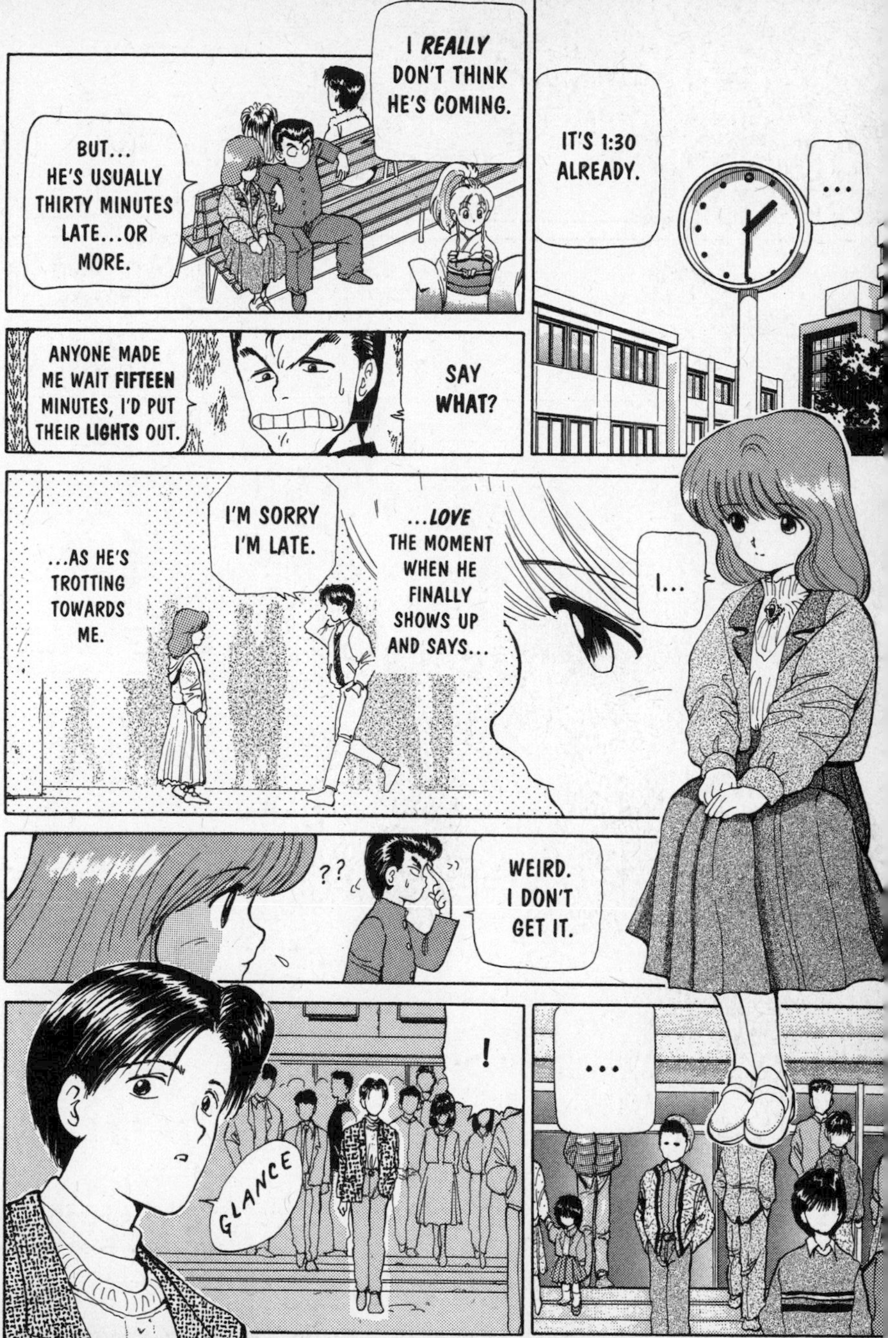

...
IT'S 1:30 ALREADY.
I REALLY DON'T THINK HE'S COMING.
BUT... HE'S USUALLY THIRTY MINUTES LATE...OR MORE.
SAY WHAT?
ANYONE MADE ME WAIT FIFTEEN MINUTES, I'D PUT THEIR LIGHTS OUT.
I...
...LOVE THE MOMENT WHEN HE FINALLY SHOWS UP AND SAYS...
I'M SORRY I'M LATE.
...AS HE'S TROTTING TOWARDS ME.
WEIRD. I DON'T GET IT.
??
...
!
GLANCE

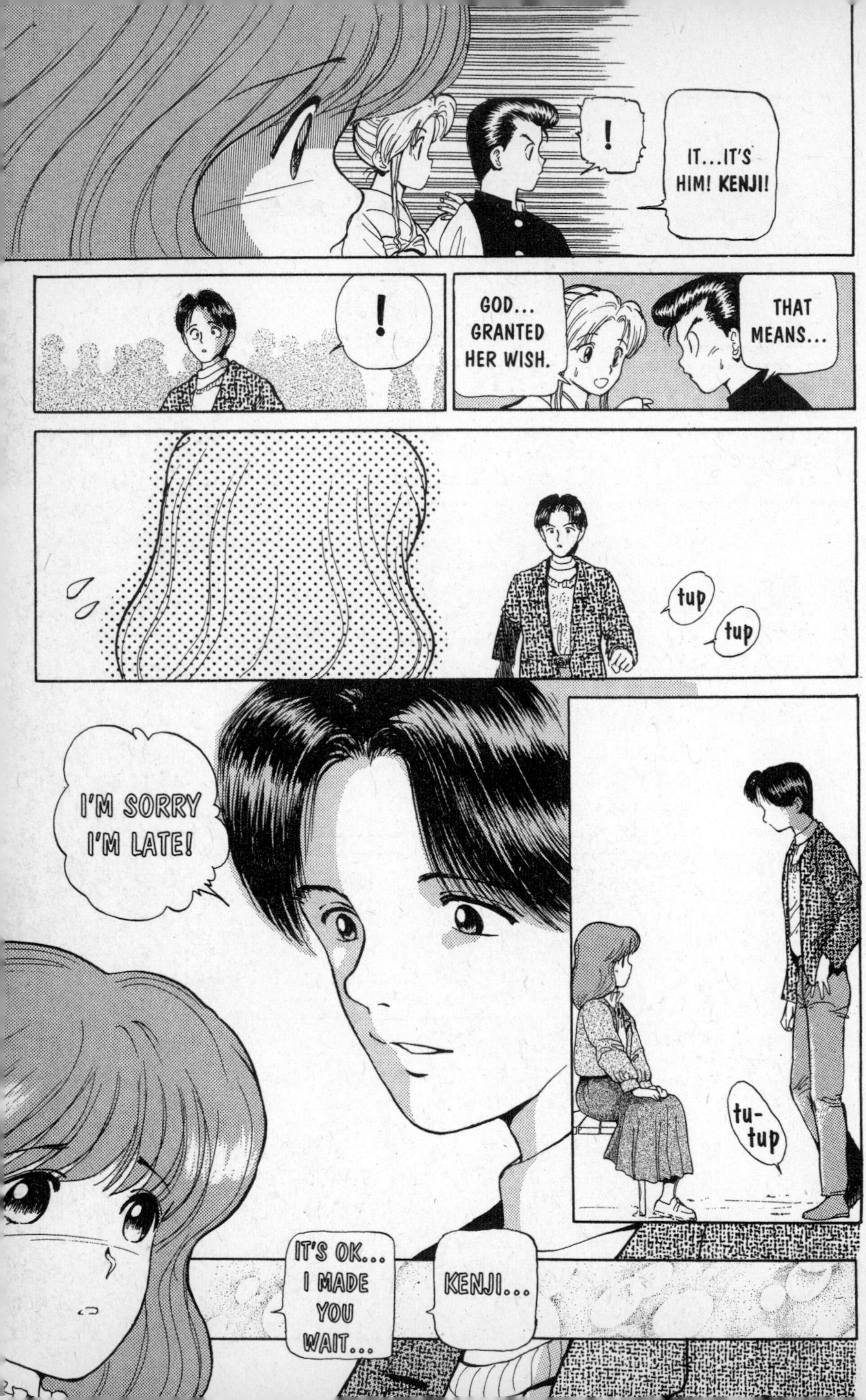
IT...IT'S HIM! KENJI!
!
THAT MEANS...
GOD... GRANTED HER WISH.
!
tup
tup
tu-tup
I'M SORRY I'M LATE!
KENJI...
IT'S OK... I MADE YOU WAIT...

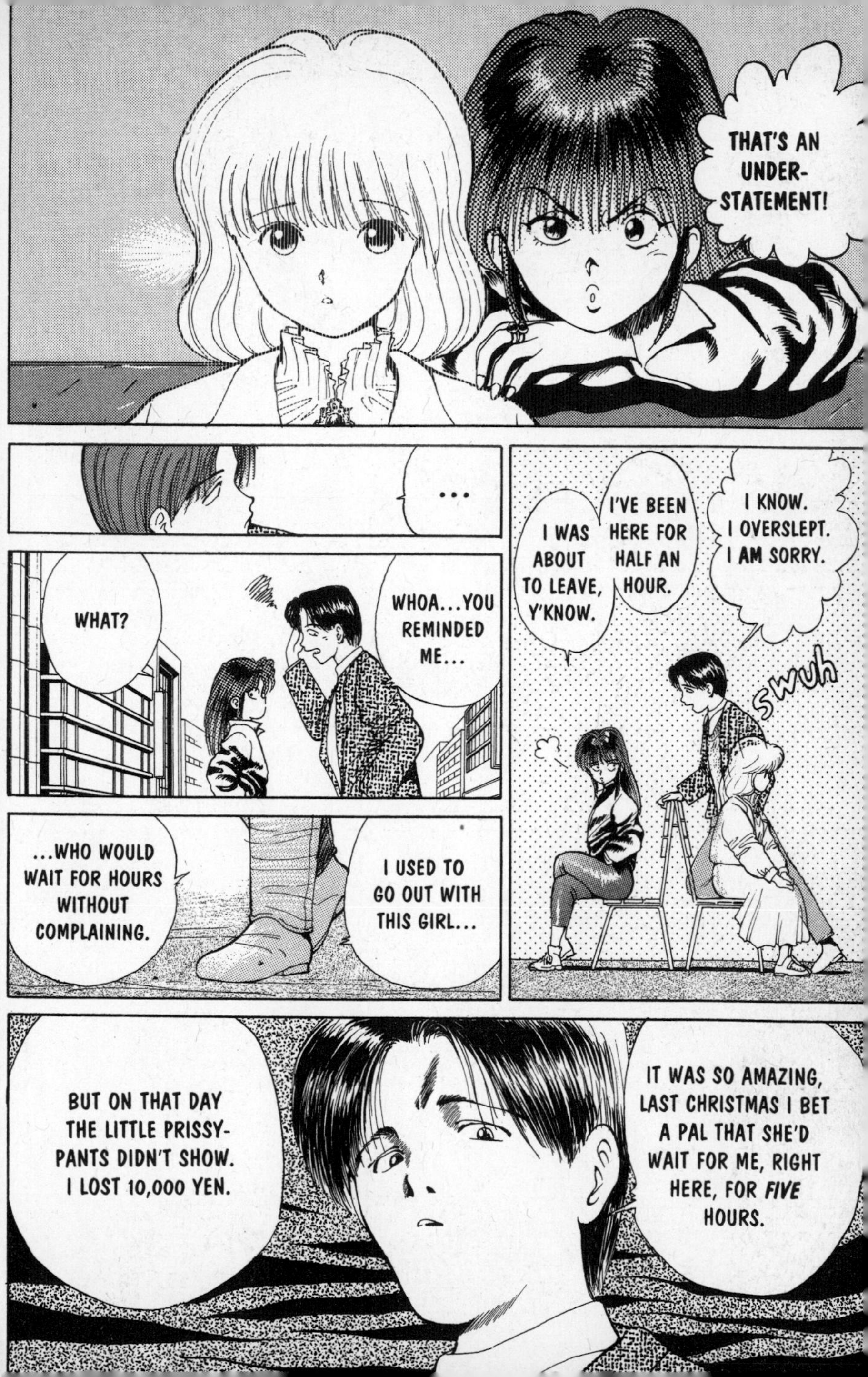
THAT'S AN UNDER-STATEMENT!
I KNOW. I OVERSLEPT. I AM SORRY.
I'VE BEEN HERE FOR HALF AN HOUR.
I WAS ABOUT TO LEAVE, Y'KNOW.
SWUH
...
WHOA...YOU REMINDED ME...
WHAT?
I USED TO GO OUT WITH THIS GIRL...
...WHO WOULD WAIT FOR HOURS WITHOUT COMPLAINING.
IT WAS SO AMAZING, LAST CHRISTMAS I BET A PAL THAT SHE'D WAIT FOR ME, RIGHT HERE, FOR *FIVE* HOURS.
BUT ON THAT DAY THE LITTLE PRISSY-PANTS DIDN'T SHOW. I LOST 10,000 YEN.

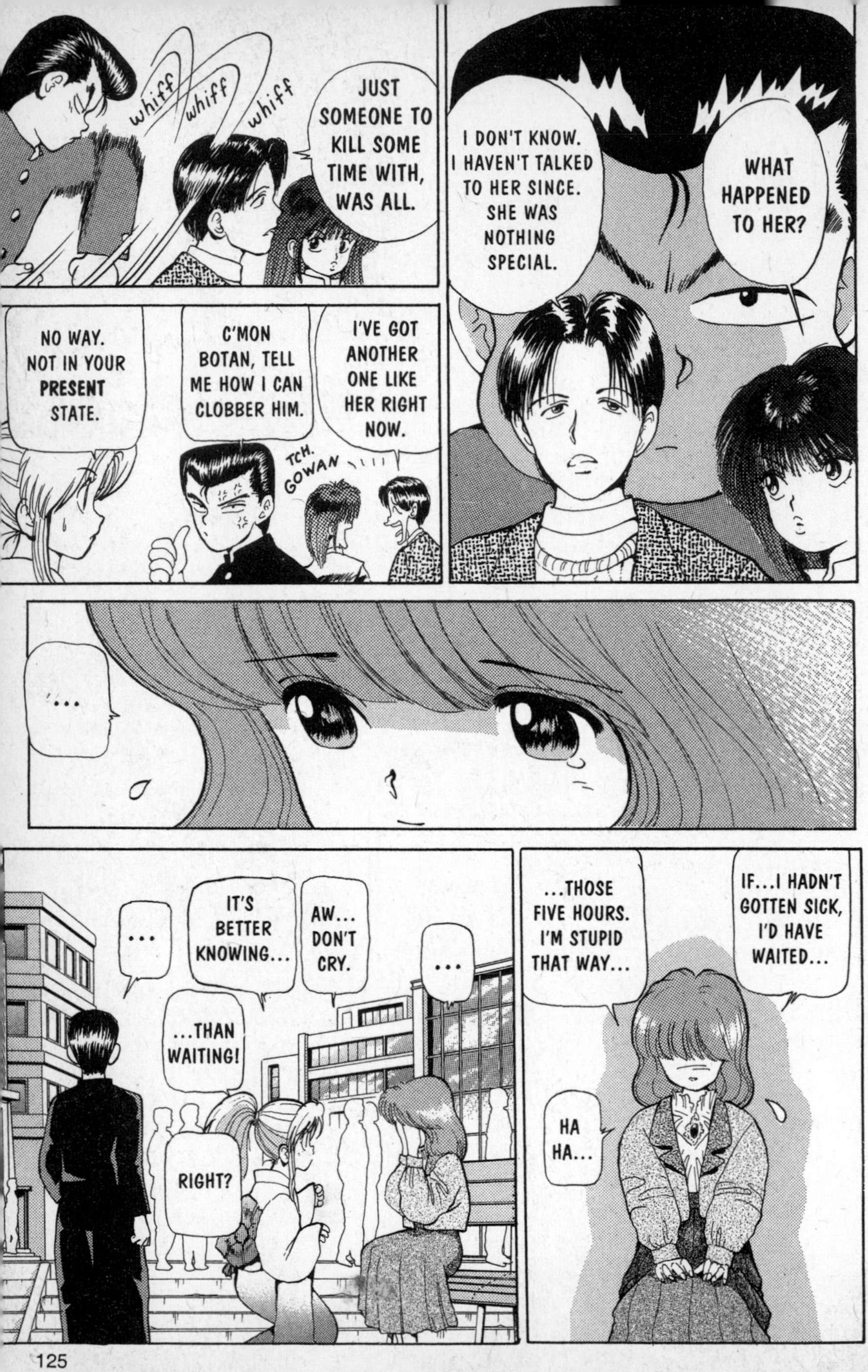

WHAT HAPPENED TO HER?
I DON'T KNOW. I HAVEN'T TALKED TO HER SINCE. SHE WAS NOTHING SPECIAL.
whiff
whiff
whiff
JUST SOMEONE TO KILL SOME TIME WITH, WAS ALL.
I'VE GOT ANOTHER ONE LIKE HER RIGHT NOW.
TCH. GOWAN
C'MON BOTAN, TELL ME HOW I CAN CLOBBER HIM.
NO WAY. NOT IN YOUR PRESENT STATE.
...
IF...I HADN'T GOTTEN SICK, I'D HAVE WAITED...
...THOSE FIVE HOURS. I'M STUPID THAT WAY...
HA HA...
...
AW... DON'T CRY.
IT'S BETTER KNOWING...
...THAN WAITING!
RIGHT?
...

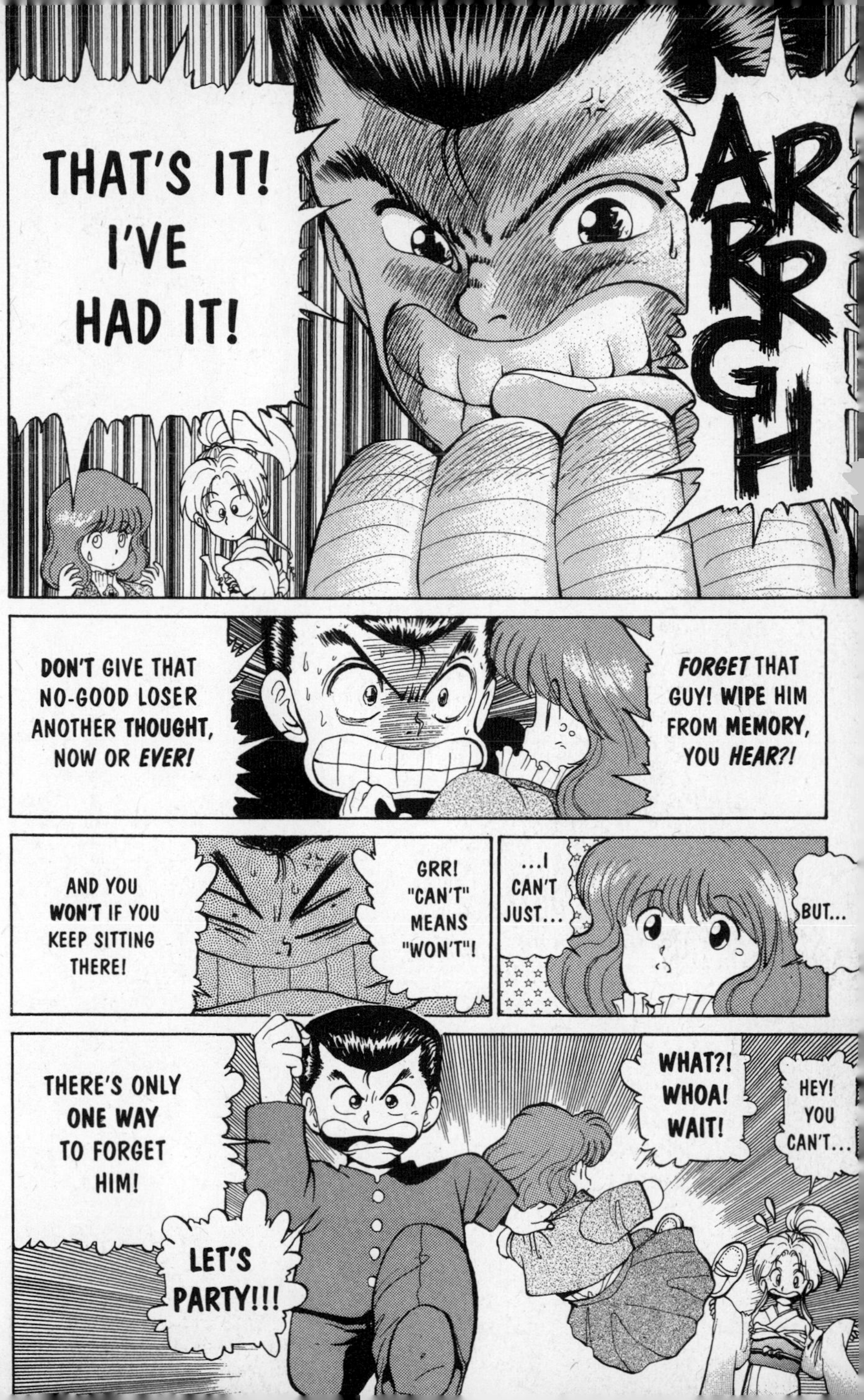
ARRRGH
THAT'S IT! I'VE HAD IT!
FORGET THAT GUY! WIPE HIM FROM MEMORY, YOU HEAR?!
DON'T GIVE THAT NO-GOOD LOSER ANOTHER THOUGHT, NOW OR EVER!
BUT...
...I CAN'T JUST...
GRR! "CAN'T" MEANS "WON'T"!
AND YOU WON'T IF YOU KEEP SITTING THERE!
HEY! YOU CAN'T...
WHAT?! WHOA! WAIT!
THERE'S ONLY ONE WAY TO FORGET HIM!
LET'S PARTY!!!

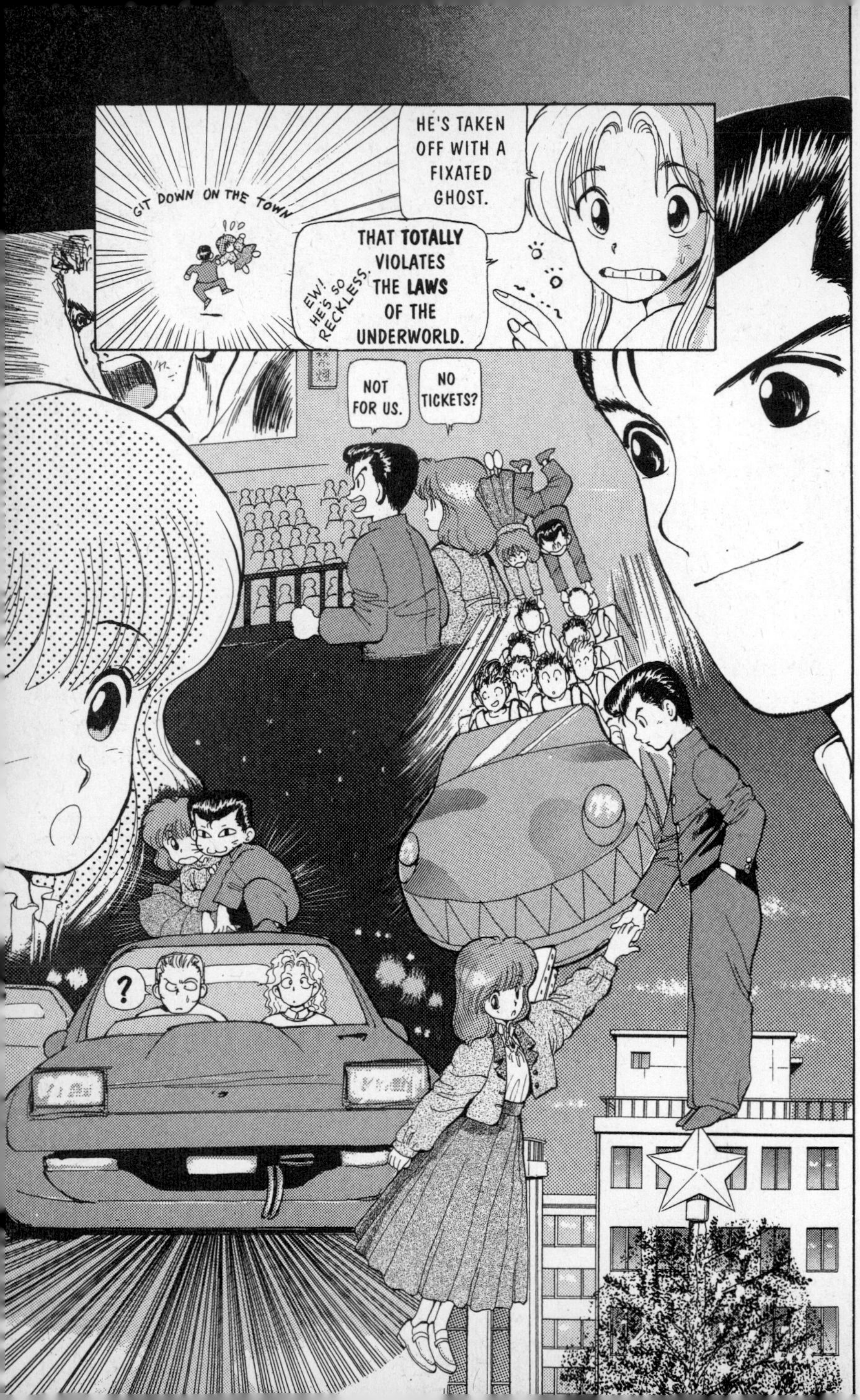
HE'S TAKEN OFF WITH A FIXATED GHOST.
THAT TOTALLY VIOLATES THE LAWS OF THE UNDERWORLD.
EW! HE'S SO RECKLESS.
GIT DOWN ON THE TOWN
NO TICKETS?
NOT FOR US.
?

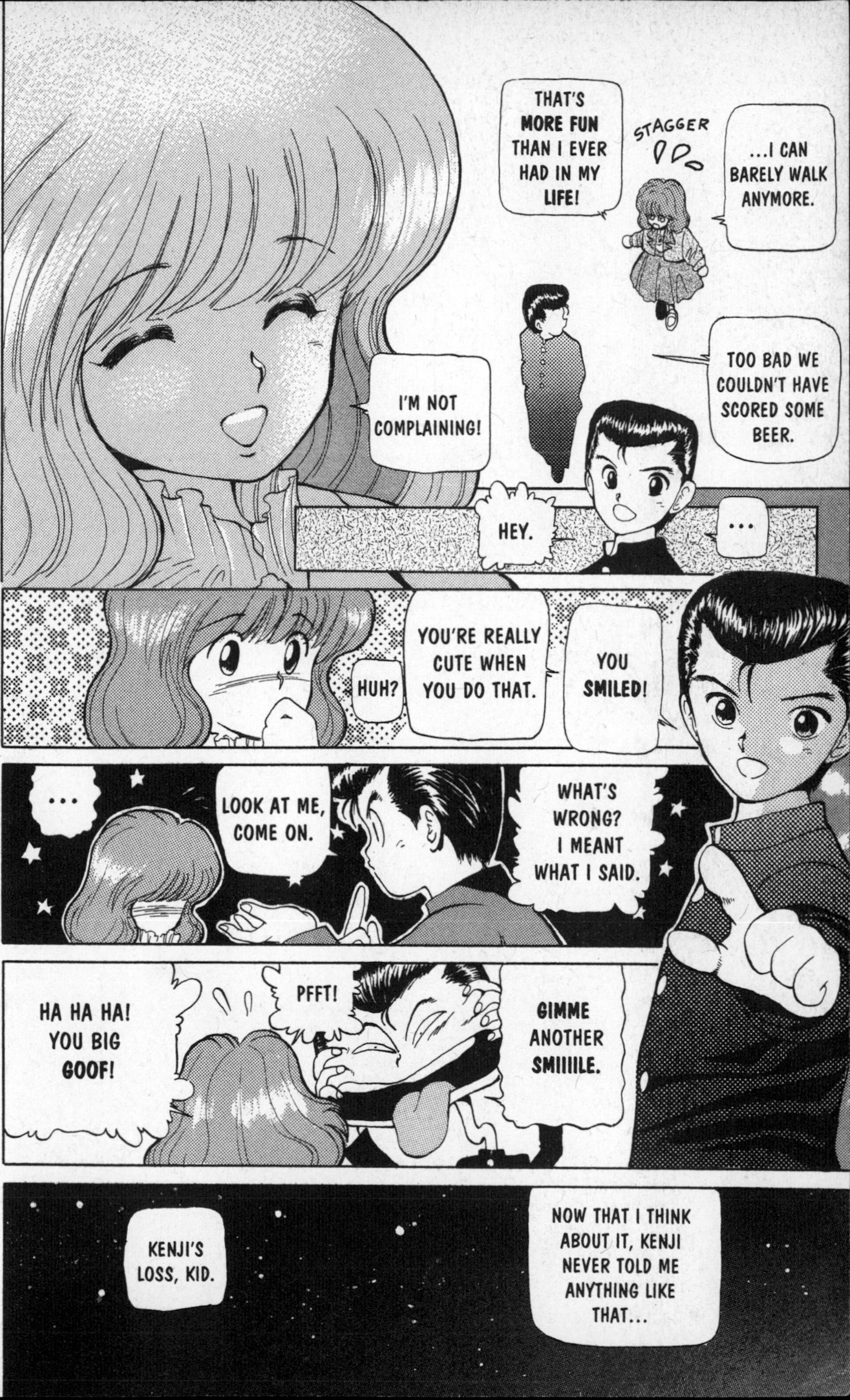
STAGGER
...I CAN BARELY WALK ANYMORE.
THAT'S MORE FUN THAN I EVER HAD IN MY LIFE!
TOO BAD WE COULDN'T HAVE SCORED SOME BEER.
I'M NOT COMPLAINING!
...
HEY.
YOU SMILED!
YOU'RE REALLY CUTE WHEN YOU DO THAT.
HUH?
WHAT'S WRONG? I MEANT WHAT I SAID.
LOOK AT ME, COME ON.
...
GIMME ANOTHER SMIIIILE.
PFFT!
HA HA HA! YOU BIG GOOF!
NOW THAT I THINK ABOUT IT, KENJI NEVER TOLD ME ANYTHING LIKE THAT...
KENJI'S LOSS, KID.

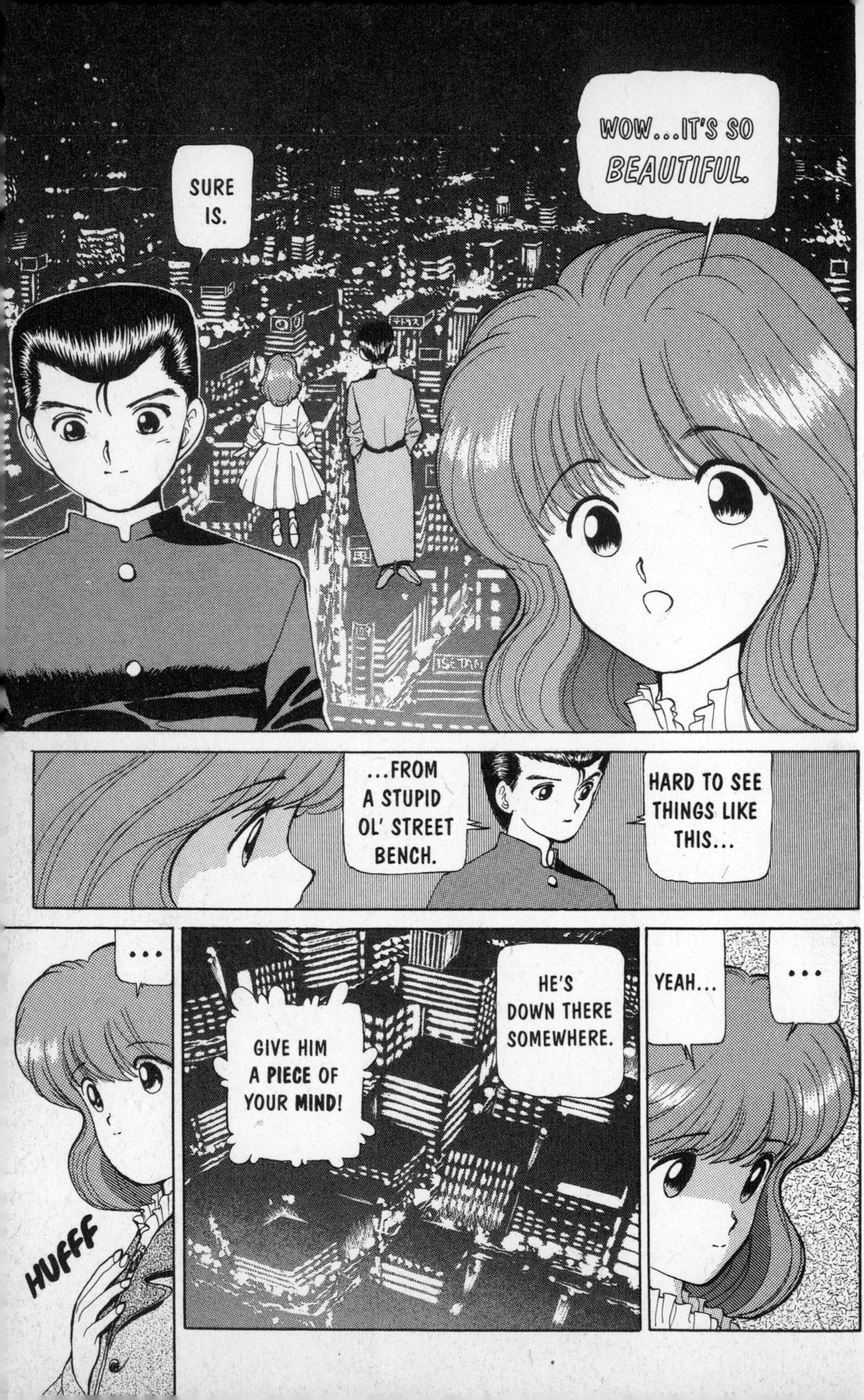
WOW...IT'S SO BEAUTIFUL.
SURE IS.
HARD TO SEE THINGS LIKE THIS...
...FROM A STUPID OL' STREET BENCH.
...
YEAH...
HE'S DOWN THERE SOMEWHERE.
GIVE HIM A PIECE OF YOUR MIND!
...
HUFFF

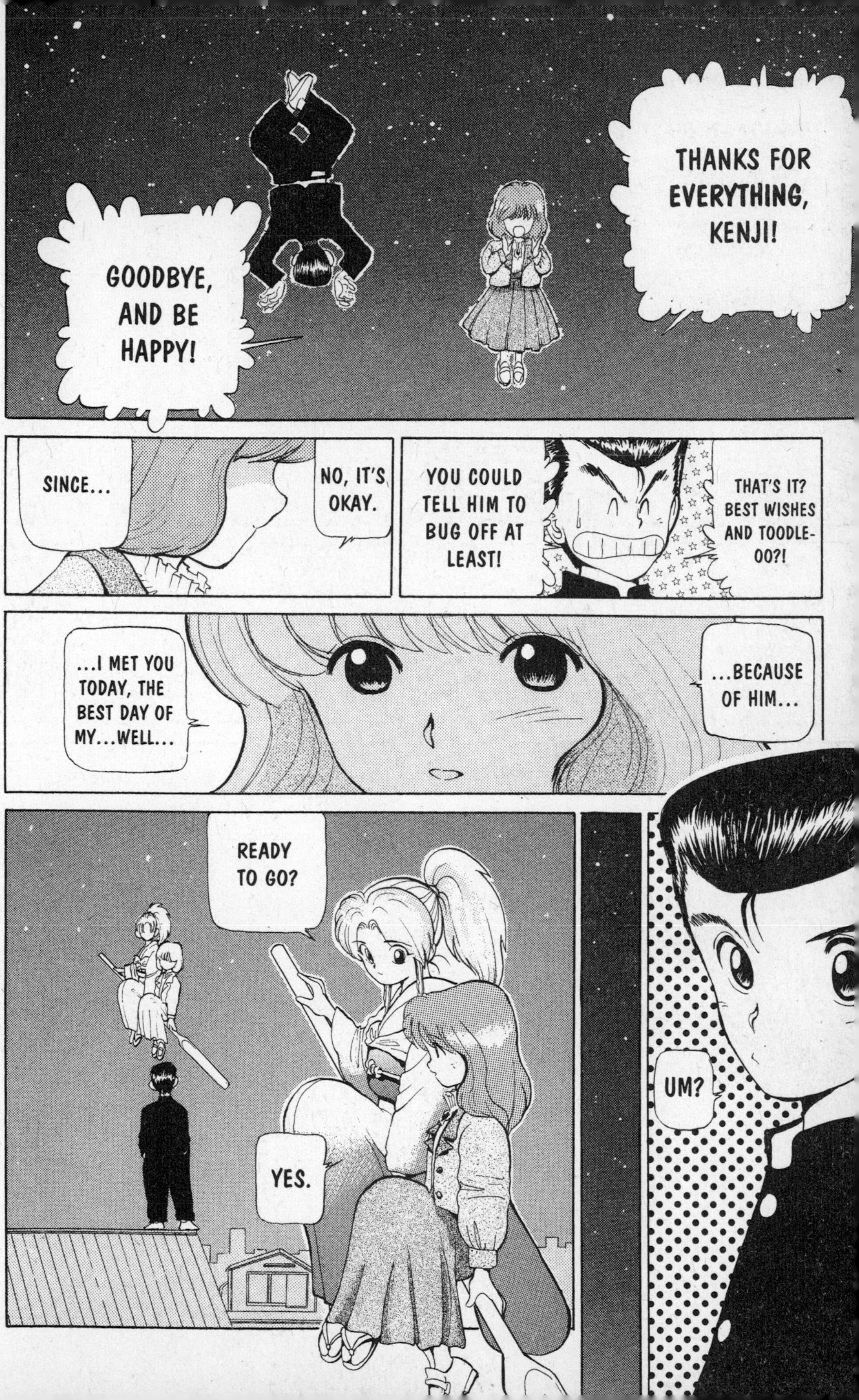
THANKS FOR EVERYTHING, KENJI!
GOODBYE, AND BE HAPPY!
THAT'S IT? BEST WISHES AND TOODLE-OO?!
YOU COULD TELL HIM TO BUG OFF AT LEAST!
NO, IT'S OKAY.
SINCE...
...BECAUSE OF HIM...
...I MET YOU TODAY, THE BEST DAY OF MY...WELL...
UM?
READY TO GO?
YES.

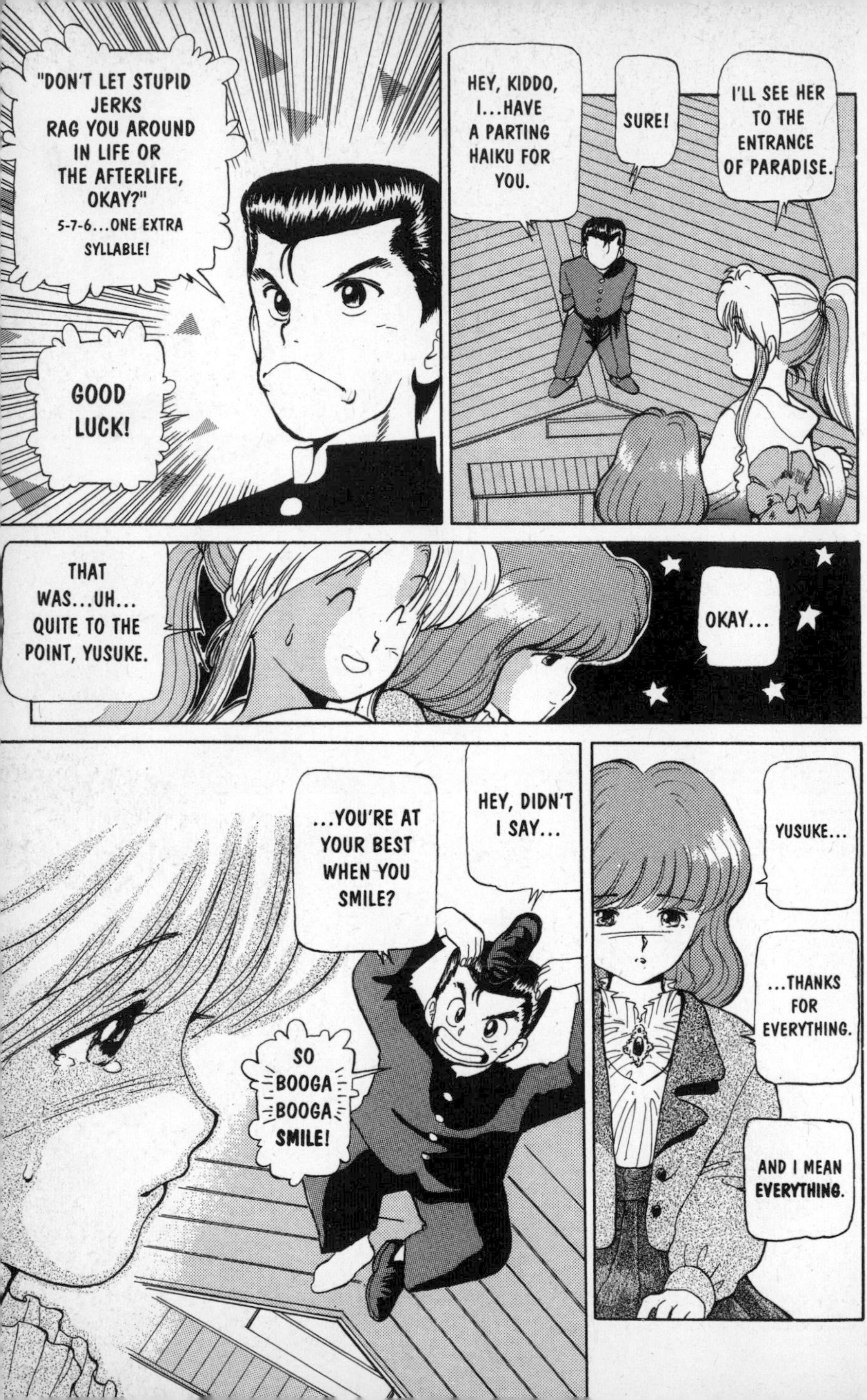
I'LL SEE HER TO THE ENTRANCE OF PARADISE.
SURE!
HEY, KIDDO, I...HAVE A PARTING HAIKU FOR YOU.
"DON'T LET STUPID JERKS RAG YOU AROUND IN LIFE OR THE AFTERLIFE, OKAY?"
5-7-6...ONE EXTRA SYLLABLE!
GOOD LUCK!
OKAY...
THAT WAS...UH... QUITE TO THE POINT, YUSUKE.
YUSUKE...
...THANKS FOR EVERYTHING.
AND I MEAN EVERYTHING.
HEY, DIDN'T I SAY...
...YOU'RE AT YOUR BEST WHEN YOU SMILE?
SO BOOGA BOOGA SMILE!

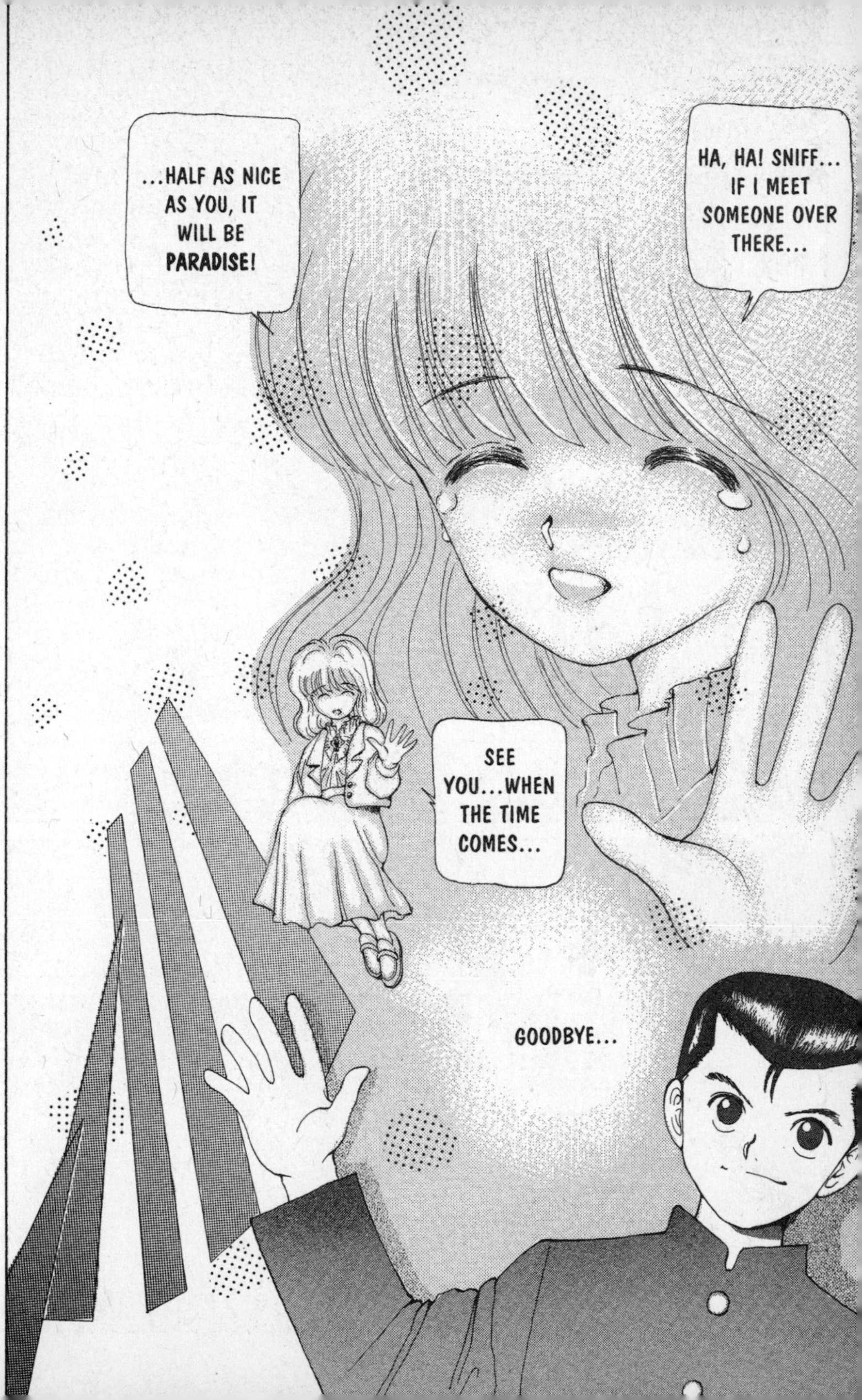
HA, HA! SNIFF... IF I MEET SOMEONE OVER THERE...
...HALF AS NICE AS YOU, IT WILL BE PARADISE!
SEE YOU...WHEN THE TIME COMES...
GOODBYE...

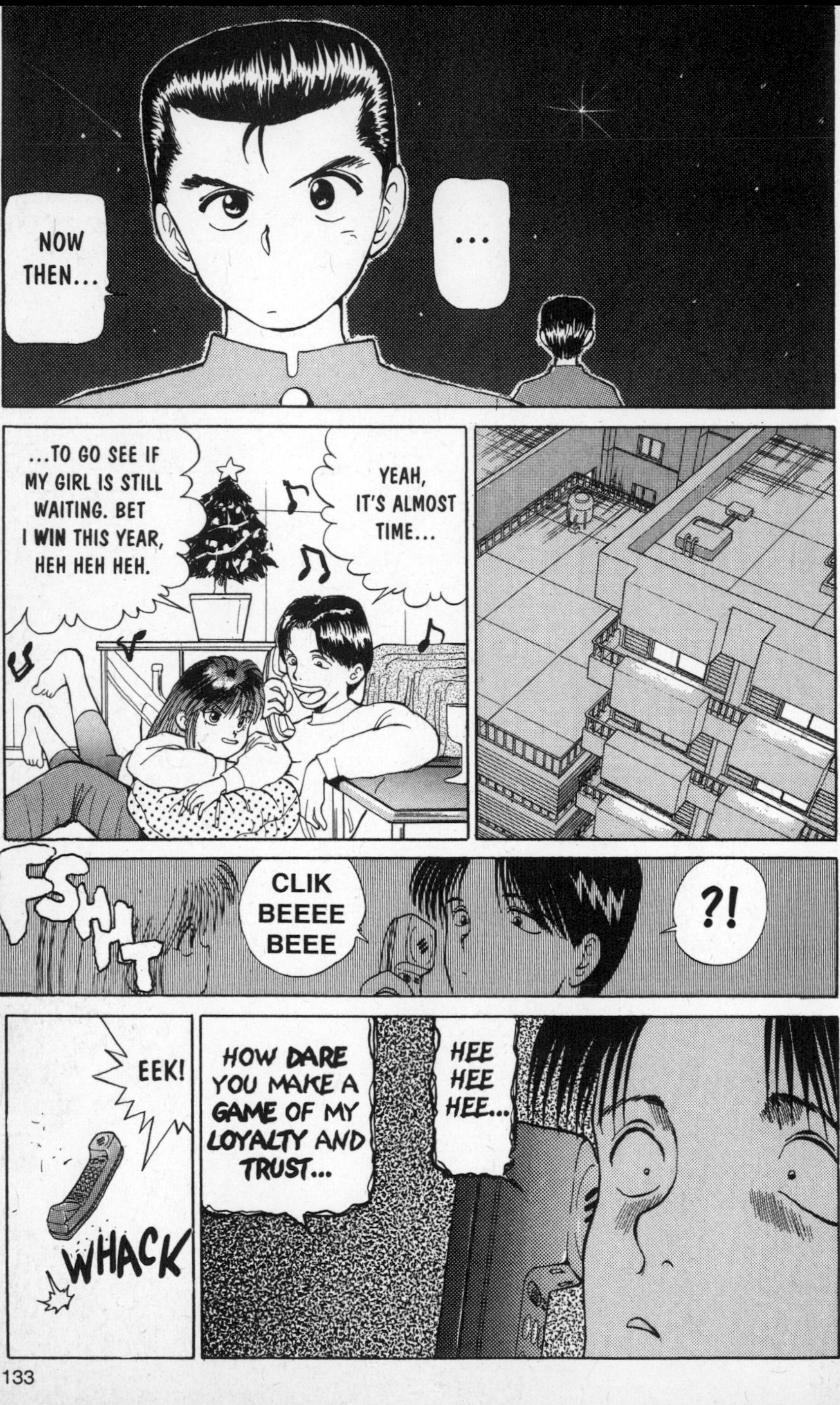
...
NOW THEN...
YEAH, IT'S ALMOST TIME...
...TO GO SEE IF MY GIRL IS STILL WAITING. BET I WIN THIS YEAR, HEH HEH HEH.
?!
CLIK BEEEE BEEE
FSHHT
HEE HEE HEE...
HOW DARE YOU MAKE A GAME OF MY LOYALTY AND TRUST...
EEK!
WHACK

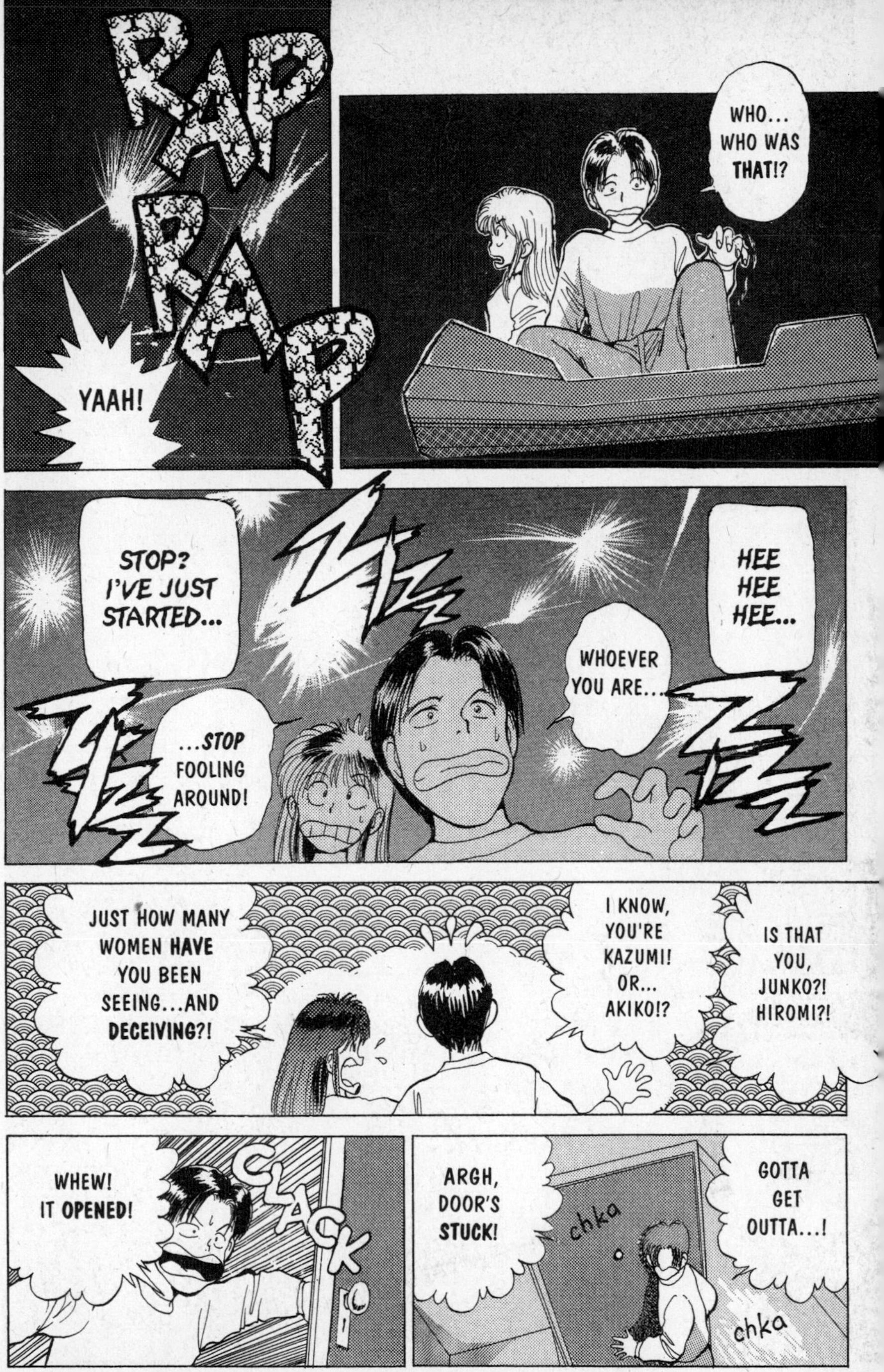
WHO... WHO WAS THAT!?
RAP RAP RAP
YAAH!
WHOEVER YOU ARE...
...STOP FOOLING AROUND!
STOP? I'VE JUST STARTED...
HEE HEE HEE...
IS THAT YOU, JUNKO?! HIROMI?!
I KNOW, YOU'RE KAZUMI! OR... AKIKO!?
JUST HOW MANY WOMEN HAVE YOU BEEN SEEING...AND DECEIVING?!
GOTTA GET OUTTA...!
chka
ARGH, DOOR'S STUCK!
chka
CLACK
WHEW! IT OPENED!

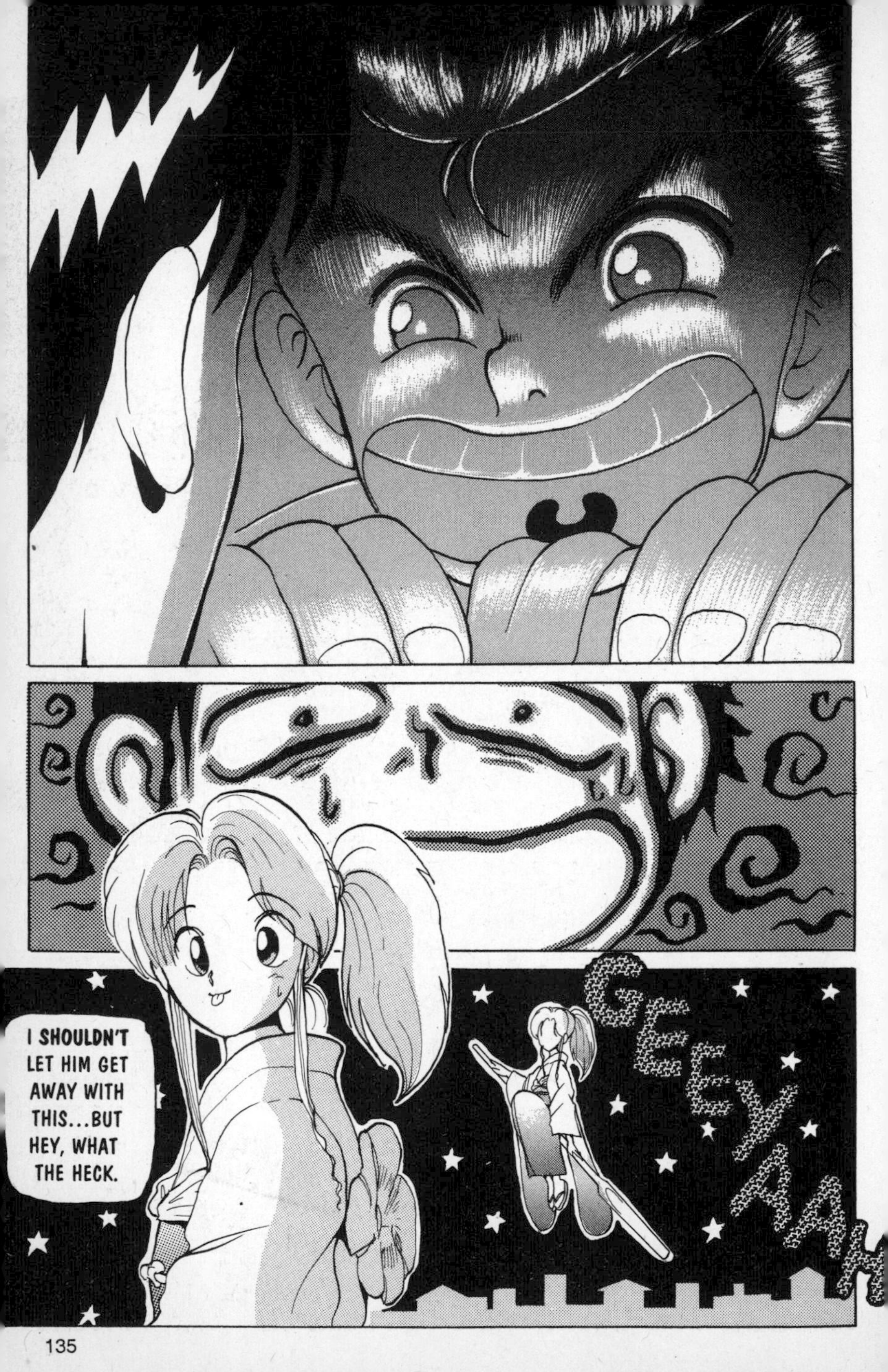
GEEEYAAH
I SHOULDN'T LET HIM GET AWAY WITH THIS...BUT HEY, WHAT THE HECK.

Seisaku Hakusho
("The Production Report")

Part 3

By Yoshihiro Togashi

GEN OTODA (male)

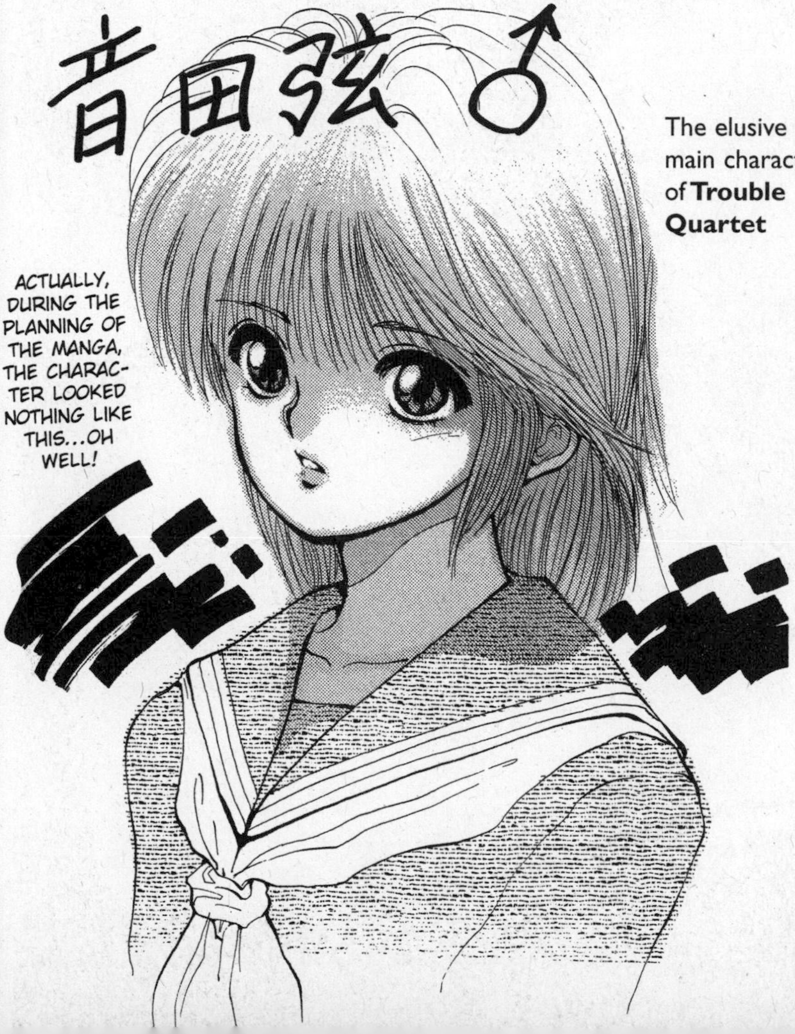

音田弦 ♂

The elusive main character of **Trouble Quartet**

ACTUALLY, DURING THE PLANNING OF THE MANGA, THE CHARACTER LOOKED NOTHING LIKE THIS...OH WELL!

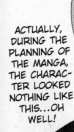

YuYu Hakusho™

by Yoshihiro Togashi

CHAPTER 6: THE LONELY JOURNEY

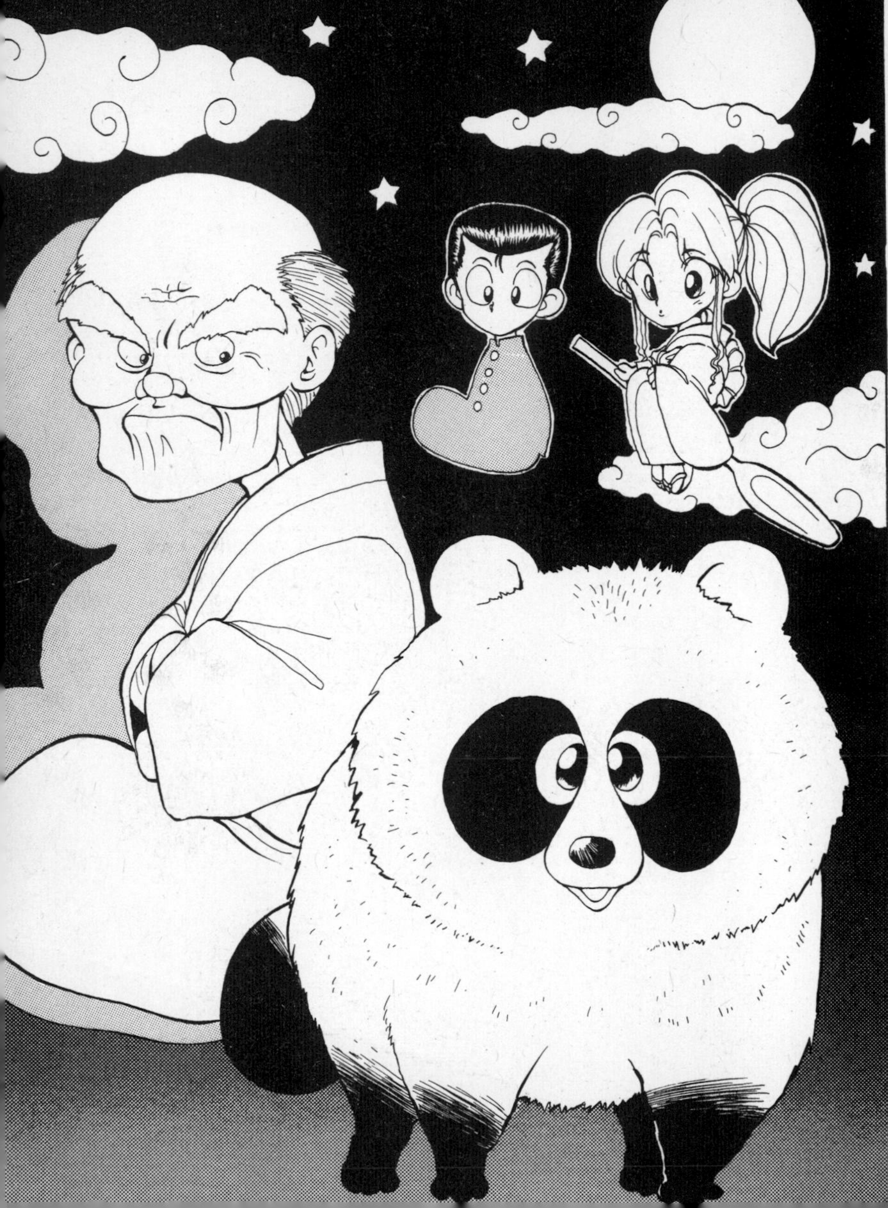

READ THIS WAY

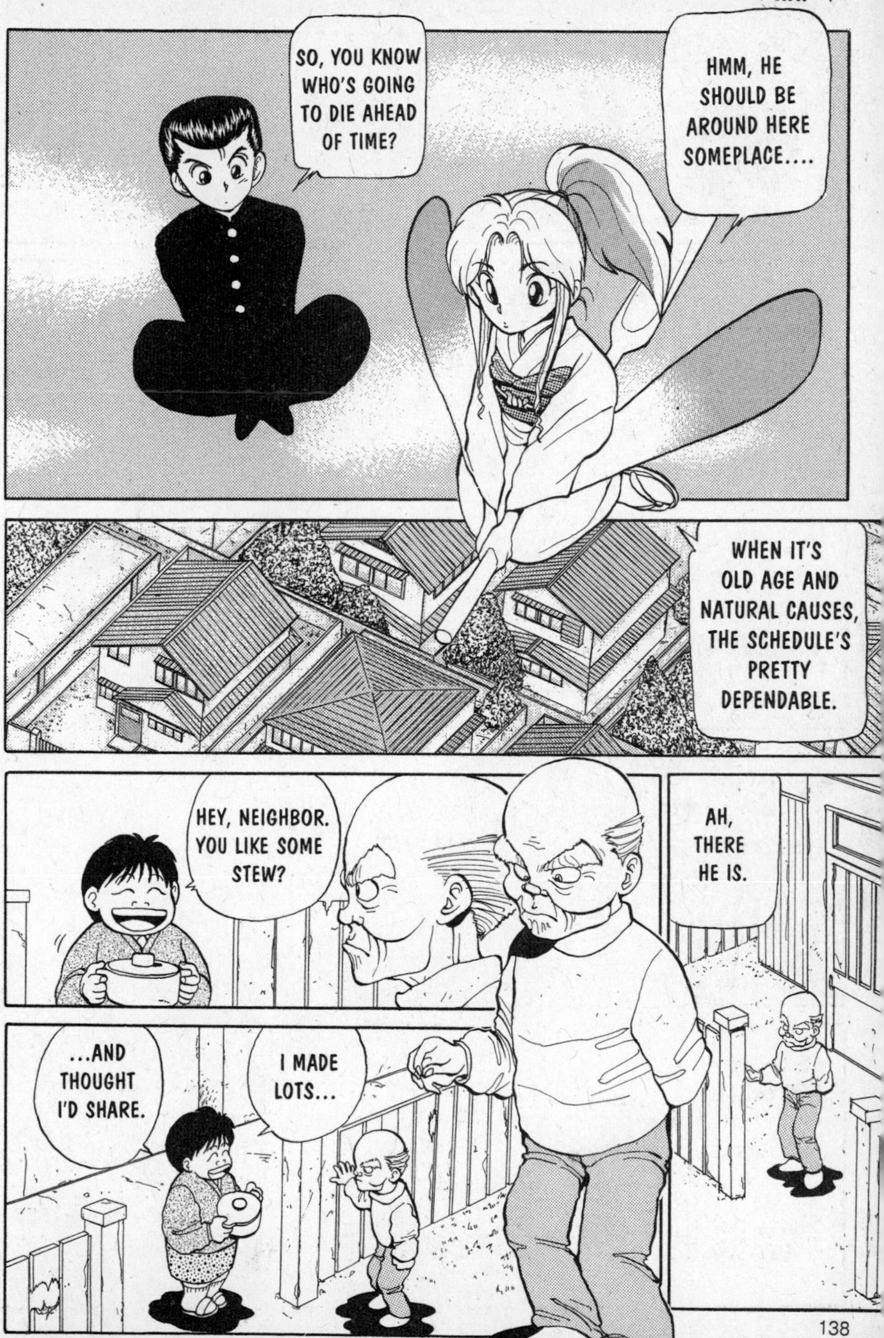
HMM, HE SHOULD BE AROUND HERE SOMEPLACE....
SO, YOU KNOW WHO'S GOING TO DIE AHEAD OF TIME?
WHEN IT'S OLD AGE AND NATURAL CAUSES, THE SCHEDULE'S PRETTY DEPENDABLE.
AH, THERE HE IS.
HEY, NEIGHBOR. YOU LIKE SOME STEW?
I MADE LOTS...
...AND THOUGHT I'D SHARE.

READ THIS WAY

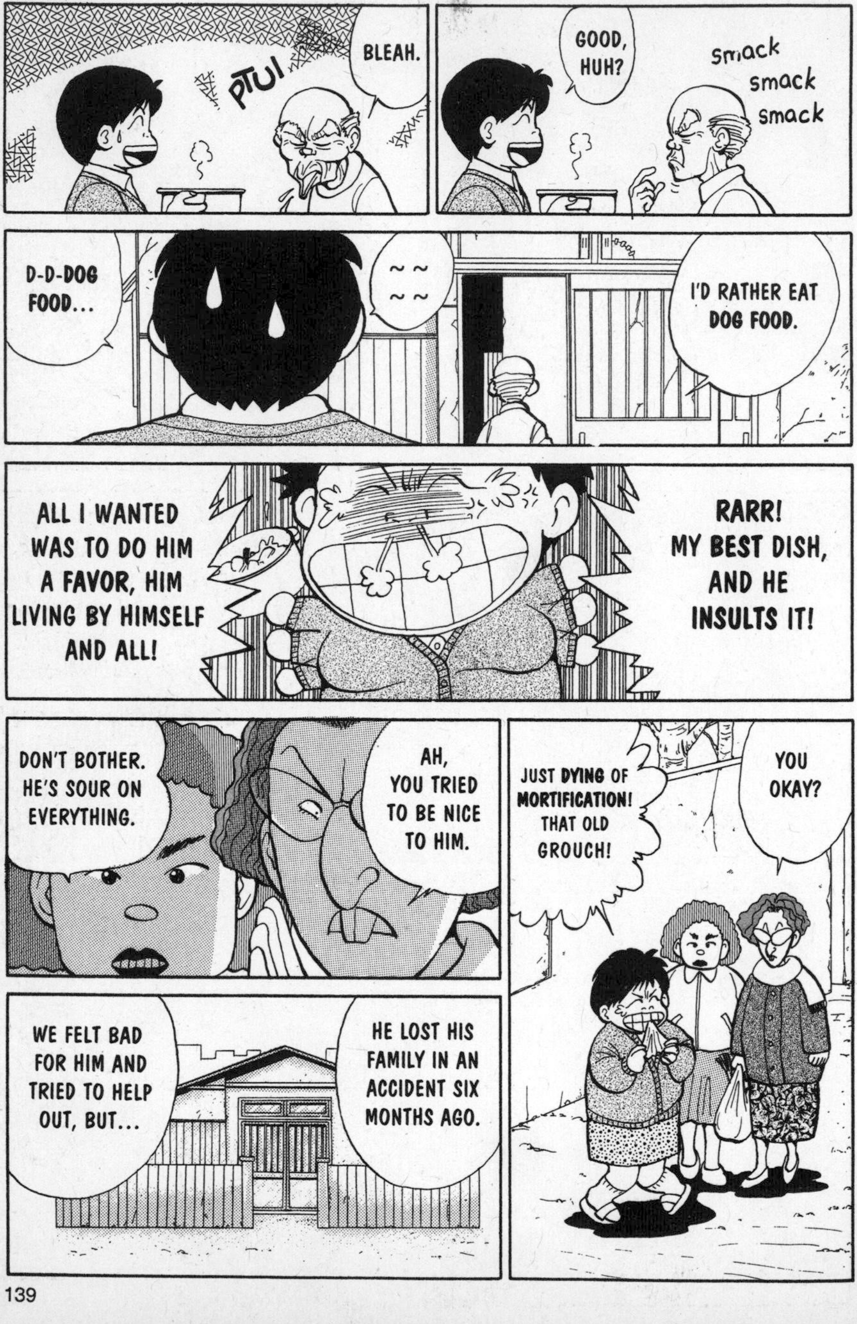
GOOD, HUH?
smack smack smack
BLEAH.
PTUI
I'D RATHER EAT DOG FOOD.
~~ ~~
D-D-DOG FOOD...
RARR! MY BEST DISH, AND HE INSULTS IT!
ALL I WANTED WAS TO DO HIM A FAVOR, HIM LIVING BY HIMSELF AND ALL!
YOU OKAY?
JUST DYING OF MORTIFICATION! THAT OLD GROUCH!
AH, YOU TRIED TO BE NICE TO HIM.
DON'T BOTHER. HE'S SOUR ON EVERYTHING.
HE LOST HIS FAMILY IN AN ACCIDENT SIX MONTHS AGO.
WE FELT BAD FOR HIM AND TRIED TO HELP OUT, BUT...

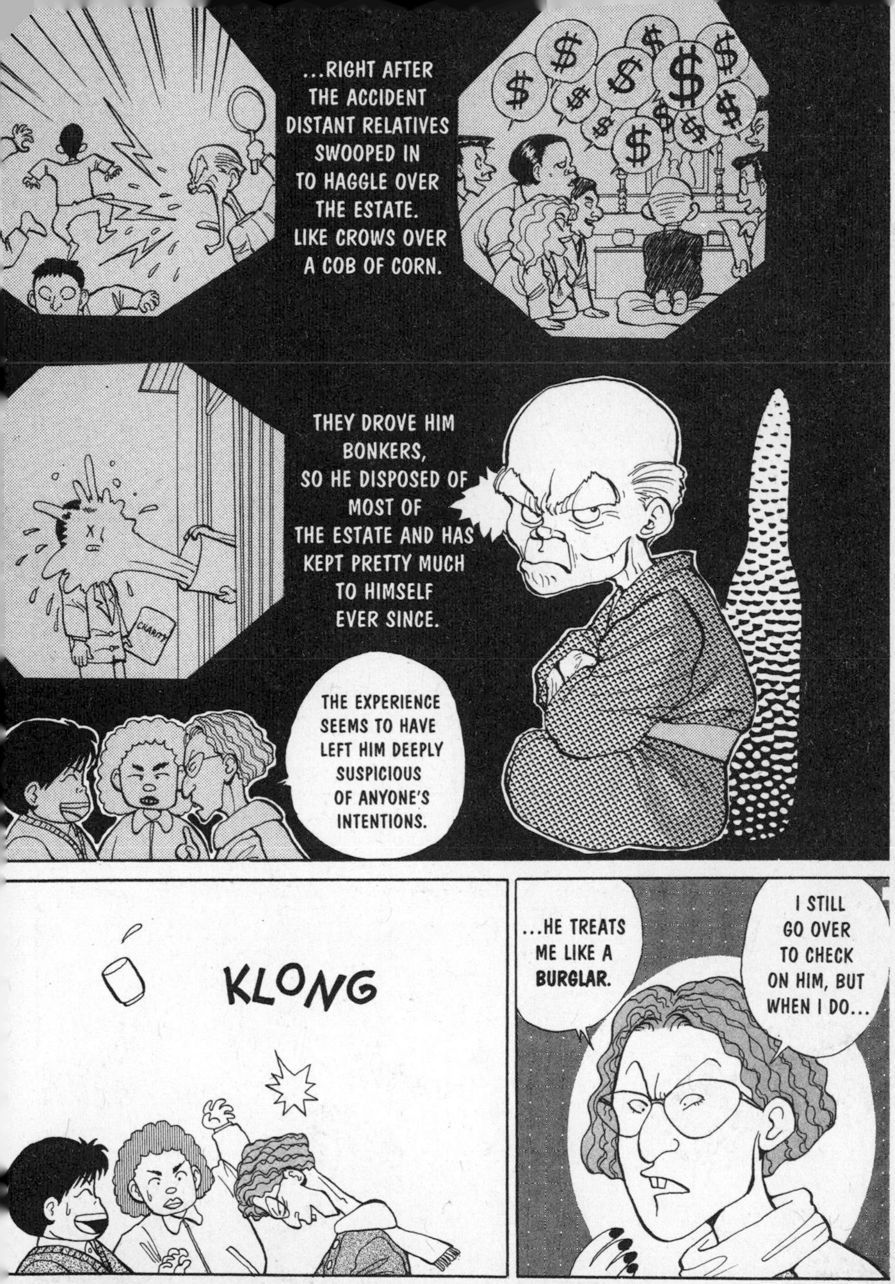
...RIGHT AFTER THE ACCIDENT DISTANT RELATIVES SWOOPED IN TO HAGGLE OVER THE ESTATE. LIKE CROWS OVER A COB OF CORN.
THEY DROVE HIM BONKERS, SO HE DISPOSED OF MOST OF THE ESTATE AND HAS KEPT PRETTY MUCH TO HIMSELF EVER SINCE.
THE EXPERIENCE SEEMS TO HAVE LEFT HIM DEEPLY SUSPICIOUS OF ANYONE'S INTENTIONS.
I STILL GO OVER TO CHECK ON HIM, BUT WHEN I DO...
...HE TREATS ME LIKE A **BURGLAR.**
KLONG

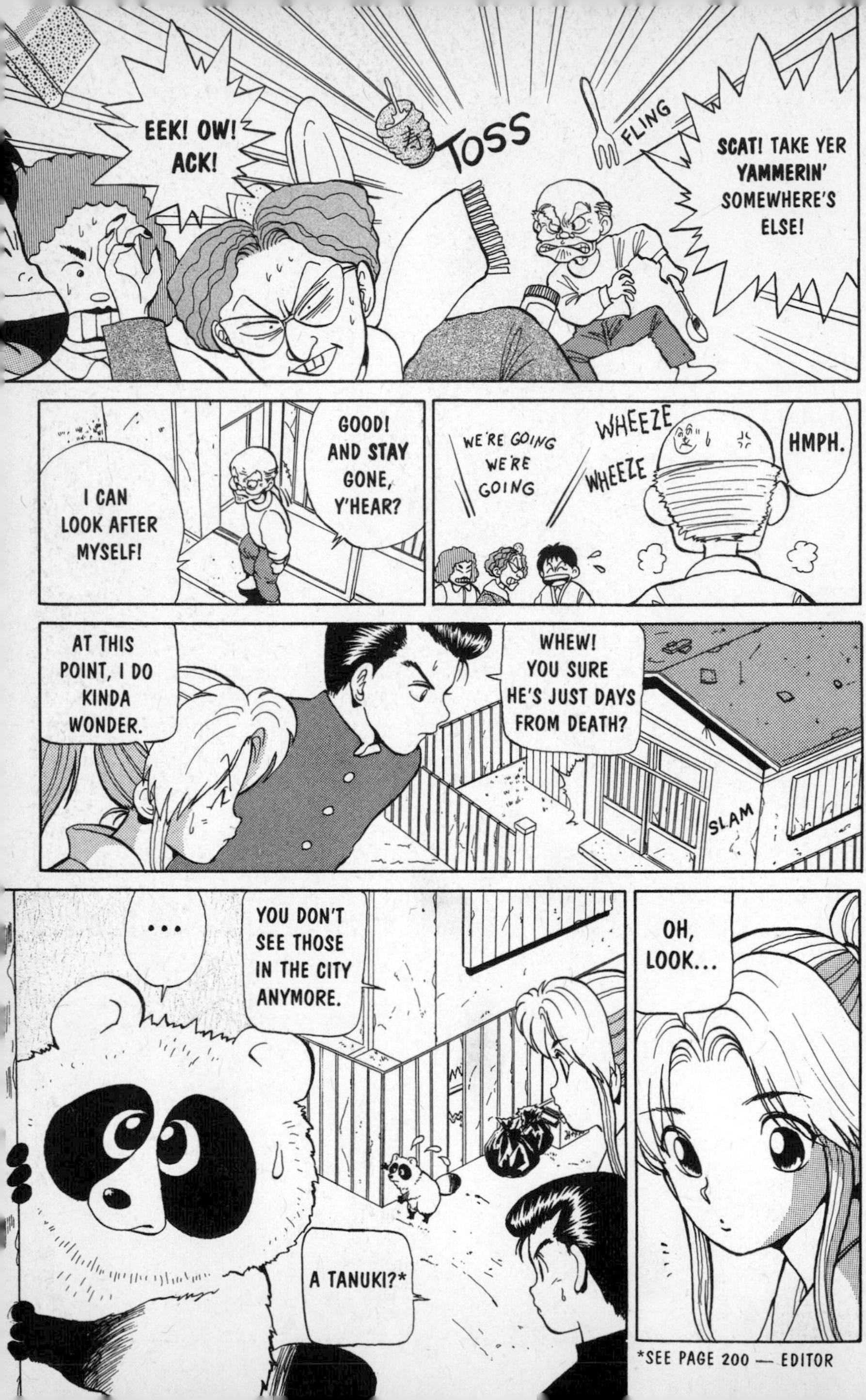
SCAT! TAKE YER YAMMERIN' SOMEWHERE'S ELSE!
FLING
TOSS
EEK! OW! ACK!
HMPH.
WHEEZE
WHEEZE
WE'RE GOING WE'RE GOING
GOOD! AND STAY GONE, Y'HEAR?
I CAN LOOK AFTER MYSELF!
WHEW! YOU SURE HE'S JUST DAYS FROM DEATH?
AT THIS POINT, I DO KINDA WONDER.
SLAM
OH, LOOK...
YOU DON'T SEE THOSE IN THE CITY ANYMORE.
...
A TANUKI?*

*SEE PAGE 200 — EDITOR

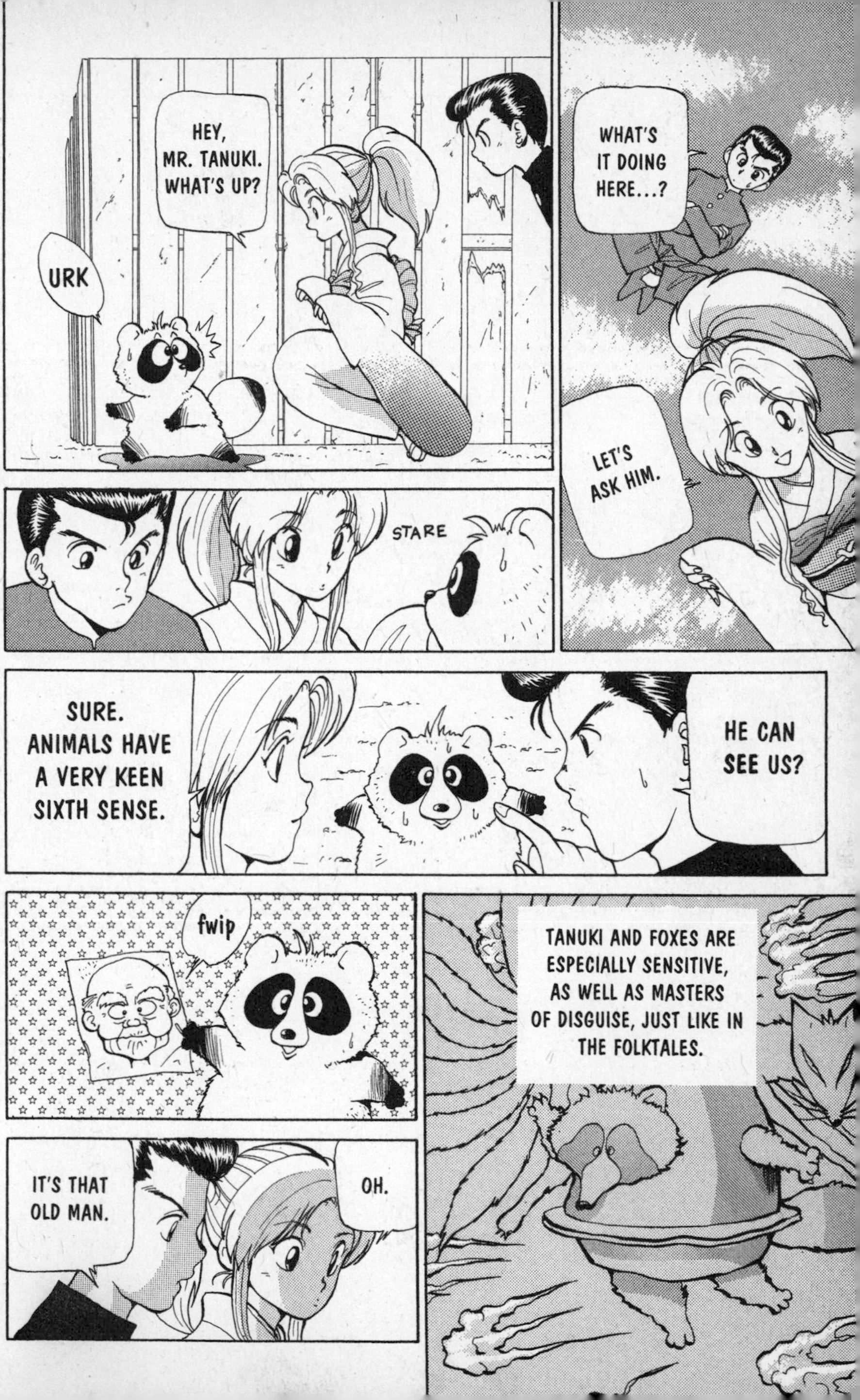
WHAT'S IT DOING HERE...?
LET'S ASK HIM.
HEY, MR. TANUKI. WHAT'S UP?
URK
STARE
HE CAN SEE US?
SURE. ANIMALS HAVE A VERY KEEN SIXTH SENSE.
TANUKI AND FOXES ARE ESPECIALLY SENSITIVE, AS WELL AS MASTERS OF DISGUISE, JUST LIKE IN THE FOLKTALES.
fwip
OH.
IT'S THAT OLD MAN.

READ THIS WAY

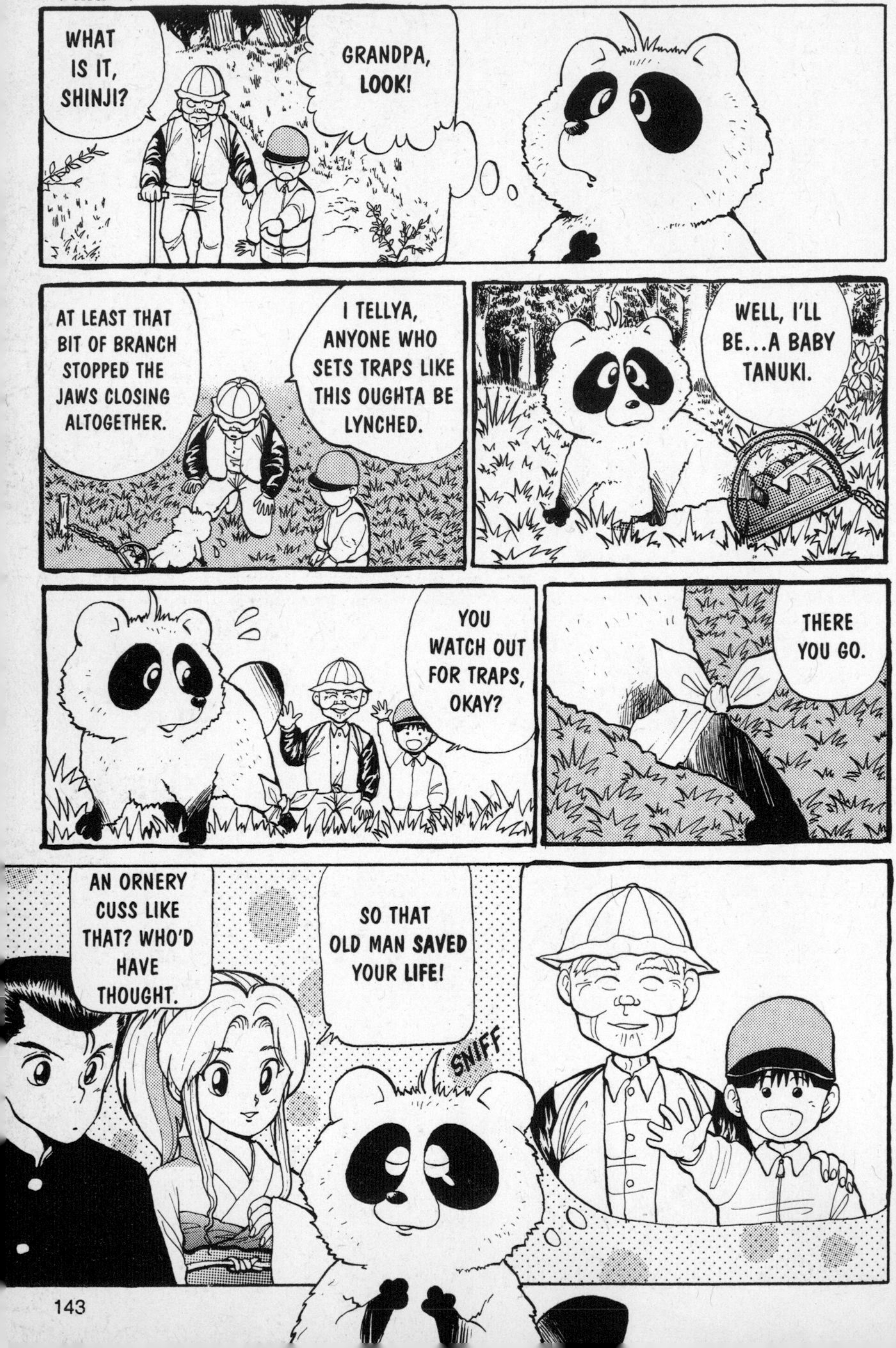
GRANDPA, LOOK!
WHAT IS IT, SHINJI?
WELL, I'LL BE...A BABY TANUKI.
I TELLYA, ANYONE WHO SETS TRAPS LIKE THIS OUGHTA BE LYNCHED.
AT LEAST THAT BIT OF BRANCH STOPPED THE JAWS CLOSING ALTOGETHER.
THERE YOU GO.
YOU WATCH OUT FOR TRAPS, OKAY?
SO THAT OLD MAN SAVED YOUR LIFE!
AN ORNERY CUSS LIKE THAT? WHO'D HAVE THOUGHT.
SNIFF

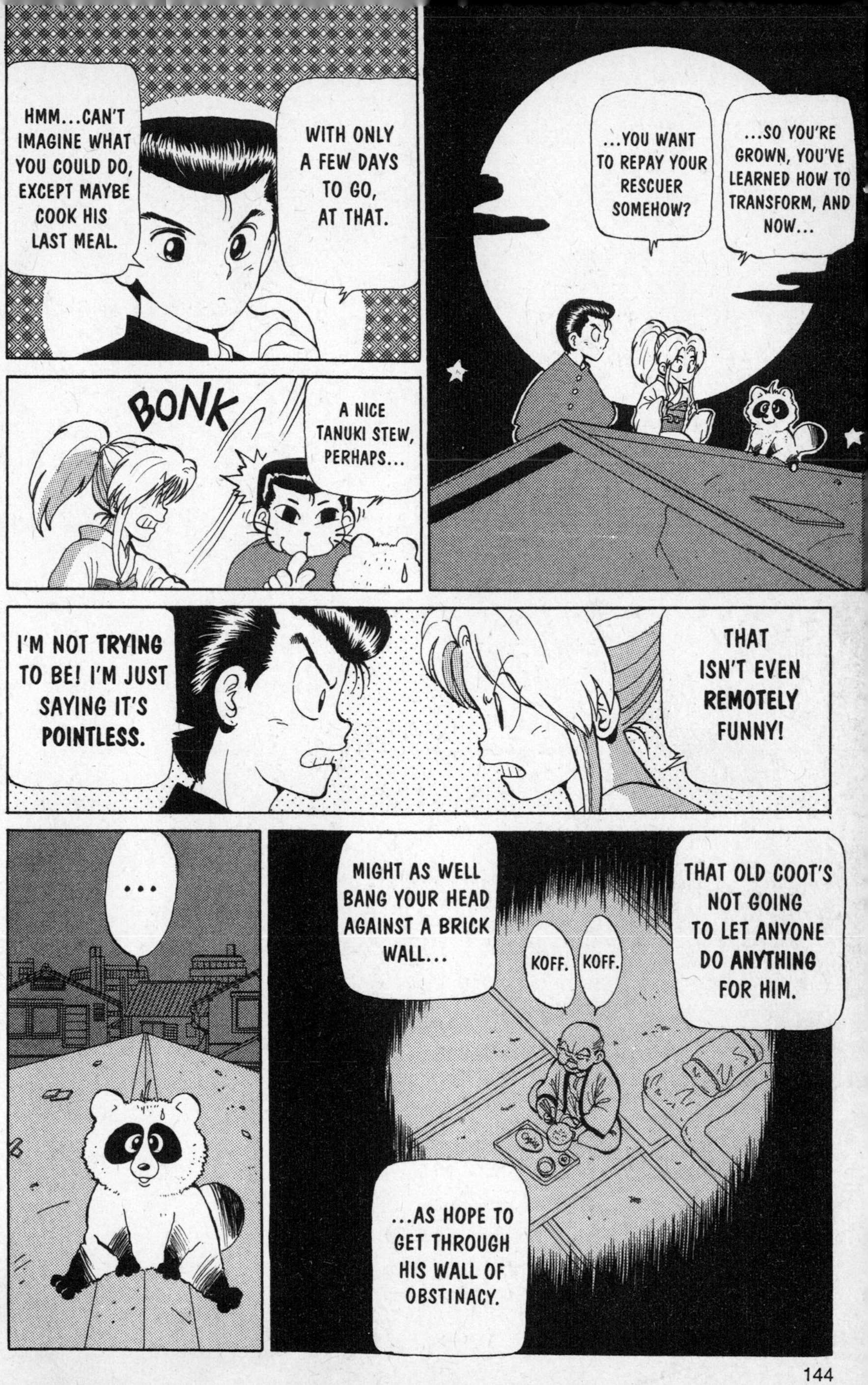
...SO YOU'RE GROWN, YOU'VE LEARNED HOW TO TRANSFORM, AND NOW...
...YOU WANT TO REPAY YOUR RESCUER SOMEHOW?
HMM...CAN'T IMAGINE WHAT YOU COULD DO, EXCEPT MAYBE COOK HIS LAST MEAL.
WITH ONLY A FEW DAYS TO GO, AT THAT.
A NICE TANUKI STEW, PERHAPS...
BONK
THAT ISN'T EVEN REMOTELY FUNNY!
I'M NOT TRYING TO BE! I'M JUST SAYING IT'S POINTLESS.
THAT OLD COOT'S NOT GOING TO LET ANYONE DO ANYTHING FOR HIM.
MIGHT AS WELL BANG YOUR HEAD AGAINST A BRICK WALL...
KOFF.
KOFF.
...AS HOPE TO GET THROUGH HIS WALL OF OBSTINACY.
...

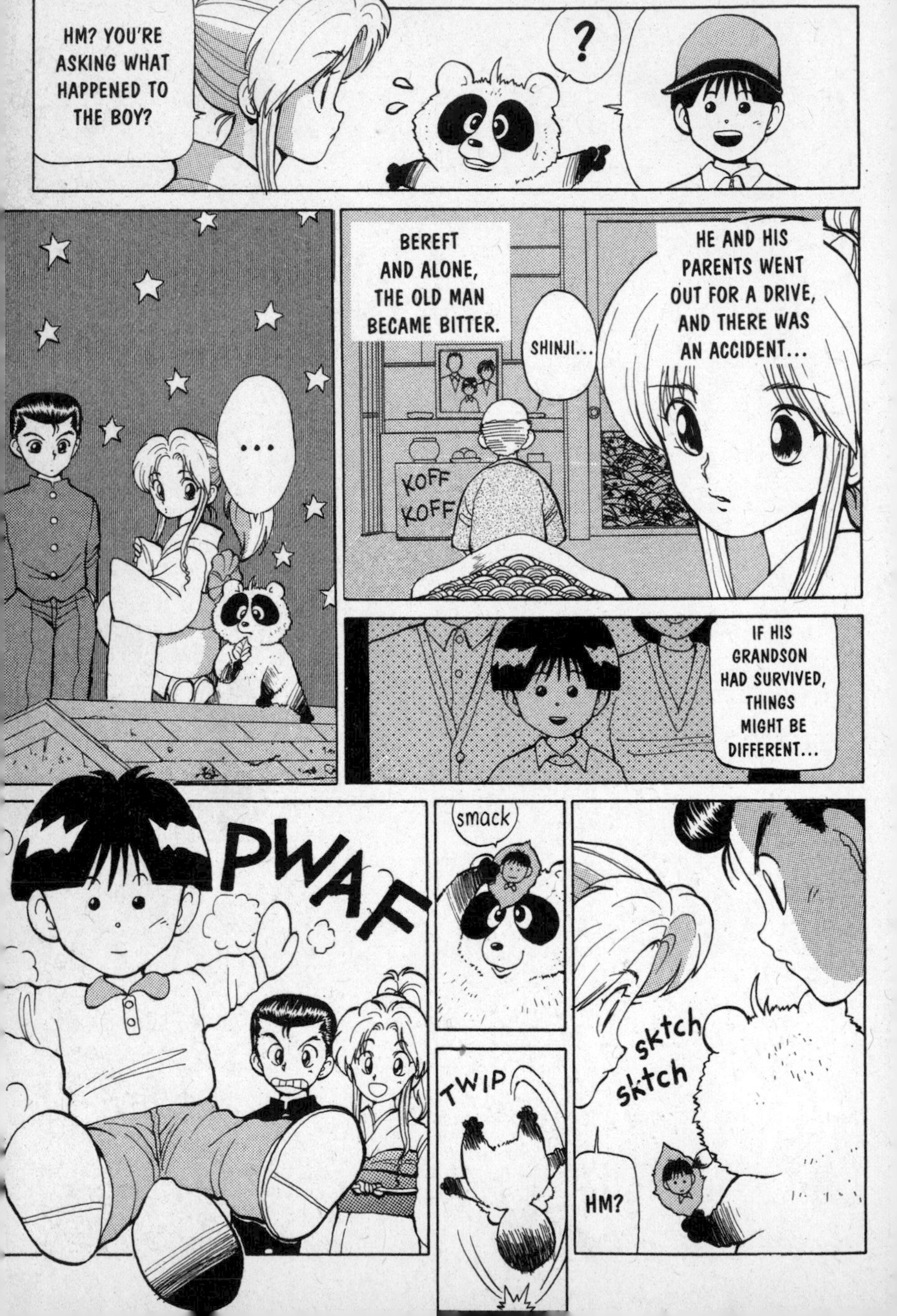
?
HM? YOU'RE ASKING WHAT HAPPENED TO THE BOY?
HE AND HIS PARENTS WENT OUT FOR A DRIVE, AND THERE WAS AN ACCIDENT...
BEREFT AND ALONE, THE OLD MAN BECAME BITTER.
SHINJI...
KOFF KOFF
IF HIS GRANDSON HAD SURVIVED, THINGS MIGHT BE DIFFERENT...
...
sktch sktch
HM?
smack
TWIP
PWAF

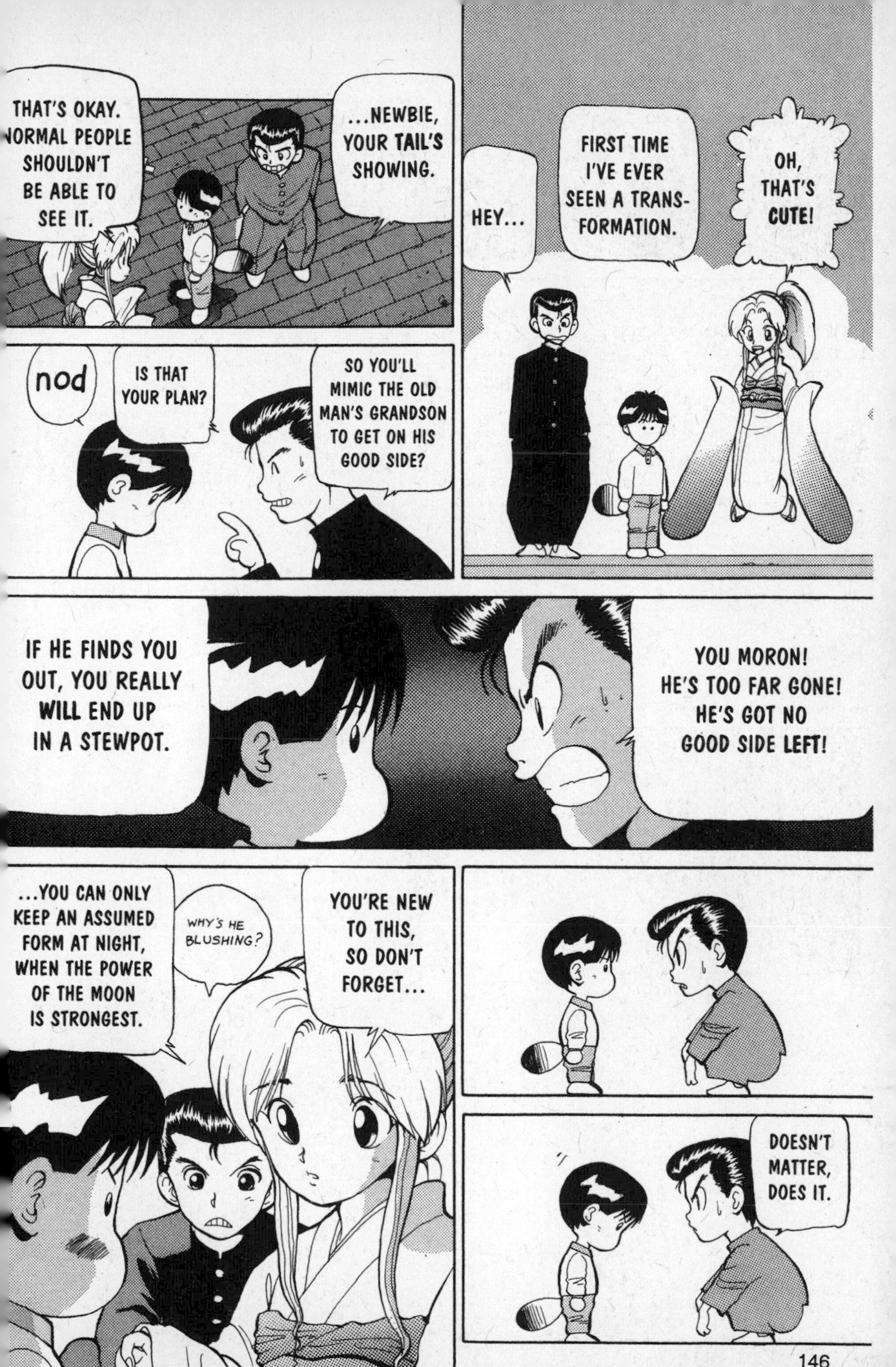
OH, THAT'S CUTE!
FIRST TIME I'VE EVER SEEN A TRANS-FORMATION.
HEY...
...NEWBIE, YOUR TAIL'S SHOWING.
THAT'S OKAY. NORMAL PEOPLE SHOULDN'T BE ABLE TO SEE IT.
SO YOU'LL MIMIC THE OLD MAN'S GRANDSON TO GET ON HIS GOOD SIDE?
IS THAT YOUR PLAN?
nod
YOU MORON! HE'S TOO FAR GONE! HE'S GOT NO GOOD SIDE LEFT!
IF HE FINDS YOU OUT, YOU REALLY WILL END UP IN A STEWPOT.
DOESN'T MATTER, DOES IT.
YOU'RE NEW TO THIS, SO DON'T FORGET...
WHY'S HE BLUSHING?
...YOU CAN ONLY KEEP AN ASSUMED FORM AT NIGHT, WHEN THE POWER OF THE MOON IS STRONGEST.

READ THIS WAY

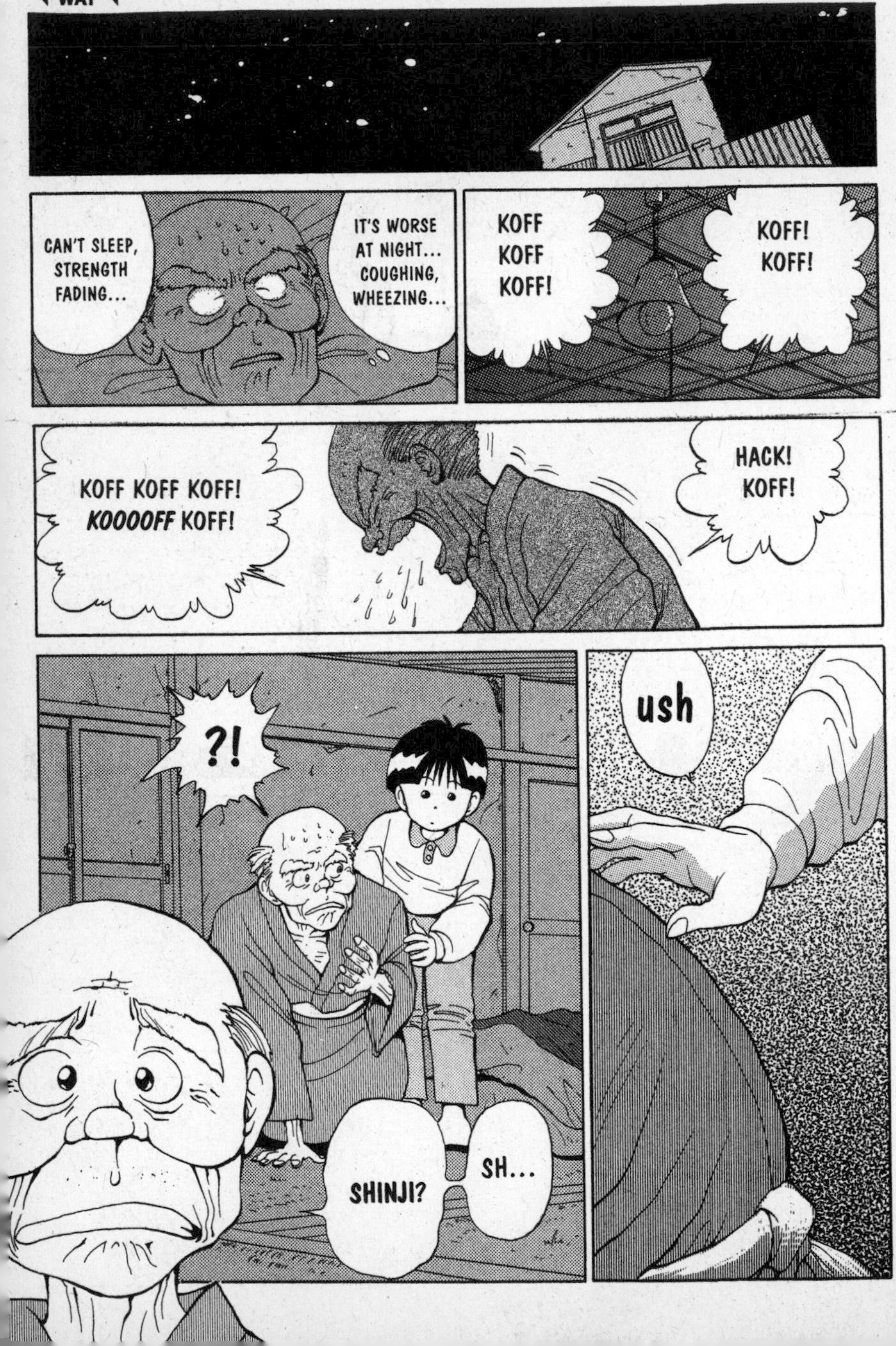
KOFF! KOFF!
KOFF KOFF KOFF!
IT'S WORSE AT NIGHT... COUGHING, WHEEZING...
CAN'T SLEEP, STRENGTH FADING...
HACK! KOFF!
KOFF KOFF KOFF! *KOOOOFF* KOFF!
ush
?!
SH...
SHINJI?

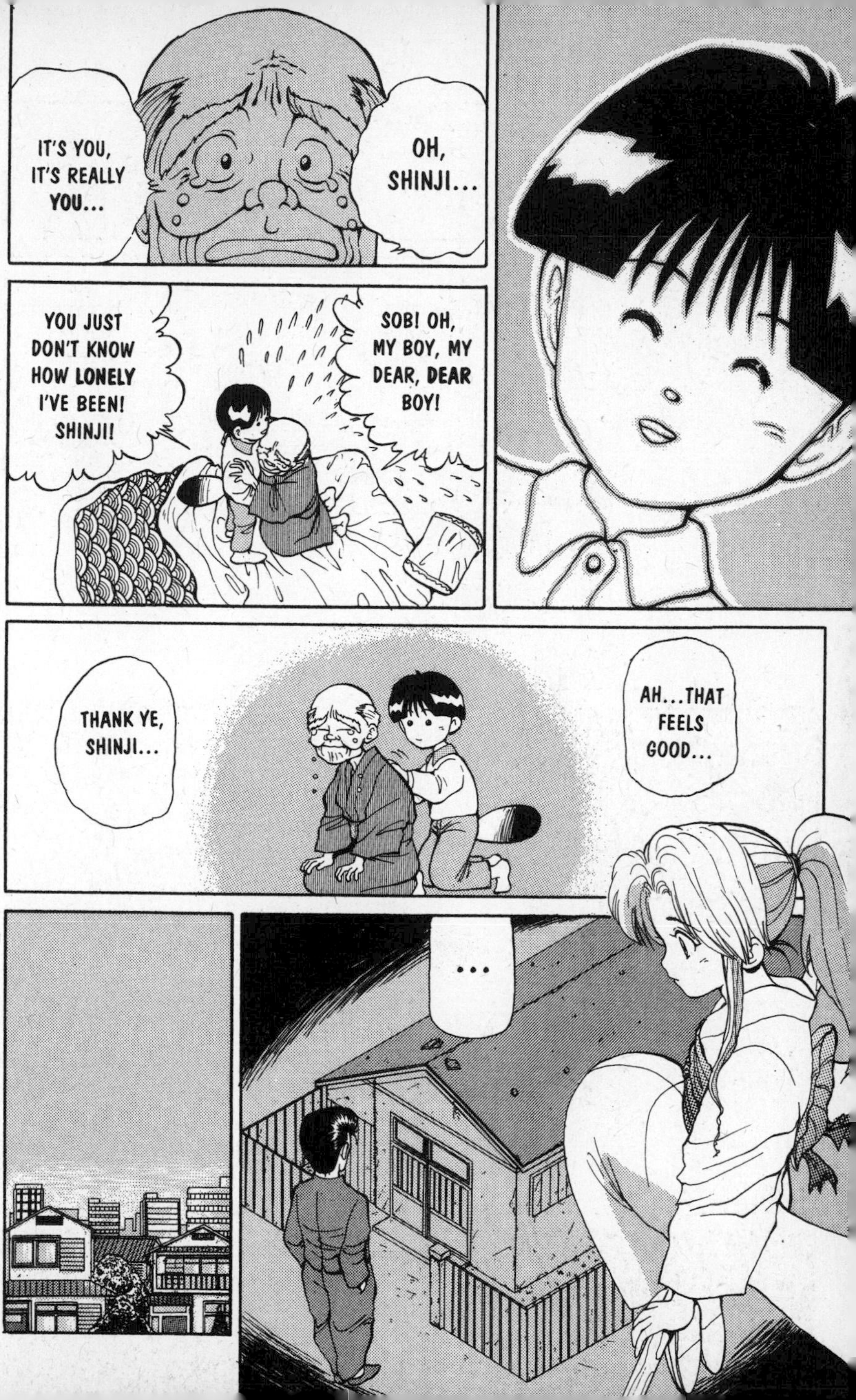
OH, SHINJI...
IT'S YOU, IT'S REALLY YOU...
SOB! OH, MY BOY, MY DEAR, DEAR BOY!
YOU JUST DON'T KNOW HOW LONELY I'VE BEEN! SHINJI!
AH...THAT FEELS GOOD...
THANK YE, SHINJI...
...

READ THIS WAY

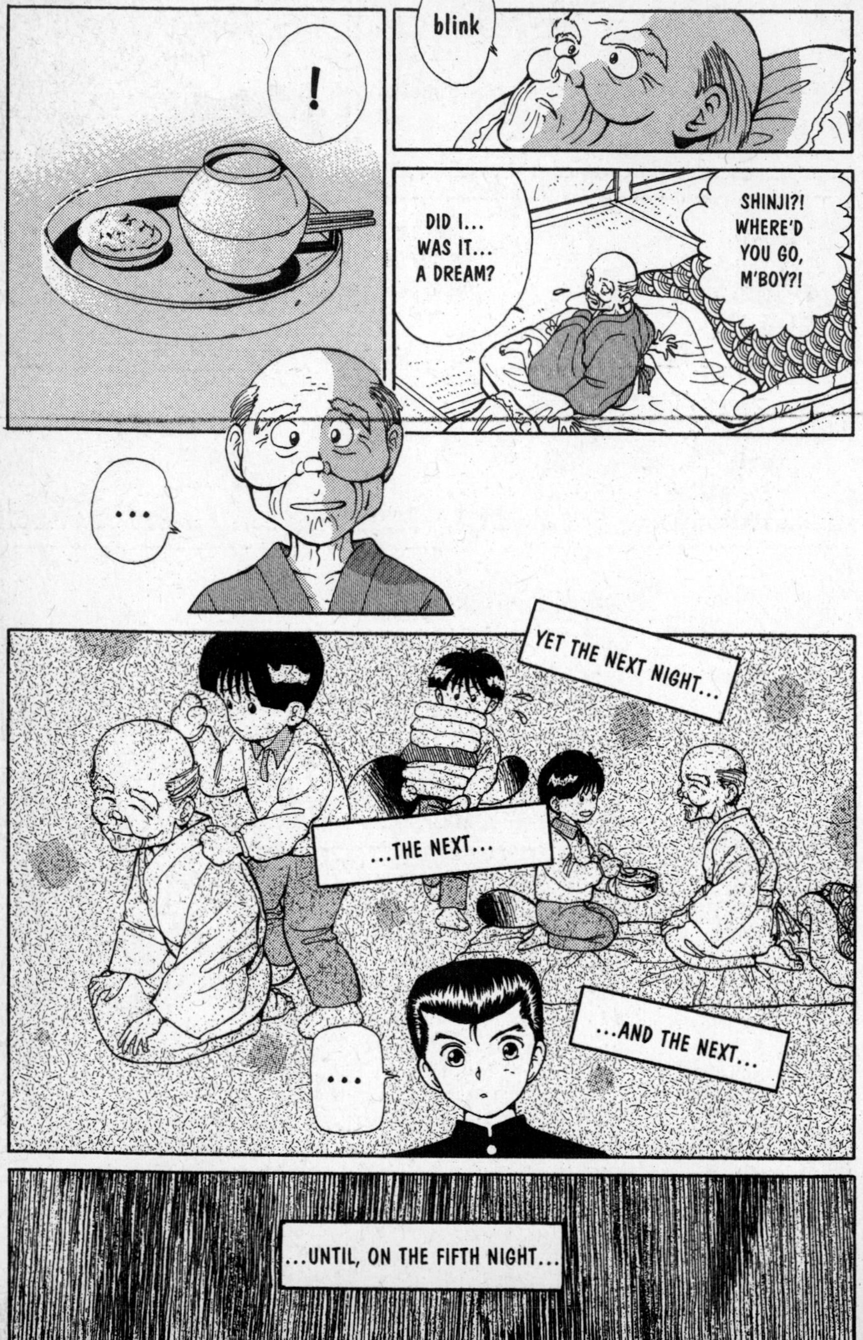
blink
SHINJI?! WHERE'D YOU GO, M'BOY?!
DID I... WAS IT... A DREAM?
!
...
YET THE NEXT NIGHT...
...THE NEXT...
...AND THE NEXT...
...
...UNTIL, ON THE FIFTH NIGHT...

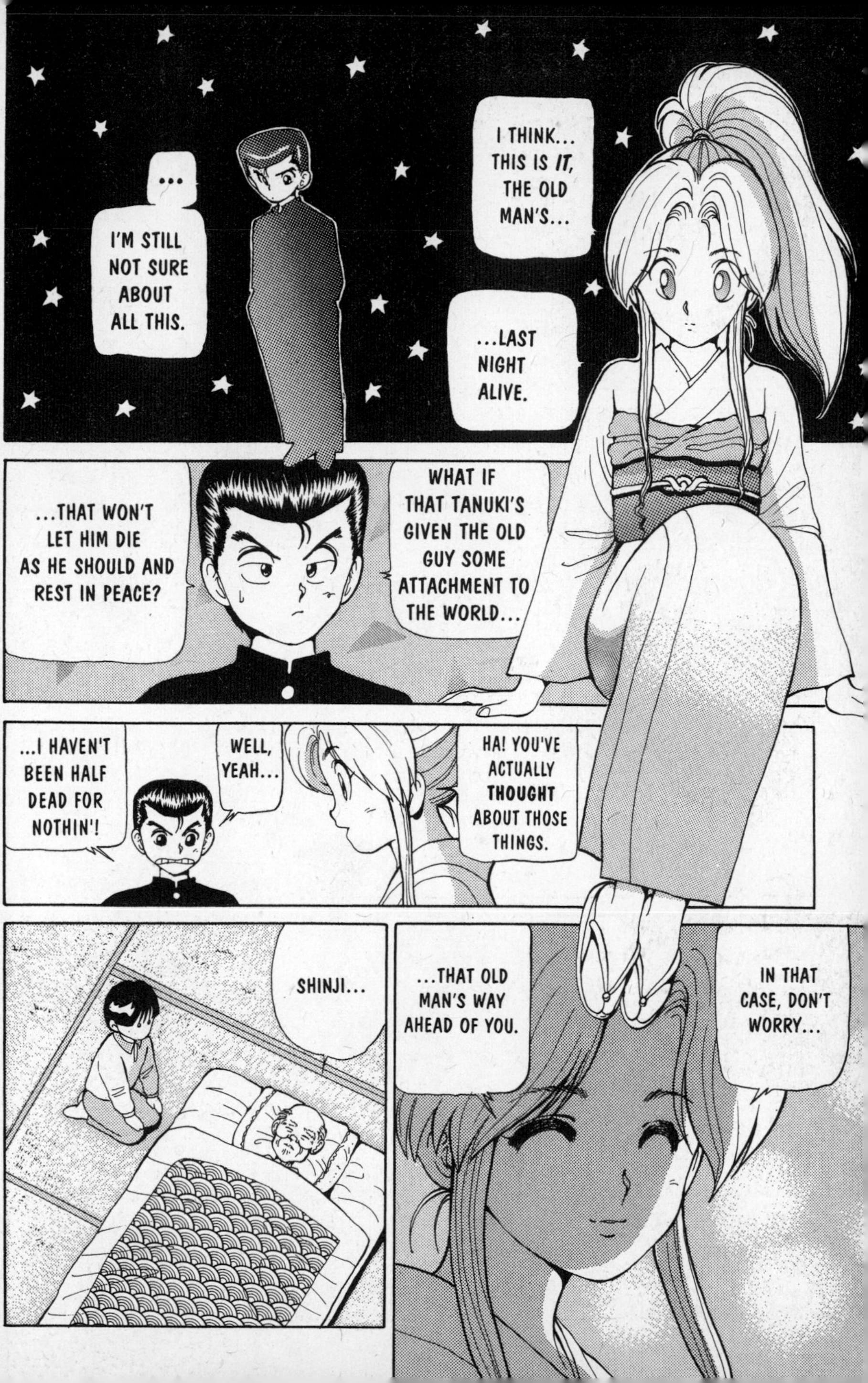
I THINK... THIS IS IT, THE OLD MAN'S...
...LAST NIGHT ALIVE.
...
I'M STILL NOT SURE ABOUT ALL THIS.
WHAT IF THAT TANUKI'S GIVEN THE OLD GUY SOME ATTACHMENT TO THE WORLD...
...THAT WON'T LET HIM DIE AS HE SHOULD AND REST IN PEACE?
HA! YOU'VE ACTUALLY THOUGHT ABOUT THOSE THINGS.
WELL, YEAH...
...I HAVEN'T BEEN HALF DEAD FOR NOTHIN'!
IN THAT CASE, DON'T WORRY...
...THAT OLD MAN'S WAY AHEAD OF YOU.
SHINJI...

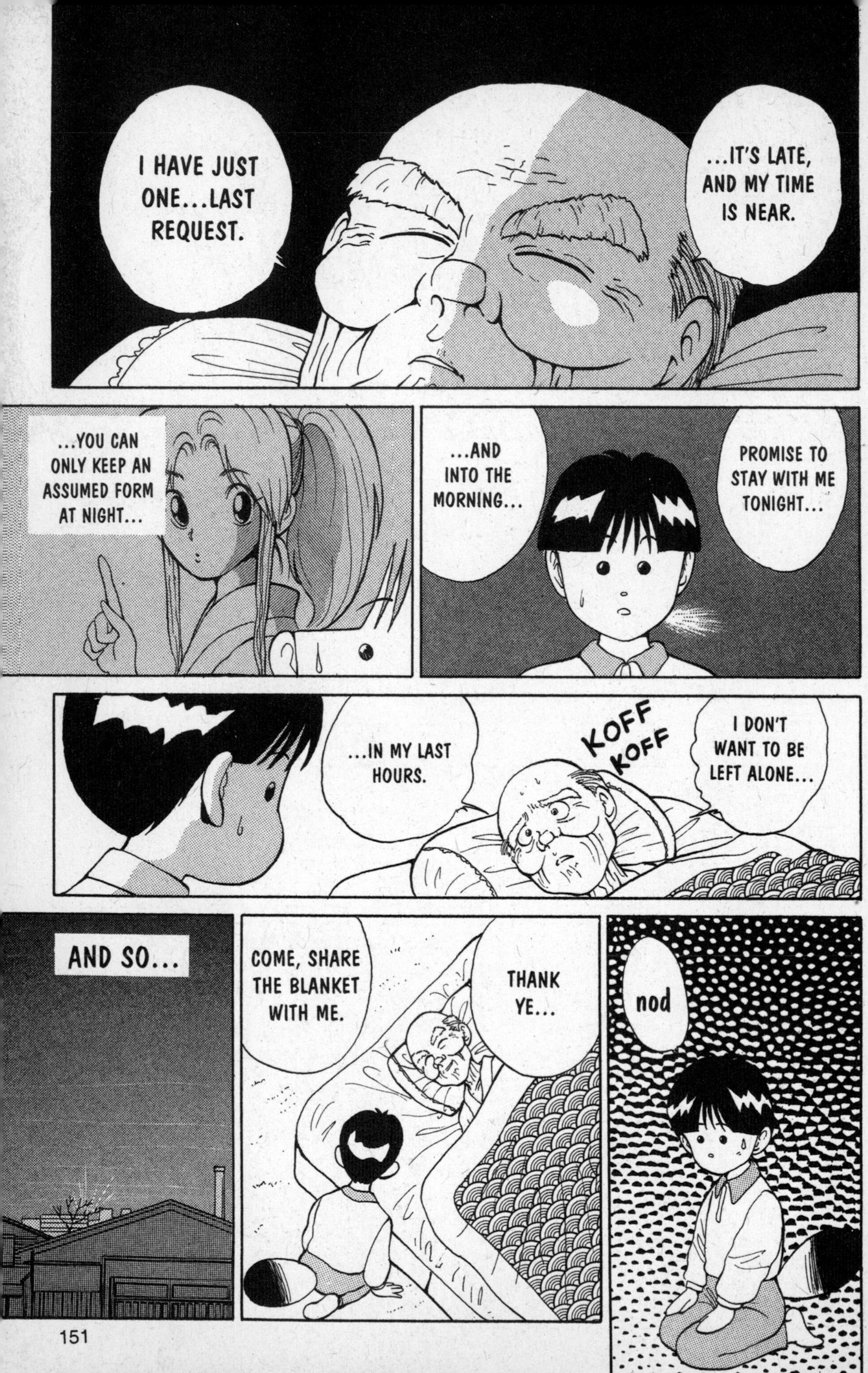
...IT'S LATE, AND MY TIME IS NEAR.
I HAVE JUST ONE...LAST REQUEST.
PROMISE TO STAY WITH ME TONIGHT...
...AND INTO THE MORNING...
...YOU CAN ONLY KEEP AN ASSUMED FORM AT NIGHT...
I DON'T WANT TO BE LEFT ALONE...
KOFF KOFF
...IN MY LAST HOURS.
nod
THANK YE...
COME, SHARE THE BLANKET WITH ME.
AND SO...

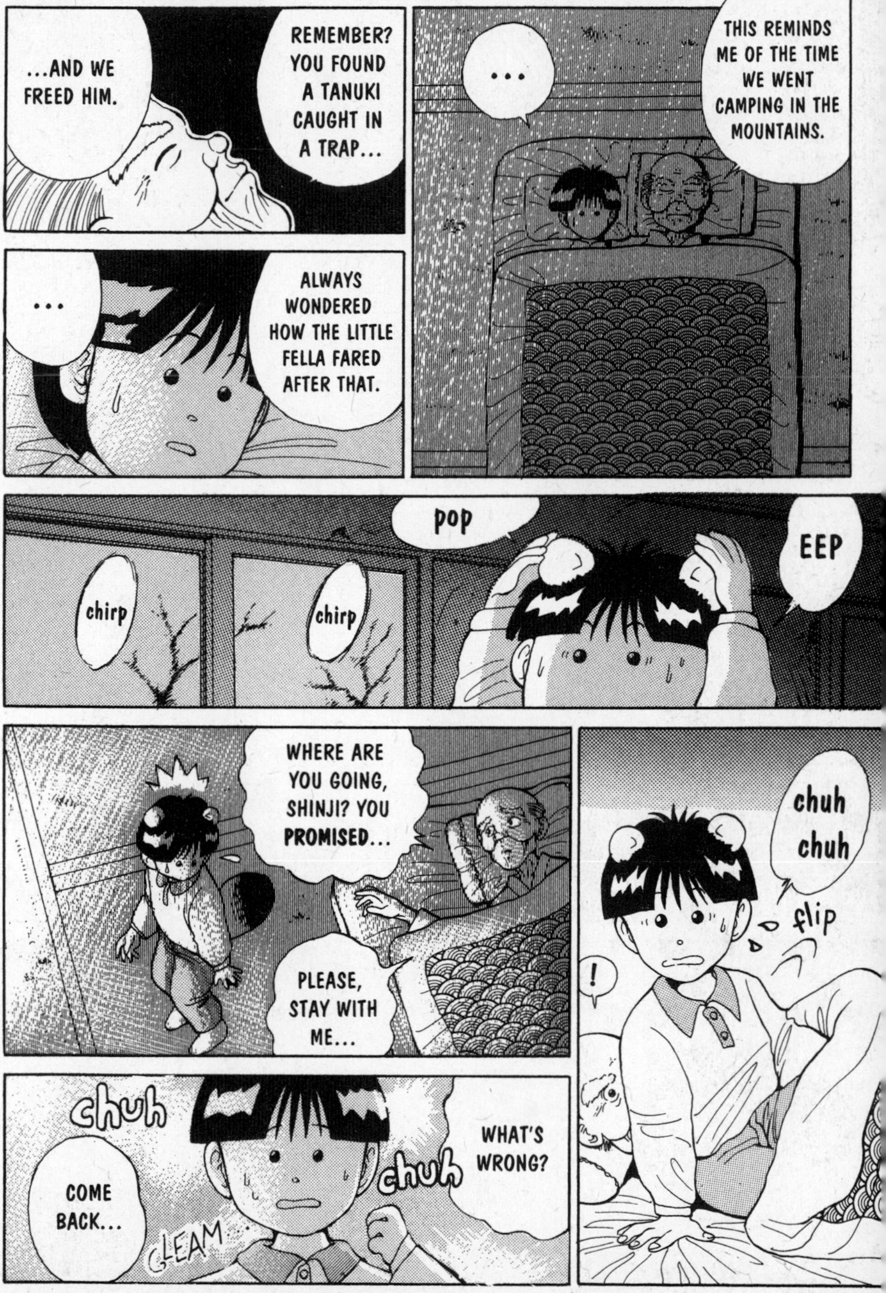
THIS REMINDS ME OF THE TIME WE WENT CAMPING IN THE MOUNTAINS.
...
REMEMBER? YOU FOUND A TANUKI CAUGHT IN A TRAP...
...AND WE FREED HIM.
ALWAYS WONDERED HOW THE LITTLE FELLA FARED AFTER THAT.
...
EEP
pop
chirp
chirp
chuh chuh
flip
!
WHERE ARE YOU GOING, SHINJI? YOU **PROMISED**...
PLEASE, STAY WITH ME...
WHAT'S WRONG?
chuh
chuh
COME BACK...
GLEAM

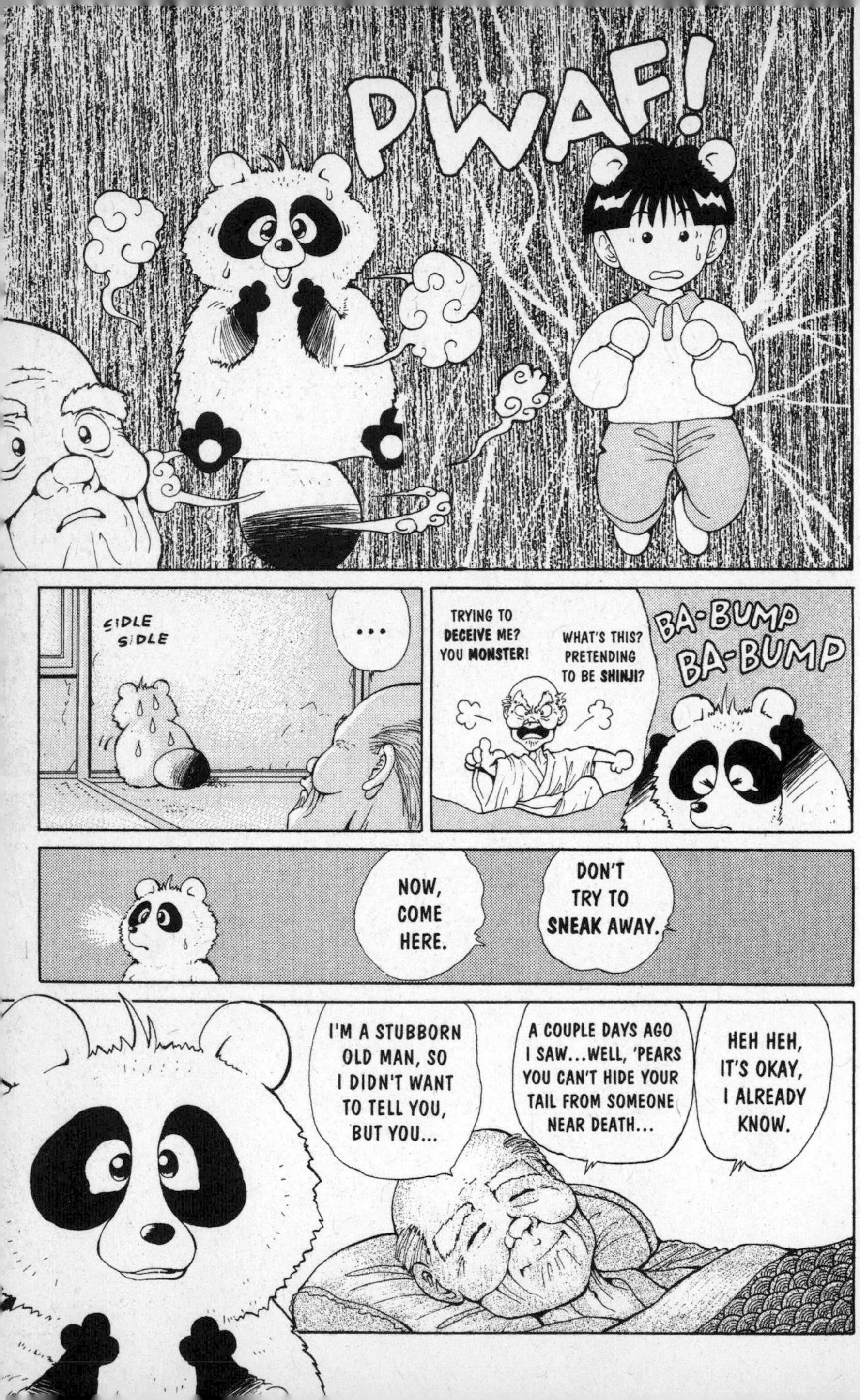
PWAF!
BA-BUMP BA-BUMP
WHAT'S THIS? PRETENDING TO BE SHINJI?
TRYING TO DECEIVE ME? YOU MONSTER!
...
SIDLE SIDLE
DON'T TRY TO SNEAK AWAY.
NOW, COME HERE.
HEH HEH, IT'S OKAY, I ALREADY KNOW.
A COUPLE DAYS AGO I SAW...WELL, 'PEARS YOU CAN'T HIDE YOUR TAIL FROM SOMEONE NEAR DEATH...
I'M A STUBBORN OLD MAN, SO I DIDN'T WANT TO TELL YOU, BUT YOU...

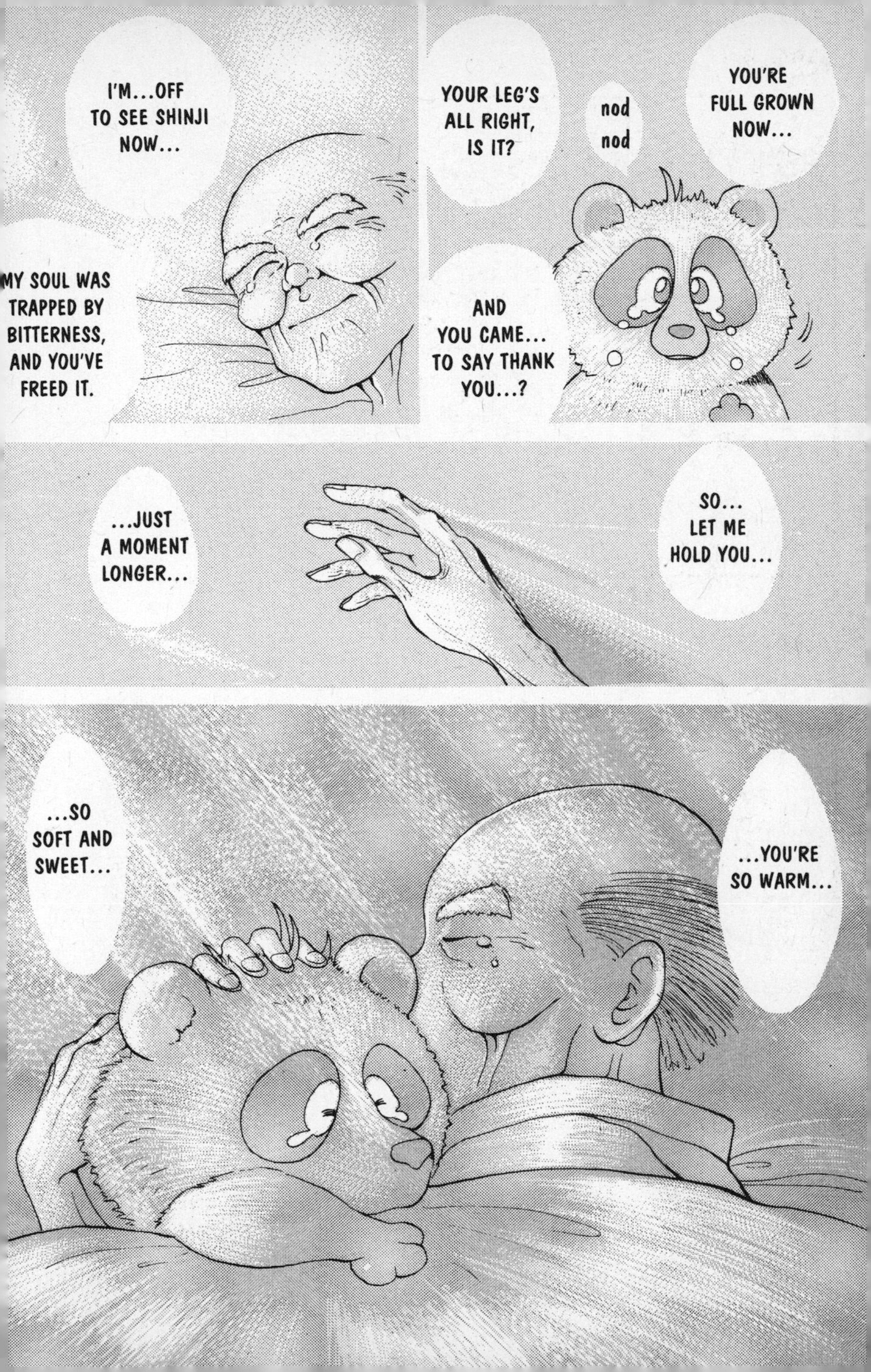
YOU'RE FULL GROWN NOW...
nod nod
YOUR LEG'S ALL RIGHT, IS IT?
AND YOU CAME... TO SAY THANK YOU...?
I'M...OFF TO SEE SHINJI NOW...
MY SOUL WAS TRAPPED BY BITTERNESS, AND YOU'VE FREED IT.
SO... LET ME HOLD YOU...
...JUST A MOMENT LONGER...
...YOU'RE SO WARM...
...SO SOFT AND SWEET...

READ THIS WAY

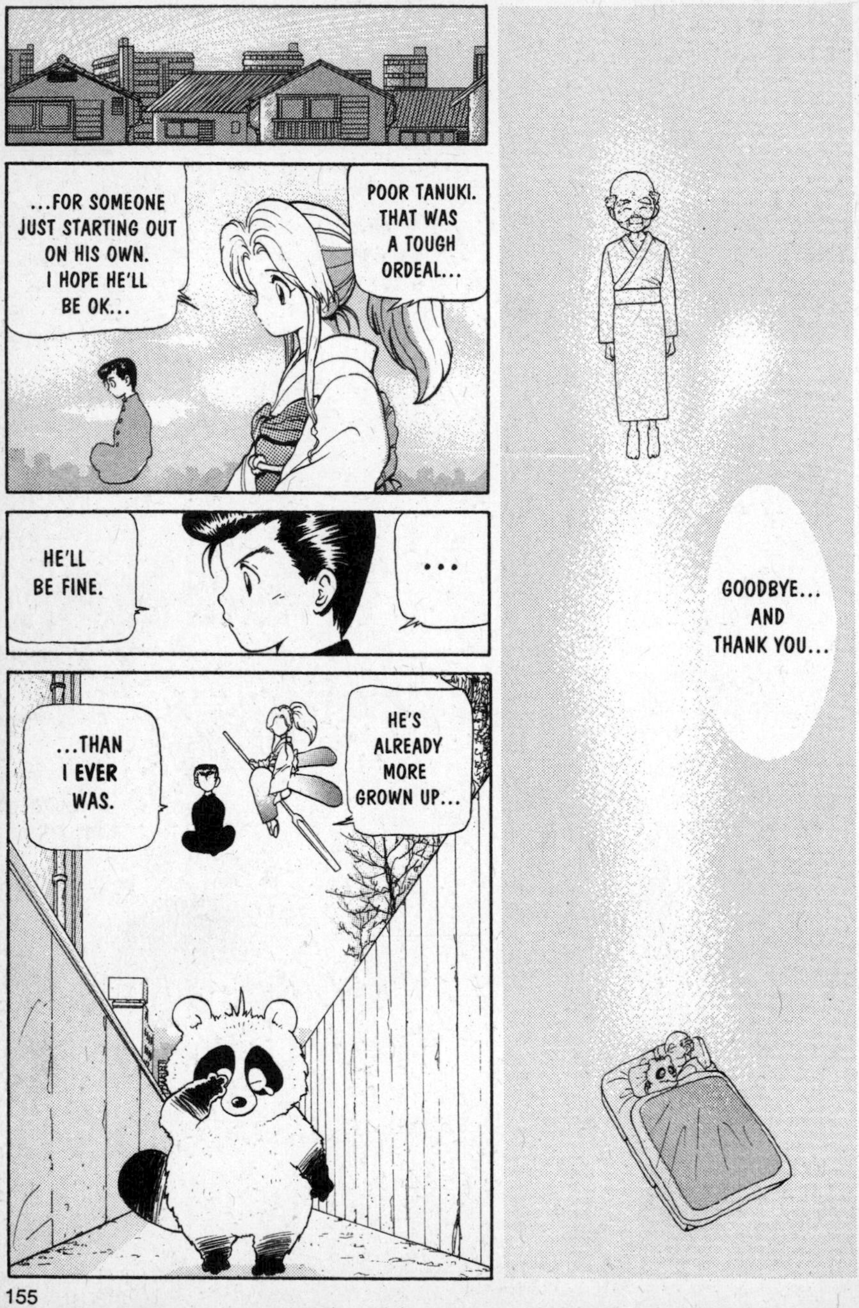

GOODBYE... AND THANK YOU...
POOR TANUKI. THAT WAS A TOUGH ORDEAL...
...FOR SOMEONE JUST STARTING OUT ON HIS OWN. I HOPE HE'LL BE OK...
...
HE'LL BE FINE.
HE'S ALREADY MORE GROWN UP...
...THAN I EVER WAS.

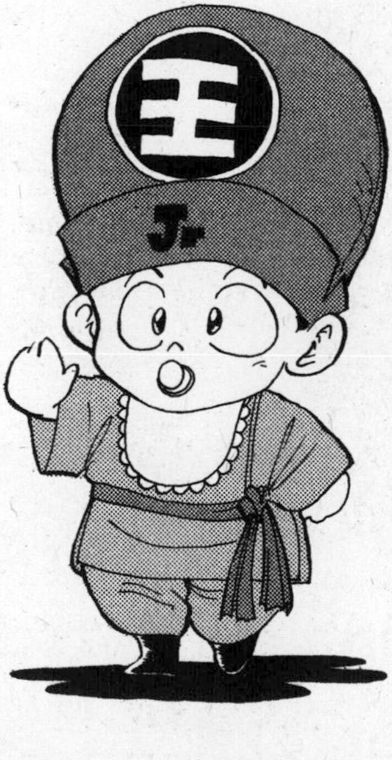
王
Jr

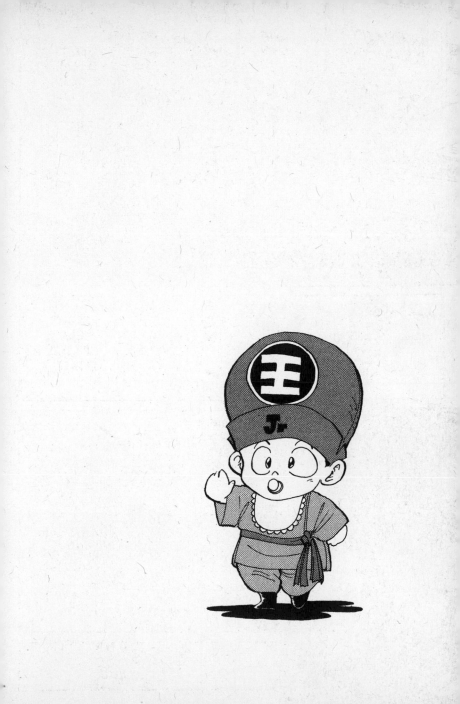

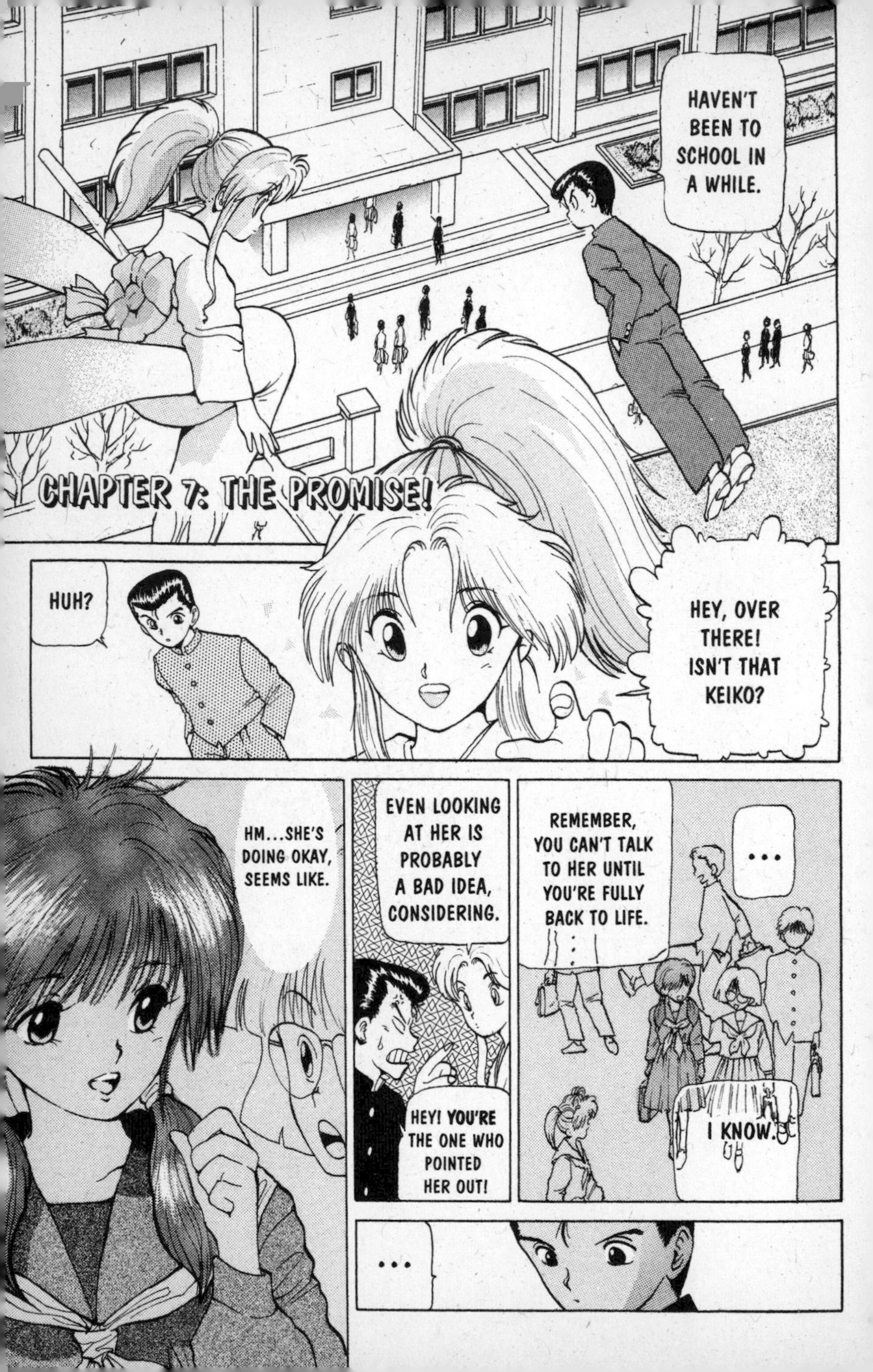

HAVEN'T BEEN TO SCHOOL IN A WHILE.
CHAPTER 7: THE PROMISE!
HUH?
HEY, OVER THERE! ISN'T THAT KEIKO?
HM...SHE'S DOING OKAY, SEEMS LIKE.
EVEN LOOKING AT HER IS PROBABLY A BAD IDEA, CONSIDERING.
HEY! YOU'RE THE ONE WHO POINTED HER OUT!
REMEMBER, YOU CAN'T TALK TO HER UNTIL YOU'RE FULLY BACK TO LIFE.
...
I KNOW.
...

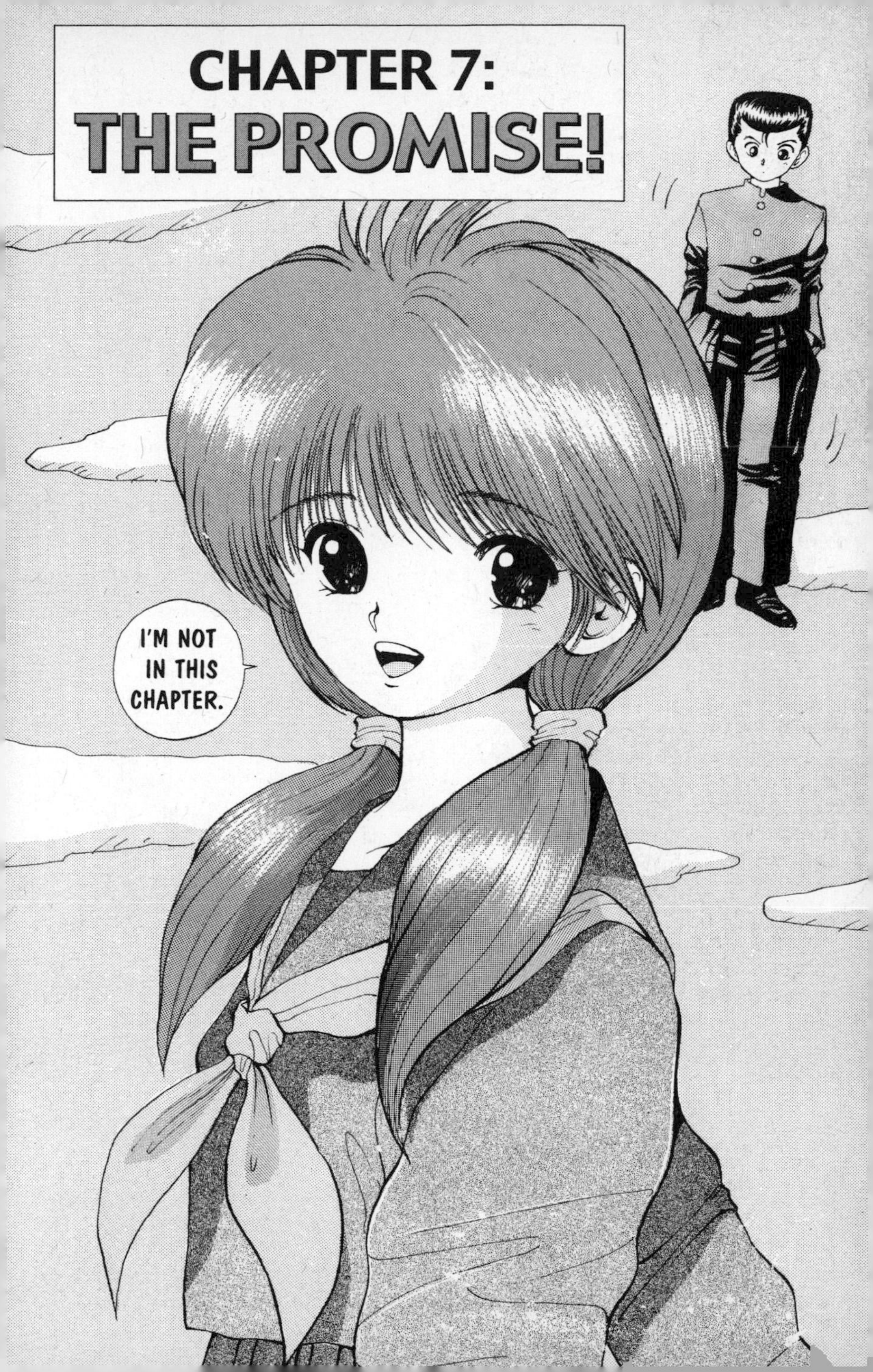
CHAPTER 7:
THE PROMISE!
I'M NOT IN THIS CHAPTER.

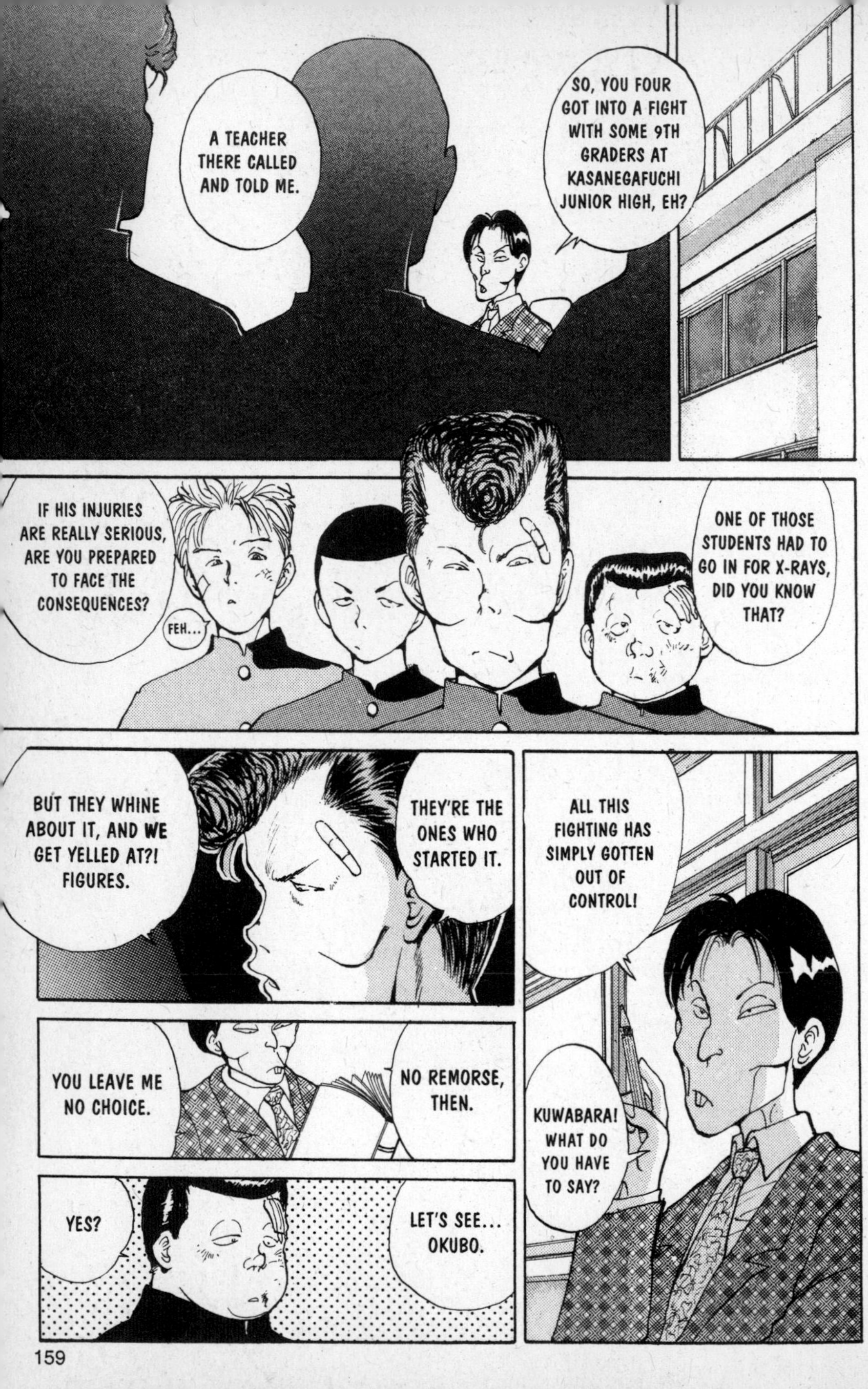
SO, YOU FOUR GOT INTO A FIGHT WITH SOME 9TH GRADERS AT KASANEGAFUCHI JUNIOR HIGH, EH?
A TEACHER THERE CALLED AND TOLD ME.
ONE OF THOSE STUDENTS HAD TO GO IN FOR X-RAYS, DID YOU KNOW THAT?
IF HIS INJURIES ARE REALLY SERIOUS, ARE YOU PREPARED TO FACE THE CONSEQUENCES?
FEH...
ALL THIS FIGHTING HAS SIMPLY GOTTEN OUT OF CONTROL!
KUWABARA! WHAT DO YOU HAVE TO SAY?
THEY'RE THE ONES WHO STARTED IT.
BUT THEY WHINE ABOUT IT, AND WE GET YELLED AT?! FIGURES.
NO REMORSE, THEN.
YOU LEAVE ME NO CHOICE.
LET'S SEE... OKUBO.
YES?

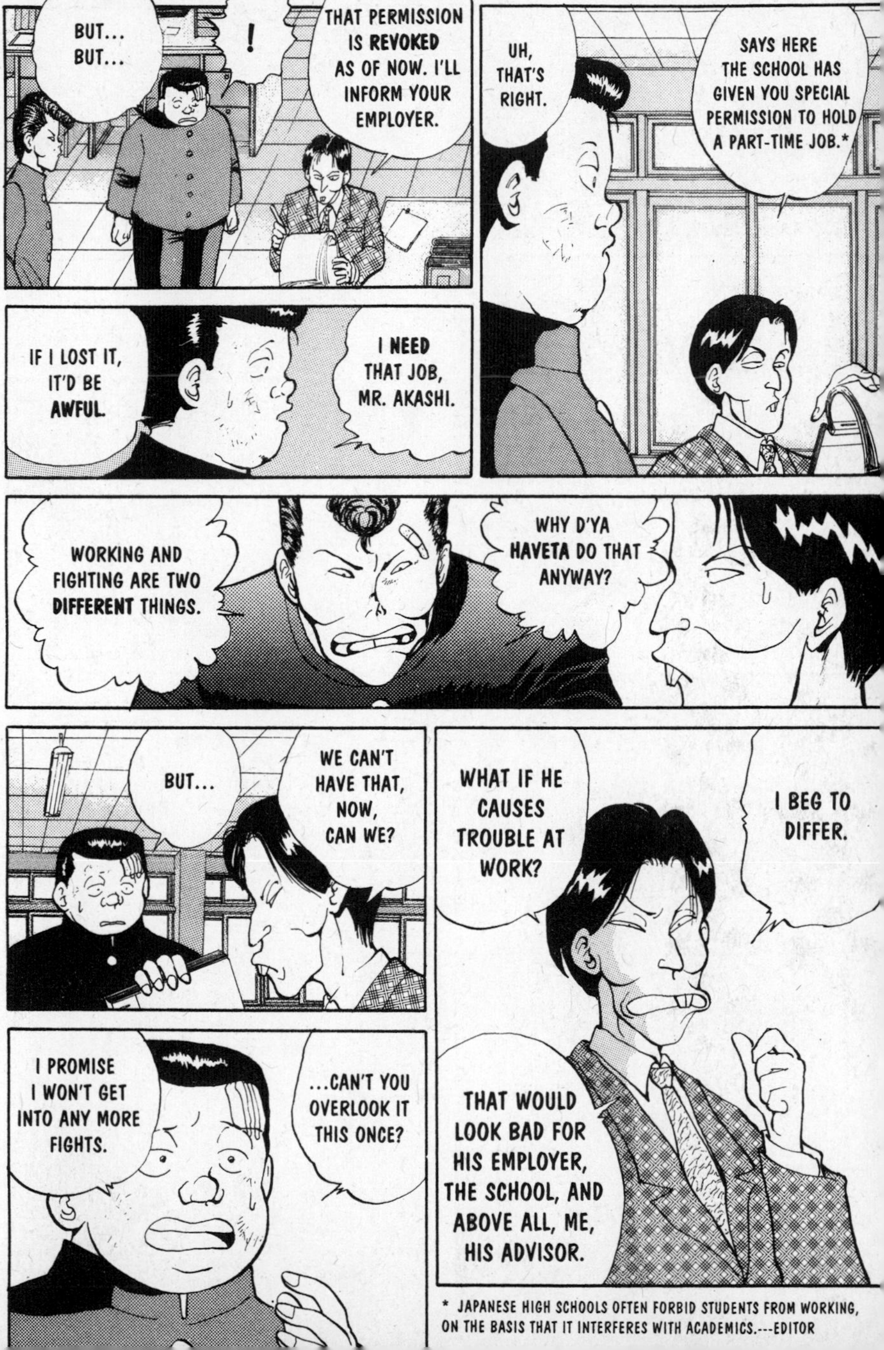
SAYS HERE THE SCHOOL HAS GIVEN YOU SPECIAL PERMISSION TO HOLD A PART-TIME JOB.*
UH, THAT'S RIGHT.
THAT PERMISSION IS REVOKED AS OF NOW. I'LL INFORM YOUR EMPLOYER.
!
BUT... BUT...
I NEED THAT JOB, MR. AKASHI.
IF I LOST IT, IT'D BE AWFUL.
WHY D'YA HAVETA DO THAT ANYWAY?
WORKING AND FIGHTING ARE TWO DIFFERENT THINGS.
I BEG TO DIFFER.
WHAT IF HE CAUSES TROUBLE AT WORK?
THAT WOULD LOOK BAD FOR HIS EMPLOYER, THE SCHOOL, AND ABOVE ALL, ME, HIS ADVISOR.
WE CAN'T HAVE THAT, NOW, CAN WE?
BUT...
...CAN'T YOU OVERLOOK IT THIS ONCE?
I PROMISE I WON'T GET INTO ANY MORE FIGHTS.

* JAPANESE HIGH SCHOOLS OFTEN FORBID STUDENTS FROM WORKING, ON THE BASIS THAT IT INTERFERES WITH ACADEMICS.---EDITOR

READ THIS WAY

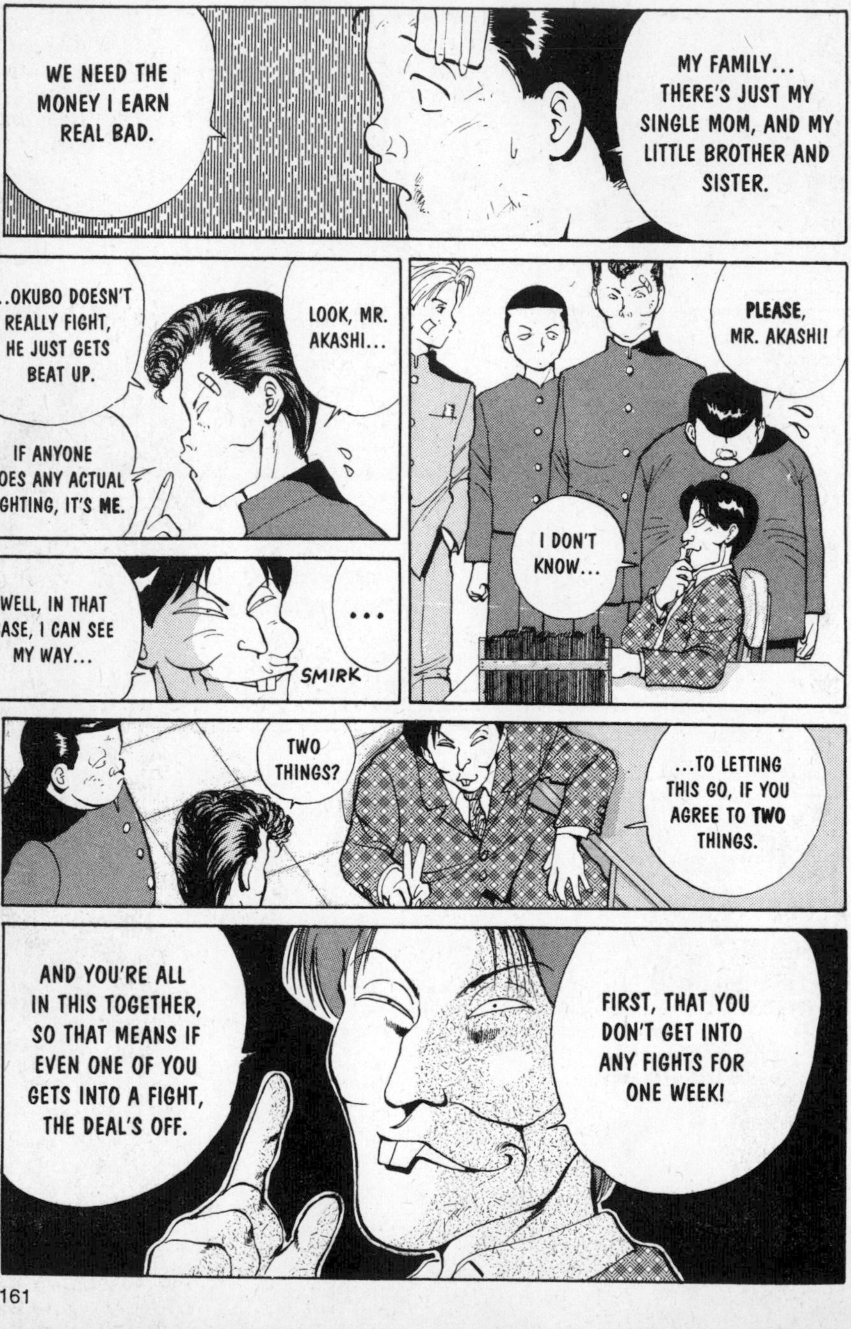

MY FAMILY... THERE'S JUST MY SINGLE MOM, AND MY LITTLE BROTHER AND SISTER.
WE NEED THE MONEY I EARN REAL BAD.
PLEASE, MR. AKASHI!
I DON'T KNOW...
LOOK, MR. AKASHI...
...OKUBO DOESN'T REALLY FIGHT, HE JUST GETS BEAT UP.
IF ANYONE DOES ANY ACTUAL FIGHTING, IT'S ME.
...
WELL, IN THAT CASE, I CAN SEE MY WAY...
SMIRK
...TO LETTING THIS GO, IF YOU AGREE TO TWO THINGS.
TWO THINGS?
FIRST, THAT YOU DON'T GET INTO ANY FIGHTS FOR ONE WEEK!
AND YOU'RE ALL IN THIS TOGETHER, SO THAT MEANS IF EVEN ONE OF YOU GETS INTO A FIGHT, THE DEAL'S OFF.

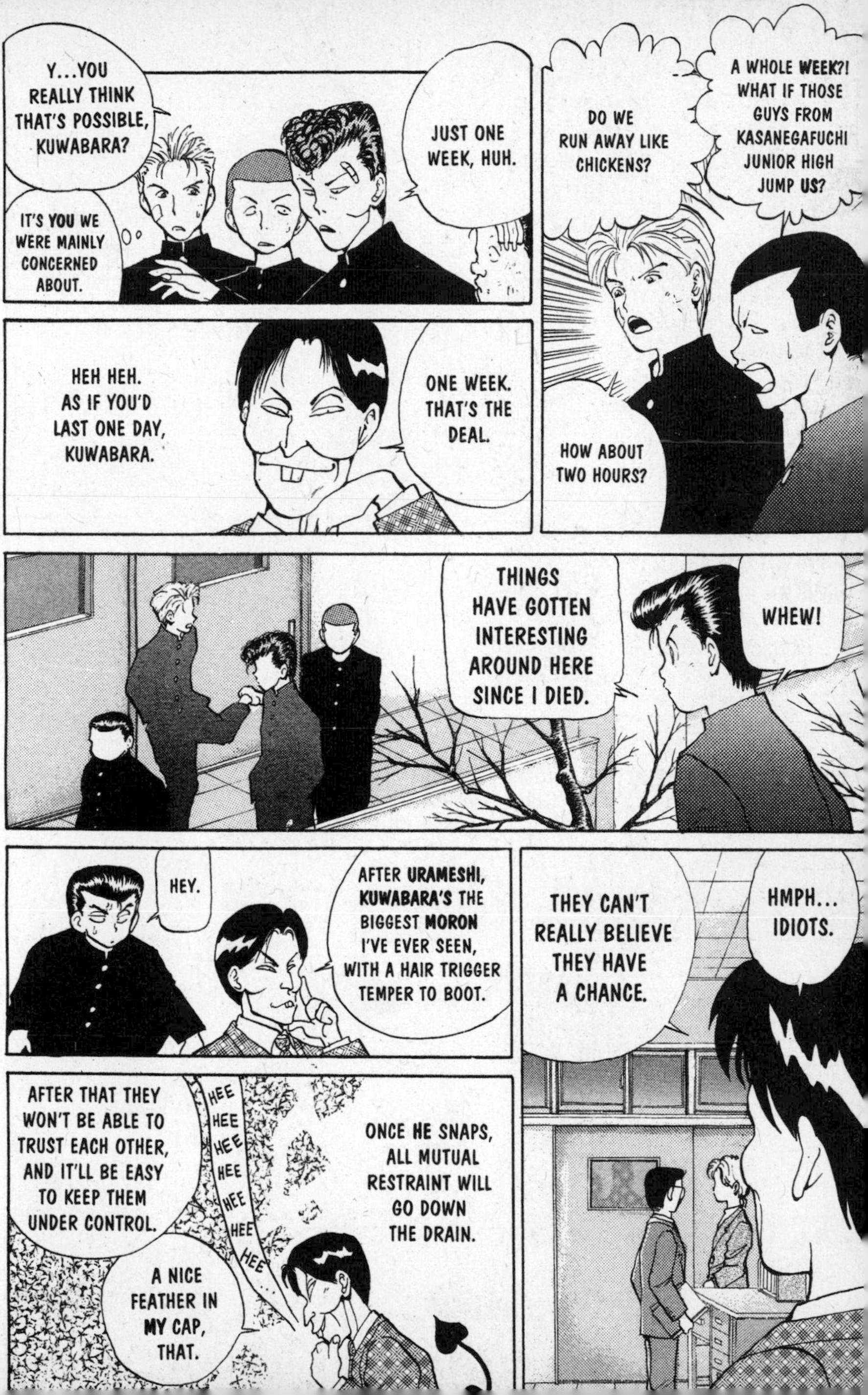
A WHOLE WEEK?! WHAT IF THOSE GUYS FROM KASANEGAFUCHI JUNIOR HIGH JUMP US?
DO WE RUN AWAY LIKE CHICKENS?
HOW ABOUT TWO HOURS?
JUST ONE WEEK, HUH.
Y...YOU REALLY THINK THAT'S POSSIBLE, KUWABARA?
IT'S YOU WE WERE MAINLY CONCERNED ABOUT.
ONE WEEK. THAT'S THE DEAL.
HEH HEH. AS IF YOU'D LAST ONE DAY, KUWABARA.
WHEW!
THINGS HAVE GOTTEN INTERESTING AROUND HERE SINCE I DIED.
HMPH... IDIOTS.
THEY CAN'T REALLY BELIEVE THEY HAVE A CHANCE.
AFTER URAMESHI, KUWABARA'S THE BIGGEST MORON I'VE EVER SEEN, WITH A HAIR TRIGGER TEMPER TO BOOT.
HEY.
ONCE HE SNAPS, ALL MUTUAL RESTRAINT WILL GO DOWN THE DRAIN.
HEE HEE HEE HEE HEE HEE HEE...
AFTER THAT THEY WON'T BE ABLE TO TRUST EACH OTHER, AND IT'LL BE EASY TO KEEP THEM UNDER CONTROL.
A NICE FEATHER IN MY CAP, THAT.

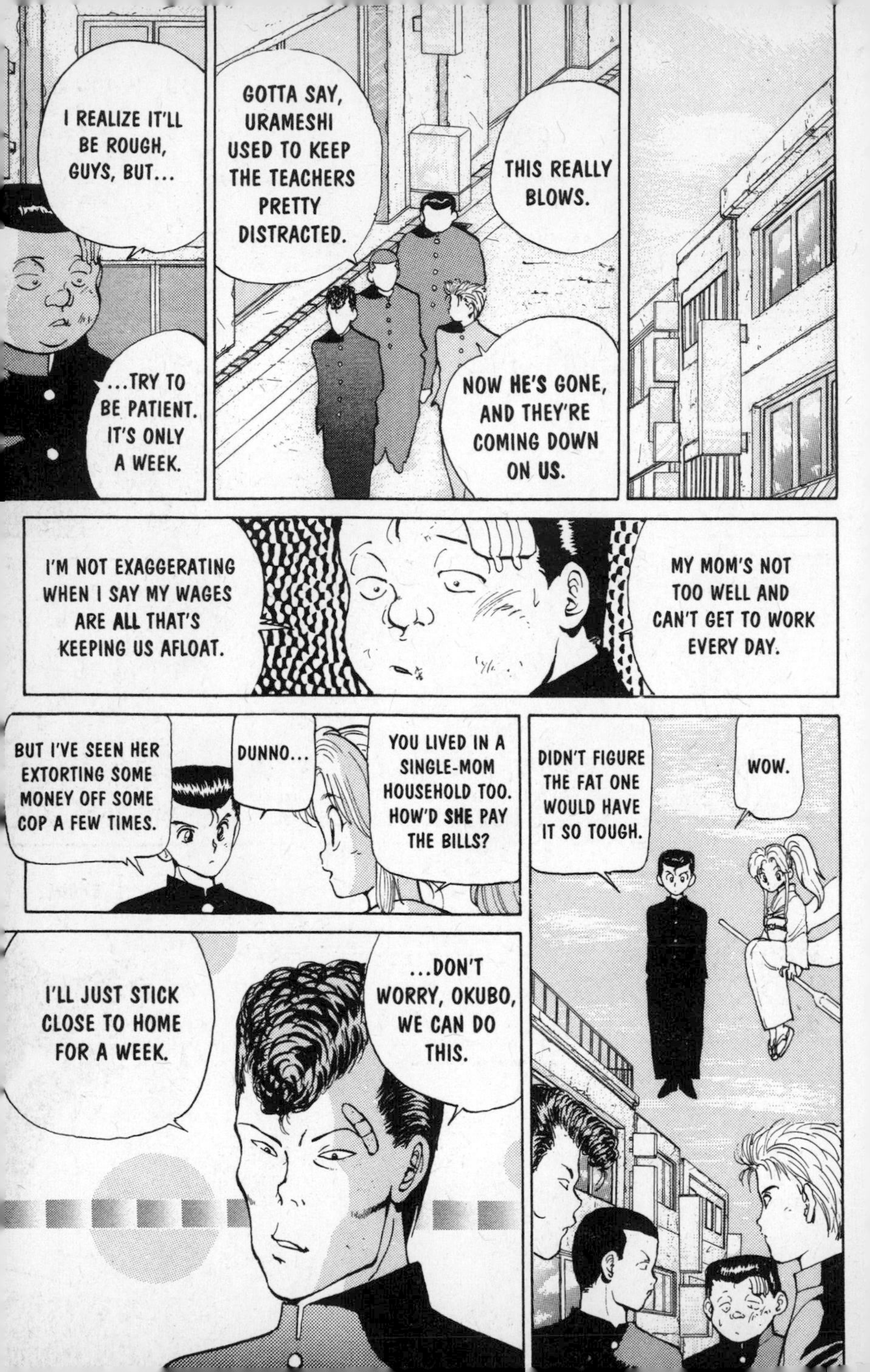
THIS REALLY BLOWS.
GOTTA SAY, URAMESHI USED TO KEEP THE TEACHERS PRETTY DISTRACTED.
NOW HE'S GONE, AND THEY'RE COMING DOWN ON US.
I REALIZE IT'LL BE ROUGH, GUYS, BUT...
...TRY TO BE PATIENT. IT'S ONLY A WEEK.
MY MOM'S NOT TOO WELL AND CAN'T GET TO WORK EVERY DAY.
I'M NOT EXAGGERATING WHEN I SAY MY WAGES ARE ALL THAT'S KEEPING US AFLOAT.
WOW.
DIDN'T FIGURE THE FAT ONE WOULD HAVE IT SO TOUGH.
YOU LIVED IN A SINGLE-MOM HOUSEHOLD TOO. HOW'D SHE PAY THE BILLS?
DUNNO...
BUT I'VE SEEN HER EXTORTING SOME MONEY OFF SOME COP A FEW TIMES.
...DON'T WORRY, OKUBO, WE CAN DO THIS.
I'LL JUST STICK CLOSE TO HOME FOR A WEEK.

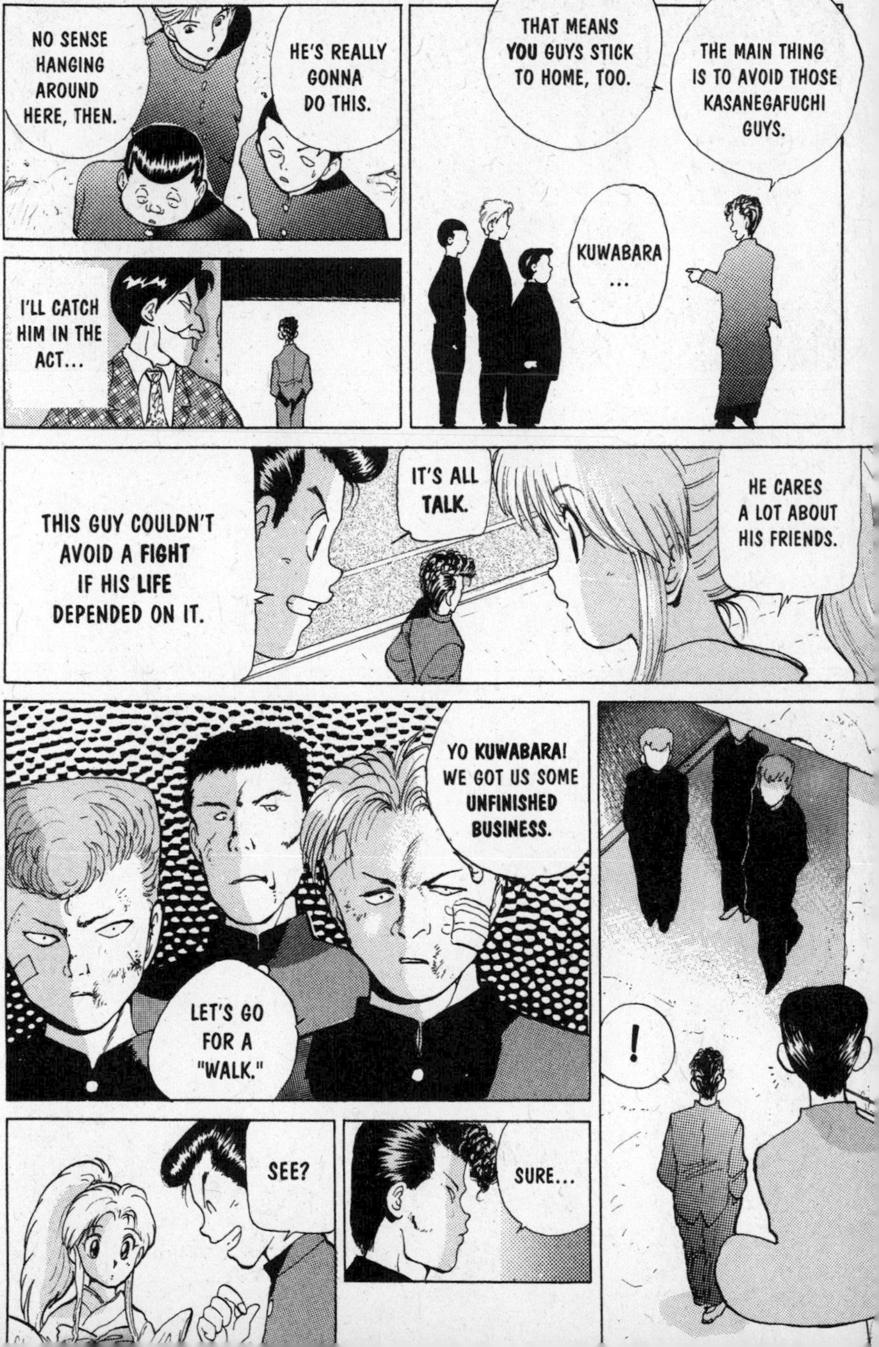
THE MAIN THING IS TO AVOID THOSE KASANEGAFUCHI GUYS.
THAT MEANS YOU GUYS STICK TO HOME, TOO.
KUWABARA...
HE'S REALLY GONNA DO THIS.
NO SENSE HANGING AROUND HERE, THEN.
I'LL CATCH HIM IN THE ACT...
HE CARES A LOT ABOUT HIS FRIENDS.
IT'S ALL TALK.
THIS GUY COULDN'T AVOID A FIGHT IF HIS LIFE DEPENDED ON IT.
!
YO KUWABARA! WE GOT US SOME UNFINISHED BUSINESS.
LET'S GO FOR A "WALK."
SURE...
SEE?

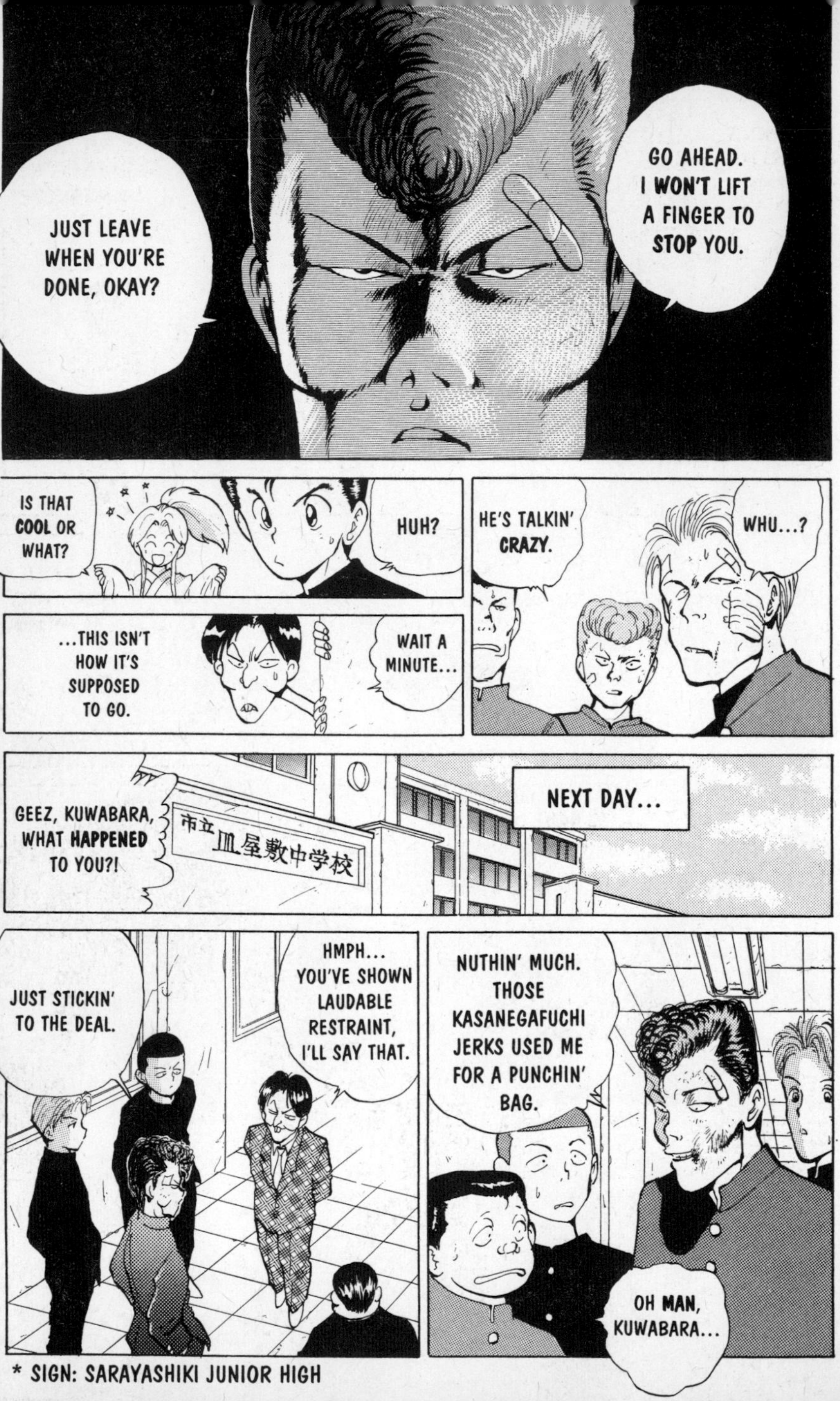
GO AHEAD. I WON'T LIFT A FINGER TO STOP YOU.
JUST LEAVE WHEN YOU'RE DONE, OKAY?
WHU...?
HE'S TALKIN' CRAZY.
HUH?
IS THAT COOL OR WHAT?
WAIT A MINUTE...
...THIS ISN'T HOW IT'S SUPPOSED TO GO.
NEXT DAY...
GEEZ, KUWABARA, WHAT HAPPENED TO YOU?!
市立 皿屋敷中学校
NUTHIN' MUCH. THOSE KASANEGAFUCHI JERKS USED ME FOR A PUNCHIN' BAG.
OH MAN, KUWABARA...
HMPH... YOU'VE SHOWN LAUDABLE RESTRAINT, I'LL SAY THAT.
JUST STICKIN' TO THE DEAL.

* SIGN: SARAYASHIKI JUNIOR HIGH

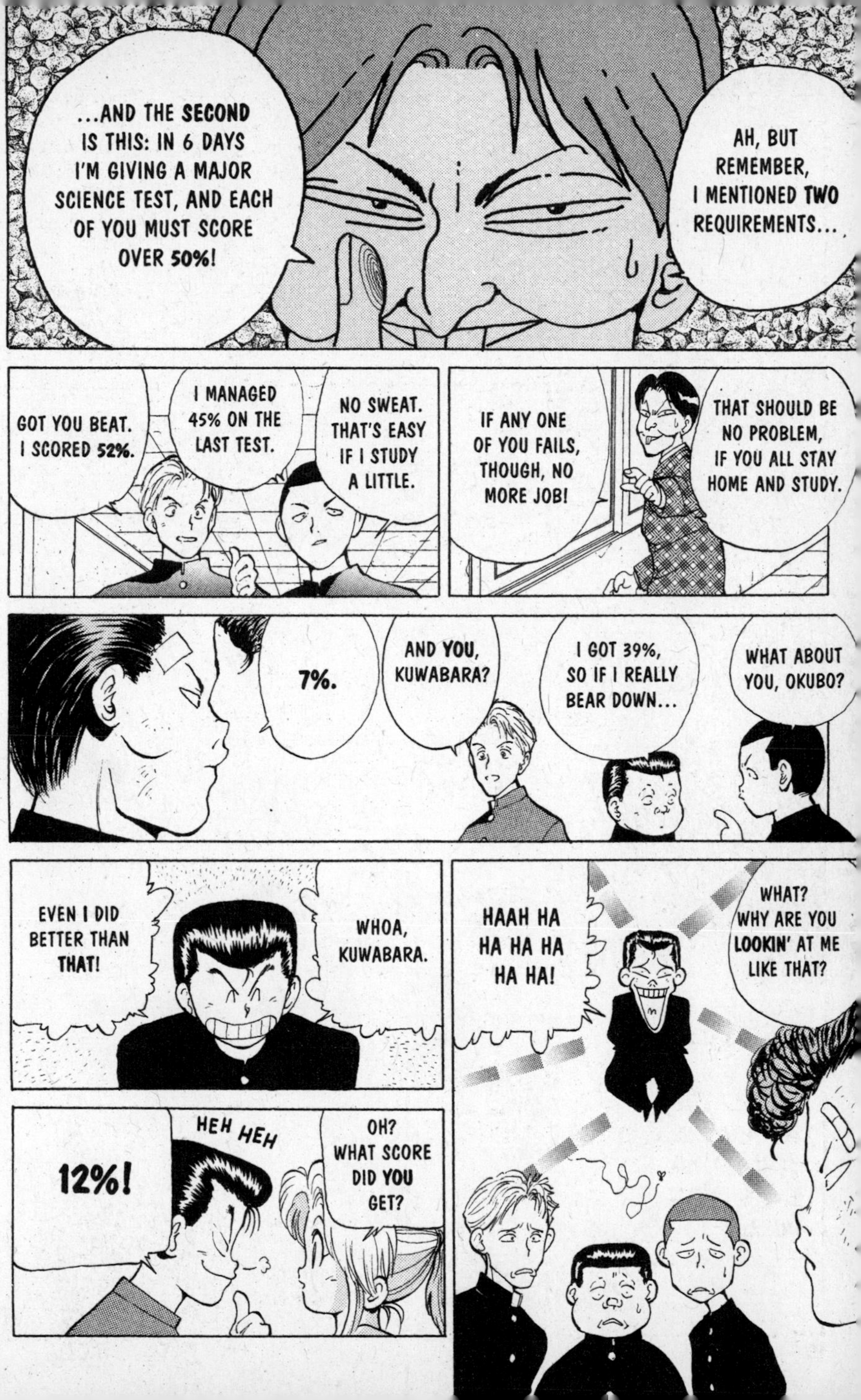
AH, BUT REMEMBER, I MENTIONED TWO REQUIREMENTS...
...AND THE SECOND IS THIS: IN 6 DAYS I'M GIVING A MAJOR SCIENCE TEST, AND EACH OF YOU MUST SCORE OVER 50%!
THAT SHOULD BE NO PROBLEM, IF YOU ALL STAY HOME AND STUDY.
IF ANY ONE OF YOU FAILS, THOUGH, NO MORE JOB!
NO SWEAT. THAT'S EASY IF I STUDY A LITTLE.
I MANAGED 45% ON THE LAST TEST.
GOT YOU BEAT. I SCORED 52%.
WHAT ABOUT YOU, OKUBO?
I GOT 39%, SO IF I REALLY BEAR DOWN...
AND YOU, KUWABARA?
7%.
WHAT? WHY ARE YOU LOOKIN' AT ME LIKE THAT?
HAAH HA HA HA HA HA HA!
WHOA, KUWABARA.
EVEN I DID BETTER THAN THAT!
OH? WHAT SCORE DID YOU GET?
HEH HEH
12%!

READ THIS WAY

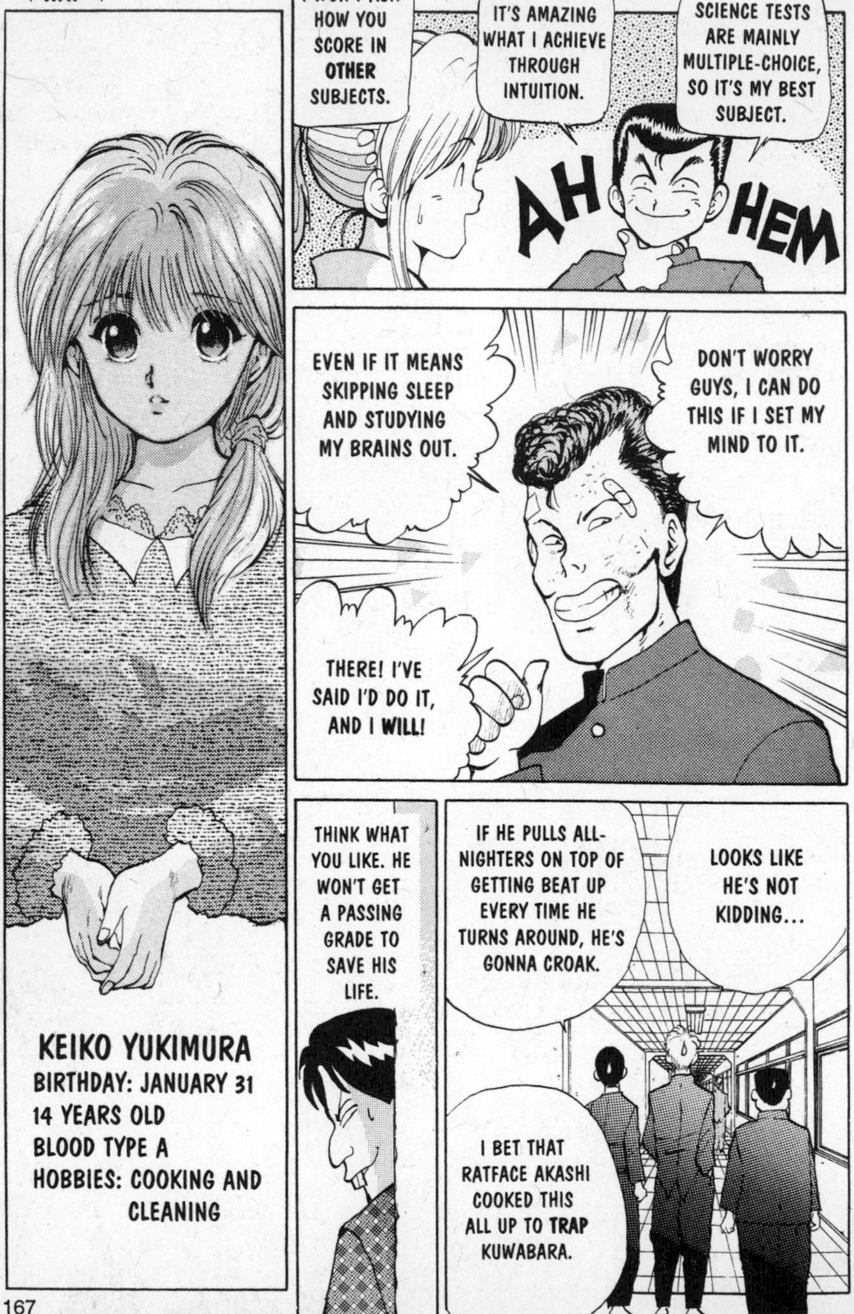
SCIENCE TESTS ARE MAINLY MULTIPLE-CHOICE, SO IT'S MY BEST SUBJECT.
IT'S AMAZING WHAT I ACHIEVE THROUGH INTUITION.
I WON'T ASK HOW YOU SCORE IN **OTHER** SUBJECTS.
AH HEM
DON'T WORRY GUYS, I CAN DO THIS IF I SET MY MIND TO IT.
EVEN IF IT MEANS SKIPPING SLEEP AND STUDYING MY BRAINS OUT.
THERE! I'VE SAID I'D DO IT, AND I **WILL**!
LOOKS LIKE HE'S NOT KIDDING...
IF HE PULLS ALL-NIGHTERS ON TOP OF GETTING BEAT UP EVERY TIME HE TURNS AROUND, HE'S GONNA CROAK.
I BET THAT RATFACE AKASHI COOKED THIS ALL UP TO **TRAP** KUWABARA.
THINK WHAT YOU LIKE. HE WON'T GET A PASSING GRADE TO SAVE HIS LIFE.
KEIKO YUKIMURA
BIRTHDAY: JANUARY 31
14 YEARS OLD
BLOOD TYPE A
HOBBIES: COOKING AND CLEANING

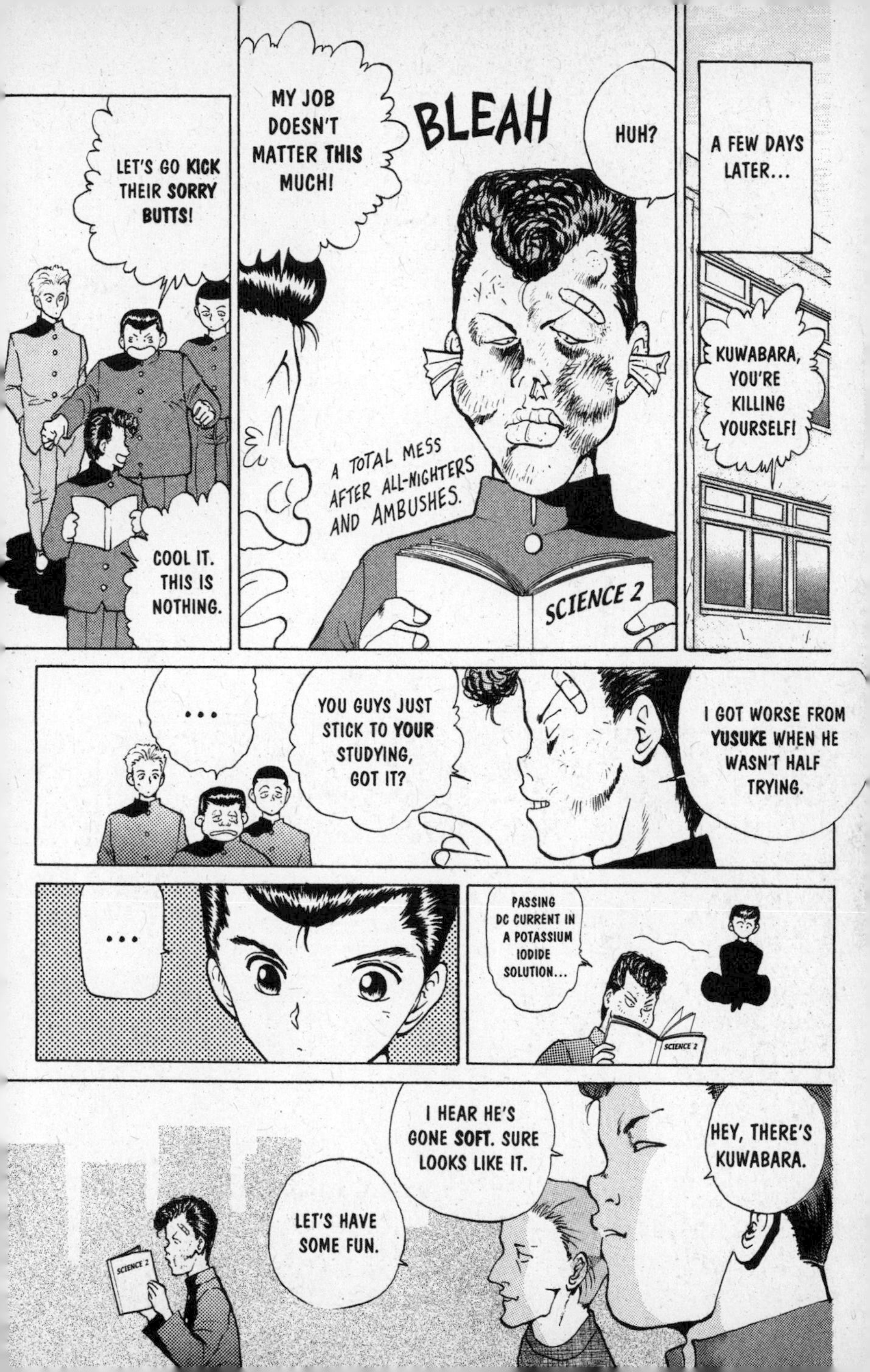
A FEW DAYS LATER...
KUWABARA, YOU'RE KILLING YOURSELF!
HUH?
BLEAH
MY JOB DOESN'T MATTER THIS MUCH!
A TOTAL MESS AFTER ALL-NIGHTERS AND AMBUSHES.
SCIENCE 2
LET'S GO KICK THEIR SORRY BUTTS!
COOL IT. THIS IS NOTHING.
I GOT WORSE FROM YUSUKE WHEN HE WASN'T HALF TRYING.
YOU GUYS JUST STICK TO YOUR STUDYING, GOT IT?
...
PASSING DC CURRENT IN A POTASSIUM IODIDE SOLUTION...
SCIENCE 2
...
HEY, THERE'S KUWABARA.
I HEAR HE'S GONE SOFT. SURE LOOKS LIKE IT.
LET'S HAVE SOME FUN.
SCIENCE 2

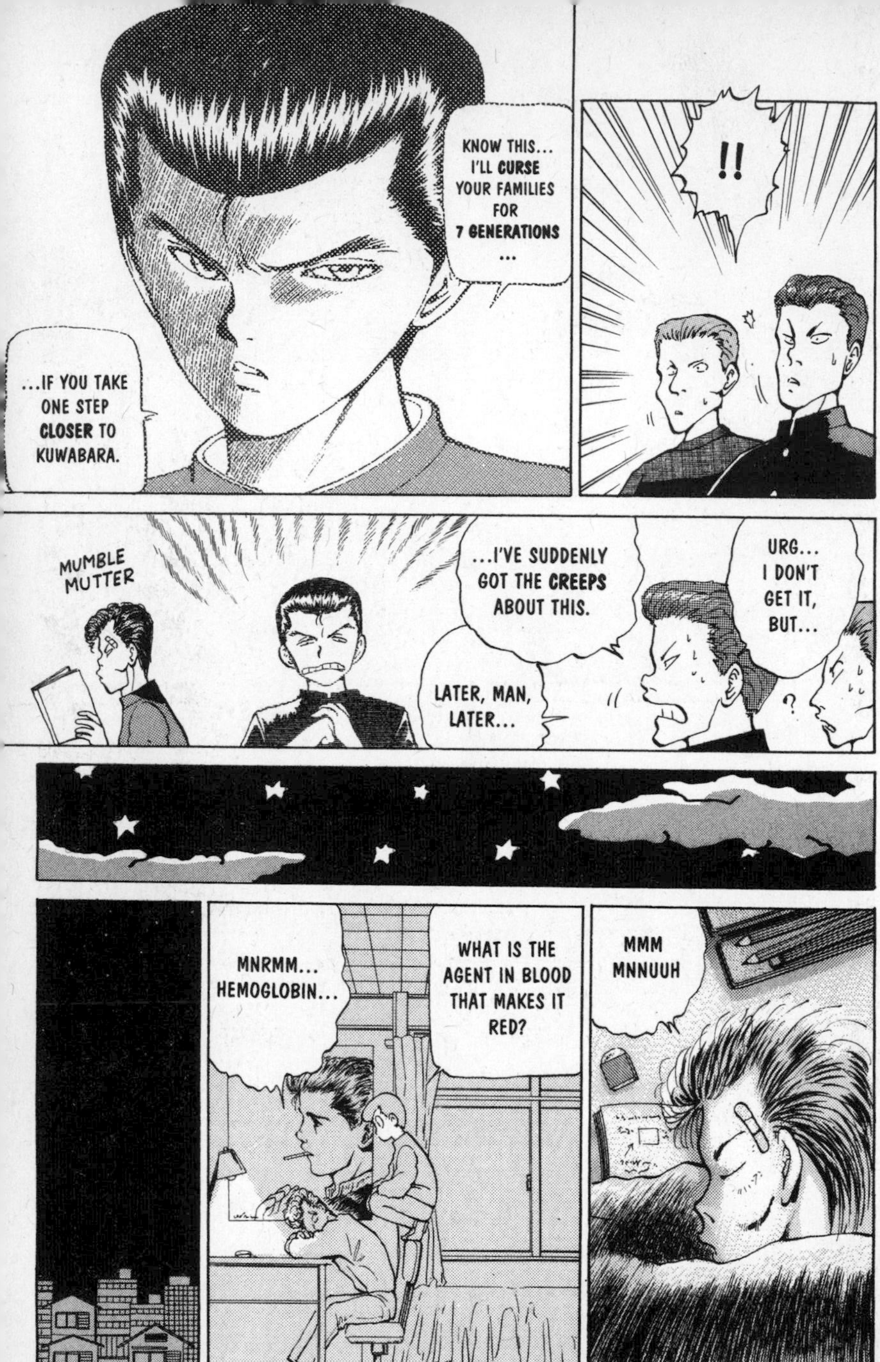
!!
KNOW THIS... I'LL CURSE YOUR FAMILIES FOR 7 GENERATIONS ...
...IF YOU TAKE ONE STEP CLOSER TO KUWABARA.
URG... I DON'T GET IT, BUT...
...I'VE SUDDENLY GOT THE CREEPS ABOUT THIS.
LATER, MAN, LATER...
MUMBLE MUTTER
MMM MNNUUH
WHAT IS THE AGENT IN BLOOD THAT MAKES IT RED?
MNRMM... HEMOGLOBIN...

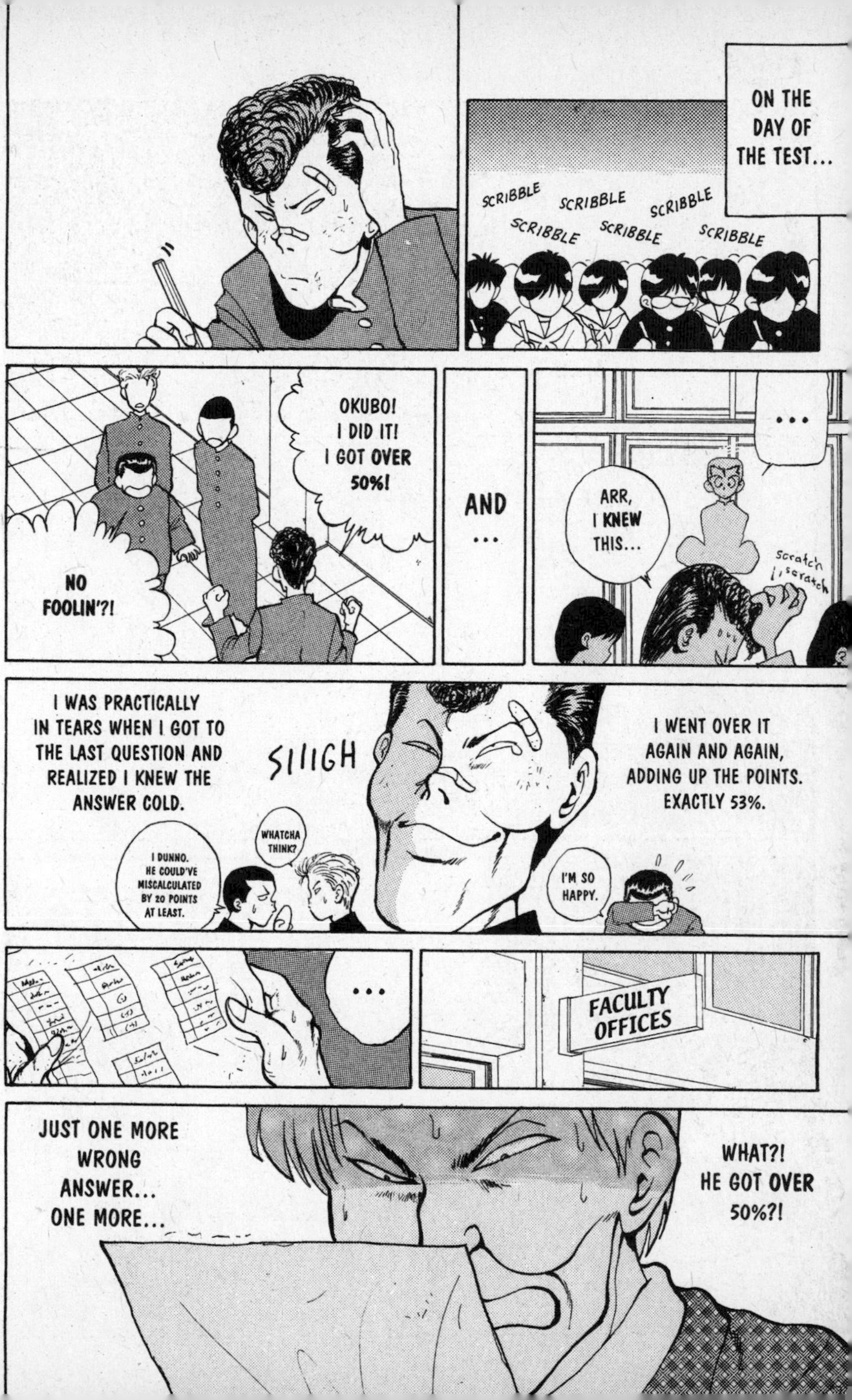
ON THE DAY OF THE TEST...
SCRIBBLE
SCRIBBLE
SCRIBBLE
SCRIBBLE
SCRIBBLE
SCRIBBLE
...
ARR, I KNEW THIS...
scratch scratch
AND ...
OKUBO! I DID IT! I GOT OVER 50%!
NO FOOLIN'?!
I WENT OVER IT AGAIN AND AGAIN, ADDING UP THE POINTS. EXACTLY 53%.
I'M SO HAPPY.
SIIIGH
I WAS PRACTICALLY IN TEARS WHEN I GOT TO THE LAST QUESTION AND REALIZED I KNEW THE ANSWER COLD.
WHATCHA THINK?
I DUNNO. HE COULD'VE MISCALCULATED BY 20 POINTS AT LEAST.
FACULTY OFFICES
...
WHAT?! HE GOT OVER 50%?!
JUST ONE MORE WRONG ANSWER... ONE MORE...

READ THIS WAY

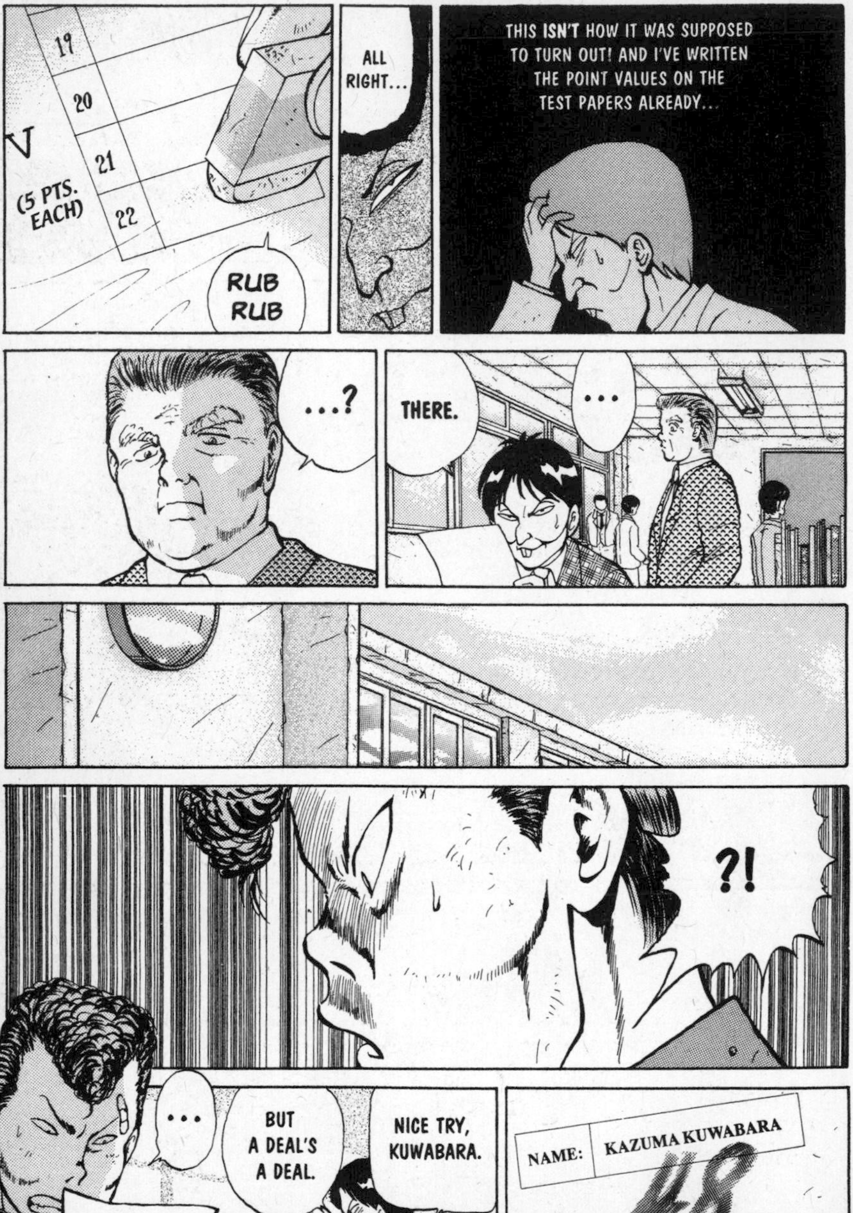
THIS ISN'T HOW IT WAS SUPPOSED TO TURN OUT! AND I'VE WRITTEN THE POINT VALUES ON THE TEST PAPERS ALREADY...
ALL RIGHT...
19
20
V
21
(5 PTS. EACH)
22
RUB RUB
...
THERE.
...?
?!
NAME: KAZUMA KUWABARA
48
NICE TRY, KUWABARA.
BUT A DEAL'S A DEAL.
...

READ THIS WAY

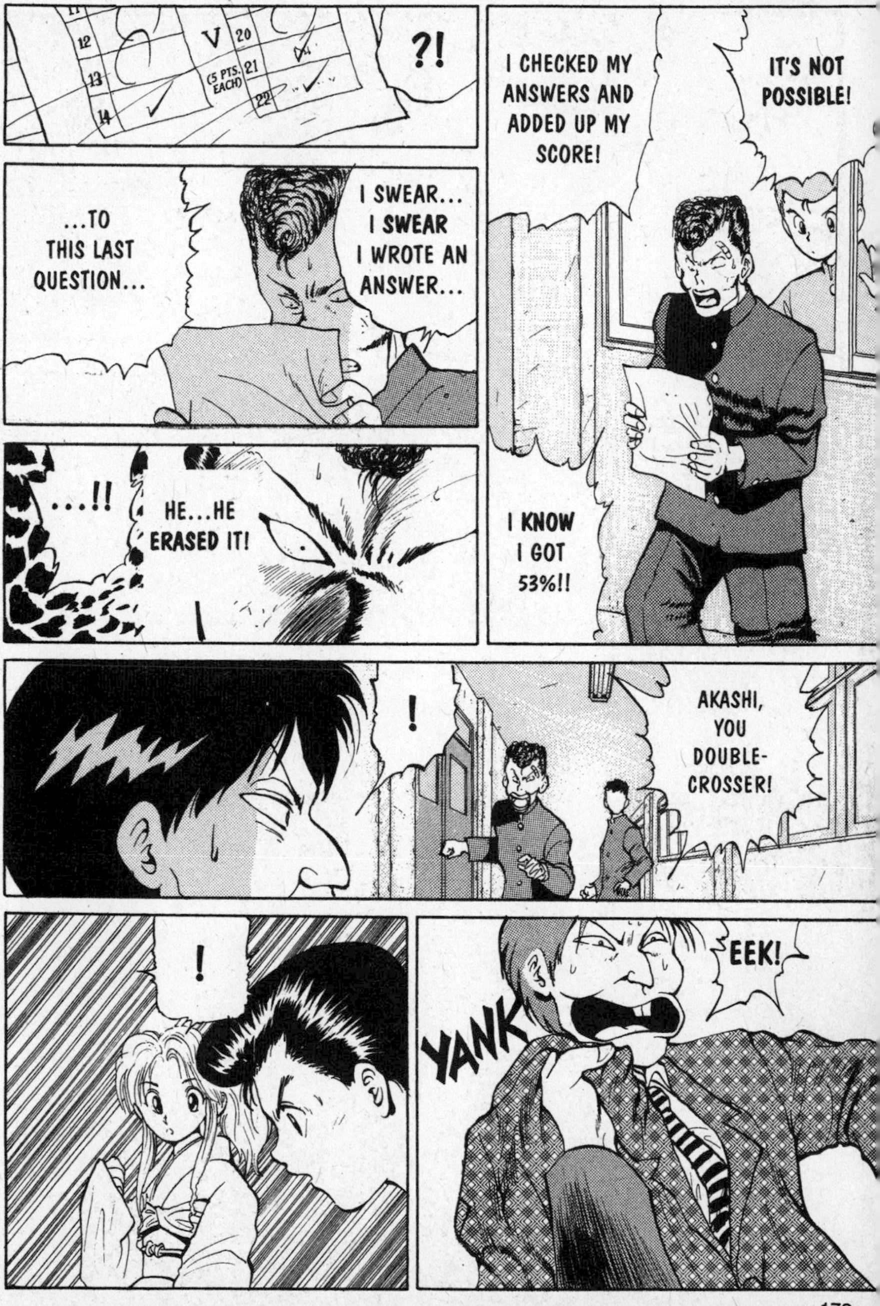

IT'S NOT POSSIBLE!
I CHECKED MY ANSWERS AND ADDED UP MY SCORE!
I KNOW I GOT 53%!!
?!
(5 PTS. EACH)
I SWEAR... I SWEAR I WROTE AN ANSWER...
...TO THIS LAST QUESTION...
HE...HE ERASED IT!
...!!
AKASHI, YOU DOUBLE-CROSSER!
!
EEK!
YANK
!

READ THIS WAY

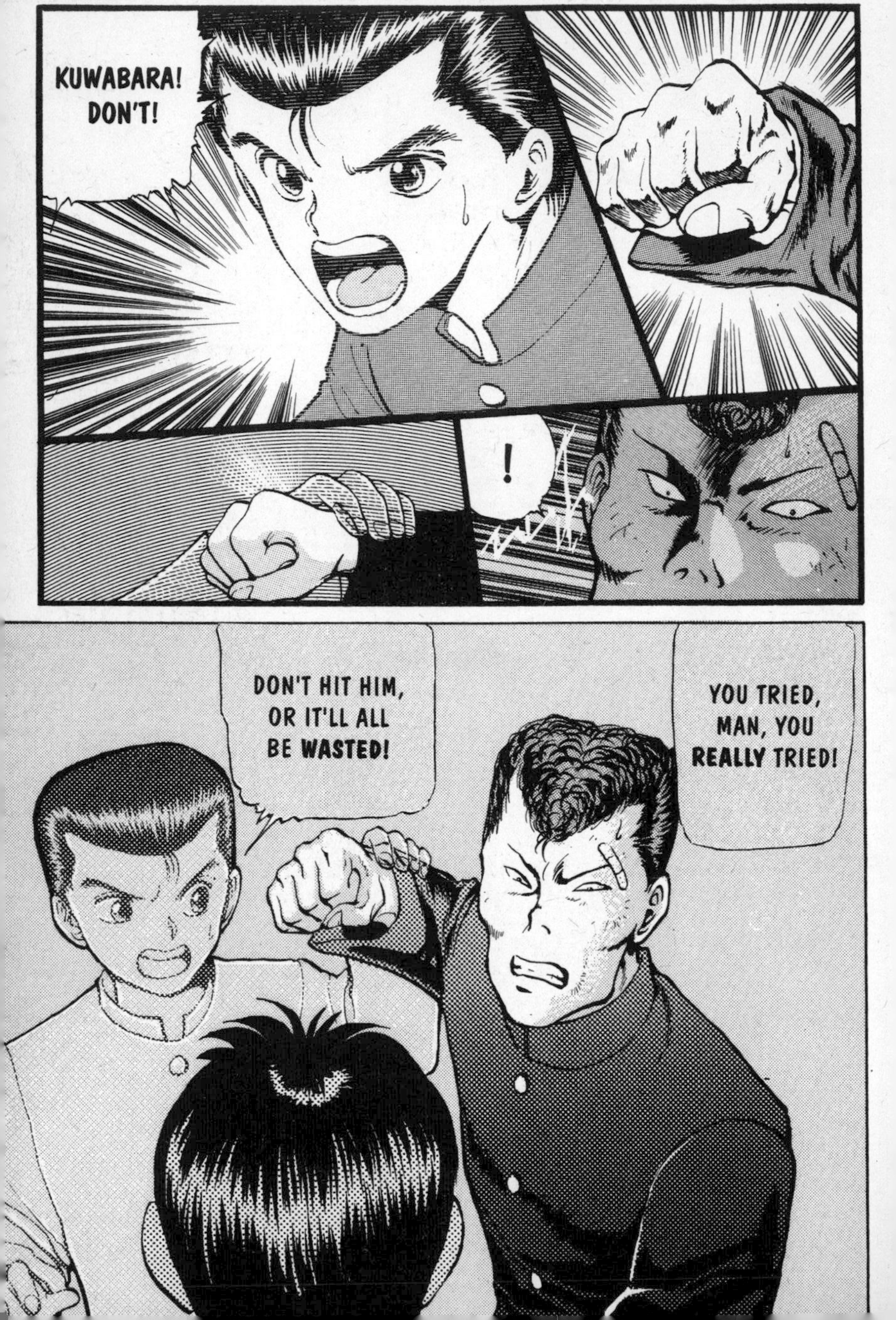
KUWABARA! DON'T!
!
YOU TRIED, MAN, YOU REALLY TRIED!
DON'T HIT HIM, OR IT'LL ALL BE WASTED!

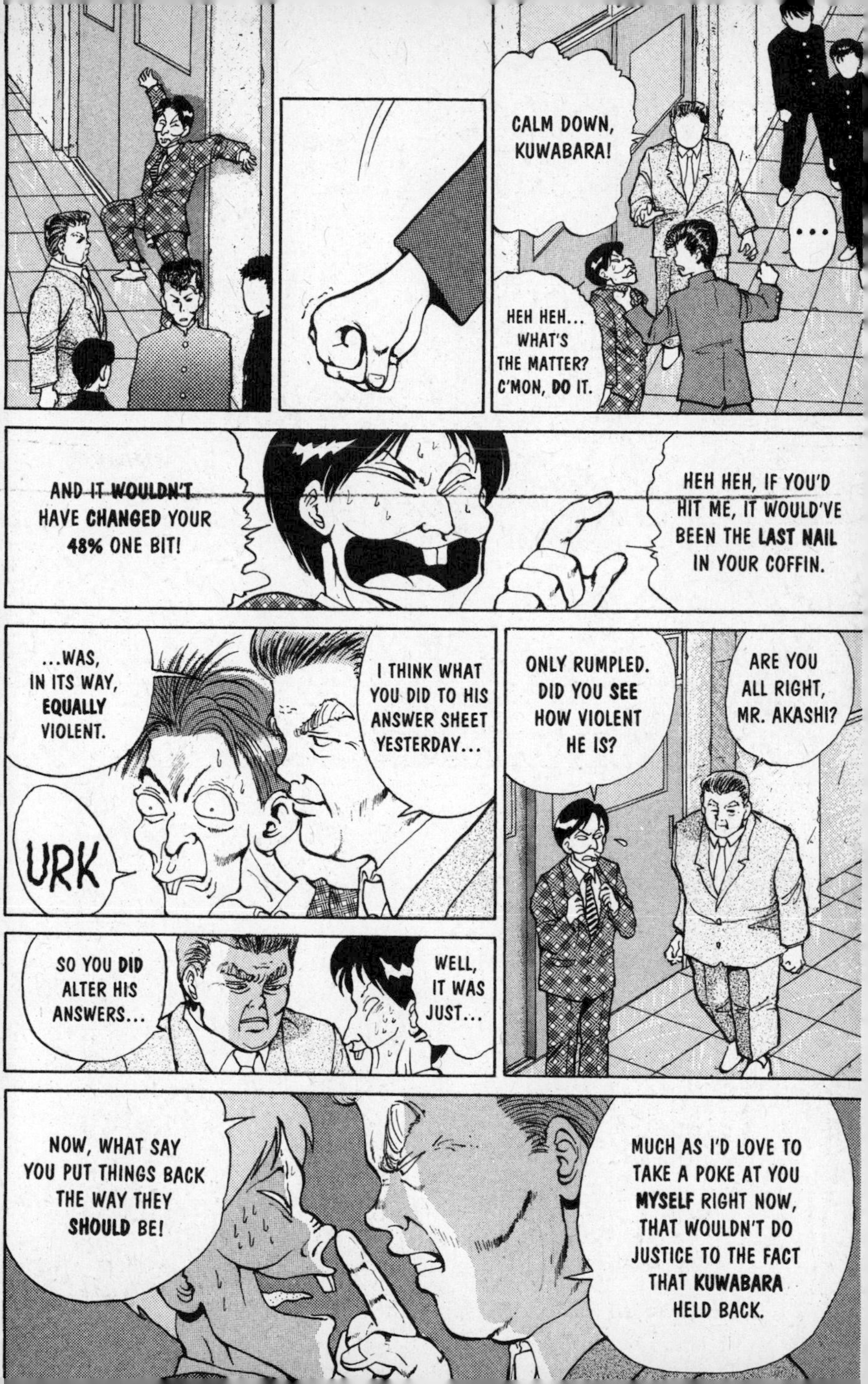
CALM DOWN, KUWABARA!
...
HEH HEH... WHAT'S THE MATTER? C'MON, DO IT.
HEH HEH, IF YOU'D HIT ME, IT WOULD'VE BEEN THE LAST NAIL IN YOUR COFFIN.
AND IT WOULDN'T HAVE CHANGED YOUR 48% ONE BIT!
ARE YOU ALL RIGHT, MR. AKASHI?
ONLY RUMPLED. DID YOU SEE HOW VIOLENT HE IS?
I THINK WHAT YOU DID TO HIS ANSWER SHEET YESTERDAY...
...WAS, IN ITS WAY, EQUALLY VIOLENT.
URK
WELL, IT WAS JUST...
SO YOU DID ALTER HIS ANSWERS...
MUCH AS I'D LOVE TO TAKE A POKE AT YOU MYSELF RIGHT NOW, THAT WOULDN'T DO JUSTICE TO THE FACT THAT KUWABARA HELD BACK.
NOW, WHAT SAY YOU PUT THINGS BACK THE WAY THEY SHOULD BE!

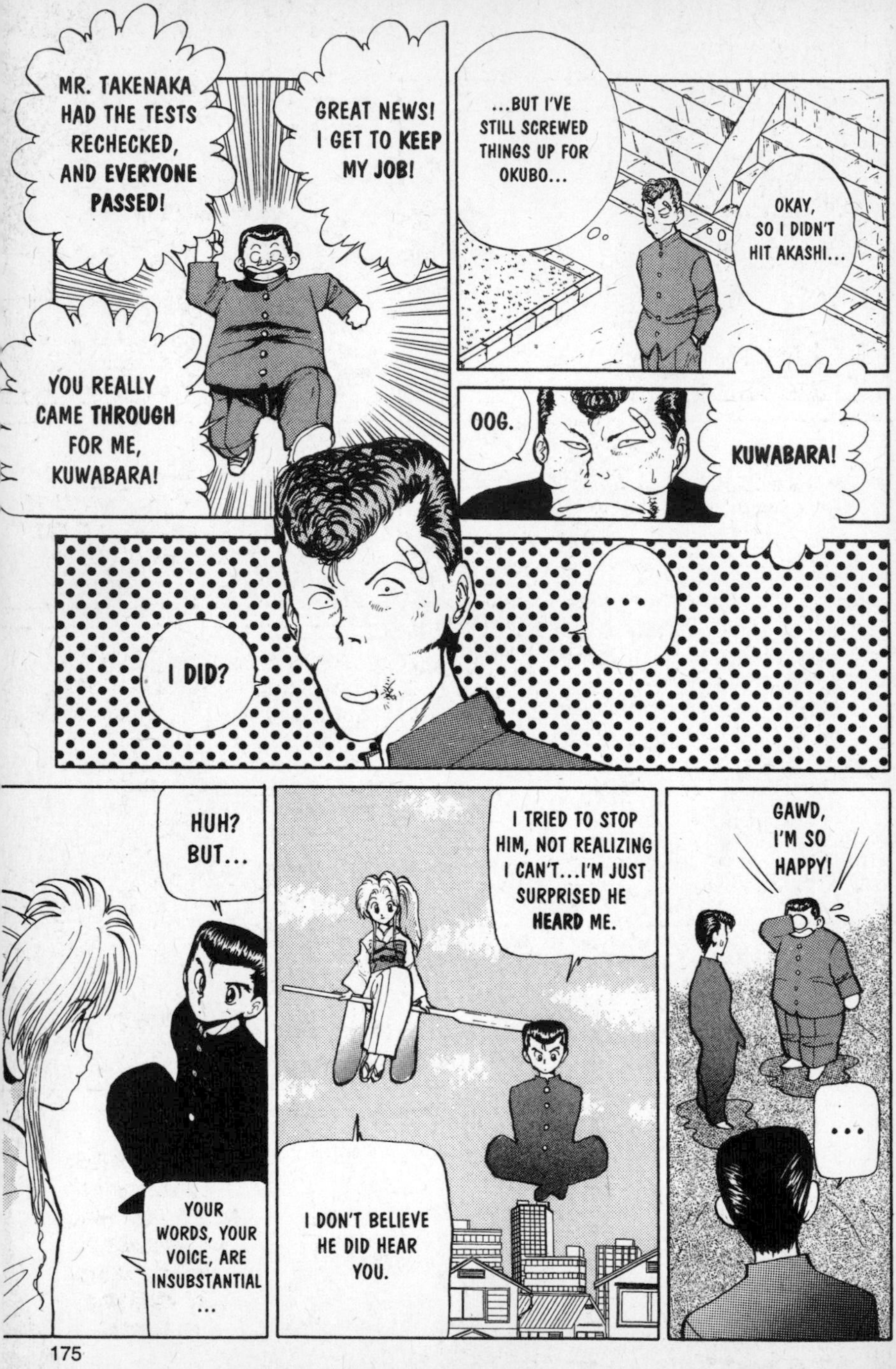
OKAY, SO I DIDN'T HIT AKASHI...
...BUT I'VE STILL SCREWED THINGS UP FOR OKUBO...
KUWABARA!
OOG.
GREAT NEWS! I GET TO KEEP MY JOB!
MR. TAKENAKA HAD THE TESTS RECHECKED, AND EVERYONE PASSED!
YOU REALLY CAME THROUGH FOR ME, KUWABARA!
...
I DID?
GAWD, I'M SO HAPPY!
...
I TRIED TO STOP HIM, NOT REALIZING I CAN'T...I'M JUST SURPRISED HE HEARD ME.
I DON'T BELIEVE HE DID HEAR YOU.
HUH? BUT...
YOUR WORDS, YOUR VOICE, ARE INSUBSTANTIAL ...

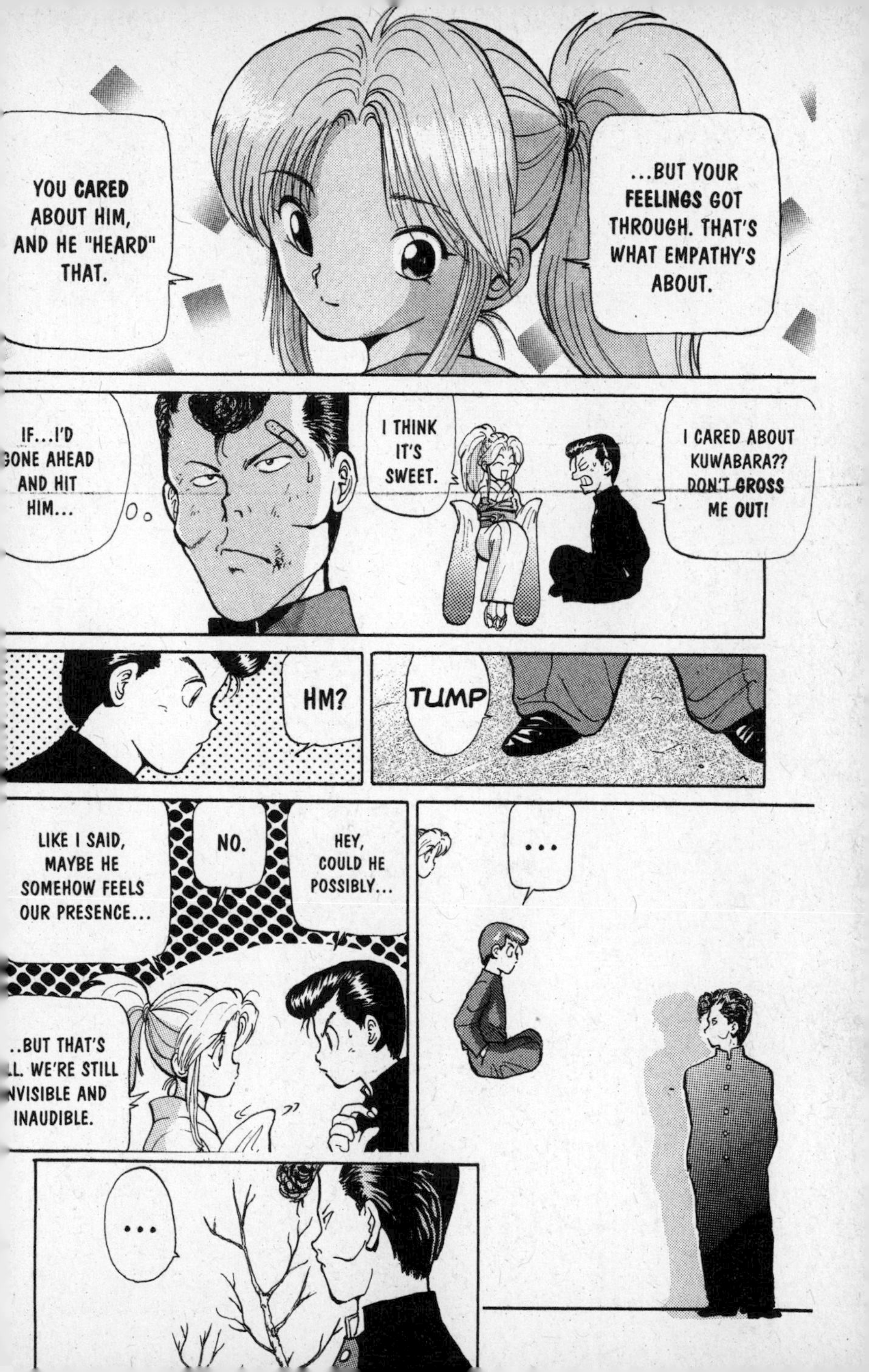
...BUT YOUR FEELINGS GOT THROUGH. THAT'S WHAT EMPATHY'S ABOUT.
YOU CARED ABOUT HIM, AND HE "HEARD" THAT.
I CARED ABOUT KUWABARA?? DON'T GROSS ME OUT!
I THINK IT'S SWEET.
IF...I'D GONE AHEAD AND HIT HIM...
TUMP
HM?
...
HEY, COULD HE POSSIBLY...
NO.
LIKE I SAID, MAYBE HE SOMEHOW FEELS OUR PRESENCE...
..BUT THAT'S LL. WE'RE STILL NVISIBLE AND INAUDIBLE.
...

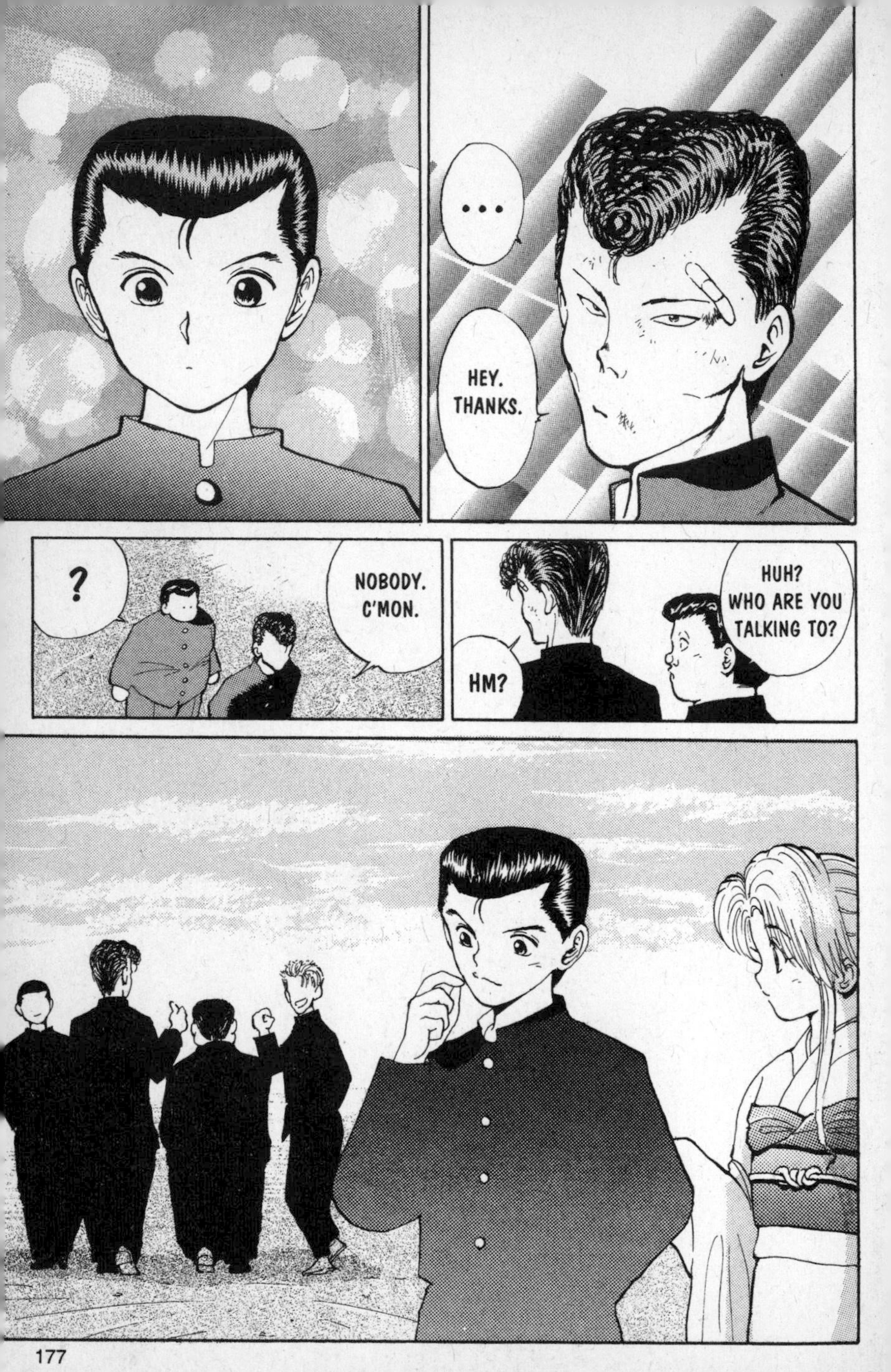
...
HEY. THANKS.
HUH? WHO ARE YOU TALKING TO?
HM?
NOBODY. C'MON.
?

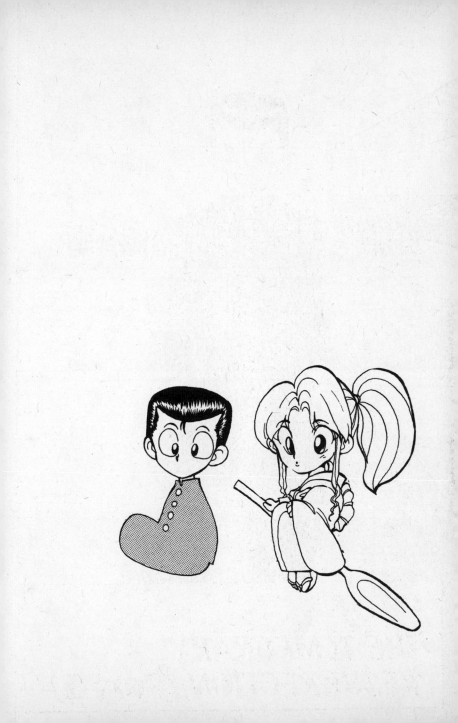

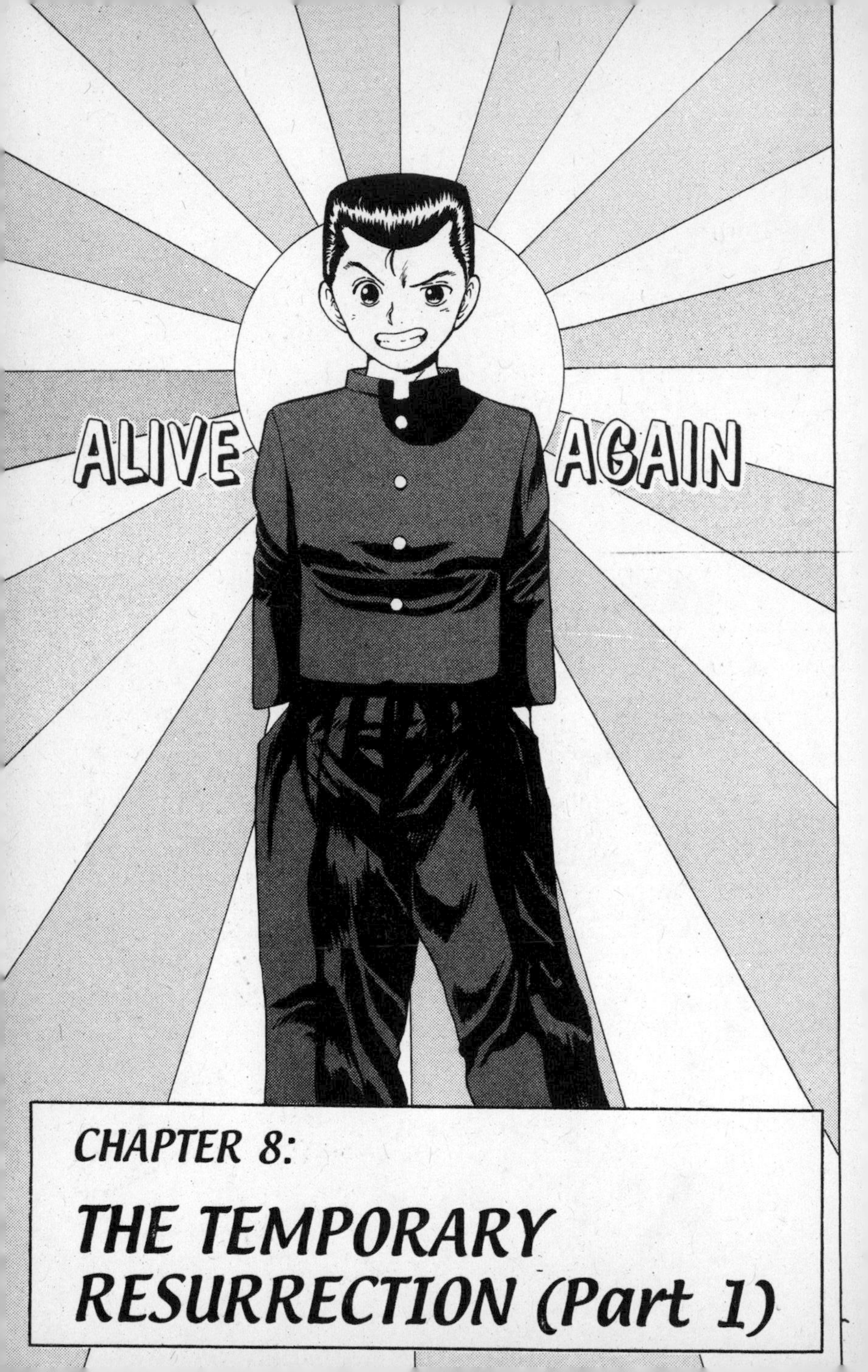
ALIVE AGAIN
CHAPTER 8:
THE TEMPORARY RESURRECTION (Part 1)

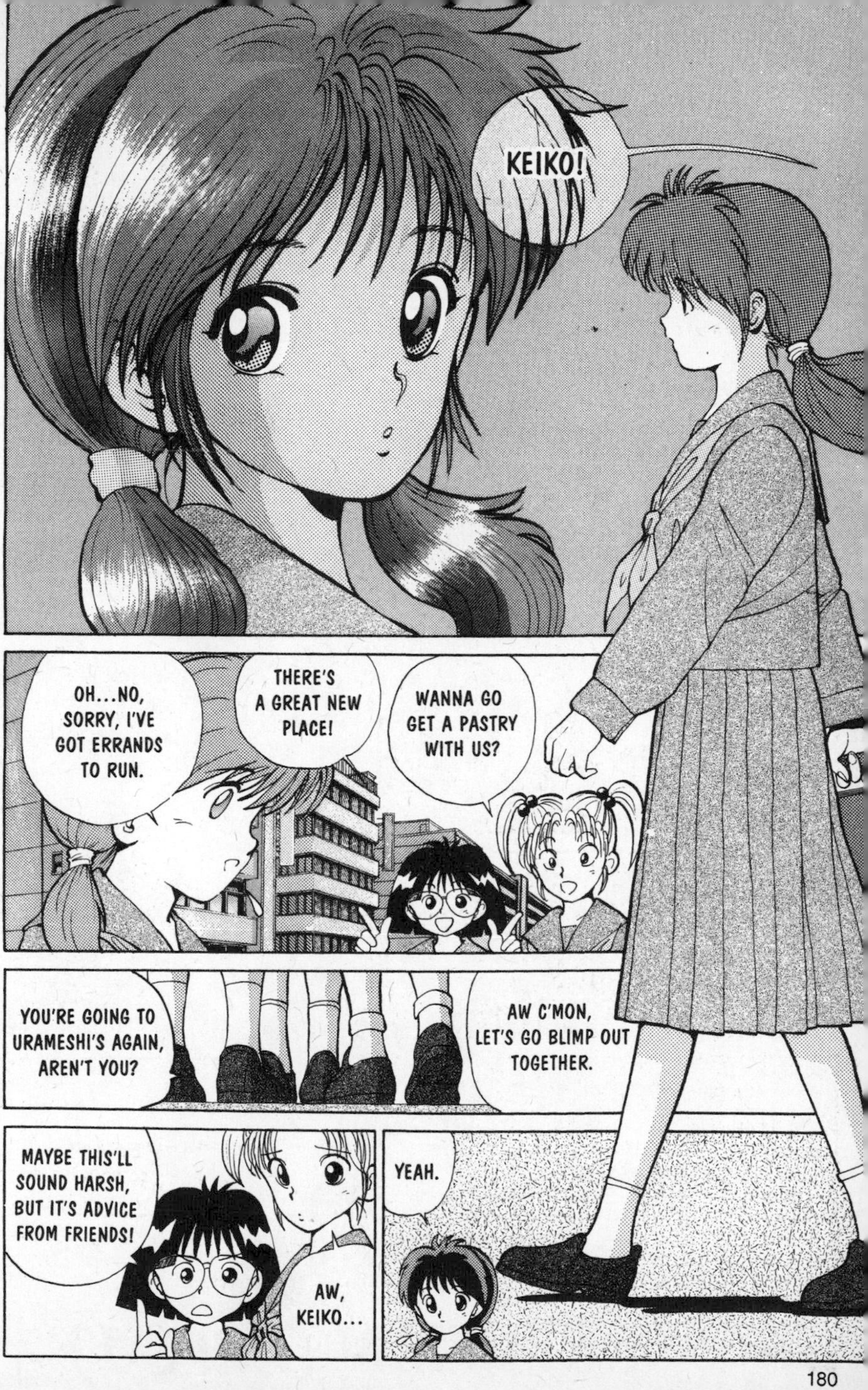
KEIKO!
WANNA GO GET A PASTRY WITH US?
THERE'S A GREAT NEW PLACE!
OH...NO, SORRY, I'VE GOT ERRANDS TO RUN.
AW C'MON, LET'S GO BLIMP OUT TOGETHER.
YOU'RE GOING TO URAMESHI'S AGAIN, AREN'T YOU?
YEAH.
MAYBE THIS'LL SOUND HARSH, BUT IT'S ADVICE FROM FRIENDS!
AW, KEIKO...

READ THIS WAY

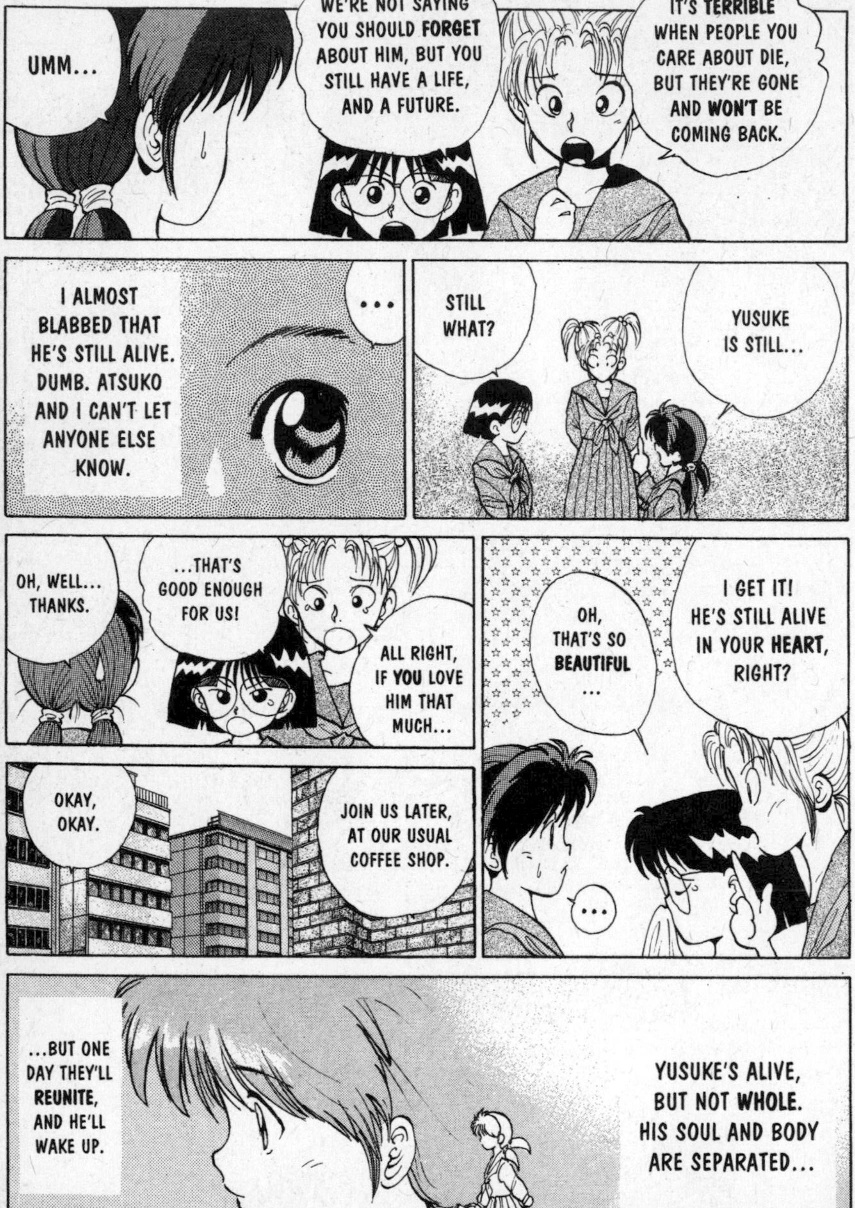

IT'S TERRIBLE WHEN PEOPLE YOU CARE ABOUT DIE, BUT THEY'RE GONE AND WON'T BE COMING BACK.
WE'RE NOT SAYING YOU SHOULD FORGET ABOUT HIM, BUT YOU STILL HAVE A LIFE, AND A FUTURE.
UMM...
YUSUKE IS STILL...
STILL WHAT?
...
I ALMOST BLABBED THAT HE'S STILL ALIVE. DUMB. ATSUKO AND I CAN'T LET ANYONE ELSE KNOW.
I GET IT! HE'S STILL ALIVE IN YOUR HEART, RIGHT?
OH, THAT'S SO BEAUTIFUL...
...
ALL RIGHT, IF YOU LOVE HIM THAT MUCH...
...THAT'S GOOD ENOUGH FOR US!
OH, WELL... THANKS.
JOIN US LATER, AT OUR USUAL COFFEE SHOP.
OKAY, OKAY.
YUSUKE'S ALIVE, BUT NOT WHOLE. HIS SOUL AND BODY ARE SEPARATED...
...BUT ONE DAY THEY'LL REUNITE, AND HE'LL WAKE UP.

READ THIS WAY

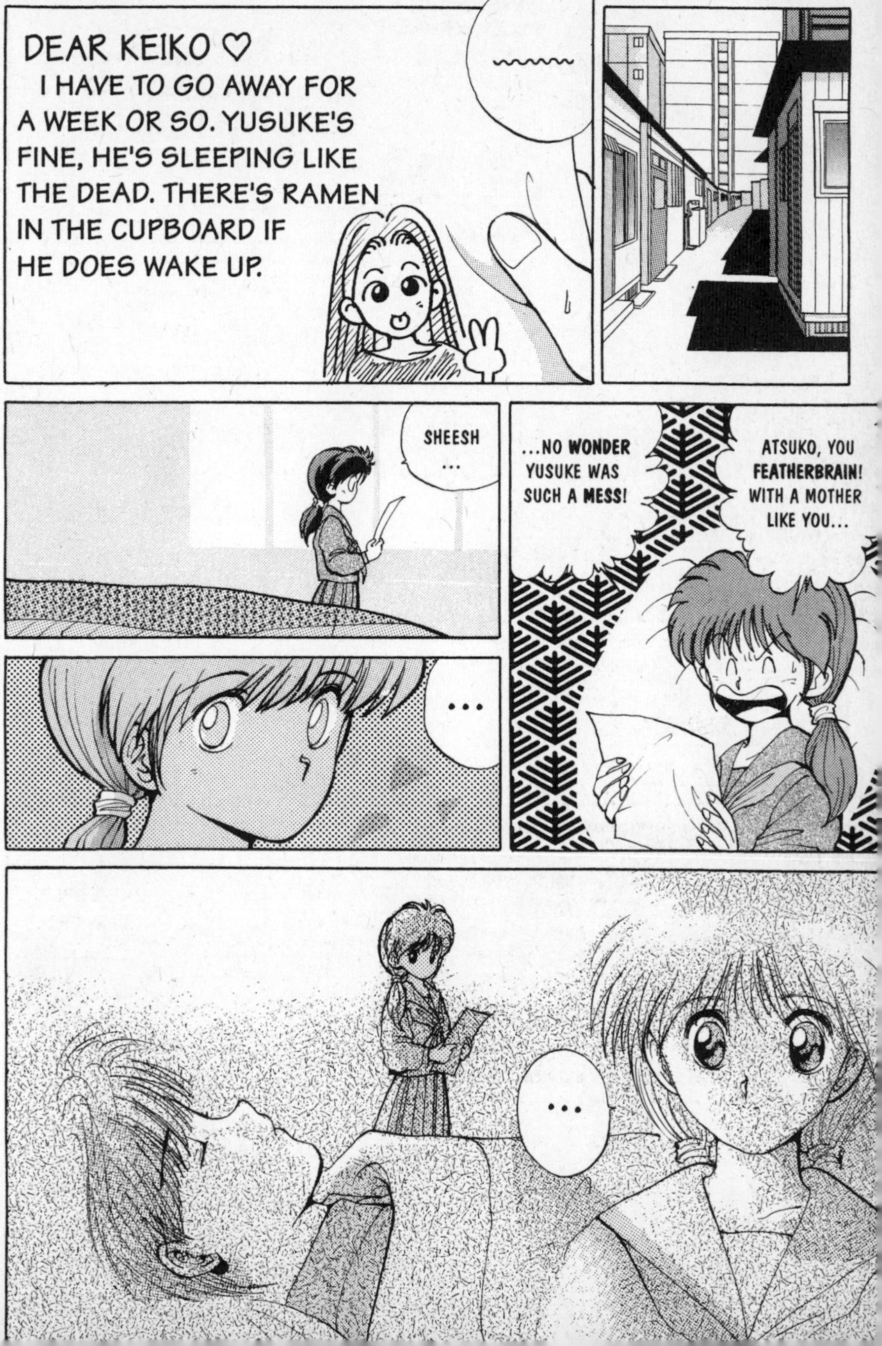
DEAR KEIKO ♡
I HAVE TO GO AWAY FOR A WEEK OR SO. YUSUKE'S FINE, HE'S SLEEPING LIKE THE DEAD. THERE'S RAMEN IN THE CUPBOARD IF HE DOES WAKE UP.
ATSUKO, YOU FEATHERBRAIN! WITH A MOTHER LIKE YOU...
...NO WONDER YUSUKE WAS SUCH A MESS!
SHEESH ...
...
...

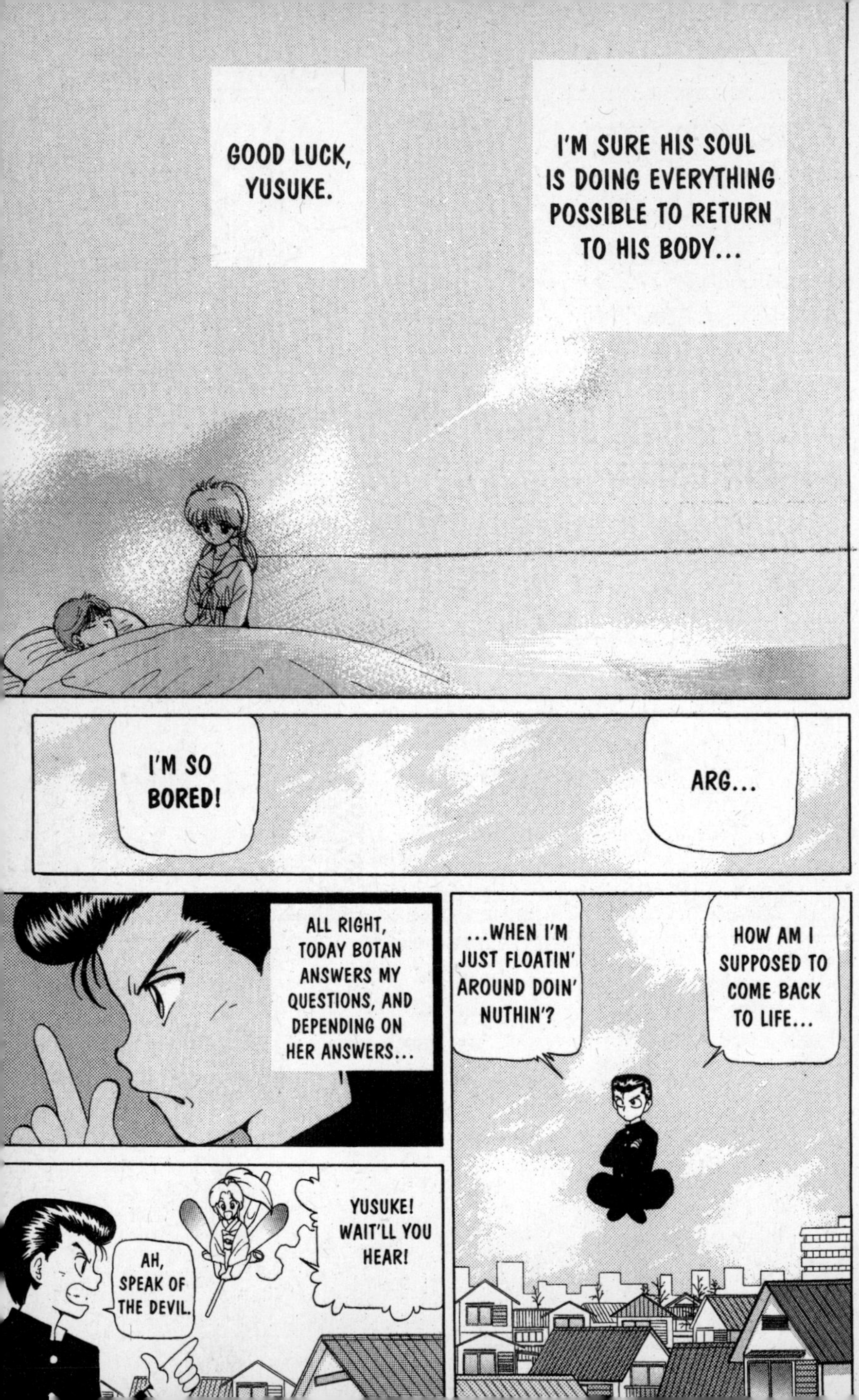
I'M SURE HIS SOUL IS DOING EVERYTHING POSSIBLE TO RETURN TO HIS BODY...
GOOD LUCK, YUSUKE.
ARG...
I'M SO BORED!
HOW AM I SUPPOSED TO COME BACK TO LIFE...
...WHEN I'M JUST FLOATIN' AROUND DOIN' NUTHIN'?
ALL RIGHT, TODAY BOTAN ANSWERS MY QUESTIONS, AND DEPENDING ON HER ANSWERS...
YUSUKE! WAIT'LL YOU HEAR!
AH, SPEAK OF THE DEVIL.

READ THIS WAY

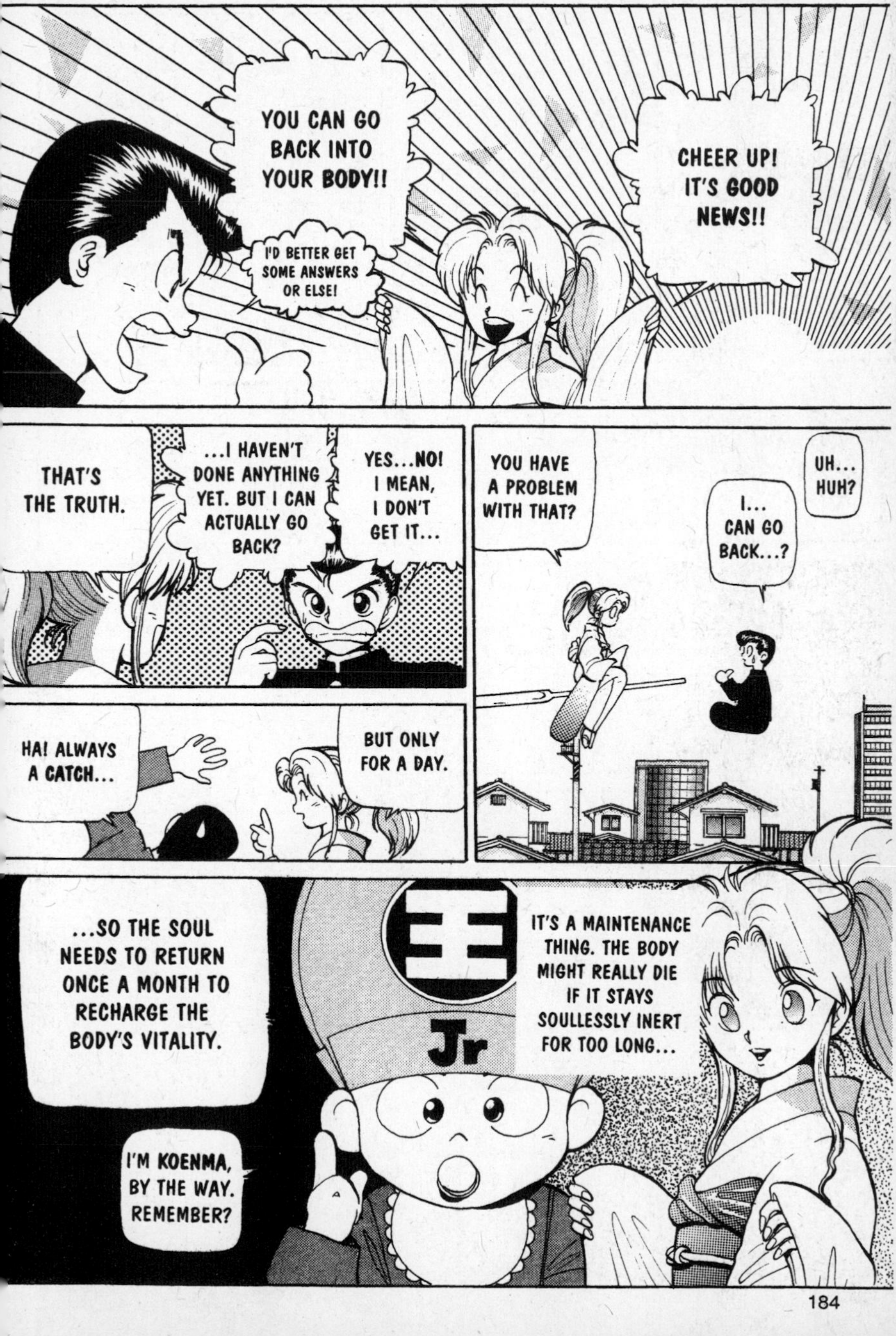
CHEER UP! IT'S GOOD NEWS!!
YOU CAN GO BACK INTO YOUR BODY!!
I'D BETTER GET SOME ANSWERS OR ELSE!
UH... HUH?
I... CAN GO BACK...?
YOU HAVE A PROBLEM WITH THAT?
YES...NO! I MEAN, I DON'T GET IT...
...I HAVEN'T DONE ANYTHING YET. BUT I CAN ACTUALLY GO BACK?
THAT'S THE TRUTH.
BUT ONLY FOR A DAY.
HA! ALWAYS A CATCH...
IT'S A MAINTENANCE THING. THE BODY MIGHT REALLY DIE IF IT STAYS SOULLESSLY INERT FOR TOO LONG...
...SO THE SOUL NEEDS TO RETURN ONCE A MONTH TO RECHARGE THE BODY'S VITALITY.
Jr
I'M KOENMA, BY THE WAY. REMEMBER?

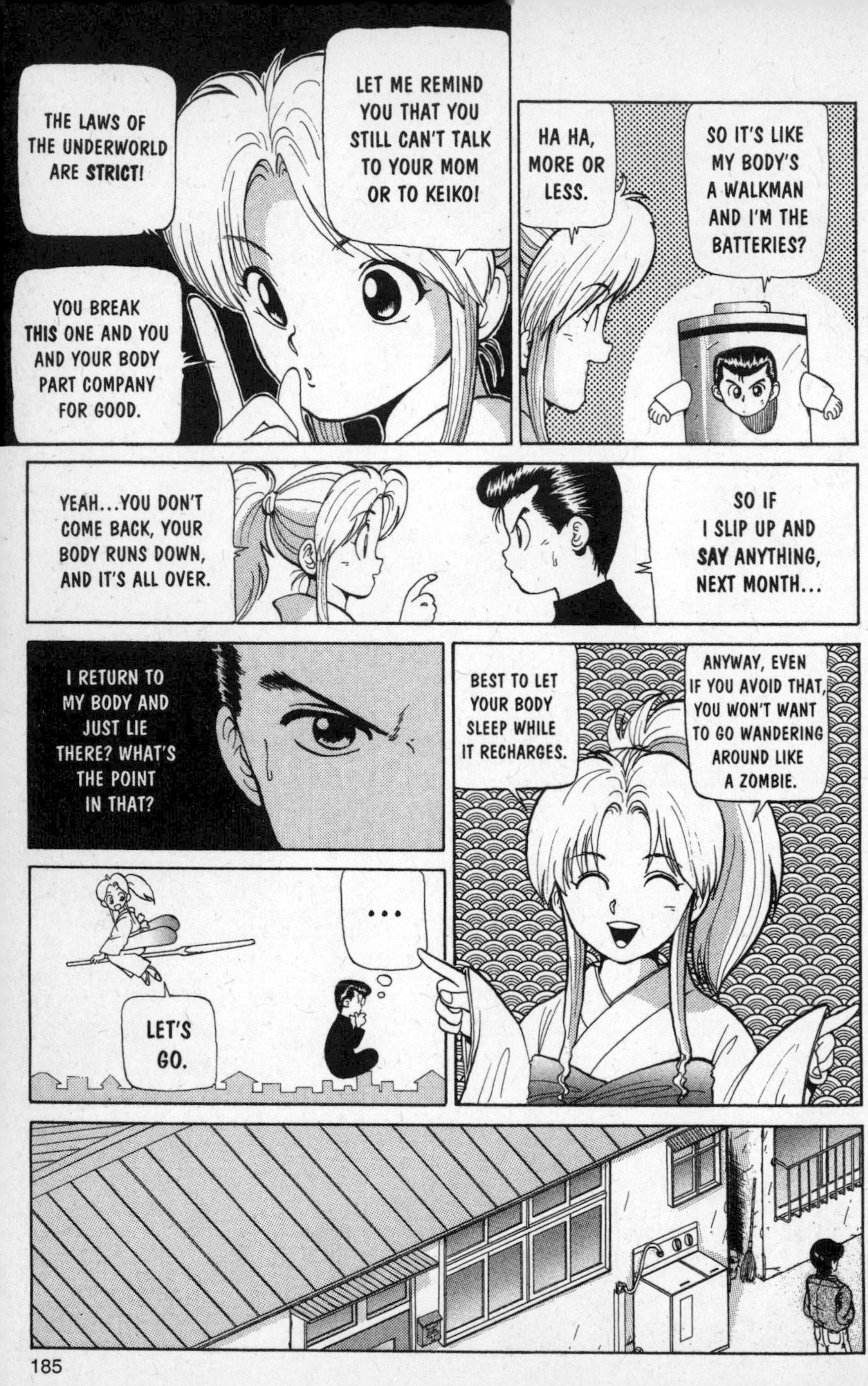
SO IT'S LIKE MY BODY'S A WALKMAN AND I'M THE BATTERIES?
HA HA, MORE OR LESS.
LET ME REMIND YOU THAT YOU STILL CAN'T TALK TO YOUR MOM OR TO KEIKO!
THE LAWS OF THE UNDERWORLD ARE STRICT!
YOU BREAK THIS ONE AND YOU AND YOUR BODY PART COMPANY FOR GOOD.
SO IF I SLIP UP AND SAY ANYTHING, NEXT MONTH...
YEAH...YOU DON'T COME BACK, YOUR BODY RUNS DOWN, AND IT'S ALL OVER.
ANYWAY, EVEN IF YOU AVOID THAT, YOU WON'T WANT TO GO WANDERING AROUND LIKE A ZOMBIE.
BEST TO LET YOUR BODY SLEEP WHILE IT RECHARGES.
I RETURN TO MY BODY AND JUST LIE THERE? WHAT'S THE POINT IN THAT?
...
LET'S GO.

READ THIS WAY

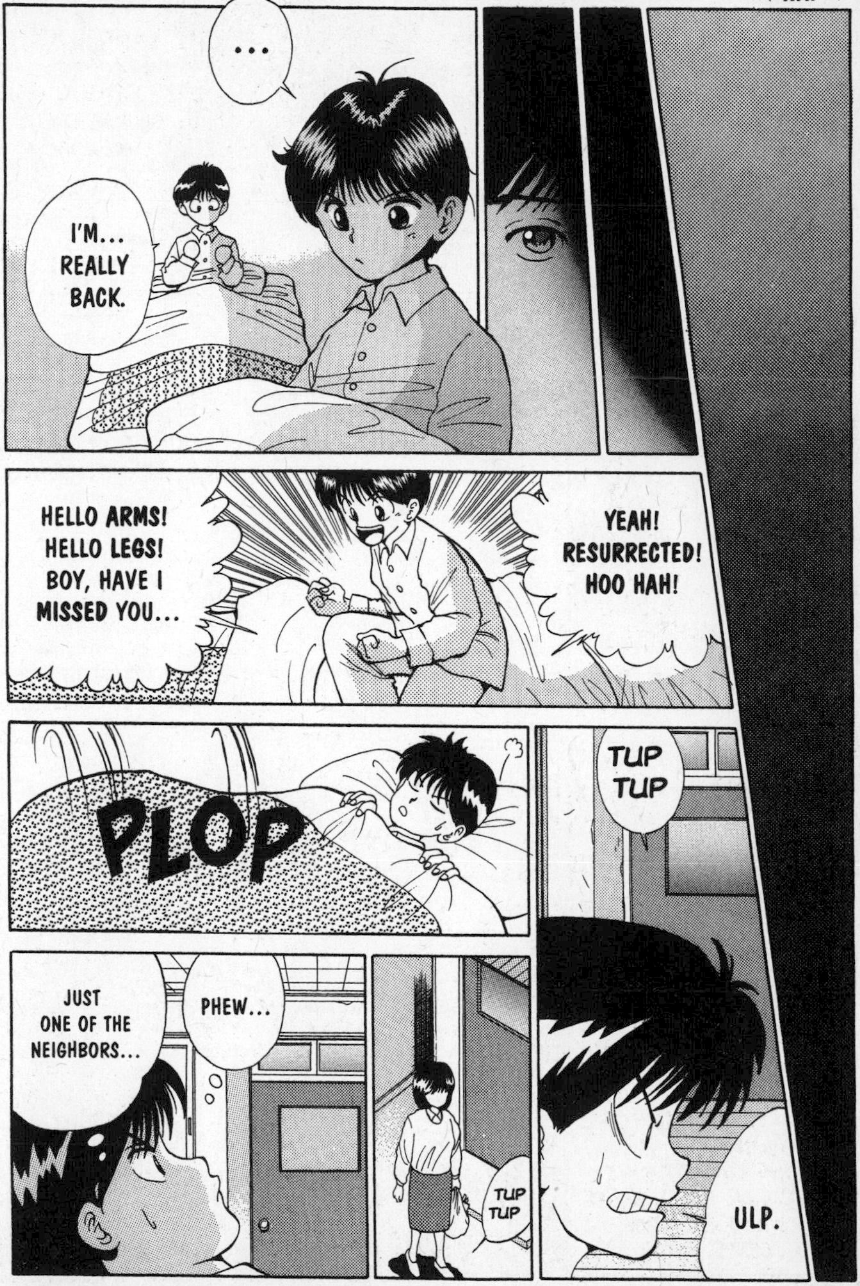
...
I'M... REALLY BACK.
YEAH! RESURRECTED! HOO HAH!
HELLO ARMS! HELLO LEGS! BOY, HAVE I MISSED YOU...
TUP TUP
ULP.
PLOP
TUP TUP
PHEW...
JUST ONE OF THE NEIGHBORS...

READ THIS WAY

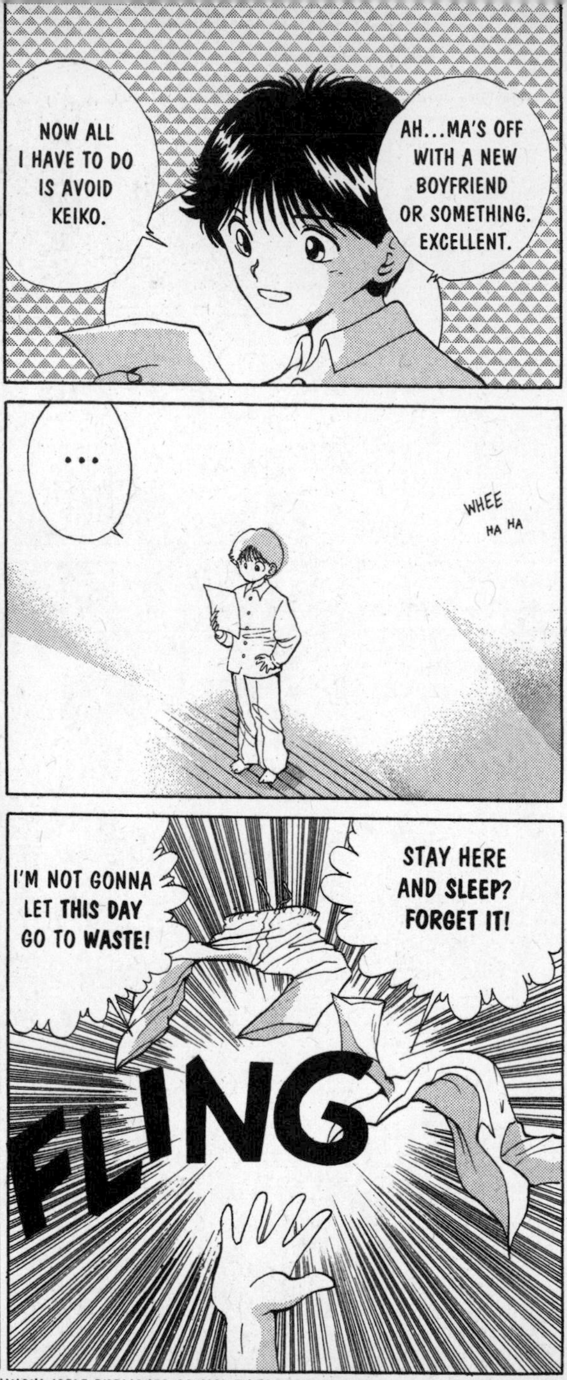
AH...MA'S OFF WITH A NEW BOYFRIEND OR SOMETHING. EXCELLENT.
NOW ALL I HAVE TO DO IS AVOID KEIKO.
...
WHEE
HA HA
STAY HERE AND SLEEP? FORGET IT!
I'M NOT GONNA LET THIS DAY GO TO WASTE!
FLING

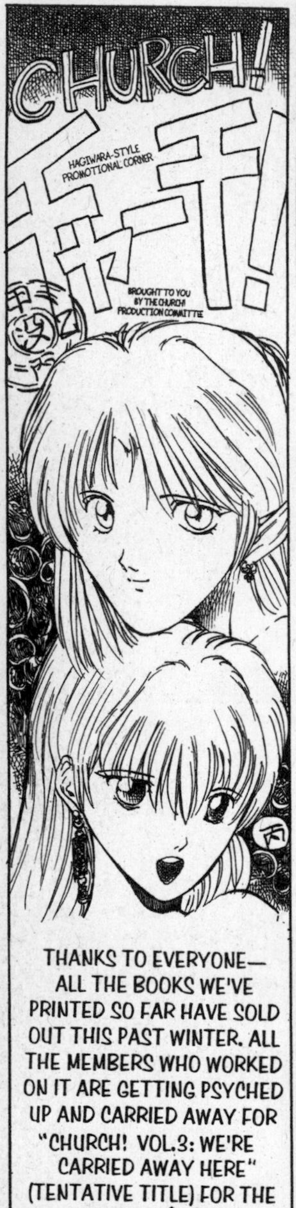
CHURCH!
HAGIWARA-STYLE PROMOTIONAL CORNER
BROUGHT TO YOU BY THE CHURCH! PRODUCTION COMMITTEE
THANKS TO EVERYONE—ALL THE BOOKS WE'VE PRINTED SO FAR HAVE SOLD OUT THIS PAST WINTER. ALL THE MEMBERS WHO WORKED ON IT ARE GETTING PSYCHED UP AND CARRIED AWAY FOR "CHURCH! VOL.3: WE'RE CARRIED AWAY HERE" (TENTATIVE TITLE) FOR THE SUMMER DÔJINSHI CONVENTION!!!

* THIS IS AN ADVERTISEMENT FOR A DÔJINSHI (SELF-PUBLISHED COMIC) BY TOGASHI AND CO. UNFORTUNATELY, THE COMIC IS NO LONGER AVAILABLE. ---EDITOR

READ THIS WAY

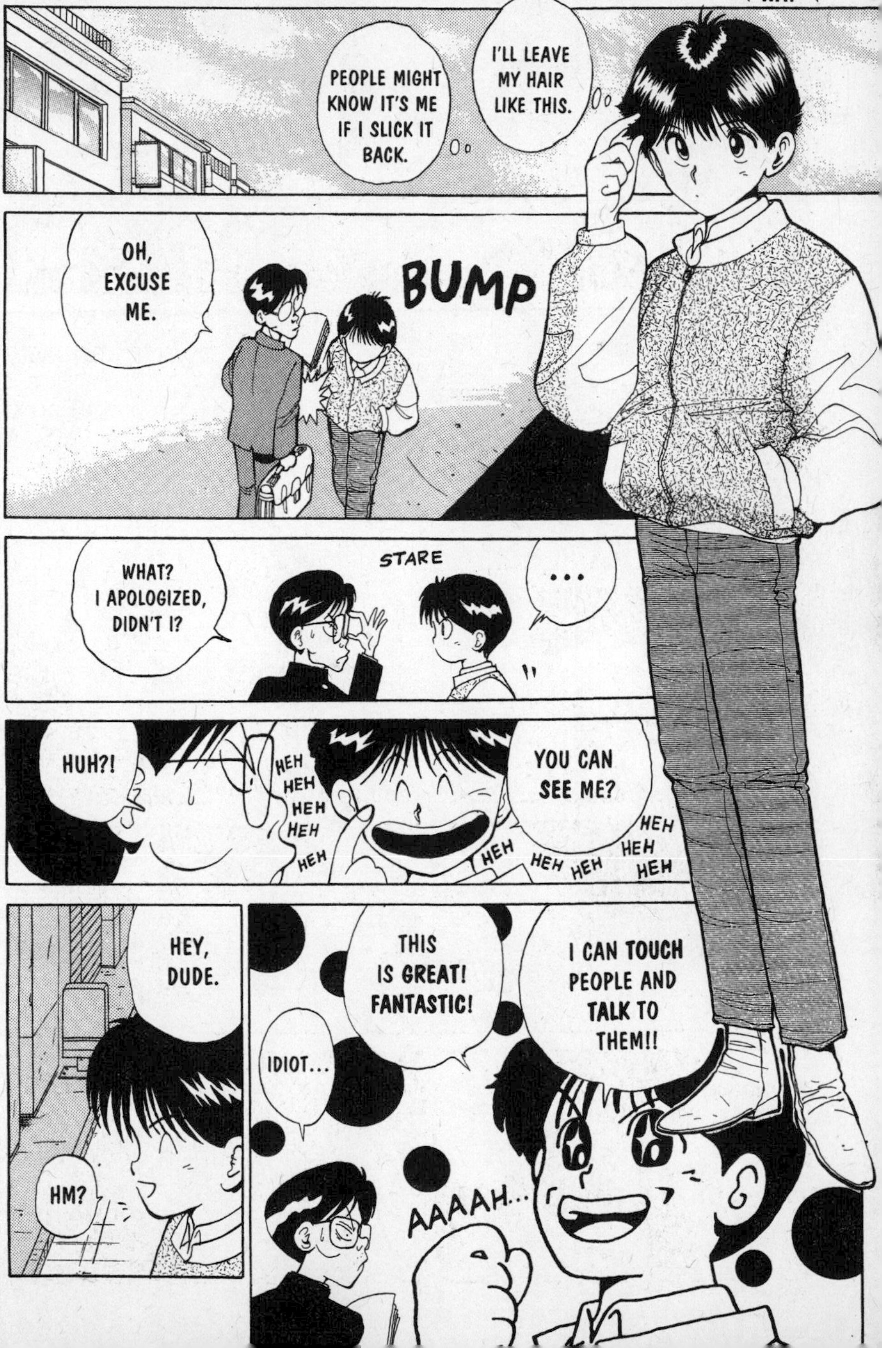
I'LL LEAVE MY HAIR LIKE THIS.
PEOPLE MIGHT KNOW IT'S ME IF I SLICK IT BACK.
BUMP
OH, EXCUSE ME.
...
STARE
WHAT? I APOLOGIZED, DIDN'T I?
YOU CAN SEE ME?
HEH HEH HEH HEH HEH
HEH HEH HEH HEH HEH HEH
HEH HEH HEH HEH HEH
HUH?!
I CAN TOUCH PEOPLE AND TALK TO THEM!!
THIS IS GREAT! FANTASTIC!
IDIOT...
AAAAH...
HEY, DUDE.
HM?

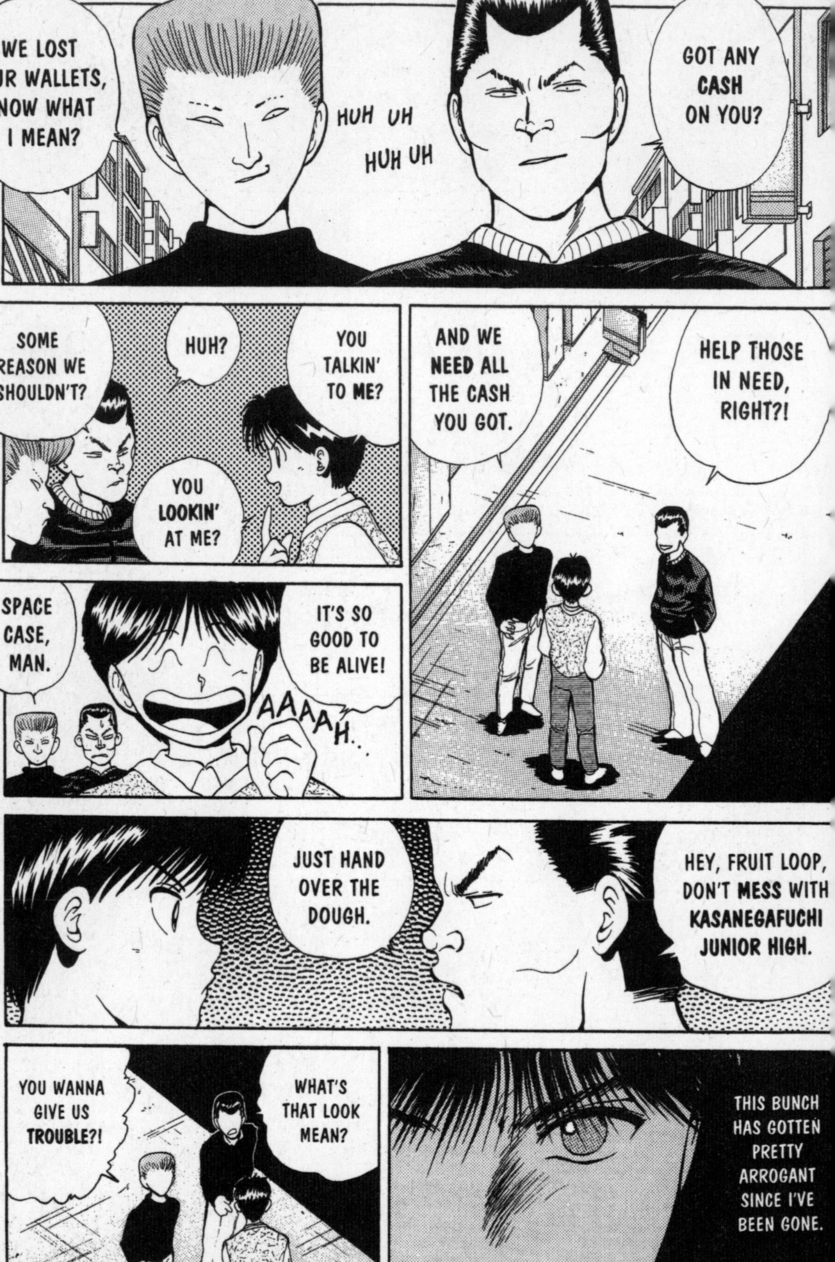
GOT ANY CASH ON YOU?
HUH UH HUH UH
WE LOST OUR WALLETS, KNOW WHAT I MEAN?
HELP THOSE IN NEED, RIGHT?!
AND WE NEED ALL THE CASH YOU GOT.
YOU TALKIN' TO ME?
HUH?
SOME REASON WE SHOULDN'T?
YOU LOOKIN' AT ME?
IT'S SO GOOD TO BE ALIVE!
AAAAH...
SPACE CASE, MAN.
HEY, FRUIT LOOP, DON'T MESS WITH KASANEGAFUCHI JUNIOR HIGH.
JUST HAND OVER THE DOUGH.
THIS BUNCH HAS GOTTEN PRETTY ARROGANT SINCE I'VE BEEN GONE.
WHAT'S THAT LOOK MEAN?
YOU WANNA GIVE US TROUBLE?!

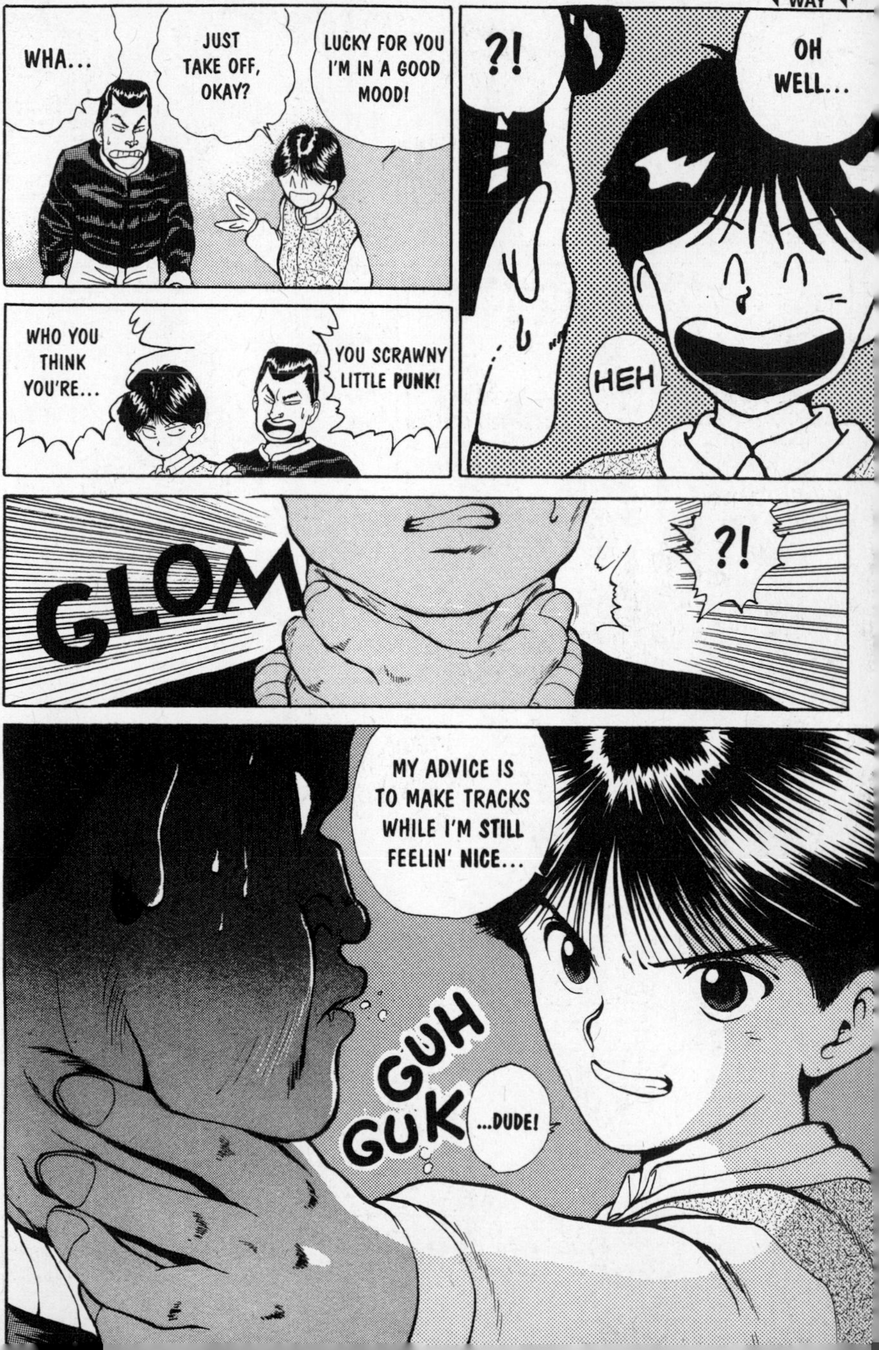
READ THIS WAY
OH WELL...
?!
HEH
LUCKY FOR YOU I'M IN A GOOD MOOD!
JUST TAKE OFF, OKAY?
WHA...
WHO YOU THINK YOU'RE...
YOU SCRAWNY LITTLE PUNK!
?!
GLOM
MY ADVICE IS TO MAKE TRACKS WHILE I'M STILL FEELIN' NICE...
GUH GUK
...DUDE!

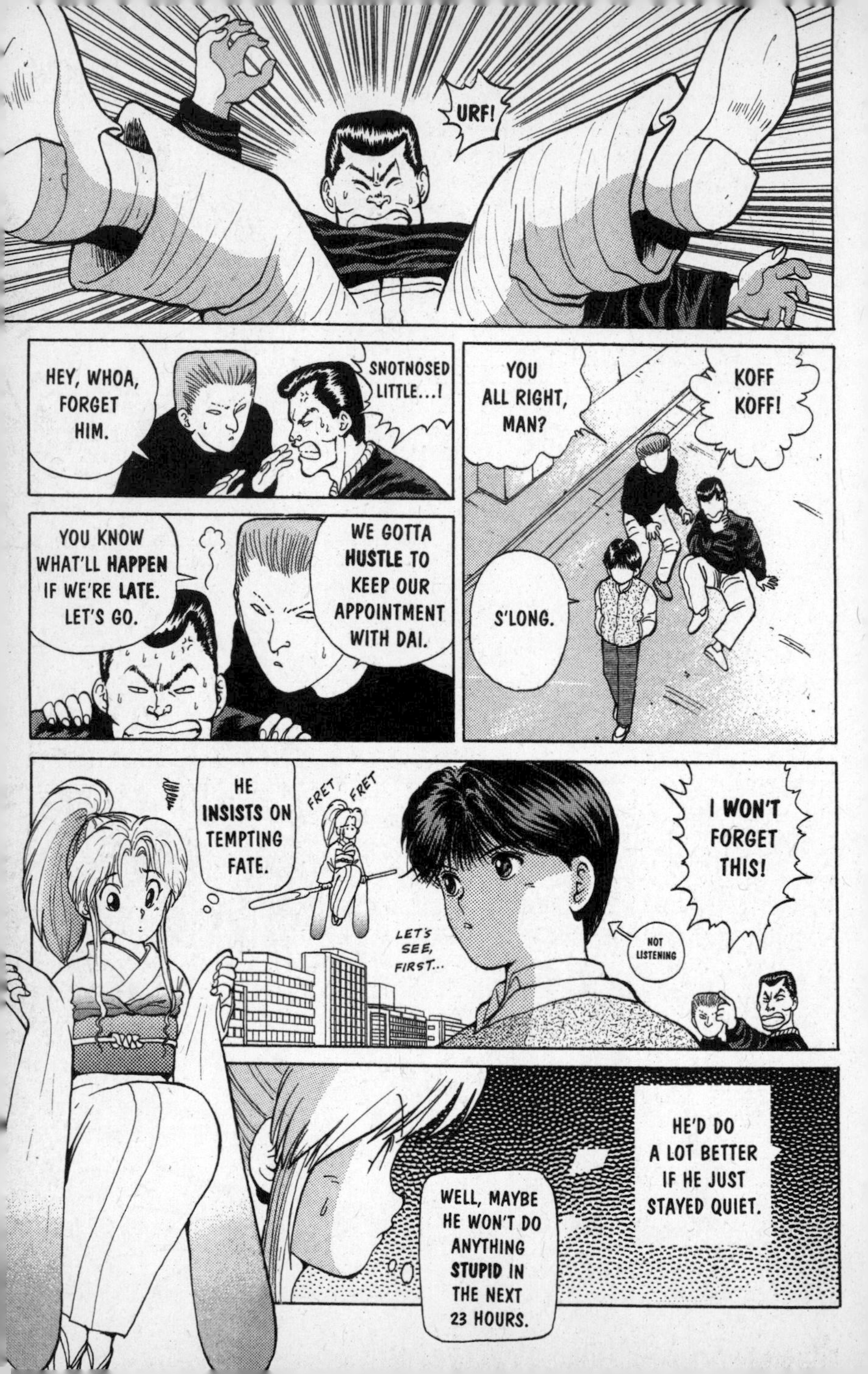
URF!
KOFF KOFF!
YOU ALL RIGHT, MAN?
S'LONG.
SNOTNOSED LITTLE...!
HEY, WHOA, FORGET HIM.
WE GOTTA HUSTLE TO KEEP OUR APPOINTMENT WITH DAI.
YOU KNOW WHAT'LL HAPPEN IF WE'RE LATE. LET'S GO.
I WON'T FORGET THIS!
NOT LISTENING
LET'S SEE, FIRST...
FRET FRET
HE INSISTS ON TEMPTING FATE.
HE'D DO A LOT BETTER IF HE JUST STAYED QUIET.
WELL, MAYBE HE WON'T DO ANYTHING STUPID IN THE NEXT 23 HOURS.

READ THIS WAY

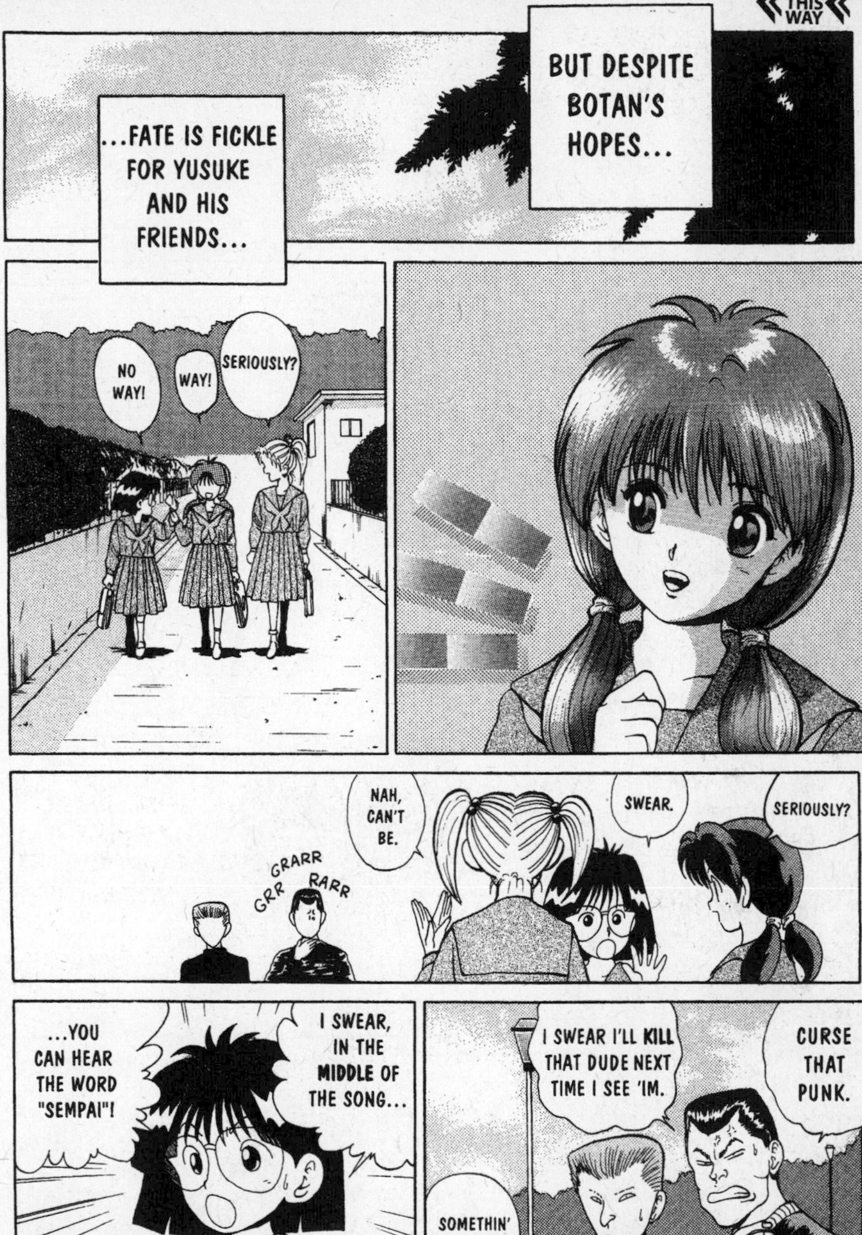

BUT DESPITE BOTAN'S HOPES...
...FATE IS FICKLE FOR YUSUKE AND HIS FRIENDS...
SERIOUSLY?
WAY!
NO WAY!
SERIOUSLY?
SWEAR.
NAH, CAN'T BE.
GRR GRARR RARR
CURSE THAT PUNK.
I SWEAR I'LL **KILL** THAT DUDE NEXT TIME I SEE 'IM.
SOMETHIN' FAMILIAR ABOUT 'IM...
I SWEAR, IN THE **MIDDLE** OF THE SONG...
...YOU CAN HEAR THE WORD "SEMPAI"!

READ THIS WAY

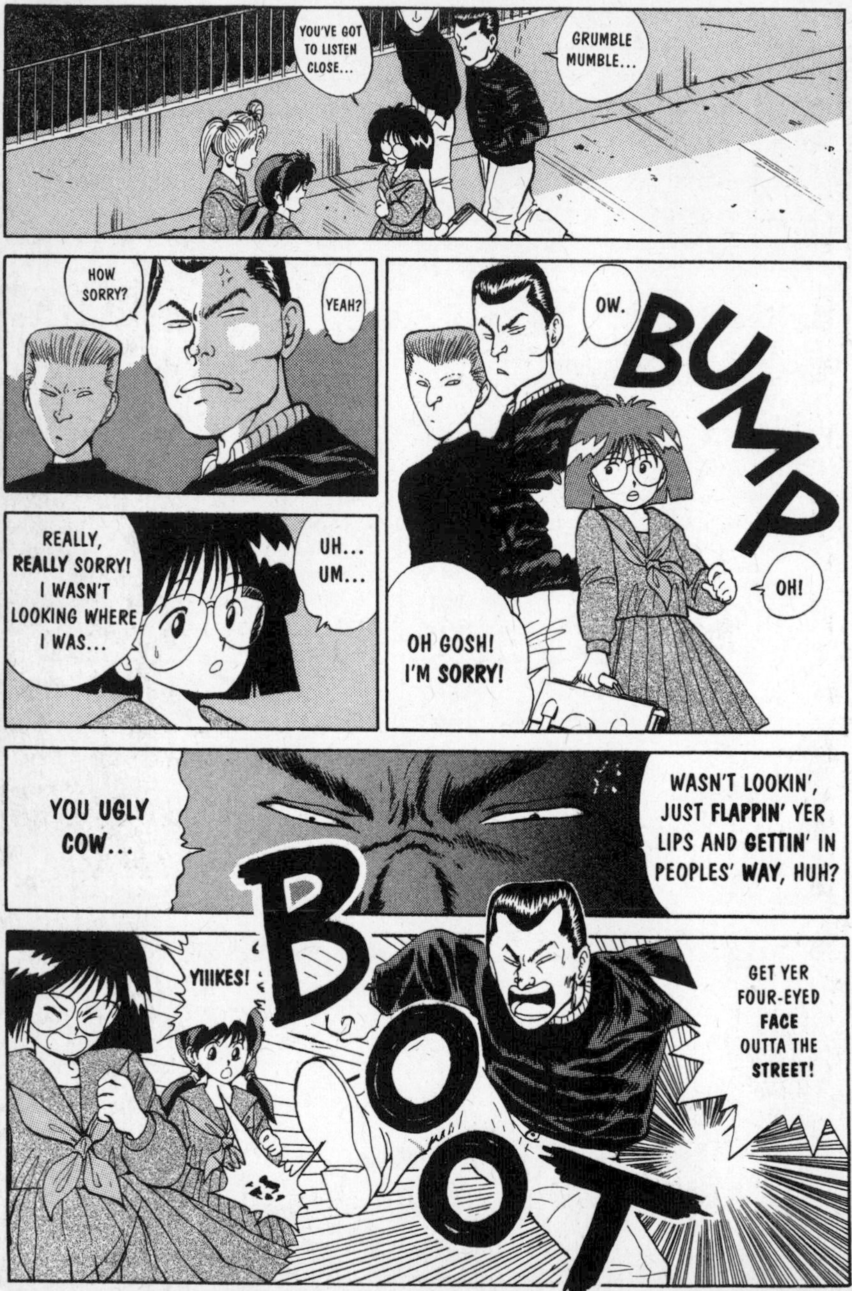
GRUMBLE MUMBLE...
YOU'VE GOT TO LISTEN CLOSE...
BUMP
OW.
OH!
OH GOSH! I'M SORRY!
YEAH?
HOW SORRY?
UH... UM...
REALLY, REALLY SORRY! I WASN'T LOOKING WHERE I WAS...
WASN'T LOOKIN', JUST FLAPPIN' YER LIPS AND GETTIN' IN PEOPLES' WAY, HUH?
YOU UGLY COW...
GET YER FOUR-EYED FACE OUTTA THE STREET!
BOOOT
YIIIKES!

READ THIS WAY

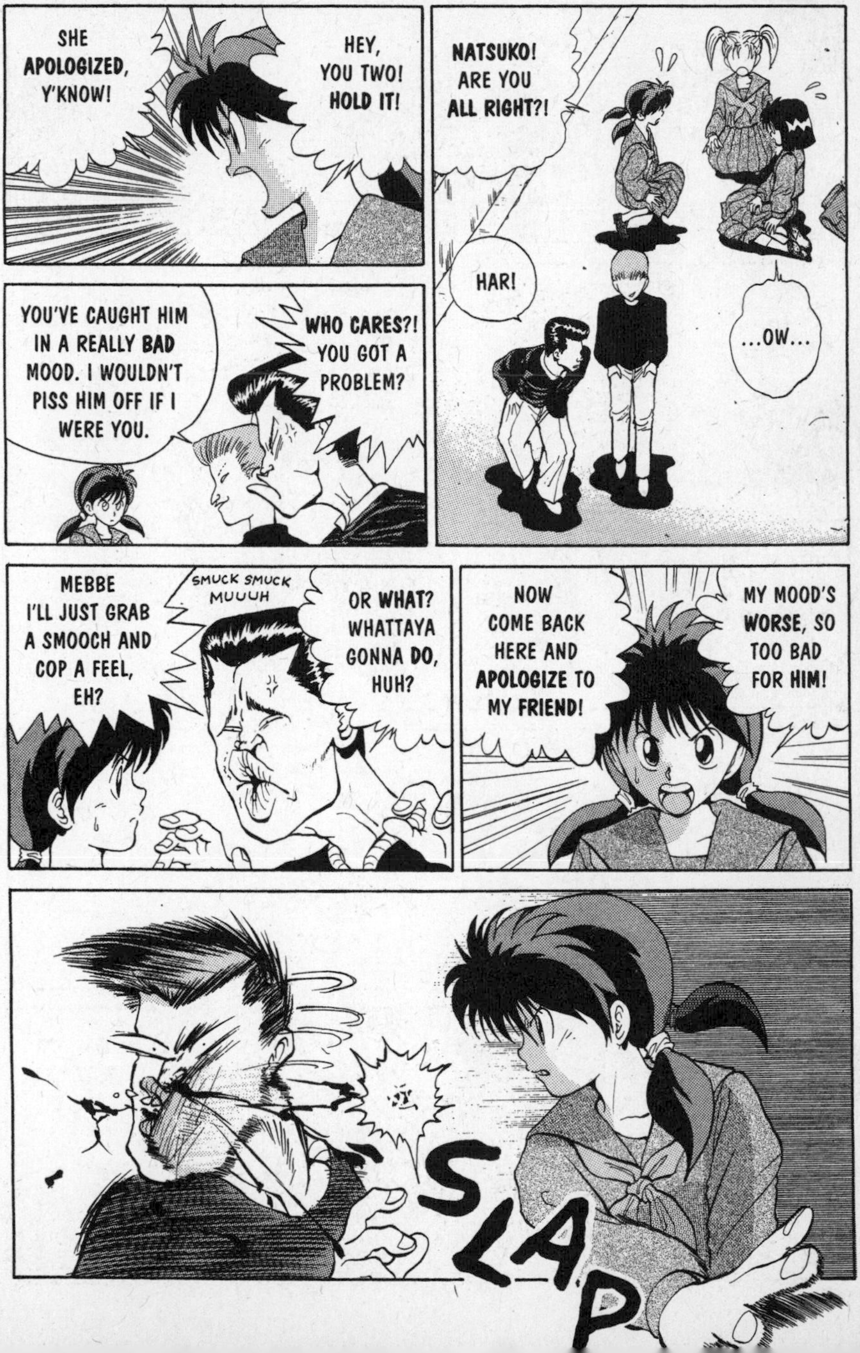

NATSUKO! ARE YOU ALL RIGHT?!
HAR!
...OW...
HEY, YOU TWO! HOLD IT!
SHE APOLOGIZED, Y'KNOW!
WHO CARES?! YOU GOT A PROBLEM?
YOU'VE CAUGHT HIM IN A REALLY BAD MOOD. I WOULDN'T PISS HIM OFF IF I WERE YOU.
MY MOOD'S WORSE, SO TOO BAD FOR HIM!
NOW COME BACK HERE AND APOLOGIZE TO MY FRIEND!
OR WHAT? WHATTAYA GONNA DO, HUH?
SMUCK SMUCK MUUUH
MEBBE I'LL JUST GRAB A SMOOCH AND COP A FEEL, EH?
SLAP

READ THIS WAY

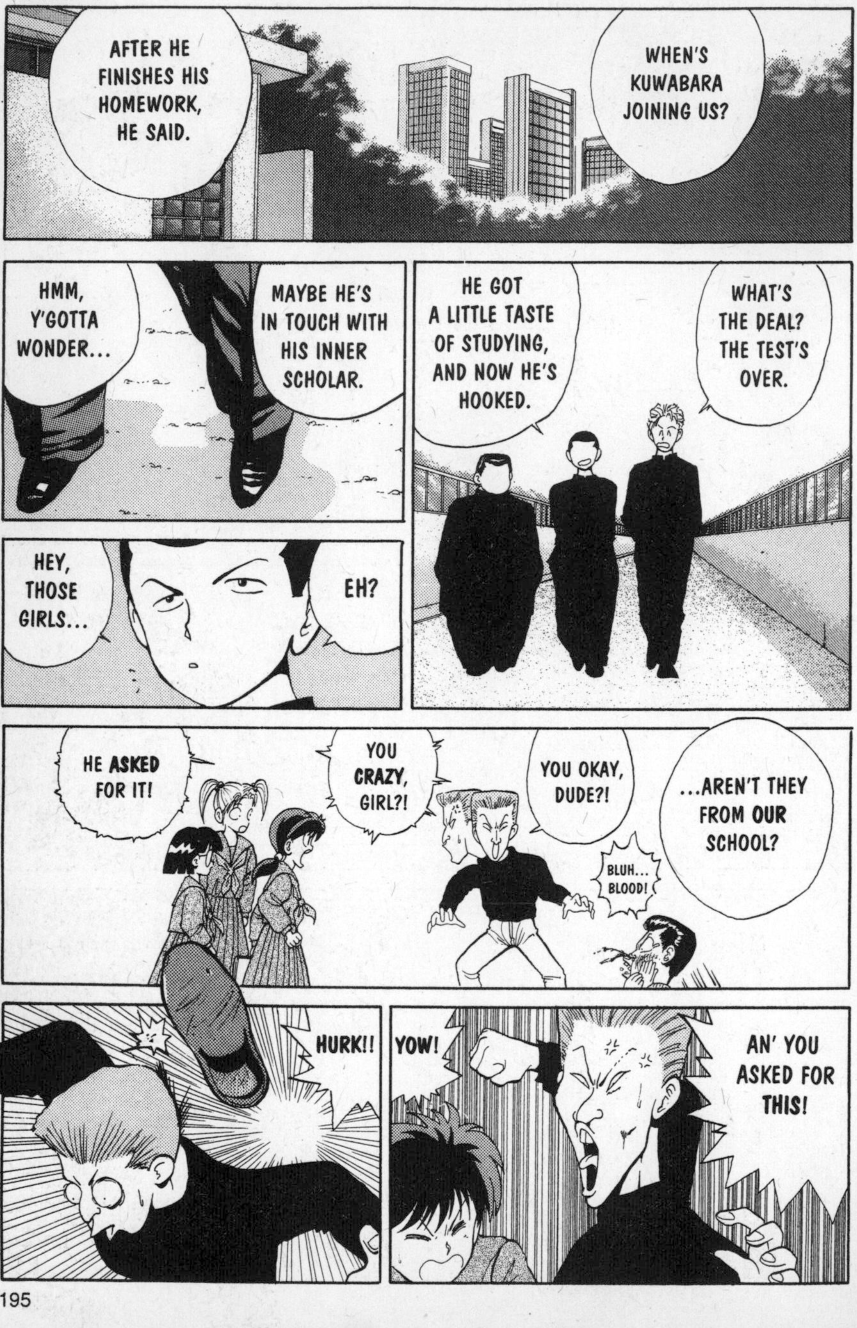

WHEN'S KUWABARA JOINING US?
AFTER HE FINISHES HIS HOMEWORK, HE SAID.
WHAT'S THE DEAL? THE TEST'S OVER.
HE GOT A LITTLE TASTE OF STUDYING, AND NOW HE'S HOOKED.
MAYBE HE'S IN TOUCH WITH HIS INNER SCHOLAR.
HMM, Y'GOTTA WONDER...
EH?
HEY, THOSE GIRLS...
...AREN'T THEY FROM OUR SCHOOL?
BLUH... BLOOD!
YOU OKAY, DUDE?!
YOU CRAZY, GIRL?!
HE ASKED FOR IT!
AN' YOU ASKED FOR THIS!
YOW!
HURK!!

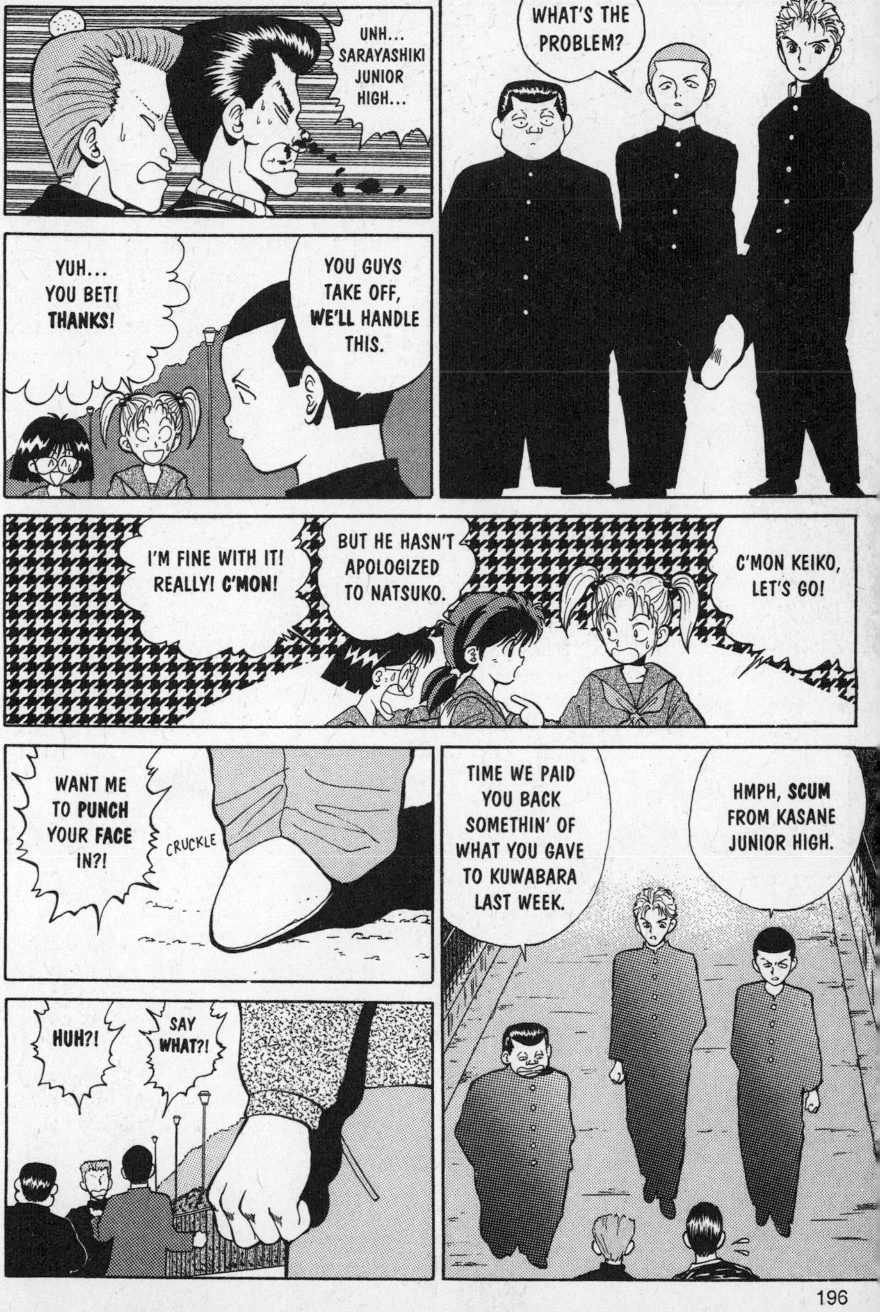
WHAT'S THE PROBLEM?
UNH... SARAYASHIKI JUNIOR HIGH...
YOU GUYS TAKE OFF, WE'LL HANDLE THIS.
YUH... YOU BET! THANKS!
C'MON KEIKO, LET'S GO!
BUT HE HASN'T APOLOGIZED TO NATSUKO.
I'M FINE WITH IT! REALLY! C'MON!
HMPH, SCUM FROM KASANE JUNIOR HIGH.
TIME WE PAID YOU BACK SOMETHIN' OF WHAT YOU GAVE TO KUWABARA LAST WEEK.
WANT ME TO PUNCH YOUR FACE IN?!
CRUCKLE
SAY WHAT?!
HUH?!

READ THIS WAY

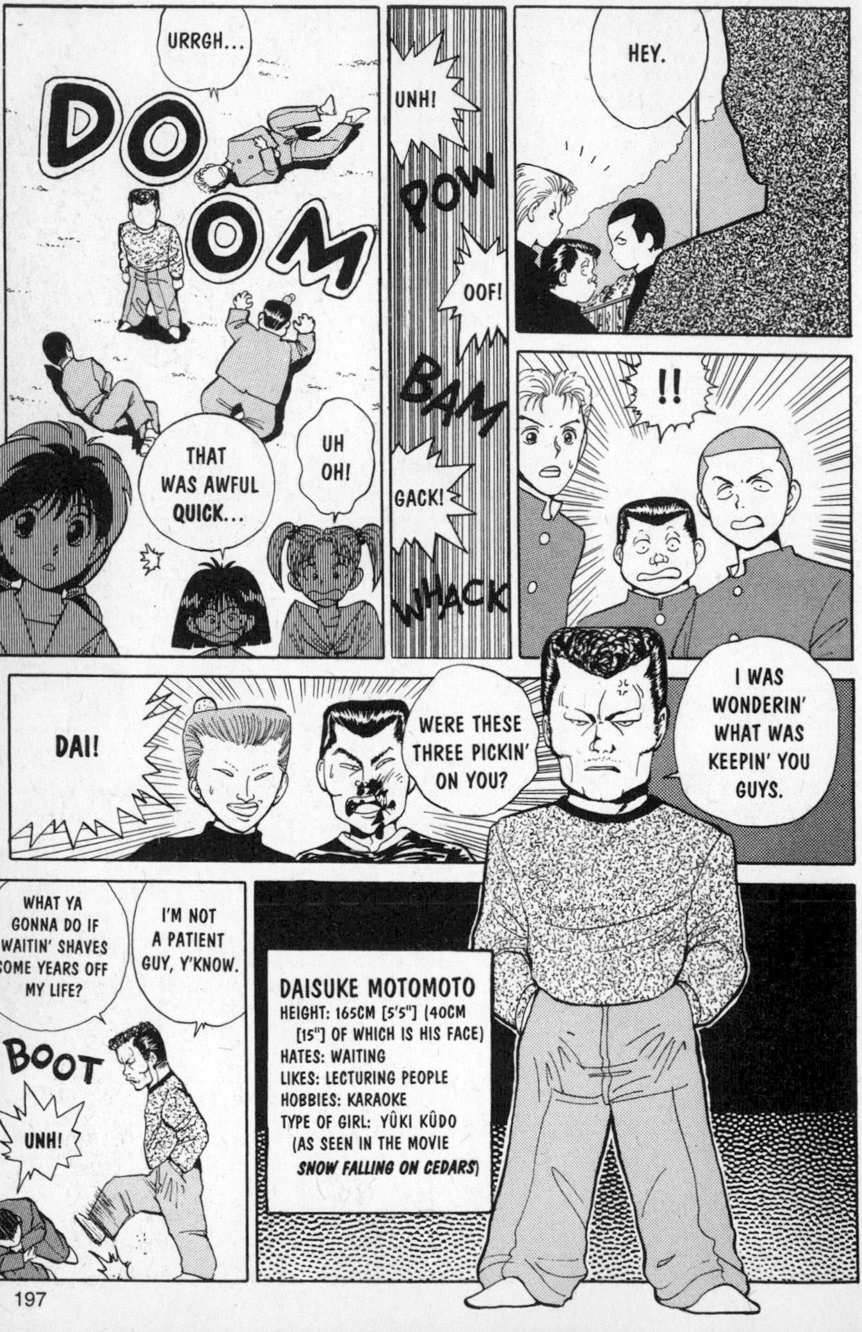
HEY.
!!
UNH!
POW
OOF!
BAM
GACK!
WHACK
URRGH...
DOOM
UH OH!
THAT WAS AWFUL QUICK...
I WAS WONDERIN' WHAT WAS KEEPIN' YOU GUYS.
WERE THESE THREE PICKIN' ON YOU?
DAI!
DAISUKE MOTOMOTO
HEIGHT: 165CM [5'5"] (40CM [15"] OF WHICH IS HIS FACE)
HATES: WAITING
LIKES: LECTURING PEOPLE
HOBBIES: KARAOKE
TYPE OF GIRL: YÛKI KÛDO (AS SEEN IN THE MOVIE *SNOW FALLING ON CEDARS*)
I'M NOT A PATIENT GUY, Y'KNOW.
WHAT YA GONNA DO IF WAITIN' SHAVES SOME YEARS OFF MY LIFE?
BOOT
UNH!

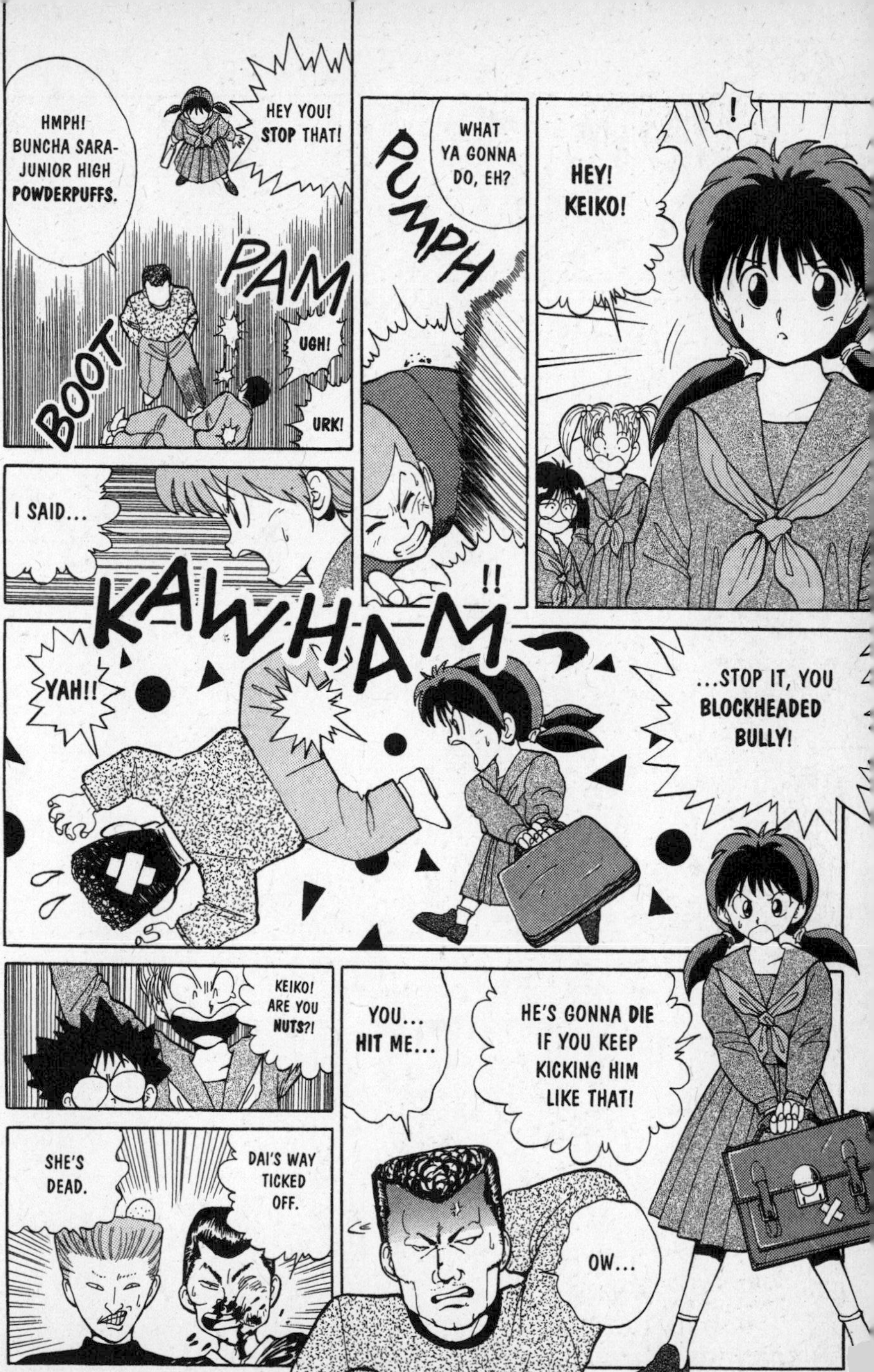
!
HEY! KEIKO!
WHAT YA GONNA DO, EH?
PUMPH
!!
HEY YOU! STOP THAT!
HMPH! BUNCHA SARA-JUNIOR HIGH POWDERPUFFS.
PAM
UGH!
BOOT
URK!
I SAID...
...STOP IT, YOU BLOCKHEADED BULLY!
KAWHAM
YAH!!
HE'S GONNA DIE IF YOU KEEP KICKING HIM LIKE THAT!
YOU... HIT ME...
OW...
KEIKO! ARE YOU NUTS?!
DAI'S WAY TICKED OFF.
SHE'S DEAD.

READ THIS WAY

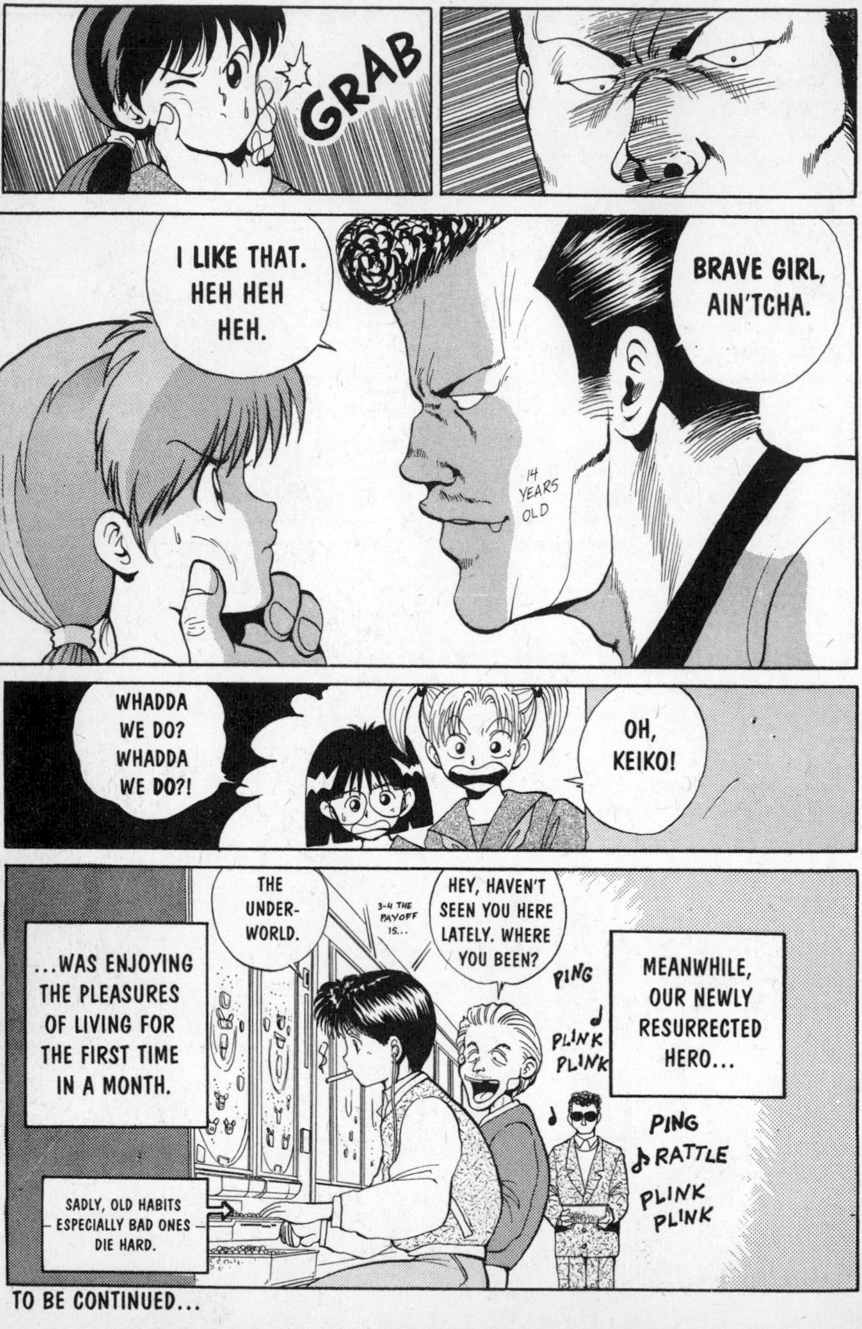
GRAB
BRAVE GIRL, AIN'TCHA.
14 YEARS OLD
I LIKE THAT. HEH HEH HEH.
OH, KEIKO!
WHADDA WE DO? WHADDA WE DO?!
MEANWHILE, OUR NEWLY RESURRECTED HERO...
...WAS ENJOYING THE PLEASURES OF LIVING FOR THE FIRST TIME IN A MONTH.
PING
PLINK PLINK
PING
RATTLE
PLINK PLINK
HEY, HAVEN'T SEEN YOU HERE LATELY. WHERE YOU BEEN?
3-4 THE PAYOFF IS...
THE UNDER-WORLD.
SADLY, OLD HABITS – ESPECIALLY BAD ONES – DIE HARD.

TO BE CONTINUED...

JAPANESE CULTURAL NOTES

YuYu Hakusho has many references to Japanese ghost stories and mythology—some serious, most not so serious. Here's a list of some of the Japanese cultural elements in this volume.

YuYu Hakusho (title)—**YuYu Hakusho** is a pun in two words: YuYu, meaning "playful ghost" or "poltergeist," and Hakusho, literally meaning "white paper." A "white paper" is a term for an official report, usually a government report on important issues. (In this case, we can safely say it's tongue-in-cheek.) In other words, a close translation of **YuYu Hakusho** would be "Ghost Files" or "Poltergeist Report."

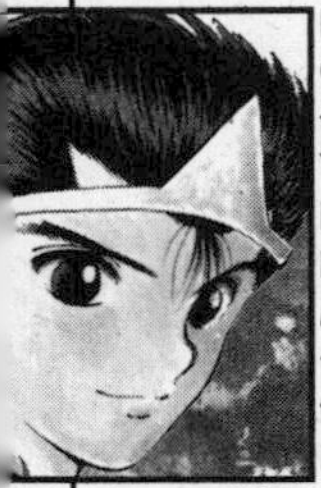

Hitaikakushi (Front and back Covers, P.1, 7, 51)—The white triangle-shaped headband Yusuke sometimes wears on his head. A traditional piece of headgear for ghosts, the *hitaikakushi* is used to adorn the dead during Buddhist funerals, and was originally intended to protect the deceased from evil spirits. Yusuke's expression on page 7 is a parody of typical "sinister ghost" expressions, including sticking out the tongue (female ghosts often have some threads of long black hair hanging down in their mouth, a traditional sign of insanity).

Hitodama (P.7, 51)—The small, ghostly flames, like will-o'-the-wisps, sometimes seen around Yusuke. Called *hitodama* ("human spirits") or *hi no tama* ("fireballs"), these flames are believed to be small flamesh. In anime, manga and other pop culture, they are often shown accompanying ghosts in human form.

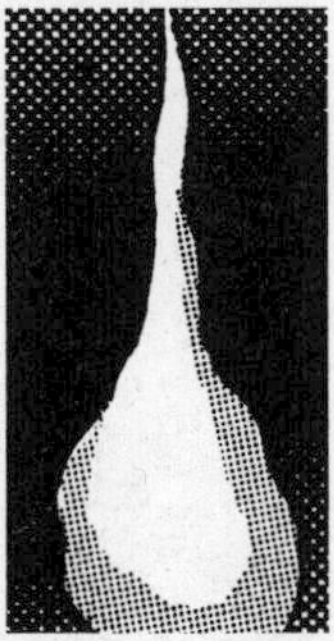

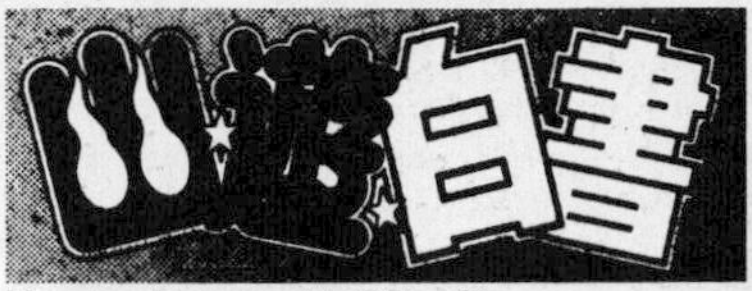

Yusuke Urameshi (P.5)—There are several puns in Yusuke's name. The "Yu" in Yusuke's name is written with the *kanji* (Japanese character) for "ghost", just like in the title of the series. Urameshi is a phrase stereotypically said by wailing ghosts ("Urameshiii…") Yusuke and Kuwabara's hair is slicked back in the classic "tough" style of Japanese gang members.

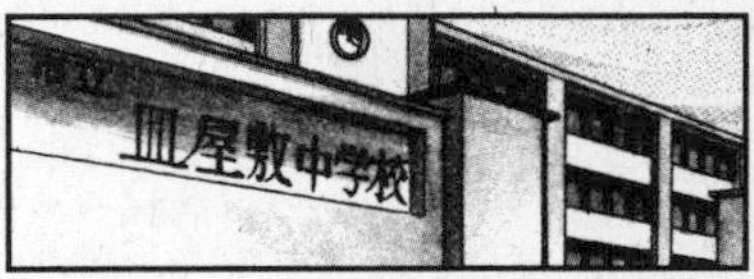
皿屋敷中学校

Sarayashiki (P.10)—The name of the main characters' high school, Sarayashiki ("Dish Mansion"), is the name of a haunted mansion in a famous Japanese ghost story, **Banchô Sarayashiki**. The original story has been adapted into several Japanese big screen and TV movies.

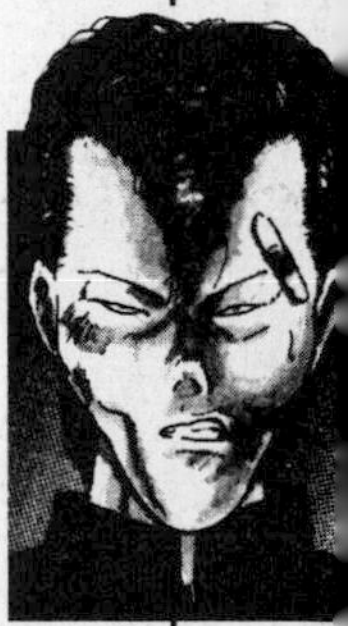

Kuwabara (P.24)—Another pun name! "Kuwabara Kuwabara" is a superstitious phrase traditionally uttered by people when they hear something scary. According to Togashi, Kuwabara's name is also a combination of the names of two Japanese pro baseball players.

Botan (P.33)—Botan's name could mean either "peony" (a type of flower) or "button."

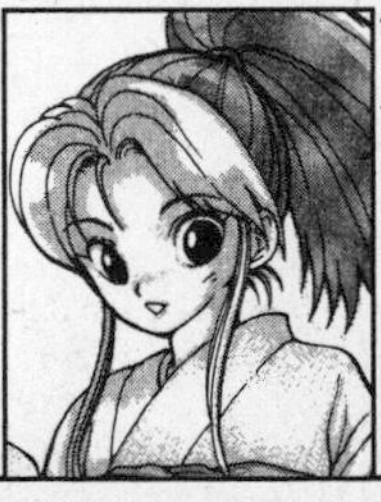

Yusuke's Funeral (P.40)—Yusuke has

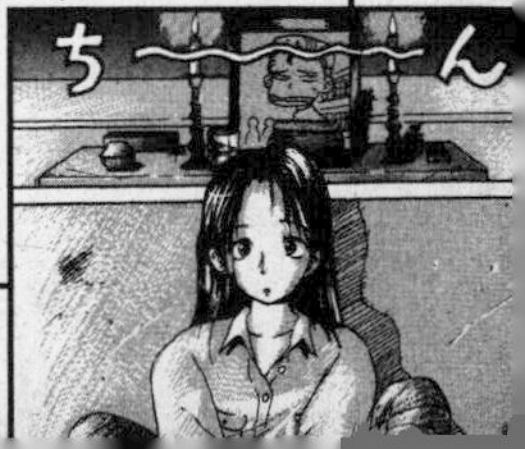
ち〜〜〜ん

been given a Buddhist funeral. The "chaiiing" sound (also see p.66) is the sound of a prayer bell ringing. In Japan, most people are cremated instead of being buried, partly for traditional reasons and partly because graveyard space is very expensive.

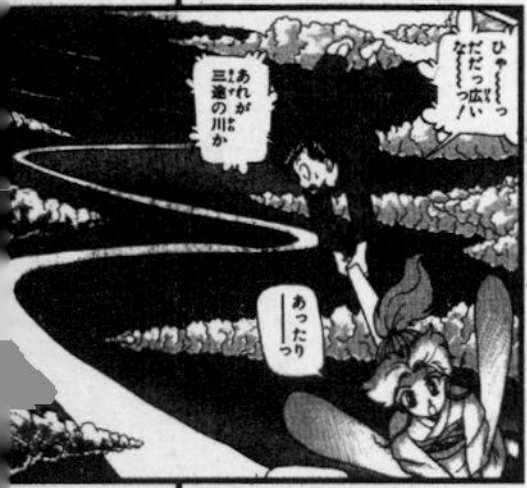
ひゃ〜〜〜っだだっ広いな〜〜〜っ!
あれが三途の川か
あったり——っ

Sanzu River (P.33, 53)—In the original Japanese edition, Botan is the guide of the Sanzu River, the Japanese equivalent of the many rivers of the underworld in world myth (such as the River Styx and the River Lethe in Greek myth). Traditionally, dead people with many sins must swim across the deep water, people with a few sins must ford through the rapids, while people without sin may cross the river on a convenient bridge. Thus, the Sanzu River means "The River of Three Crossings." Because Botan guides souls across the river, she rides an oar.

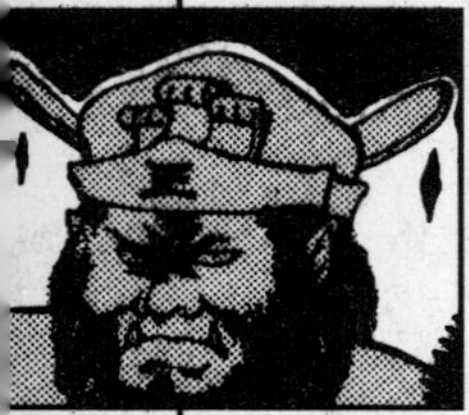

King Enma, Koenma (P.54)—The Ruler of the Underworld and Judge of the Dead in Japanese mythology. Enma is the leader of the Ten Kings of Hell who weigh the deeds of the dead and determine their fate. The belief in Enma originated in Indian Hinduism (where his name was written in Sanskrit as "Yama") before spreading to China and Japan, and he is depicted differently in different countries. The name of Koenma, King Enma's son in the manga, is a combination of Enma and ko, the Japanese word for "child."

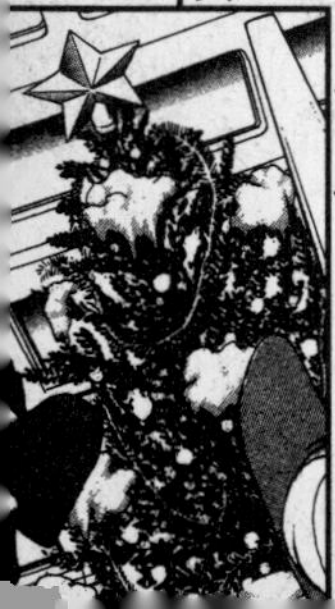

Christmas Eve (P.117)—In Japan, Christmas eve has developed the connotation of a "romantic holiday for couples." On the other hand, New Year's (which, in Japan, is a bigger holiday than Christmas) is the "family holiday."

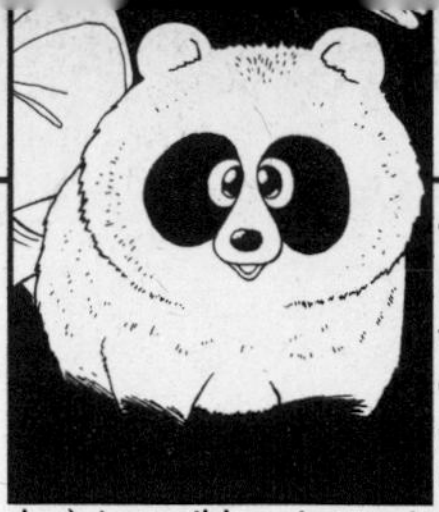

Tanuki (P.137)—In real life the tanuki, or "raccoon dog" (though it isn't really related to a dog), is a wild canine native to Japan and parts of Asia. In Japanese folklore, they are believed to be friendly tricksters and bumbling shapeshifters, associated with gluttony, virility and good cheer. Tanuki statues are often seen outside Japanese restaurants, depicting the animal dressed as a wandering monk with a cone-shaped hat, a jug of sake—and really large testicles which touch the floor. (The tanuki in **YuYu Hakusho** is unusually discreet, or maybe it's just young.)

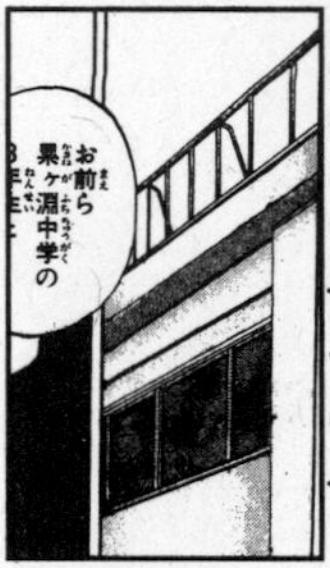
お前ら

Kasanegafuchi (P.159)—Like Sarayashiki, Kasanegafuchi High School is named after a haunted mansion in a classic Japanese ghost story, **Kaidan Kasanegafuchi**. The original story has been adapted into several Japanese big screen and TV movies.

Pachinko (P.199)—The game Yusuke is playing is pachinko, where players pay money for steel balls which randomly tumble through a pinball-like playing field and into different holes. Depending on which holes the balls land in, players accumulate points which can be traded in to the pachinko parlor staff for various prizes and merchandise. Some people go on to trade the prizes for money at certain outlets (although this is technically illegal), and this element of gambling contributes to pachinko's popularity.

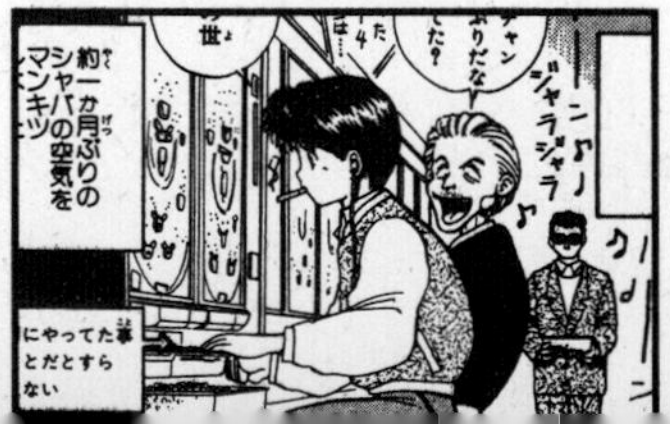
ジャラジャラ
約一カ月ぶりのシャバの空気を
にやってた事とだとすらない

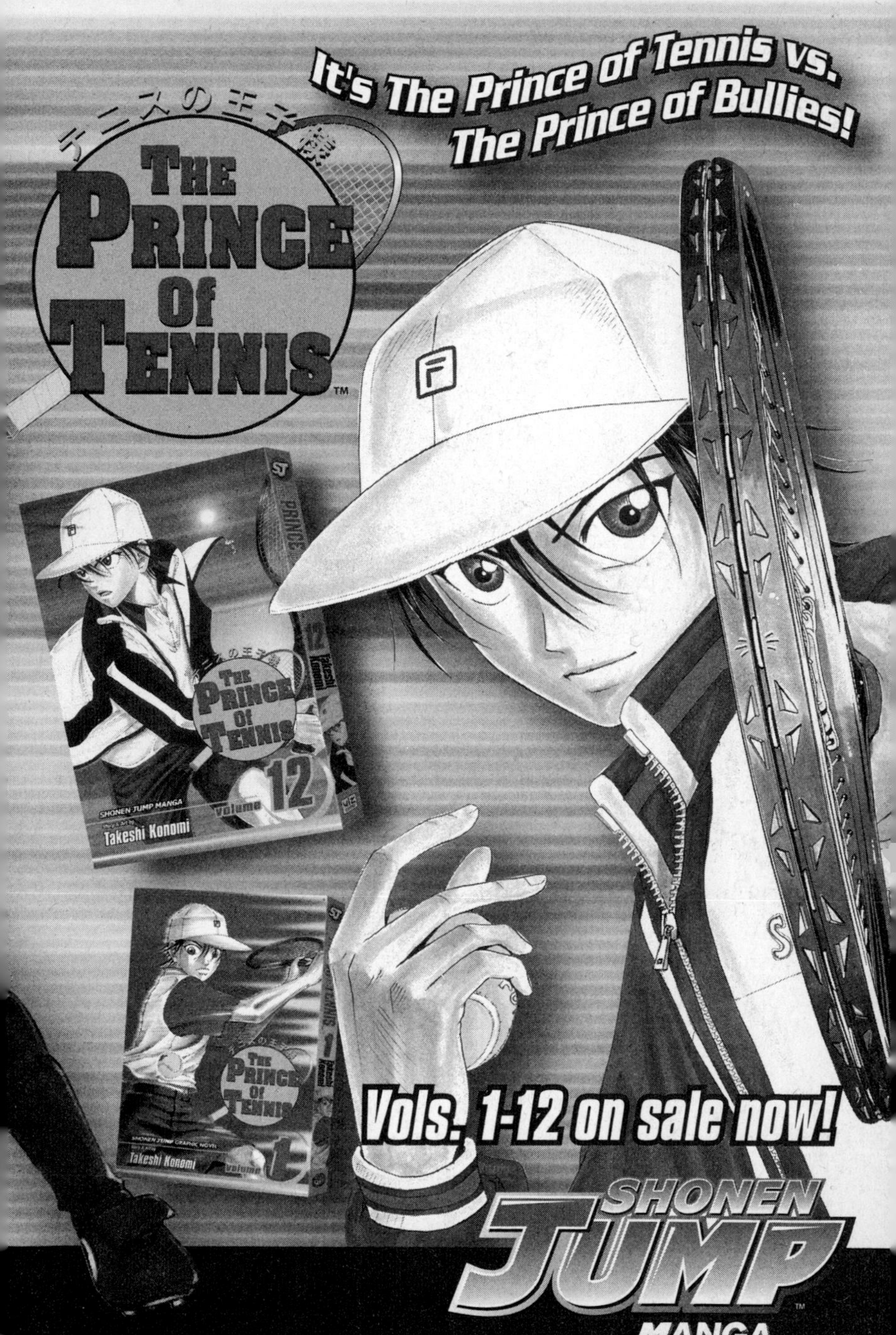
It's The Prince of Tennis vs.
The Prince of Bullies!
THE PRINCE OF TENNIS™
SHONEN JUMP MANGA
Takeshi Konomi
12
Takeshi Konomi
1
Vols. 1-12 on sale now!
SHONEN JUMP
MANGA

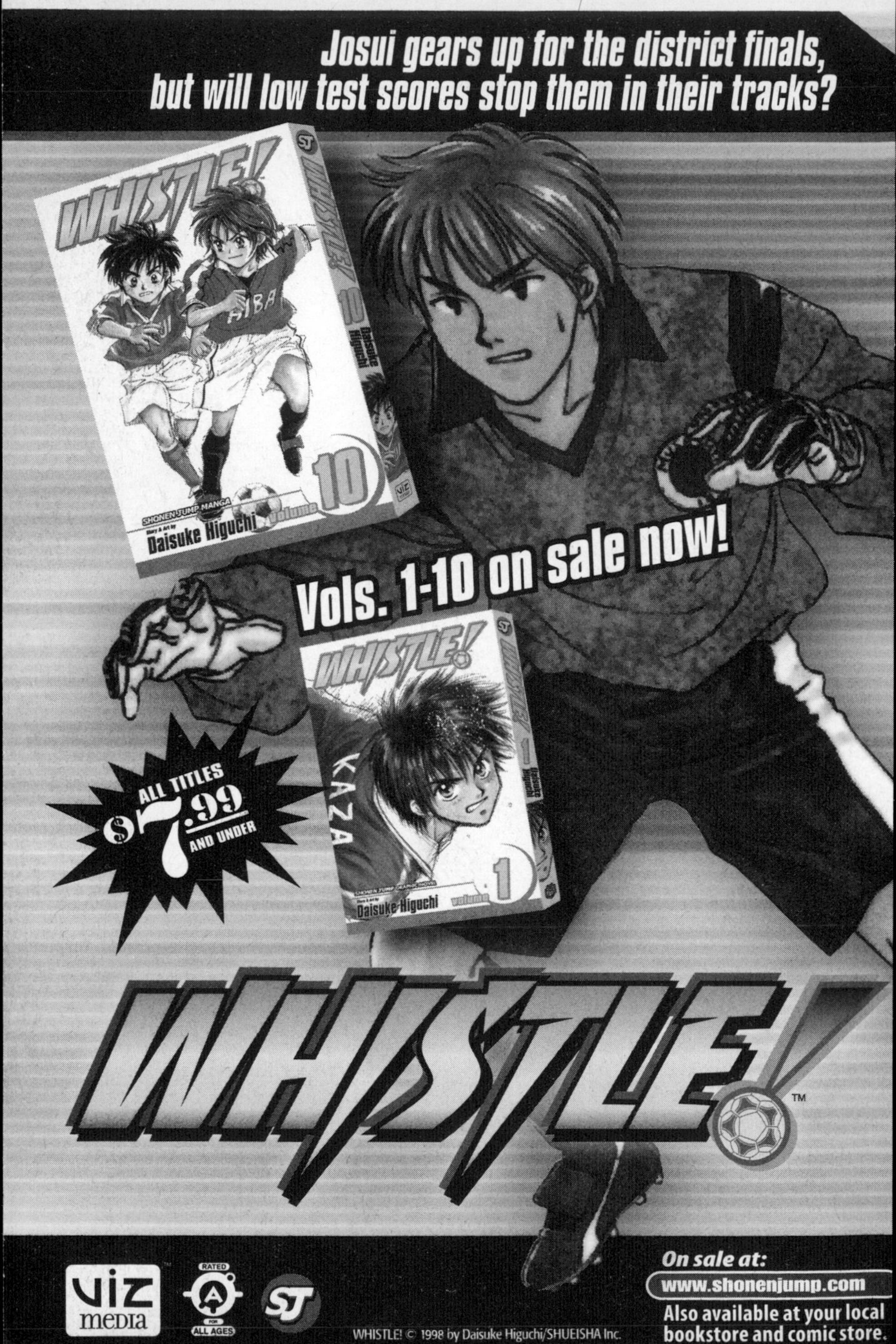
Josui gears up for the district finals, but will low test scores stop them in their tracks?
WHISTLE!
SHONEN JUMP MANGA
Daisuke Higuchi
volume 10
Vols. 1-10 on sale now!
WHISTLE!
KAZA
Daisuke Higuchi
volume 1
ALL TITLES $7.99 AND UNDER
WHISTLE! ™
On sale at:
www.shonenjump.com
Also available at your local bookstore and comic store.
viz media
RATED A FOR ALL AGES
SJ
WHISTLE! © 1998 by Daisuke Higuchi/SHUEISHA Inc.

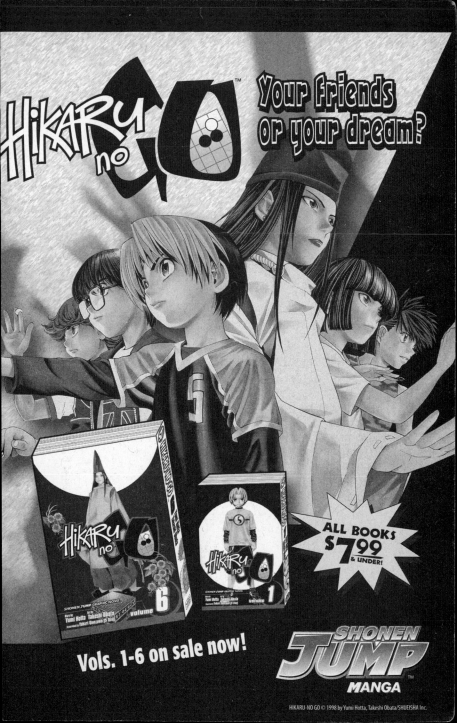

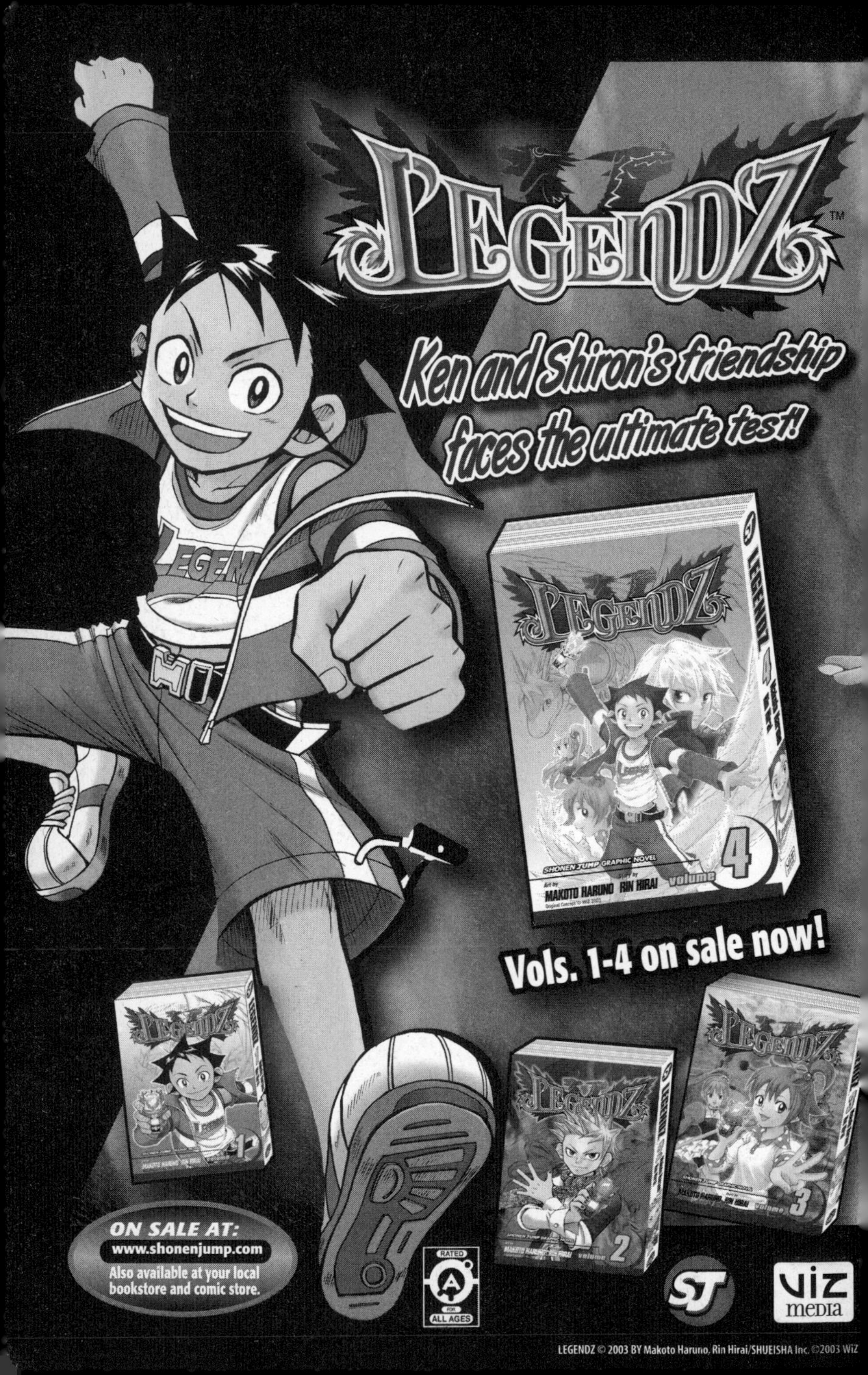
LEGENDZ™
Ken and Shiron's friendship faces the ultimate test!
LEGENDZ
SHONEN JUMP GRAPHIC NOVEL
Art by MAKOTO HARUNO Story by RIN HIRAI
volume 4
Vols. 1-4 on sale now!
ON SALE AT:
www.shonenjump.com
Also available at your local bookstore and comic store.
RATED A FOR ALL AGES
SJ
VIZ media
LEGENDZ © 2003 BY Makoto Haruno, Rin Hirai/SHUEISHA Inc. ©2003 WiZ

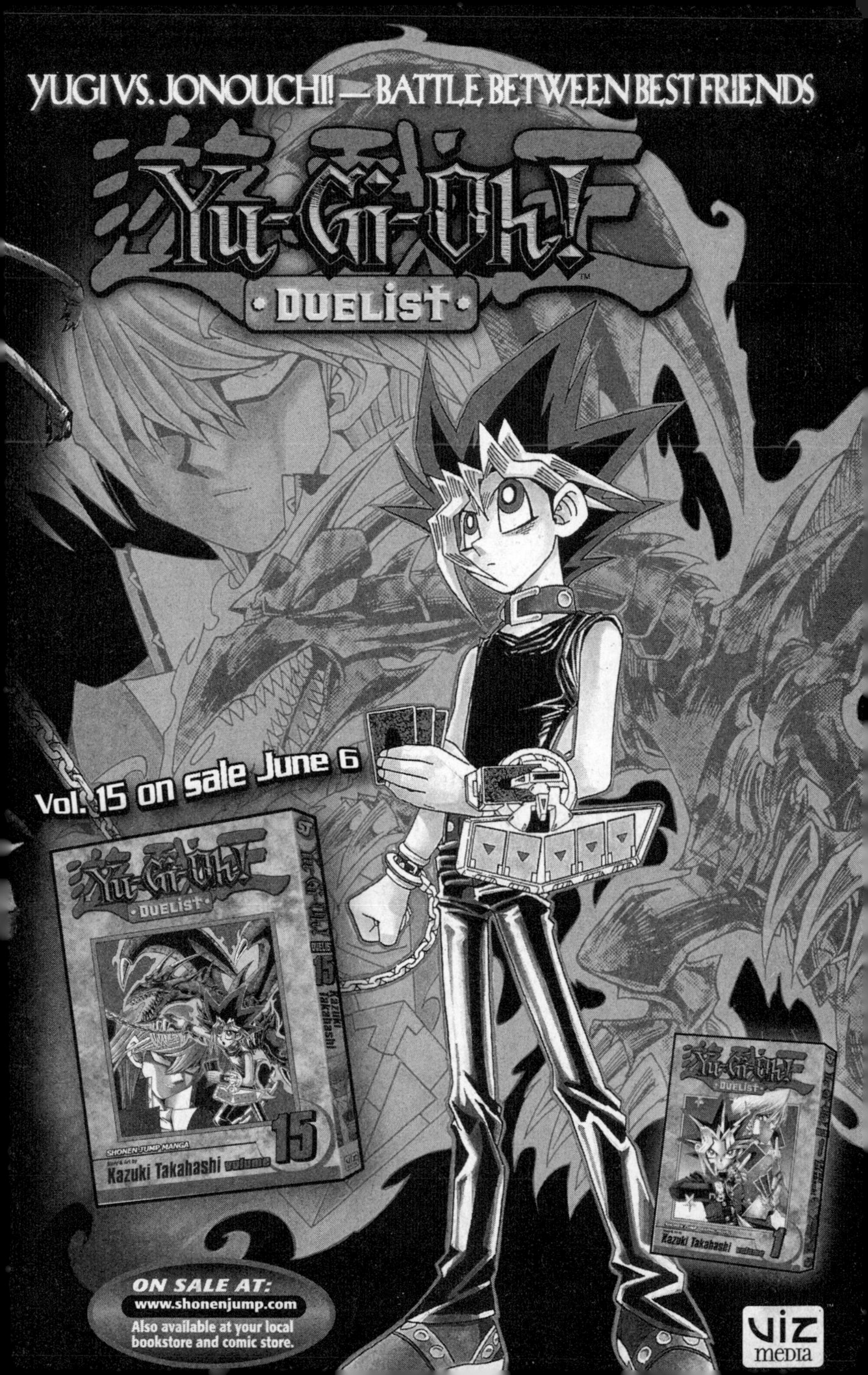
YUGI VS. JONOUCHI! — BATTLE BETWEEN BEST FRIENDS
Yu-Gi-Oh!™
DUELIST
Vol. 15 on sale June 6
Yu-Gi-Oh! DUELIST
SHONEN JUMP MANGA
Kazuki Takahashi volume 15
Yu-Gi-Oh! DUELIST
Kazuki Takahashi volume 1
ON SALE AT:
www.shonenjump.com
Also available at your local bookstore and comic store.
VIZ media

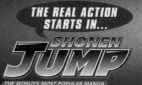

Check us out
on the web!

www.shonenjump.com

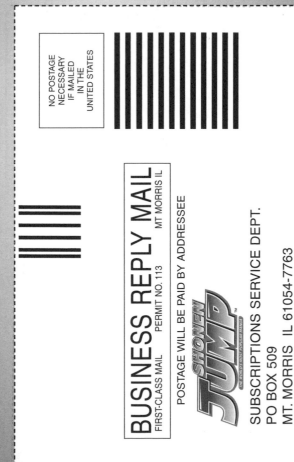

SHONEN JUMP
THE WORLD'S MOST POPULAR MANGA

COMPLETE OUR SURVEY AND LET US KNOW WHAT YOU THINK!

☐ Please do NOT send me information about VIZ Media and SHONEN JUMP products, news and events, special offers, or other information.

☐ Please do NOT send me information from VIZ Media's trusted business partners.

Name: ______________________________

Address: ______________________________

City: ________________ **State:** ________ **Zip:** ________

E-mail: ______________________________

☐ **Male** ☐ **Female** **Date of Birth** (mm/dd/yyyy): ___/___/______ (**Under 13? Parental consent required.**)

1 Do you purchase SHONEN JUMP magazine?

☐ Yes ☐ No

If **YES**, do you subscribe?

☐ Yes ☐ No

If **NO**, how often do you purchase SHONEN JUMP magazine?

☐ 1-3 issues a year ☐ 4-6 issues a year ☐ more than 7 issues a year

2 Which SHONEN JUMP Volume 1 manga did you purchase this time? ______________

Will you purchase subsequent volumes?

☐ Yes ☐ No

3 How did you learn about this title? (check all that apply)

☐ Favorite title ☐ Advertisement ☐ Article

☐ Gift ☐ Recommendation ☐ Special offer

☐ Through TV animation ☐ Read excerpt in SHONEN JUMP magazine

☐ Website ☐ Other ______________

4 Of the titles that are serialized in SHONEN JUMP magazine, have you purchased the paperback manga volumes?

☐ Yes ☐ No

If **YES**, which ones have you purchased? (check all that apply)

☐ Hikaru no Go ☐ Naruto ☐ One Piece ☐ Shaman King

☐ Yu-Gi-Oh!: Millennium World ☐ YuYu Hakusho

If **YES**, what were your reasons for purchasin

- ☐ A favorite title
- ☐ A favorite cre
- ☐ There are extras that aren't in the magazine
- ☐ I want to read it in one go
- ☐ The quality of printing is better than the magazine
- ☐ I want to read it over and over again
- ☐ Recommendation
- ☐ Special offer
- ☐ Other

If **NO**, why did/would you not purchase it?

- ☐ I'm happy just reading it in the magazine
- ☐ It's not worth buying the manga volume
- ☐ All the manga pages are in black and white, unlike the magazine
- ☐ There are other manga volumes that I prefer
- ☐ There are too many to collect for each title
- ☐ It's too small
- ☐ Other ____________

5 Of the titles NOT serialized in the magazine, which ones have you purchased?
(check all that apply)

☐ Beet the Vandel Buster	☐ Black Cat	☐ Bleach	☐ Bobobo-bo Bo-bobo
☐ Claymore	☐ D.Gray-man	☐ Death Note	☐ Dragon Ball
☐ Dragon Ball Z	☐ Dr. Slump	☐ Eyeshield 21	☐ Hunter x Hunter
☐ I"s	☐ JoJo's Bizarre Adventure	☐ Knights of the Zodiac	☐ Legendz
☐ The Prince of Tennis	☐ Rurouni Kenshin	☐ Ultimate Muscle	☐ Whistle!
☐ Yu-Gi-Oh!	☐ Yu-Gi-Oh!: Duelist	☐ None	☐ Other ________

If you did purchase any of the above, what were your reasons for purchasing?

- ☐ A favorite title
- ☐ A favorite creator/artist
- ☐ Read a preview in SHONEN JUMP magazine and wanted to read the rest of the story
- ☐ Recommendation
- ☐ Other

Will you purchase subsequent volumes if available?

- ☐ Yes
- ☐ No

6 Of the following, what manga-related books would you like to buy? (check all that apply)

- ☐ Art books
- ☐ Character profile books
- ☐ Novels/Novelizations
- ☐ None of these

7 What race/ethnicity do you consider yourself? (please check one)

- ☐ Asian/Pacific Islander
- ☐ Black/African American
- ☐ Hispanic/Latino
- ☐ Native American/Alaskan Native
- ☐ White/Caucasian
- ☐ Other

THANK YOU! Please send the completed form to:

VIZ Media Survey
42 Catharine St.
Poughkeepsie, NY 12601

VIZ media

All information provided will be used for internal purposes only. We promise not to sell or otherwise divulge your information.